Companion to *Colossus Reborn*

MODERN WAR STUDIES

Theodore A. Wilson
General Editor

Raymond A. Callahan
J. Garry Clifford
Jacob W. Kipp
Jay Luvaas
Allan R. Millett
Carol Reardon
Dennis Showalter
David R. Stone
Series Editors

Companion to *Colossus Reborn*

KEY DOCUMENTS AND STATISTICS

David M. Glantz

University Press of Kansas

© 2005 by the University Press of Kansas
All rights reserved

Published by the University Press of Kansas (Lawrence, Kansas 66049), which was organized by the Kansas Board of Regents and is operated and funded by Emporia State University, Fort Hays State University, Kansas State University, Pittsburg State University, the University of Kansas, and Wichita State University

Library of Congress Cataloging-in-Publication Data

Glantz, David M.
  Companion to Colossus reborn : key documents and statistics / David M. Glantz.
    p. cm. — (Modern war studies)
  Includes bibliographical references and index.
  ISBN 0-7006-1359-5 (cloth : alk. paper)
  1. Glantz, David M. Colossus reborn. 2. Soviet Union. Raboche-Krest'ëñanskaëñìa Krasnaëñìa Armiëñìa—Organization. 3. Soviet Union. Raboche-Krest'ëñanskaëñìa Krasnaëñìa Armiëñìa—Equipment and supplies—Statistics. 4. Soviet Union. Armed Forces—Weapons systems—Statistics.
5. World War, 1939–1945—Campaigns—Eastern Front—Sources. 6. Soviet Union—History, Military—Sources. I. Title. II. Series.
  D764.G55583 2005
  940.54'1247—dc22   2004013597

British Library Cataloguing-in-Publication Data is available.

Printed in the United States of America

10 9 8 7 6 5 4 3 2 1

The paper used in this publication meets the minimum requirements of the American National Standard for Permanence of Paper for Printed Library Materials Z39.48-1984.

Contents

Preface	ix
APPENDIX 1. RED ARMY DOCUMENTS, 1941–1943	1
NKO Directive No. 0308 (20 August 1941)	1
Stavka Order No. 089 (9 February 1942)	2
GKO Decree No. 169ss (16 July 1941)	3
NKO Order No. 158/24 (6 April 1943)	4
NKO Order No. 0413 (21 August 1943)	5
NKO Order No. 0099 (8 October 1941)	6
NKO Order No. 0058 (25 March 1942)	7
NKO Order No. 0284 (13 April 1942)	8
NKO Order No. 0296 (18 April 1942)	9
NKO Order No. 0320 (25 August 1941)	10
GKO Decree No. 1227ss (11 May 1942)	11
NKO Order No. 0883 (13 November 1942)	11
NKO Order No. 0169 (3 March 1942)	13
NKO Order No. 307 (9 October 1942)	15
Extract from NKO Order No. 219 (23 June 1941)	16
NKO Order No. 227 (28 July 1942)	17
Extract from NKO Order No. 298 (28 September 1942)	21
NKO Order No. 323 (16 October 1942)	22
NKO Order No. 0860 (29 October 1942)	25
NKO Order No. 47 (30 January 1943)	27
APPENDIX 2. RED ARMY SENIOR COMMAND CADRE, 1941–1945	29
Main Commands of Strategic Directions [Axes]	29
Fronts	30
Defense Lines and Defense Zones	43
Field (Combined-Arms) Armies	43
Tank Armies	65
Sapper Armies	67
Air Armies	68

Military Districts	71
Operational Groups	75
Defense Zones and Regions	75
Mechanized Corps (1st Formation)	76
Cavalry Corps	80
Tank Corps	84
Mechanized Corps (2nd Formation)	93
Artillery Penetration Corps	96
PVO Fronts, Armies, Corps	97
Aviation Corps	101
Special Corps of Railroad Forces	111

APPENDIX 3. NKVD FORCES AND OTHER SPECIALIZED RED ARMY FORCES IN WARTIME   113

Identified Wartime NKVD Divisions	113
Identified Wartime NKVD Brigades	131
Identified Wartime Separate NKVD Regiments	132
Identified Wartime Red Army (NKPS) Railroad Brigades	135
Selected Red Army Wartime Military Road, Auto-Transport, and Road Service Forces	136
Representative Red Army Wartime Construction Forces	138

APPENDIX 4. CHARACTERISTICS OF RED ARMY WARTIME WEAPONRY AND EQUIPMENT (INCLUDING LEND-LEASE)   139

Pistols	139
Rifles	139
Submachine Guns	140
Machine Guns, 1941–1943	140
Antitank Rifles, 1941–1943	140
Tanks	141
Field Artillery and Mortar Systems	143
Antitank Guns	144
Antiaircraft Guns	144
Multiple Rocket Launcher (Guards-Mortar) Systems	145
Self-Propelled Guns	146
Aircraft (Soviet-Produced)	147
Aircraft (Lend-Lease)	148
Mines	149
Mine-Clearing Equipment	149
River-Crossing Equipment (Tactical Bridging)	150
Radios	151

Military-Field Telephones	152
Field Telephone Switchboards	152
Radio-Telegraph Apparatuses	152
Other Mobile Communication Means	153
"Flame Bottles" ("Molotov Cocktails")	153
Backpacked Flamethrowers	154
Tank-Mounted Flamethrowers	154
Smoke Generators	155
APPENDIX 5. RED ARMY ORDERS OF BATTLE, 1941–1943	156
22 June 1941	157
1 January 1942	165
1 July 1942	182
1 February 1943	204
1 July 1943	234
31 December 1943	270
Abbreviations	307

Preface

This volume enriches and amplifies the documentary and statistical foundation for my presentation in *Colossus Reborn: The Red Army at War, 1941–1943*, the second volume of a trilogy that includes *Stumbling Colossus* (1998) and *Colossus Triumphant* (forthcoming). *Colossus Reborn* presents an epic narrative of the initial years of a titanic war between Germany and the Soviet Union, encompassing a region of nearly 600,000 square miles, killing as many as 35 million soldiers and civilians, and inflicting unimaginable destruction throughout Eastern and Central Europe. Nevertheless, out of the great tragic conflict Russians describe as the Great Patriotic War, an almost decimated Red Army resurrected itself from the disasters of 1941 to stop and then reverse the German offensive and, in so doing, become one of the world's premier fighting forces.

Prejudiced by a literature dominated by the views of Western historians (primarily English, German, French, and American historians), readers for too many years have had difficulty seeing and/or articulating just how crucial this turnaround was to ending the German threat to the Allies and the rest of the world. Ideology, political motivations, and persistent Cold War shibboleths, which have prevented many Soviet and Russian historians from providing a fuller and much more credible understanding of those battles, operations, campaigns, and leaders (both good and bad) directly affecting their country and influencing the war's final outcome, have further obscured our collective vision.

Recovering that lost history, as well as rewriting previous inaccurate accounts, has been at the very heart of my work on the Soviet-German campaigns during World War II. That recovery and rewriting, however, has required decades of painstaking research to document as precisely as possible exactly what actually happened. Amassing that vital documentary evidence has required extended access to previously unavailable or neglected Soviet, Russian, and German archival sources, especially during those periods of "openness" when foreign scholars were allowed (if not always welcomed) into Soviet repositories and aided by a great many of my Russian friends (many Red Army veterans) whose Herculean efforts have produced so much valuable information on my behalf. It has also required getting past the natural tendency among Russians to avoid probing too deeply into their own history for fear of what they might encounter. A number of my books, such as *Zhukov's Greatest Defeat*, have no doubt reinforced such fears.

I see the situation quite differently. Like any committed historian, I would hope that this effort has been made to ascertain the truth of the past. As long as this truth remains completely hidden or partially lost, we are all thereby limited and diminished. Often a clear-headed look at the past can indeed reveal terrible events we wished we could not claim as our own. At the same time, however, and this is so true for the Soviet experience in World War II, we can also rediscover a bond to ancestors and countrymen (and women) whose sacrifices and heroism fully merit our memorialization.

Thus, I have sought to compile the most factually accurate and complete record possible based on the sources available to me. To this end I offer in this companion volume key documents regarding the everyday lives of the army's soldiers, a full roster of the Red Army's senior command cadre during wartime, a description of the army's wartime weaponry and equipment, and a detailed listing of the Red Army's and NKVD's order of battle at six crucial points during the period from 22 June 1941 through 31 December 1943. I do so hoping that their presentation here will further clarify the historical record for the period and places described in *Colossus Reborn* and at the same time honor the heroic efforts of the Russian people in World War II.

APPENDIX 1

Red Army Documents, 1941–1943

NKO DIRECTIVE NO. 0308 (20 AUGUST 1941)

*Concerning the Replacement of Junior Command Cadre
and Young Soldiers in Rear Service Units and Installations*

In order to employ military personnel of noncommissioned officer rank and soldiers who are assigned to the service and rear subunits of combat units, military-training organizations, central and district apparatuses, local rifle forces, construction battalions, local military command organs, warehouses, medical-sanitary battalions, hospitals, veterinary services, and other rear facilities in more expedient fashion, I order:

1. Remove all young Red Army men and noncommissioned officers from all rear service subunits, medical and veterinary facilities, and warehouses in military units and also from construction battalions and send them to military units at the disposal of the military councils of *fronts* and armies and replace them with 2nd category [low-quality] soldiers who are more than 35 years of age and who are suited for only limited combat duty.

2. Remove from all internal [military] districts:
   a. All noncommissioned officers from central and district apparatuses, construction units formed on the declaration of mobilization, military commissariats, warehouses, and other rear facilities and replace them with 2nd category [soldiers] and civilian personnel who have military obligations;
   b. All noncommissioned officers and soldiers from the service subunits of military-training institutions and medical and veterinary facilities and replace them with 2nd category [soldiers] who have military obligations;
   c. During the first month, 50 percent of the on-hand personnel from local rifle units and replace them with 2nd category [soldiers] who have military obligations, and, after one month, replace the remaining military of young age;
   d. Transfer all of the noncommissioned officers and soldiers who have been replaced to newly formed reserve rifle brigades and regiments in the [military] districts for subsequent training and assignment to the front as march battalions;

3. The military councils of the *fronts,* armies, and military districts will complete carrying out these measures by 1 September 1941. Report to me by 2 September 1941 about the quantity of noncommissioned officers and soldiers who have been replaced with regard to their composition and state of training.

Provide corrections on the status of the replaced personnel to the chief of the Main Directorate for the Formation and Manning of the Red Army every five days.

I. Stalin, People's Commissar of Defense[1]

STAVKA ORDER NO. 089 (9 FEBRUARY 1942)

To the Chiefs of Staff of the Voronezh, Southwestern, Don, Stalingrad, and Trans-Caucasus Fronts Concerning the Conscription of Civilians Inhabiting Territories Liberated from the Occupiers into the Red Army

While conducting their heroic struggle at the front against the fascist occupiers, the forces of the operating armies must simultaneously obtain personnel reinforcements. The force contingents available to our country are abundantly providing for the complete satisfaction of all our requirements in terms of both reinforcements and new formations. However, because of transportation difficulties, large masses of our reinforcements that have already been prepared for duty at the front are very frequently being held up en route or are late and join the operating units in untimely fashion.

Meanwhile, in addition to the main source of reinforcements alluded to above, there is an important though as yet unexploited opportunity in the sectors of the operating armies to regulate the influx of personnel into the force right on the spot. This opportunity involves the use of conscripts of military age not yet serving in the army who have been liberated from Soviet regions and districts under German occupation. The Soviet population in the occupied territories is burning with hatred for the invader and a desire to participate in the subsequent liberation of their Soviet motherland with weapons in their hands.

I order:

1. In order to reinforce their units with personnel, the military councils of operating armies are obliged to conscript Soviet citizens into the ranks of the Red Army. Citizens in the liberated territories between the ages of 17 and 45 who have not been conscripted into the Red Army during the previous months of the war are subject to conscription;

2. Immediately form reserve rifle regiments in all armies, which, in practice, must select, conscript, and combat-train these contingents within their armies' operational sectors.

3. Implement this order immediately by transmitting it by telegraph.

4. The Main Directorate for the Formation and Manning of Red Army Forces will provide detailed instructions to the armies regarding the best way to implement this order.

I. V. Stalin, People's Commissar of Defense[2]

GKO DECREE NO. 169SS (16 JULY 1941)

The GKO has determined that, in a majority of instances while in combat with the German invaders, Red Army units are holding the great banner of Soviet authority high and are behaving satisfactorily, and sometimes openly heroically, while fighting for their motherland against the fascist plunderers.

However, at the same time, the GKO must acknowledge that individual commanders and soldiers are displaying unsteadiness, panic, and disgraceful cowardice, and, by throwing down their weapons and forgetting about their debt to the motherland, they are crudely violating their oath, transforming themselves into herds of sheep, and running away in panic before the impudent enemy.

While rendering honor and fame to the brave soldiers and commanders, at the same time, the GKO [State Defense Committee] considers it necessary to employ severe measures against cowards, panic-mongers, and deserters.

Panic-mongers, cowards, and deserters are worse than the enemy because they not only undermine our cause but also discredit the honor of the Red Army. Therefore, dealing with panic-mongers, cowards, and deserters, and reestablishing military discipline is our sacred duty if we wish to protect unsullied the great profession of the Red Army soldier.

Therefore, as a result of recommendations by the main [direction] commander, and by the commanders of *fronts* and armies, the GKO has arrested and brought to trial by military tribunal [the following] for cowardice that disgraced the profession of command, criminal negligence of authority, mismanagement, breakdown of command and control, handing over weapons to the enemy without a fight, and willfully abandoning their combat positions. . . .

While giving their due to the brave and courageous commanders who have covered themselves in glory in the struggles with the fascist invaders, at the same time, the GKO is providing notice that, henceforth, it will stop any manifestation of cowardice or disorganization in the ranks of the Red Army with an iron hand, remembering that iron discipline in the Red Army is the most important condition for victory over the enemy.

The GKO demands that commanders and political workers at all levels systematically strengthen the spirit of discipline and good organization in the ranks of the Red Army so that they inspire the soldiers to great feats by personal examples of bravery and courage, so that they prevent scaremongers, cowards, and disorganizers from discrediting the great standard of the Red Army, and so that they give short shrift to them as well as to those who infringe upon their oath and become traitors to the homeland.

Chairman of the GKO, I. Stalin[3]

NKO ORDER NO. 158/24 (6 APRIL 1943)

Concerning Procedures for the Early Removal of Loss of Rights [Disenfranchisement] with Regard to Those Persons Who Have Served Most of Their Punishment and Whose Age Subjects Them to Conscription or Mobilization

I order:

1. In cooperation with local councils, NKVD [People's Commissariat of Internal Affairs] organs, and the militia, *oblast'* [district], city, and regional military commissariats will call up all males of up to 50 years of age who have not yet been conscripted into the army because of their loss of rights, excluding those persons who have been serving sentences for counterrevolutionary crimes (those who have actually carried out the crimes) and banditry.

2. All of those conscripted will undergo a medical examination in accordance with NKO [People's Commissariat of Defense] Order No. 336 of 1942, and, with regard to those persons who have been designated as fit for line [combat] service and fit for non-line service, will report to the local people's court with a statement concerning their relief from loss of rights.

The statement will indicate the last [family], first, and middle names of the person who has lost his rights, his year of birth and place of residence, and when, at which court, and for what period the rights were lost.

3. The court will examine the statement submitted to it by the military commissariat within a period of three days and will immediately inform the appropriate military commissariat about the decision it reaches.

If the people's court perceives from the submitted materials that the question of relief from the loss of rights relates to the competency of another court, then it will immediately send the materials to the appropriate court without returning the materials to the military commissariat, while informing the military commissariat about what it has done.

4. After reaching a decision about the relief from loss of rights, the court will take a signed statement from the person whose rights are being restored concerning his immediate appearance at the military commissariat for call-up on a force roster.

5. Upon receiving information concerning relief from loss of rights from the people's court, the military commissariat will immediately enroll all per-

sons who have been released from this measure of punishment on the military roster and call them up into the army on a general basis.

6. At the same time, also register all males of up to 55 years of age who have lost their rights while serving the full measure of their sentence (besides counterrevolutionary crimes and banditry) and who have been designated by medical certification as unfit for military service but fit for physical work.

7. Complete all work called for by this order by 15 May 1943.

8. The military councils of the districts [*fronts*] will report about the progress of this work every 10 days beginning on 15 April. Submit a complete accounting by 20 May.

Include in these reports: (a) a total of how many males of conscription age who lost their rights after release from punishment showed up, and how many of them had their rights restored; and (b) the total number of those whose rights were restored, (1) how many of them were recognized as fit for line duty, and how many of them were called up into the army; and (2) how many were recognized as unfit for line duty, and how many of these were called up into the army.

Show separately how many males of up to 55 years of age, during the medical certification process, were accepted on the rolls and recognized as unfit for military service but fit for physical work and, of this number, how many were under 50 years of age, and how many were from 51 up to 55 years of age.

9. Transmit this order to the military councils of the districts [*fronts*] by telegraph.

Deputy People's Commissar of Defense
Colonel General E. Shchadenko
People's Commissar of Justice of the USSR
Rychkov[4]

NKO ORDER NO. 0413 (21 AUGUST 1943)

Concerning the Granting of Rights to Unit and Formation Commanders to Send Sergeants and Rank-and-File Soldiers within Their Authority Who Have Been Found Guilty of Some Types of Crimes to Penal Companies without Trial

1. By virtue of their authority and without trial, the commanders of regiments (separate units) in the operating armies and the commanders of divisions (separate brigades) and their equivalents in the military districts and nonoperating *fronts* are granted the right to send sergeants and rank-and-file soldiers who are guilty of absence without leave, desertion, disobedience of orders, squandering and theft of property, violation of regulations of the

guards service, and other military crimes to penal units of the operating army, in those instances when normal disciplinary measures for these misdemeanors have proved inadequate.

2. By virtue of their authority, those chiefs of garrisons who enjoy rights no lower than regimental commander are granted the right to send, without trial, all sergeants and rank-and-file soldiers who have been arrested for desertion and who have deserted from units of the operating army and from other garrisons to penal units of the operating army.

If the chief of the garrison does not enjoy the rights of a regimental commander or higher, then the dispatch of the arrested deserter to penal units will be carried out on the instructions of the commander of the formation (or district military commissariat) to which the garrison commander is subordinate by order of the former.

3. In order to establish the fact of the crime, conduct an inquiry in accordance with NKO Order No. 357 of 1942.[5]

Arrange dispatch to penal units by units in the established manner in accordance with NKO Orders Nos. 298 and 323 of 1942.

4. In those cases when more severe means of punishment must be used against the guilty, the inquiry will be directed to the military prosecutor in order to bring the guilty [parties] to trial before a military tribunal.

People's Commissar of Defense
Marshal of the Soviet Union I. Stalin[6]

NKO ORDER NO. 0099 (8 OCTOBER 1941)

Concerning the Formation of Women's Aviation Regiments in the Red Army VVS [Air Force]

For the purpose of employing women flight-technical cadre, I order the formation and preparation for combat work by 1 December 1941 of:

1. The 586th Fighter Aviation Regiment located at the town of Engels, which will be equipped with Iak-1 aircraft in accordance with *Shtat* No. 015/174;

2. The 587th Close Bomber Aviation Regiment, which will be equipped with Su-2 aircraft in accordance with *Shtat* No. 015/159. Form the regiment by using the 10th Reserve Aviation Regiment at Kamenka; and

3. The 588th Night Bomber Aviation Regiment located at the town of Engels, which will be equipped with U-2 aircraft on the basis of *Shtat* No. 015/186.

4. The commander of the Red Army Air Force will complete the formation of the aviation regiments with aircraft and flight-technical personnel from among the women's cadre of the VVS, Red Army, Navy, and OSOAVIAKHIM [Society for Assistance to Defense, Aviation and Chemical Structuring of the USSR].

5. Organize and conduct retraining of the personnel on the new equipment [as follows]:

- Flight personnel—at the formation points for the aviation regiments;
- Technical personnel—in Moscow—where the flight-technical personnel are assembling; and
- Navigators and headquarters commanders—at the 2nd Ivanovo Higher School for Red Army VVS Navigators.

6. The chief quartermaster of the Red Army and the chief of the central directorates of the USSR's NKO will support the formation of the aviation regiments with all types of agreed-upon allowances.

I. Stalin, People's Commissar of Defense[7]

NKO ORDER NO. 0058 (25 MARCH 1942)

Concerning the Conscription of Women-Komsomol Members into PVO [Air Defense] Forces

I order:

1. Dispatch the conscripted girl-Komsomol members to PVO Strany forces to replace Red Army men in the following specialties:
    a. In antiaircraft artillery—instrument operators, telephone operators, range finders, radio operators, and air scout-observers, for a total of 45,000 men;
    b. In antiaircraft machine-gun units—communicators, 40 percent of the machine-gun operators, and scouts, for a total of 3,000 men;
    c. In antiaircraft projector [searchlight] units—telephone operators, radio operators, scouts, and 60 percent of the crews of associated stations, for a total of 7,000 men;
    d. In aerostatic obstacle balloon units—60 percent of the aerostatic crews and telephone operators, for a total of 5,000 men;
    e. In VNOS [early warning] service units—all observers, telephone operators, and VNOS observation posts, for a total of 40,000 men; and
    f. In all units of PVO Strany forces—medical orderlies and helpers, clerks, cooks, and individual drivers and warehouse personnel.
2. Replace the Red Army male soldiers with girl-Komsomol members during the [following] periods:
    a. In service subunits—immediately after their conscription;
    b. Specialists for antiaircraft artillery units—no later than one and one-half months after their conscription;
    c. Specialists for antiaircraft projector units—two months after their conscription;

d. Specialists for aerostatic obstacles—one and one-half months after their conscription;
   e. Machine gunners—one and one-half months after their conscription; and
   f. Observers and telephone operators for the VNOS service posts—two months after their conscription. . . .

                              I. Stalin, People's Commissar of Defense[8]

NKO ORDER NO. 0284 (13 APRIL 1942)

Concerning the Mobilization of Women to Replace Red Army Men in Signal Forces

I order:

1. Send the conscripted women to the signal forces to replace Red Army men with the following military specialists in *front,* army, and rear service signal units:
   a. BODO [encoded telegraph], ST-35, and Morse [code] operators, telephone and radio operators, telegraph operators and technicians, radio technicians, film-radio mechanics and technicians, and field postal workers and clerks who require special training, for a total of 24,144 men; and
   b. Draftsmen, clerks, secretaries, cooks, warehouse clerks, medical assistants, librarians, tailors, metalworkers, lathe operators, and other service personnel, for a total of 5,856 men;

2. Comrade Peresypkin, the chief of the Red Army's Main Signal Directorate, will replace [the following] during the period from 25 April through 1 September:
   a. 5,856 men serving in signal forces located at the front and in the rear by 1 May of this year;
   b. 2,042 telephone operators, 920 clerks at telegraph stations, and 500 senior and 500 junior inspectors at field postal stations and bases, for a total of 4,462 men, by 1 July of this year;
   c. 6,595 telegraph and Morse operators and 1,050 junior inspectors at field postal stations and bases, for a total of 7,465 men, by 1 July 1942;
   d. 3,000 telegraph operators, 250 section chiefs and their assistants, and 1,200 senior inspectors at field postal stations and bases, for a total of 4,450 men, by 1 August of this year; and
   e. 5,315 radio operators, 300 radio repairmen, 872 BODO operators, and 1,100 technicians, film-radio, and telegraph mechanics, for a total of 7,587 men, by 1 September of this year.

Overall, replace 30,000 men during this period. . . .

After their replacement with women, use the replaced Red Army signalmen from the *fronts'* and armies' signal units, first and foremost, to fill out and replace the losses of signalmen in rifle divisions and rifle brigades and in artillery, tank, and mortar units that are situated at the front. Use the remaining excess of specialist-signalmen to fill out communications units in rifle divisions and rifle brigades that have been withdrawn from the front in accordance with Glavupraform's plans. . . .

Deputy People's Commissar of Defense E. Shchadenko[9]

NKO ORDER NO. 0296 (18 APRIL 1942)

Concerning the Truncation of the Tables of Organization of Rear Service Units and Installations and the Replacement of Military Servicemen with Women in Duty Positions in Red Army Military Units and Installations

I order:

1. Send the conscripted women to air force units, where they will replace Red Army soldiers and noncommissioned officers in the following specialties:

    a. BODO, ST-35, and Morse operators, telephone, radio, and telegraph operators, clerks and other communications specialists requiring special training, for a total of 11,000 men;

    b. Drivers (except for special auto transport), tractor operators, and weapons gunners (Red Army men for cleaning guns and packing rounds), who require special training, for a total of 14,000 men in all; and

    c. Warehouse managers and assistant managers, warehouse men, product managers, office workers, cooks, mess hall managers, firemen, librarians, bookkeepers, accountants, and other specialists in administrative-housekeeping services, for a total of 15,000 men.

2. The commander of the Red Army Air Force will replace [the following] male soldiers during the period from 25 April through 1 August 1942:

    a. 15,000 men in the male duty positions indicated at paragraph 1 (b) by 15 May 1942; and

    b. 5,000 men in the male duty positions of weapons gunners (Red Army men for cleaning guns and packing rounds) by 1 July 1942.

3. In accordance with the needs of the Red Army Air Force commander, the chief of the Red Army's Glavupraform will prepare and transfer 9,000 female drivers and tractor drivers to the Red Army Air Force by 1 July 1942.

4. In accordance with the needs of the Red Army Air Force commander, the chief of the Red Army's Main Signal Directorate will prepare and transfer

11,000 female BODO, S-35, and Morse operators, telephone, radio, and telegraph operators, clerks, and other signal specialists to the air force by 1 August 1942.

5. The commander of the Red Army Air Force will complete replacing the 40,000 male duty positions indicated in paragraph 1 by 1 August 1942.

6. After their replacement by women, use the freed-up Red Army soldiers and noncommissioned officers from the air force units located at the front to fill out *front* ground and air units at the direction of the *front* commanders and in the military districts under the overall supervision of Glavupraform. . . .

I. Stalin, People's Commissar of Defense[10]

NKO ORDER NO. 0320 (25 AUGUST 1941)

Concerning the Issue of 100 Grams of Vodka per Day to Servicemen in the Operating Army's First Line

In fulfillment of GKO Decree No. 562ss, dated 22 August 1941, I order:

1. Issue 100 grams of 40 proof vodka per day to Red Army soldiers and command cadre in the forward line of the operating armies beginning on 1 September 1941.

Issue vodka equal to that of the forward line units to Red Army VVS flight crews that are carrying out combat missions, and to engineer-technical personnel who are serving at the operating armies' field airfields.

2. The military councils of the *fronts* and armies will:
    a. Organize the issuance of vodka only to those contingents designated by the GKO decree and strictly control its exact fulfillment;
    b. Provide for the timely delivery of vodka to the forward line of operating forces and organize reliable security of its reserves in field conditions;
    c. Assign special individuals who will be responsible for the proper distribution of portions of vodka, accounting for the vodka distribution, and for the conduct of receipt and distribution accounting; and
    d. Order the *front* quartermaster to provide information concerning the leftover [vodka] to the Main Quartermaster Directorate every 10 days and the requirement for the requisite quantity of vodka on the twenty-fifth day.

3. The Red Army's chief quartermaster will determine the demand for vodka during the month of September without the *fronts* presenting their requirements.

Implement this order by telegraph.

Deputy People's Commissar of Defense,
Lieutenant General of the Quartermaster Service Khrulev[11]

GKO DECREE NO. 1227SS (11 MAY 1942)

Concerning the Issuing of Vodka to Forces of the Operating Army

1. Cease the massive daily issue of vodka to personnel in the operating armies' forces on 15 May 1942.

2. Maintain a daily ration of vodka only for forward line soldiers in units that have achieved success in combat operations against the German invaders by increasing the norm for the distribution of vodka to the soldiers in these units up to 200 grams per man per day.

To this end, allocate vodka based on 20 percent of the monthly strength of *front* and army forces located along the forward line at the direction of *front* and separate army commanders.

3. Issue vodka to all remaining soldiers in the forward line on the basis of 100 grams per person on the following revolutionary and social holidays: the Anniversary of the Great October Socialist Revolution, 7 and 8 November; Constitution Day, 5 February; New Year's Day, 1 January; Red Army Day, 23 February; International Workers Holiday Day, 1 and 2 May; All-Union Physical Culture Day, 19 July; All-Union Aviation Day, 16 August; International Youth Day, 6 September; and also the day of the regiment's (unit's) formation.

Representative of the GKO, I. Stalin[12]

NKO ORDER NO. 0883 (13 NOVEMBER 1942)

Concerning the Issue of Vodka to Force Units of the Operating Army
from 25 November 1942

1. In accordance with GKO Decree No. 2507s, dated 12 November 1942, beginning on 25 November of this year, start issuing vodka to the field armies' combat units in the following manner:

    a. 100 grams per person per day to subunits of units that are conducting direct combat operations and are located in trenches in the forward positions, to subunits conducting reconnaissance, to artillery and mortar units that are attached to and supporting the infantry and are located in firing positions, and to combat aircraft crews upon the fulfillment of their combat missions; and

b. 50 grams per person per day to regimental and division reserves; to combat security subunits and units that are working in the forward positions, to units that are fulfilling responsible missions in special cases (constructing and repairing bridges and roads, and others in special working conditions under enemy fire), and, on the instructions of doctors, to the wounded who are located in medical service field installations.

2. Issue a ration of 100 grams of vodka per person per day to all servicemen in the operating armies on revolutionary or people's holidays as designated by GKO Decree No. 1889, dated 6 June 1942.

3. In the Trans-Caucasus Front, issue 200 grams of fortified wine or 300 grams of table wine instead of the 100 grams of vodka, and, in place of the 50 grams of vodka, 100 grams of fortified wine or 150 grams of table wine.

4. The military councils of the *fronts* and armies will establish the monthly limits of [daily] vodka rations for their armies and units in accordance with *front* and army orders, and the distribution will take place within the limit established for each month.

5. After they have consumed their monthly limit of vodka, each *front* will report to the Main Directorate for Food Supply of the Red Army for receipt of a [new] limit for the following month.

In the event the *fronts* fail to present an accounting and the vodka is used up by the tenth of the previous month, during the next month, the chief of the Red Army's Main Directorate for Food Supply will not ship the vodka to each *front* that failed to present an accounting.

6. Establish a limit on the consumption of vodka by the *fronts* from 25 November through 31 December 1942 in accordance with the [following] attachment.

7. Brigade engineer Comrade Pavlov, the chief of the Red Army's Main Directorate for Food Supply, and Major General of Technical Forces Comrade Kovalev, the chief of the Red Army's Military Communications [Routes], will supply vodka in quantities within the indicated limits to the Southwestern, Don, and Stalingrad Fronts by 16 November and to the remaining *fronts* by 20 November of this year.

8. The chief of the Red Army's Main Directorate for Food Supply will establish continuous control over the consumption of vodka in strict accordance with this order.

9. The military councils of the *fronts* and armies will organize the return of the used packaging from the vodka to the vodka factories and to the casking

points of the People's Commissariat for the Food Industry, which are attached to the *fronts*.

Force units that fail to return the packaging will not be issued vodka.

10. Implement this order by telegraph.

Deputy People's Commissar of Defense,
Lieutenant General of the Quartermaster Service Khrulev[13]

Attachment:

Limit on the Consumption of Vodka for Force Units of the Operating Armies, 25 November through 31 December 1942 (in liters)

Front *and Separate Army*	*Consumption Limit (in liters)* (% of total allocated vodka)°
Karelian	364,000 (6.4)
7th Separate Army	99,000 (1.7)
Leningrad	533,000 (9.4)
Volkhov	407,000 (7.2)
Northwestern	394,000 (6.9)
Kalinin	690,000 (12.1)
Western	980,000 (17.2)
Briansk	414,000 (7.3)
Voronezh	381,000 (6.7)
Southwestern	478,000 (8.4)
Don	544,000 (9.6)
Stalingrad	407,000 (7.1)
Total	5,691,000 (100)
Trans-Caucasus	1,200,000 (wine)

°Percentages of the whole added by the author.

NKO ORDER NO. 0169 (3 MARCH 1942)

Concerning the Improvement of Security and Punitive Measures to Eliminate the Misappropriation and Squandering of Military Uniforms

Disgraceful incidents of misappropriation and squandering of military uniforms and kit have been pointed out recently in the *fronts* and frontal regions. The people's property is often stolen by persons who are directly responsible for its safety and storage, such as the warehouse workers accompanying the cargo and the drivers of the cargo vehicles and the transports. A considerable amount of military clothing is also being wasted from neglect at storehouses and during transport and cart transport.

Various sorts of hostile elements who have entered the Red Army are plundering vitally necessary supplies—meat, canned goods, sugar, fuel, clothing, and footwear. By exploiting the lack of oversight by and permissiveness on the part of the military chiefs, the same elements are throwing away considerable quantities of military property at stations, along the roads, and at crossings.

In addition, great quantities of food and military property in the operating armies are being scattered around, disappearing, and damaged as a result of bad management or ignorance of management. It is known to all that valuable packing—bags, sacks, barrels, and vessels from vodka are subject to return to the people's economy, but apparently because they believe that our Socialist economy is a bottomless vessel, they are not looked after and are not being given back.

All of this is occurring, first, because food, clothing and kit, fuel, and other military property are being stored in helter-skelter fashion during transport, at unloading stations, at temporary field warehouses, and at crossing points, while even the most rudimentary provisions for [its] storage, shelter, and protection are not being carried out, and because, while in field conditions, military goods are poorly protected at their storage sites and en route along the road during transport and evacuation.

Second, this is occurring because the drivers of the cargo trucks and other conveyances, and frequently those who are escorting them, do not know what they are responsible for since they have no documents with them that can establish what kind and what quantity of cargo they are carrying, and when and to whom they are to deliver it.

Exploiting this muddle, individual escorts, drivers, and cargo handlers are intentionally falling behind their transports and columns and halting at this or that place, where they are committing their dirty business.

Third, this is occurring because the accounting for military goods and foodstuffs, which must reflect the calculated value of these goods each day and in any situation—at bases, warehouses, and other places of storage—is being done in very slipshod fashion.

Finally, proper attention is not being given in the *fronts* and frontal regions to the selection of people to whom items with the greatest value to the government—military property—is being directly entrusted. It is a fact that there are still rogues and other unreliable elements in the military warehouses and bases, as well as in the forces' transportation organizations, who are undermining the power of the Red Army and about whom some commanders, political workers, and supply workers in the army do not want to comprehend and with whom they do not want to reckon.

All of this perversion is frequently occurring before the very eyes of commanders, military commissars, political workers, and chiefs of services who are responsible for the uninterrupted support of forces, for the security and lawful use of military supplies, and for the placement of people in management positions, but who have actually lost their sense of obligation to the motherland for the people's property entrusted to them. The commandants of railroad sectors, stations, and automobile roads, and the commanders of road exploitation units along the roads, who are responsible for controlling the passage of trains, transports, columns, single vehicles, and transports with military cargoes, are not only failing to combat plunderers but, in some instances, are themselves committing these unlawful actions.

Criminal elements and all sorts of direct or indirect enemy stooges are revealing and will continue to reveal themselves in the many-million-man Red Army. The foremost mission of commanders, military commissars, political workers, and suppliers is to prevent theft and bad management, expose thieves, swindlers, and ne'er-do-wells in timely fashion, and punish them mercilessly to the full extent of Soviet law.

I. Stalin, People's Commissar of Defense[14]

NKO ORDER NO. 307 (9 OCTOBER 1942)

Concerning the Establishment of Single-Command and the Disbanding of the Institute of Military Commissars in the Red Army

In accordance with a decree of the Presidium of the Supreme Soviet of the USSR, dated 9 October 1942, "Concerning the Establishment of Full Unity of Command and the Dissolution of the Institute of Commissars in the Red Army," I order:

1. Free up the commissars of units, formations, headquarters, military-educational institutions, and of the NKO's central and main directorates, as well as the political workers in subunits from their assigned duty positions, and assign them as deputies to the corresponding commanders (chiefs) for political affairs.

2. Within one month, the military councils of the *fronts* and armies will confer military command ranks on these political workers within the limits of the rights assigned to them. The military councils of the *fronts* will submit attestation materials for the award of military command ranks to political workers, beginning with senior battalion commissars and higher, to the NKO through the Red Army's Main Political Directorate no later than 15 November 1942.

3. The commanders of formations and the military councils of the armies and *fronts* will promote political workers who are trained in the military respect

to command positions, particularly at the level of company and battalion commander, more decisively.

4. By 20 October the military councils of *fronts* will organize two-month-long *front* command courses numbering 150–250 men each for training company commanders from political workers who are the most capable for command work. Conduct the selection for the courses in accordance with GlavPU [Main Political Directorate] orders.

5. Beginning on 1 November, the Red Army's Main Cadre Directorate will form two-month-long training courses within the Vystrel courses for commissars and political workers who possess the best military knowledge so as to train 200 regimental commanders and 600 battalion commanders from among them. . . .

People's Commissar of Defense, I. Stalin[15]

EXTRACT FROM NKO ORDER NO. 219 (23 JUNE 1941)

Regulations Concerning Military Tribunals in Localities Where a Military State [Condition] Has Been Declared and in Regions of Combat Operations

8. Military tribunals will examine matters that are related to their jurisdiction under Article 27 of the RSFSR Criminal-Legal Code and corresponding articles of the criminal-legal codes of the other union republics.

9. In addition, the military tribunals in the [military] districts, *fronts,* fleets, armies, and flotillas will examine matters related to their jurisdiction under the Regulation of the Central Executive Committee (TsIK) of the USSR of 10 July 1943.

10. As envisioned in Articles 8 and 9 of this Regulation, matters of jurisdiction [include]:

    a. To military tribunals under the auspices of divisions—to company commander inclusively and persons equivalent to them, in accordance with their official position;

    b. To military tribunals under the auspices of corps—to battalion commanders inclusively and persons equivalent to them, in accordance with their official position;

    c. To military tribunals under the auspices of armies—to assistant regimental commanders inclusively and persons who correspond to them; and

    d. To military tribunals under the auspices of military districts, *fronts,* and fleets—to inseparable brigades inclusively and persons who correspond to them.[16]

11. Military tribunals are granted the right to investigate matters beginning 24 hours after the accused is handed over for confinement.

12. Military tribunals consisting of three permanently assigned members will examine matters.

13. The chairmen of the military tribunals will periodically inform the military councils of the districts, *fronts,* and armies and the commanders of corps and divisions about the work of military tribunals in the struggle with crime in appropriate military formations.

14. The sentences of military tribunals are not subject to appeal and can be abrogated or changed only by legal means (Paragraph 407 of the RSFSR Legal Code and corresponding articles of the legal codes of other union republics).

15. The military councils of the districts, *fronts,* and armies (fleets and flotillas) and also the commanders of districts, *fronts,* and armies (fleets and flotillas) can exercise the right of suspending death sentences (by shooting) by simultaneously notifying the chairman of the Military Collegium of the USSR Supreme Court and both the Chief Military Prosecutor of the Red Army and the Chief Prosecutor of the Navy by telegraph through proper channels of his opinion concerning the matter for further resolution.

16. The military tribunal will immediately notify the chairman of the Military Collegium of the USSR Supreme Court and both the Chief Military Prosecutor of the Red Army and the Chief Prosecutor of the Navy by telegraph through proper channels about each sentence involving the death penalty.

In the event the addressee of the telegraphic report does not receive telegrams concerning the suspension of the sentence from the chairman of the Military Collegium of the USSR Supreme Court or the Chief Military Prosecutor of the Red Army or the Chief Prosecutor of the Navy within 72 hours from the moment of its delivery, it [the sentence] will be carried out.

The remaining sentences of the military tribunals carry the force of law from the moment of their proclamation, and they will be implemented immediately.

Chairman of the Presidium of the Supreme Soviet of the USSR
M. Kalinin
Secretary of the Presidium of the Supreme Soviet of the USSR
A. Gorkin[17]

NKO ORDER NO. 227 (28 JULY 1942)

Concerning Measures for the Strengthening of Discipline and Order in the Red Army and Preventing Unauthorized Retreat from Combat Positions

The enemy is throwing new forces forward to the front and, despite increasing losses, is thrusting forward, bursting into the depths of the Soviet Union, capturing new regions, devastating and smashing our cities and villages, and raping, robbing, and murdering our population. . . .

Some foolish people at the front are consoling themselves with discussions that we can retreat farther to the east since we have great territories, much land, and a large population, and that we will always have an abundance of bread [grain]. By doing so, they wish to justify their shameful behavior at the front. However, such talk is spurious and false through and through, and it is advantageous only for our enemy.

Each commander, soldier, and political worker must understand that our resources are not boundless. The territory of the Soviet state is not a desert, and its people, the workers, the peasants, and the intelligentsia are our fathers, mothers, wives, brothers, and children. The territory of the USSR, which the enemy is seizing and striving to seize, [represents] the bread [grain] and other products for the army and the rear, the metal and oil for industry, the mills and factories that are supplying the army with arms and munitions, and the railroads.

After the loss of the Ukraine, Belorussia, the Baltic region, the Donbas, and other regions, our territory has become far less, and, therefore, we have far fewer people, bread, metal, factories, and mills. We have lost more than 70 million of our population, more than 800 million poods [a pood equals 36 pounds] of grain per year, and more than 10 million tons of metal per year. We do not now have predominance over the enemy either in personnel resources or in reserves of bread. Further retreat means ruin for ourselves and, in addition, ruin for our motherland. Each new shred of territory abandoned by us will strengthen the enemy to the utmost and weaken our defense and our motherland to the utmost.

Therefore, we must radically nip in the bud the talk that we have an opportunity to retreat without end and that our great territory, our great and rich country, and our large population and bread will always be in abundance. Such talk is false and harmful, and it weakens us and strengthens the enemy because, if the retreat does not cease, we will be left without bread, without oil, without metal, without raw materials, without mills and factories, and without railroads.

From all of this, it follows that it is time to end the retreat.

Not a step back! This should now be our main slogan.

We must stubbornly defend every position and every meter of Soviet territory to the last drop of our blood and cling to every shred of Soviet land and fight for it to the utmost.

Our motherland has lived through trying days. We must stop and then throw back and destroy the enemy at whatever the cost. The Germans are not as strong as it seems to our panic-mongers. They are straining every last nerve. To endure their blow now means victory for us during the next several months.

Can we endure their blow and then throw the enemy back to the west? Yes, we can because our mills and factories in the rear are working splendidly and our front is receiving ever more and more aircraft, tanks, artillery, and mortars.

What are we short of?

We are short of order and discipline in our companies, battalions, regiments, and divisions, in our tank units, and in our aviation squadrons. This is now our main shortcoming. We must institute the strictest of order and iron discipline in our army if we wish to save the situation and defend our homeland.

We can no longer tolerate commanders, commissars, and political workers whose units and formations willfully abandon their positions. We can no longer tolerate it when commanders, commissars, and political workers permit a few panic-mongers to determine the situation on the field of battle so that they entice other soldiers to retreat and open up the front to the enemy.

Panic-mongers and cowards must be exterminated on the spot.

Henceforth, in accordance with the iron rule of discipline, the requirement for every commander, Red Army soldier, and political worker must be not a step back without an order from his higher commands.

Company, battalion, regimental, and division commanders and associated commissars and political workers who retreat from their combat positions without orders from higher commands are enemies of the homeland. We must treat such commanders and political workers as enemies of the homeland.

Such is the slogan of our motherland.

To fulfill this slogan means to defend our land, to save the motherland, and to exterminate and conquer the hated enemy.

After its winter retreat under the pressure of the Red Army, when discipline broke down in German forces, the Germans undertook several severe measures to restore discipline, which led to good results. They formed more than 100 penal [*shtrafnye*] companies from soldiers who were guilty of violating discipline due to cowardice or unsteadiness, they placed them in dangerous sectors of the front, and they ordered them to redeem their sins with their blood. Further, they formed tens of penal battalions from commanders who had violated discipline through cowardice or unsteadiness, they stripped them of their awards and decorations, they placed them in still more dangerous sectors of the front, and they ordered them to redeem their sins with their blood. Finally, they formed special blocking detachments, they deployed them behind the unstable divisions, and they ordered them to shoot panic-mongers on the spot in the event of attempts to withdraw willfully from their positions or in the event of attempts to surrender.

As is well known, these measures took effect, and now the German forces are fighting better than they fought during the winter. Now it turns out that the German forces have good discipline, although they do not have the lofty goal of defending their fatherland; they have only one predatory aim—to subjugate someone else's country—and our forces, which have the lofty aim of defending their desecrated motherland, do not have such discipline and are suffering defeat because of it.

Does it not follow that we should learn from our enemy in this matter just as our ancestors learned from the enemy and then achieved victory over him in the past?

I think that we should.

The Red Army High Command orders:

1. The military councils of *fronts* and, first and foremost, the *front* commanders will:
   a. Unconditionally liquidate the mood of retreat in the forces and halt the propaganda that we must and can supposedly retreat farther to the east and that such a retreat will supposedly not be harmful;
   b. Unconditionally relieve from their posts army commanders who permit unauthorized retreats by their forces from occupied positions without an order from the *front* commander and send them to the *Stavka* for trial by military court; and
   c. Form from one to three (depending on the situation) penal battalions (of 800 men each) within the *fronts,* assign all junior and senior commanders and corresponding political workers from all types of forces who have been guilty of violating discipline by their cowardice or unsteadiness to them, and place them in the most dangerous sectors of the front to give them the opportunity to redeem themselves with their blood for their crimes against the homeland.

2. The military councils of armies and, first and foremost, all army commanders will:
   a. Unconditionally relieve from their posts corps and division commanders and commissars who have permitted the willful retreat of their forces from occupied positions without an order from the army commander and send them to the *front* military council for military trial;
   b. Form three to five well-armed blocking detachments (of up to 200 men each) within the armies, place them in the immediate rear of unsteady divisions, and, in the event of panic and unauthorized retreat of divisional units, oblige them to shoot the panic-mongers and cowards on the spot. With their help, the soldiers of the division will fulfill their duty to the homeland with honor.
   c. Form from 5 to 10 (depending on the situation) penal companies (of 150–200 men each) within the armies, assign common soldiers and noncommissioned officers who have been guilty of violating discipline by cowardice and unsteadiness to them, and place them in dangerous army sectors to provide them the opportunity to re-

deem themselves with their blood for their crimes against the homeland.
3. Corps and division commanders and commissars will:
   a. Unconditionally relieve from their posts regimental and battalion commanders and commissars who have permitted willful retreat from their occupied positions without an order from their corps and division commanders, confiscate their orders and medals, and send them to the *front* military council for trial by military court.
   b. Render any sort of assistance and support to the army blocking detachments in the matter of strengthening order and discipline in the units.

Read this order in all companies, squadrons, batteries, air squadrons, commands, and headquarters.

People's Commissar of Defense of the USSR I. Stalin[18]

EXTRACT FROM NKO ORDER NO. 298
(28 SEPTEMBER 1942)

An Announcement about the Situation Concerning Penal Battalions and Companies, the Headquarters of Penal Battalions and Companies, and Blocking Detachments of the Red Army

11. Before being dispatched to a penal battalion, the *shtrafnik* is stood before the ranks of his unit (subunit) [his company, battery, squadron, etc.], the order of the division or brigade (or appropriate corps, army, or *front*) [regiment] is read, and the essence of his crime is explained completely.

The *shtrafnik's* orders and medals are taken away and, during the duration of his assignment to the penal battalion, are handed over to the *front's* cadre section for storage.

12. The *shtrafnik* is issued a special type of Red Army book [identity papers].

13. The command and political cadre of a penal battalion are obliged to use every measure of action up to and including execution [shooting] on the spot for disobedience to an order, self-mutilation, and fleeing from the field of battle or an attempt to desert to the enemy.

14. *Shtrafniki* can be appointed to the duty positions of noncommissioned officers with award of the rank of corporal, junior sergeant, or sergeant by order of the penal battalion [company].

Shtrafniki who have been appointed to the duties of noncommissioned officers are paid an allowance according to their duty position, and the remaining *shtrafniki* [are paid] in the sum of 8 rubles, 50 kopeks per month. *Shtrafniki* are not paid field allowances.

The payment of money to the families [of penal soldiers] by monetary certificate ceases, and it is allocated in a manner established for the families of Red Army men and noncommissioned officers in accordance with the regulations of the Presidium of the Supreme Soviet of the USSR, dated 26 June 1941 and 19 July 1942.

15. A *shtrafnik* can be freed ahead of time for combat distinction by a written statement of the penal battalion [company] commander approved by the *front* military council.

In addition, the *shtrafnik* can be presented with a governmental award for performing with special combat distinction.

Before leaving the penal battalion [company], those freed ahead of time will be stood in front of the battalion's [company's] formation, an order will be read about the early release, and the nature of the exploit he performed will be explained.

16. Upon expiration of the designated period [of sentence], the battalion commanders introduces the *shtrafniki* to the *front's* military council [by written statement] with the objective of release, and [the *shtrafniki*] are released from the penal battalion [company] upon confirmation of the written statement.

17. All who are released from the penal battalion [company] are restored in rank and in all rights.

18. *Shtrafniki* who have been wounded in battle are considered to have served their sentences, are restored in rank and all rights, and, after recovering, are sent for further service, and invalids are allocated pensions in accordance with the rate of pay authorized them in their last duties before being enrolled in the penal battalion [company].

19. The families of *shtrafniki* who have perished in combat are allocated pensions on a same basis as all commanders' families in accordance with the rate of pay authorized them in their last duties before being enrolled in the penal battalion [company].

"Approved by"
Deputy People's Commissar of Defense of the USSR
Army General G. Zhukov[19]

NKO ORDER NO. 323 (16 OCTOBER 1942)

Concerning the Sending of Soldiers Convicted by Military Tribunals with Deferred Execution of Their Sentences until War's End to Penal Units

"We are short of order and discipline in our companies, our battalions, our regiments, and our divisions, in our tank units, and in our aviation squadrons. This is now our main shortcoming."

These words of People's Commissar of Defense Comrade Stalin concerning forces in the operating army also apply utterly and completely to forces in the internal organs. Good breeding and discipline in reserve units, in training centers, in training brigades and regiments, in local rifle units and new formations, and in military schools is still at a low level. To a considerable degree, this is occurring because, in some instances, command cadre and chiefs are not serving as examples of discipline and are not demanding enough, and they themselves are not fully exercising the authority that is vested in them and are not demanding their subordinates exercise it [authority]. As a result, disorganization and laxity, and, as a consequence, faint-heartedness and cowardice in the face of the enemy, desertion, and other crimes are being brought along to the front.

Many deserters, as well as plunderers of military property, drunkards, malicious violators of military discipline and other unstable elements, and those convicted by military tribunals the execution of whose sentence has been delayed until war's end, are, in fact, avoiding their punishment.

Those who have been convicted find themselves in reserve units and are sent to the operating army together with worthy soldiers as a part of march columns. While located in the reserve units and also en route to the front, these persons often carry on demoralizing work and, after arriving at their duty station, sow dissension in the masses, and many of them conceal their convictions.

Thus, the judicial sentence does not achieve its aims, it undermines the authority of the court, and, in essence, it inflicts harm on the force units to which these people are assigned.

In accordance with Order No. 227 of People's Commissar of Defense Comrade Stalin, dated 28 July 1942, and the regulations concerning the penal battalions and companies of the operating armies (NKO Order No. 298), I order:

1. Send all soldiers who have been convicted by military tribunal for military and other crimes, the execution of whose sentence has been deferred until war's end (note 2 to paragraph 28 of the RSFSR Criminal Code) to penal units in the operating army for a period of from one to three months: Red Army men and noncommissioned officers to penal companies, and persons from the command and administrative cadre to penal battalions.

If the duration of stay in the penal unit has not been determined in the court sentence, then it will be established by order of the commander of the force unit in which the convicted is located (or the garrison chief), in conformation with the designated measure of punishment by the military tribunal.

The duration of stay in penal units is calculated from the actual moment those convicted arrive in the penal unit.

2. The dispatch of those convicted by military tribunals of the operating army to penal units is the responsibility of the unit commanders and, in instances of conviction outside of the place where their units are located, of the chiefs of garrisons.

3. For dispatching those who have been convicted by the military tribunals of internal [military] districts to penal units, assemble them into special march companies (or commands) at points designated by the military councils of the districts, from which they, along with by-name rosters with copies of the sentences and orders attached, will be immediately placed at the disposal of the military council of the *front* for further assignment to penal units.

Designate experienced and energetic commanders, noncommissioned officers, and Red Army soldiers who are capable of maintaining strict order and discipline en route to escort the penal troops.

4. In instances when the military tribunal has not demoted the convicted to the rank of private by its sentence and has not submitted a petition concerning the deprivation of orders and medals, the demotion and confiscation of orders and medals will be carried out according to the established instructions regarding penal units

5. March companies (commands) of convicted soldiers from the internal military districts will be sent to [the following]: from the Arkhangel'sk Military District to the Karelian Front; from the Far Eastern Military District and Trans-Baikal Front to the Leningrad Front; from the Siberian Military District to the Northwestern Front; from the Ural Military District to the Kalinin Front; from the Moscow Military District to the Western and Briansk Fronts; from the Volga Military District to the Voronezh Front; from the Southern Ural Military District to the Don Front; from the Central Asian Military District to the Stalingrad Front.

6. Immediately inform *front* headquarters about the dispatch of each march company (command) of *shtrafniki,* and report the appointed time of dispatch, the number of trains, and the quantity of people to the chief of the Red Army's Glavupraform.

7. When those convicted who have not been deprived of their rank and orders by the military tribunal's verdict have served their designated time in penal units, restore their rank and their right to wear orders and medals and send them for further regular service.

8. The expunging of the conviction of a person sent to penal units is carried out in a general manner by petition of the command of the penal unit or of that force unit where the convict arrived upon his liberation from the penal unit.

Deputy Commissar of Defense of the USSR
Army Commissar 1st Rank E. Shchadenko[20]

NKO ORDER NO. 0860 (29 OCTOBER 1942)

Concerning Measures to Strengthen Force Discipline on Garrisons and along Communications Routes

Recently, numerous instances of violations of military discipline have been noticed in a number of rear-area garrisons and, in particular, at railroad stations. Soldiers are drinking heavily, crudely violating dress codes and regulation requirements when addressing chiefs and seniors, and wandering in groups along the streets and markets. Instances have been noted where soldiers have sold clothing and products in the market, as well as instances of begging, despite the fact that all sorts of rascals and dubious elements often engage in begging under the guise of soldiers.

The wounded and sick who have been discharged from hospitals and soldiers who have deserted from the front are responsible for a considerable portion of the violations of military discipline and these instances of disgraceful conduct.

This situation exists because of the low expectations of commanders with regard to their subordinates, their weak attentiveness to disciplinary matters, and the failure by command cadre and NKO organs to properly combat these unsatisfactory phenomena.

To establish strict order and discipline in garrisons and along communications routes and to struggle decisively with desertion, I order:

1. Establish "halting point–blocking commands [*komendatura*]" along the railroad on the basis of existing halting point commands in accordance with the attached *shtat*.

2. The list of railroad stations and water and sea staging areas at which halting point–blocking commands will be formed is approved (see attachment 2).

3. The halting point–blocking commands and pass-control points along military automobile roads (VAM) and the garrison chiefs (and commandants) of cities and towns will:

    (1) Detain, send to the garrison guardhouse, and hold under strict arrest: (a) deserters; (b) those absent without leave from trains and commands; (c) malicious violators of military discipline who discredit the Red Army, namely, hooligans, drunkards, and those who begin to argue with commanders; and (d) soldiers who, when following orders given by the commands, clearly violate the established regulations of the command;

    (2) Detain soldiers who do not salute their chiefs and seniors, as well as the slovenly and those dressed not according to form, and impose on them disciplinary penalties in accordance with paragraphs 35–39 of the disciplinary regulations;

(3) Arrest soldiers who are guilty of begging and, after conducting an investigation, turn them over to the proper military authorities and arrest and hand over for trial all civilians who are engaged in begging under the guise of soldiers;
(4) Arrest and hand over to trial by military tribunal all militarily obligated civilians who are detained for evading military registration or summons for military service; and
(5) Arrest and hand over for judgment by military tribunals all soldiers found guilty of selling items of military clothing.

4. The military prosecutor and military tribunal will examine matters concerning those held in garrison guardhouses within three days after their detention.

Immediately send those who have been sentenced by military tribunals, together with an application for delay in the execution of the sentence until the end of the war, to penal units of the operating army on the basis of NKO Order No. 323 of 16 October 1942.

5. To fulfill the missions indicated in point 3 of this order, the chiefs of garrisons will send daily patrols to the marketplaces, to food and goods stores, to canteens, etc., as well as to stations and wharfs where there are no halting point–blocking commands.

6. Establish strict internal routines within NKO hospitals and the People's Commissariat of Health system. The chiefs of hospitals are categorically forbidden from releasing the wounded or the sick from medical facilities during the period of their medical treatment.

7. Send those who are recovering and being sent to combat units or to convalescent battalions, as well as those who have been released from all service because of their invalid status, from the hospital in organized fashion, such as:
   a. Depending on the location of the medical facility, with exception to command cadre, when sending soldiers to units, require the units dispatch escorts to accompany those being discharged.
   b. On the day of release, issue train tickets at the hospital location to those leaving for other points to prevent crowds of those being discharged at the stations and aimless wandering around the city. The military commandant of the stations and wharfs will satisfy the requirements of the hospitals for train tickets in the first place.

8. When sending soldiers on orders or leave, military units and formations, the chiefs of military hospitals and hospitals of the People's Commissariat for Health, and the chiefs of evacuation points will provide their authorized quantities of food as well as documentation [papers] in the case of an unforeseen delay of the servicemen en route. . . .

Deputy People's Commissar of Defense of the USSR
Lieutenant General of the Quartermaster Service
Khrulev[21]

NKO ORDER NO. 47 (30 JANUARY 1943)

Concerning the Demotion to Private and Dispatch to a Penal Battalion of Junior Lieutenant S. O. Karamal'kin for Criticism of His Commanders

In a letter he sent to the editor of the newspaper *Red Star* [*Krasnaia zvezda*], Junior Lieutenant Karamal'kin of the 1082nd Rifle Regiment urgently requested that he be summoned to Moscow to report "serious facts that expose great people."

After being summoned to Moscow, Karamal'kin presented notes that subjected the actions of all of his commanders to criticism, beginning with his company commander and ending with his army and *front* commanders. While doing so and without presenting any proof whatsoever, Karamal'nik declared that many commanders groped their way through their command duties, only to exploit their great authority and save their skin.

After receiving a barely perceptible scratch on his hand, Karamal'nik himself hastily beat it [ran away] from the front.

Although he was not an immediate participant in the battle, by exploiting every sort of rumor and gossip, Karamal'nik tried to bring false accusations against his command. Furthermore, Karamal'nik engaged in discussions with his subordinates regarding how his senior commanders sent people into the attack without assigning them with proper missions, that the commanders were drunk, and so forth.

I order:

Junior Lieutenant Semen Osipovich Karamal'nik of the 1082nd Rifle Regiment to be sent to a penal battalion for three months with reduction in rank to private for fault-finding and an attempt to slander his commanders and undermine the discipline in his subunit.

Deputy People's Commissar of Defense of the USSR
Colonel General E. Shchadenko[22]

Notes

1. V. A. Zolotarev, ed., "Prikazy narodnogo komissara oborony SSSR 22 iiunia 1941 g. – 1942" [Orders of the People's Commissar of Defense of the USSR 22 June 1941–1942], in *Russkii arkhiv: Velikaia Otechestvennaia* [The Russian archives: The Great Patriotic (War)], 13, 2 (2) (Moscow: Terra, 1997), 71. Hereafter cited as Zolotarev, "NKO 1941," with appropriate page(s).

2. See V. A. Zolotarev, ed., "Stavka VGK: Dokumenty i materialy 1942" [The *Stavka* VGK: Documents and materials 1942], in *Russkii arkhiv: Velikaia Otechestvennaia* [The Russian archives: The Great Patriotic (War)], 16, 5 (2) (Moscow: Terra, 1996), 88–89.

3. N. S. Gishko, "GKO postanovliaet" [The GKO decrees], *VIZh*, no. 4–5 (April–May 1992): 19–20.

4. V. A. Zolotarev, ed., "Prikazy narodnogo komissara oborony SSSR 1943–1945 gg. [Orders of the People's Commissar of Defense of the USSR 1943–1945], in *Russkii*

arkhiv: Velikaia Otechestvennaia [The Russian archives: The Great Patriotic (War)], 13, 2 (3) (Moscow: Terra, 1997), 109–10. Hereafter cited as Zolotarev, "NKO 1943," with appropriate page(s).

5. NKO Order No. 357 of 12 November 1942 announced instructions for investigative organs of the Red Army.
6. Zolotarev, "NKO 1943," 198.
7. Zolotarev, "NKO 1941," 113.
8. Ibid., 184–85. The GKO decree was numbered 1488ss and dated 25 March 1942.
9. Ibid., 212–13. The GKO decree was numbered 1595ss and dated 13 April 1942.
10. Ibid., 214–15. The GKO decree was numbered 1618ss and dated 18 April 1942.
11. Zolotarev, "NKO 1941," 73.
12. Ibid., 228–29. This NKO order was numbered 0373.
13. Ibid., 365–66. This NKO order was numbered 0883.
14. Ibid., 165–66.
15. Ibid., 326–27.
16. Ibid., 15–16.
17. Ibid., 16.
18. Ibid., 276–79.
19. Ibid., 312–14.
20. Ibid., 332–33.
21. Ibid, 350–51.
22. Zolotarev, "NKO 1943," 45–46.

APPENDIX 2

Red Army Senior Command Cadre, 1941–1945

MAIN COMMANDS OF STRATEGIC DIRECTIONS [AXES]

Western

Formed on 10 July 1941 to control the Western Front and Pinsk Military Flotilla, later the Western, Reserve, and Central Fronts, disbanded on 10 August 1941, reestablished in February 1942 to control the Kalinin and Western Fronts, disbanded on 5 May 1942. Commanders: Marshal of the Soviet Union S. K. Timoshenko (July–August 1941) and Army General G. K. Zhukov (February–May 1942). Commissars: Lieutenant General N. A. Bulganin (July–August 1941 and February–May 1942). Chiefs of Staff: Lieutenant General G. K. Malandin (July 1941) and Lieutenant General V. D. Sokolovsky (July–August 1941 and February–May 1942).

Northwestern

Formed on 10 July 1941 to control the Northern and Northwestern Fronts and the Northern and Baltic Fleets, and the Leningrad Front on 23 August, disbanded on 28 August 1941. Commander: Marshal of the Soviet Union K. E. Voroshilov. Commissar: Secretary of the Leningrad Communist Party and member of the Communist Party Central Committee A. A. Zhadov. Chiefs of Staff: Major General M. V. Zakharov (July 1941) and Major General A. S. Tsvetkov (August 1941).

Southwestern

Formed on 10 July 1941 to control the Southwestern and Southern Fronts, later the Briansk Front and Black Sea Fleet, relinquished control over the Southwestern and Southern Fronts on 6 September 1941, resumed control over both *fronts* on 16 October 1941 and the Briansk Front from 24 December 1941 to 1 April 1942, relinquished control over the Black Sea Fleet on 1 April 1942, disbanded on 21 June 1942. Commanders: Marshal of the Soviet Union S. M. Budenny (July–September 1941) and Marshal of the Soviet Union S. K. Timoshenko (September 1941 to June 1942, who simultaneously

29

commanded the Southwestern Front September–December 1941 and April–June 1942). Commissar: Secretary of the Ukrainian Communist Party N. S. Khrushchev. Chiefs of Staff: Major General A. P. Pokrovsky (July–October 1941); Major General (Lieutenant General in December 1941) P. I. Boldin; and Lieutenant General I. Kh. Bagramian (December 1941 to June 1942).

North Caucasus

Formed on 21 April 1942 to control the Crimean Front, Sevastopol' Defense Region, North Caucasus Military District, Black Sea Fleet, and Azov Military Flotilla, disbanded in May 1942. Commander: Marshal of the Soviet Union S. M. Budenny. Commissars: Secretary of the Krasnodar Communist Party Committee P. I. Seleznev and Deputy Main Commander for Naval Units, 1st Deputy People's Commissar of the Navy, Admiral I. S. Isakov (April–May 1942). Chief of Staff: Major General G. F. Zakharov (April–May 1942).[1]

FRONTS

Northern

Formed from the Leningrad Military District on 24 June 1941, divided into the Leningrad and Karelian Fronts on 23 August 1941. Commander: Lieutenant General M. M. Popov. Commissar: Corps Commissar N. N. Klement'ev. Chiefs of Staff: Major General D. N. Nikishev (June–August 1941) and Colonel N. V. Gorodetsky (August 1941).

Karelian

Formed from the Northern Front's northern wing on 23 August 1941, disbanded on 15 November 1944, headquarters transferred to the Far East in April 1945 to become the Coastal Group of Forces, later, the 1st Far Eastern Front. Commanders: Lieutenant General (Colonel General in April 1943) V. A. Frolov (September 1941 to February 1944) and Army General (Marshal of the Soviet Union) K. A. Meretskov (February–November 1944). Commissars: Corps Commissar A. S. Zheltov (September 1941 to July 1942); Brigade Commissar (Division Commissar in October 1942) G. N. Kupriianov (July–November 1942); and Division Commissar (Major General in December 1942) P. K. Batrakov (November 1942 to February 1944). Chiefs of Staff: Colonel (Major General in November 1941) L. S. Skvirsky (September 1941 to May 1943) and Major General (Lieutenant General in October 1943) B. A. Pigarevich (May 1943 to August 1944).

Leningrad

Formed from the Northern Front's southern wing on 23 August 1941, reorganized into the Leningrad Military District on 24 July 1945. Commanders: Lieutenant General M. M. Popov (August–September 1941); Army General G. K. Zhukov (September–October 1941); Major General I. I. Fediuninsky (October 1941); Lieutenant General M. S. Khozin (October 1941 to June 1942); and Lieutenant General of Artillery (Colonel General in January 1943 and Army General in November 1943) L. A. Govorov (June 1942 to July 1945). Commissars: Corps Commissar N. N. Klement'ev (August–September 1941) and Secretary of the Communist Party Central Committee (Lieutenant General in February 1943) A. A. Zhdanov (September 1941 to July 1945). Chiefs of Staff: Colonel N. V. Gorodetsky (August–September 1941); Lieutenant General M. S. Khozin (September–October 1941); Major General (Lieutenant General in March 1942) D. N. Gusev (October 1941 to April 1944); and Colonel General M. M. Popov (April 1944 to February 1945 and April–July 1945).

Volkhov

Formed from the Leningrad Front's left wing on 17 December 1941, reorganized as the Leningrad Front's Volkhov Operational Group on 23 April 1942, and as the Volkhov Front on 9 June 1942, disbanded on 15 February 1944, its armies transferred to the Leningrad and 2nd Baltic Fronts and its headquarters to the RVGK [Stavka Reserve]. Commander: Army General K. A. Meretskov. Commissars: Army Commissar 1st Rank A. I. Zaporozhets (December 1941 to April 1942 and June–October 1942); Corps Commissar (Lieutenant General in December 1942) L. Z. Mekhlis (October 1942 to April 1943); and Major General (Lieutenant General in August 1943) T. F. Shtykov (April 1943 to February 1944). Chiefs of Staff: *Kombrig* (Major General in December 1941) G. D. Stel'makh (December 1941 to April 1942 and June–October 1942); Lieutenant General M. N. Sharokhin (October 1942 to June 1943); and Major General (Lieutenant General in September 1943) F. P. Ozerov (June 1943 to February 1944).

Northwestern

Formed from the Baltic Special Military District on 22 June 1941, disbanded on 20 November 1943, its headquarters assigned to the RVGK. Commanders: Colonel General F. I. Kuznetsov (June–July 1941); Major General P. P. Sobennikov (July–August 1941); Lieutenant General (Colonel General in August 1941) P. A. Kurochkin (August 1941 to October 1942 and June–

November 1943); Marshal of the Soviet Union S. K. Timoshenko (October 1942 to March 1943); and Colonel General I. S. Konev (March–June 1943). Commissars: Corps Commissar P. A. Dibrova (June 1941) (repressed); Corps Commissar (Lieutenant General in December 1942) V. N. Bogatkin (June 1941 to May 1943); and Lieutenant General F. E. Bokov (May–November 1943). Chiefs of Staff: Lieutenant General P. S. Klenov (June 1941) (executed for treason); Lieutenant General N. F. Vatutin (June 1941 to May 1942); Major General I. T. Shlemin (May–August 1942); Lieutenant General M. N. Sharokhin (August–October 1942); Lieutenant General V. M. Zlobin (October 1942 to March 1943); Lieutenant General A. N. Bogoliubov (March–November 1943); and Major General P. I. Igolkin (November 1943).

Kalinin

Formed from the Western Front's right wing on 17 October 1941, reorganized as the 1st Baltic Front on 20 November 1943. Commanders: Colonel General I. S. Konev (October 1941 to August 1942); Lieutenant General (Colonel General in November 1942) M. A. Purkaev (August 1942 to April 1943); and Colonel General (Army General in August 1943) A. I. Eremenko (April–October 1943). Commissar: Corps Commissar (Lieutenant General in December 1942) D. S. Leonov (October 1941 to October 1943). Chiefs of Staff: Major General I. I. Ivanov (October–November 1941); Major General E. P. Zhuravlev (November 1941); Colonel A. A. Katsnel'son (November–December 1941); Major General (Lieutenant General in May 1942) M. V. Zakharov (January 1942 to April 1943); and Lieutenant General V. V. Kurasov (April–October 1943).

1st Baltic

Formed from the Kalinin Front on 20 October 1943, reorganized as the 3rd Belorussian Front's Zemland Group of Forces on 24 February 1945. Commanders: Army General A. I. Eremenko (October–November 1943) and Army General I. Kh. Bagramian (November 1943 to February 1945). Commissars: Lieutenant General D. S. Leonov (October 1943 to November 1944) and Lieutenant General M. V. Rudakov (November 1944 to February 1945). Chief of Staff: Lieutenant General V. V. Kurasov.

Western

Formed from the Western Special Military District on 22 June 1941, divided into the 2nd and 3rd Belorussian Fronts on 24 April 1944. Commanders: Army General D. G. Pavlov (June 1941) (executed for treason); Marshal of the Soviet Union S. K. Timoshenko (July–September 1941); Lieutenant General (Colonel General in September 1941) I. S. Konev (September–October 1941 and August 1942 to February 1943); Army General G. K. Zhukov (October 1941 to August 1942); and Colonel General (Army General in August 1943) V. D. Sokolovsky (February 1943 to April 1944) (relieved for dereliction of duty). Commissars: Corps Commissar A. Ia. Fominykh (June–July 1941); Secretary Belorussian Communist Party P. K. Ponomarenko (June–July 1941); Communist Party Secretary (Lieutenant General in December 1942) N. A. Bulganin (July 1941 to December 1943); and Lieutenant General L. Z. Mekhlis (December 1943 to April 1944). Chiefs of Staff: Major General V. E. Klimovskikh (June 1941) (executed for treason); Lieutenant General G. K. Malandin (July 1941); Lieutenant General (Colonel General in June 1942 V. D. Sokolovsky (July 1941 to January 1942 and May 1942 to February 1943); Major General V. S. Golushkevich (January–May 1942); and Lieutenant General A. P. Pokrovsky (February 1943 to April 1944).

Briansk

Formed from the Central Front's right wing on 16 August 1941, disbanded on 10 November 1941, but immediately reformed from the Southwestern Front's right wing, disbanded on 12 March 1943, reestablished from the Orel Front on 28 March, reorganized into the Baltic Front on 10 October 1943. Commanders: Lieutenant General A. I. Eremenko (August–October 1941); Major General G. F. Zakharov (October–November 1941); Colonel General Ia. T. Cherevichenko (December 1941 to April 1942); Lieutenant General F. I. Golikov (April–July 1942); Lieutenant General K. K. Rokossovsky (July–September 1942); Lieutenant General (Colonel General in January 1943) M. A. Reiter (September 1942 to June 1943); and Colonel General M. M. Popov (June–October 1943). Commissars: Division Commissar P. I. Mazepov (August–November 1941); Corps Commissar A. F. Kolobiakov (December 1941 to April 1942); Corps Commissar (Major General of Tank Forces in December 1942 and Lieutenant General of Tank Forces in March 1943) I. Z. Susaikov (April 1942 to July 1943); and Lieutenant General L. Z. Mekhlis (July–October 1943). Chiefs of Staff: Major General F. G. Zakharov (August–October 1941); Colonel, Major General (and Lieutenant General in February 1943) L. M. Sandalov (October–November 1941 and September 1942 to October 1943); Major General V. Ia. Kolpakchi (December 1941 to January 1942); Major General M. I. Kazakov (January–July 1942); and Major General M. S. Malanin (July–September 1942).

Baltic

Formed from the Briansk Front (3rd formation) on 10 October 1943, renamed the 2nd Baltic Front on 20 October 1943. Commander: Army General M. M. Popov. Commissar: Lieutenant General L. Z. Mekhlis. Chief of Staff: Major General N. P. Sidel'nikov.

2nd Baltic

Formed from the Baltic Front on 20 October 1943, disbanded on 1 April 1945, its forces transferred to the Leningrad Front. Commanders: Army General M. M. Popov (October 1943 to April 1944); Army General A. I. Eremenko (April 1944 to February 1945); and Marshal of the Soviet Union L. A. Govorov (February–March 1945). Commissars: Lieutenant General L. Z. Mekhlis (October–December 1943); Lieutenant General N. A. Bulganin (December 1943 to April 1944); and Lieutenant General V. N. Bogatkin (April 1944 to March 1945). Chiefs of Staff: Lieutenant General L. M. Sandalov (October 1943 to March 1945) and Colonel General M. M. Popov (March 1945).

3rd Baltic

Formed from the 20th Army headquarters and armies on the Leningrad Front's left wing on 21 April 1944, disbanded on 16 October 1944, its forces transferred to the Leningrad and 1st and 2nd Baltic Fronts. Commander: Colonel General (Army General in July 1944) I. I. Maslennikov. Commissar: Lieutenant General M. V. Rudakov. Chief of Staff: Lieutenant General V. R. Vashkevich.

Voronezh

Formed from the Briansk Front's left wing on 7 July 1942, renamed the 1st Ukrainian Front on 20 October 1943. Commanders: Lieutenant General (Colonel General in January 1943) F. I. Golikov (July 1942 and October 1942 to March 1943) and Lieutenant General (Colonel General in December 1942 and Army General in February 1943) N. F. Vatutin (July–October 1942 and March–October 1943). Commissars: Corps Commissar I. Z. Susaikov (July–September 1942); Corps Commissar L. Z. Mekhlis (September–October 1942); Army Commissar 2nd Rank (Lieutenant General in December 1942) F. F. Kuznetsov (October 1942 to March 1943); Lieutenant General N. S. Khrushchev (March–October 1943); and Major General K. V. Krainiukov (October 1943). Chiefs of Staff: Major General F. I. Shevchenko (July 1942); Lieutenant General M. I. Kazakov (July 1942 to February 1943); Major General A. P. Pilipenko (February–March 1943); Major General F. K. Korzhenivich (March–May 1943); and Lieutenant General S. P. Ivanov (May–October 1943).

1st Ukrainian

Formed from the Voronezh Front on 20 October 1943, disbanded on 10 June 1945, its headquarters forming the Central Group of Forces (CGF). Commanders: Army General N. F. Vatutin (October 1943 to March 1944); Marshal of the Soviet Union G. K. Zhukov (March–May 1944); and Marshal of the Soviet Union I. S. Konev (May 1944 to May 1945). Commissars: Lieutenant General N. S. Khrushchev (October 1943 to August 1944) and Lieutenant General K. V. Krainiukov (October 1943 to June 1945). Chiefs of Staff: Lieutenant General S. P. Ivanov (October–November 1943); Lieutenant General A. N. Bogoliubov (November 1943 to April 1944); Army General V. D. Sokolovsky (April 1944 to April 1945); and Army General I. E. Petrov (April–June 1945).

Don

Formed from the Stalingrad Front on 28 September 1942, formed the nucleus of the Central Front on 15 February 1943. Commander: Lieutenant General (Colonel General in January 1943) K. K. Rokossovsky. Commissars: Corps Commissar A. S. Zheltov (September–October 1942); Brigade Commissar A. I. Kirpichenko (October–December 1942); and Major General K. F. Telegin (December 1942 to February 1943). Chief of Staff: Major General (Lieutenant General in December 1942) M. S. Malanin.

Central

Formed from the Western Front's right wing and the 4th Army's headquarters on 24 July 1941, encircled, and destroyed near Chernigov, disbanded on 25 August 1941, its forces transferred to the Briansk Front, reformed from the Don Front's headquarters and reserve armies on 15 February 1943, renamed the Belorussian Front on 20 October 1943. Commanders: Colonel General F. I. Kuznetsov (July–August 1941); Lieutenant General M. G. Efremov (August 1941); and Colonel General (Army General in April 1943) K. K. Rokossovsky (February–October 1943). Commissars: Secretary of the Belorussian Communist Party P. K. Ponomarenko (July–August 1941 and March–April 1943); Major General (Lieutenant General in August 1943) K. F. Telegin (February–October 1943). Chiefs of Staff: Colonel L. M. Sandalov (July–August 1941); Lieutenant General G. G. Sokolov (August 1941); and Lieutenant General (Colonel General in September 1943) M. S. Malanin (February–October 1943).

Belorussian

Formed from the Central Front on 20 October 1943, renamed the 1st Belorussian Front on 17 February 1944. Commander: Army General K. K. Rokossovsky. Commissar: Lieutenant General K. F. Telegin. Chief of Staff: Colonel General M. S. Malanin.

1st Belorussian

Formed from Belorussian Front's headquarters and forces from the Belorussian and Western Fronts on 17 February 1944, disbanded on 10 June 1945, its headquarters forming the Group of Soviet Forces Germany (GSFG). Commanders: Army General (Marshal of the Soviet Union in June 1944) K. K. Rokossovsky (February–November 1944) and Marshal of the Soviet Union G. K. Zhukov (November 1944 to June 1945). Commissars: Lieutenant General K. F. Telegin (February–May 1944 and November 1944 to June 1945) and Colonel General N. A. Bulganin (May–November 1944). Chief of Staff: Colonel General M. S. Malanin.

2nd Belorussian

Formed from the Northwestern Front's headquarters and armies from the Belorussian Front on 17 February 1944, disbanded on 5 April 1944, its headquarters reverting to the RVGK and its armies to the Belorussian Front, second formation from the 10th Army's headquarters and armies from the Western Front on 24 April 1944, disbanded on 10 June 1945, its headquarters forming the Northern Group of Forces (NGF). Commanders: Colonel General P. A. Kurochkin (February–April 1944); Colonel General I. E. Petrov (April–June 1944); Colonel General (Army General in July 1944) G. F. Zakharov (June–November 1944); and Marshal of the Soviet Union K. K. Rokossovsky (November 1944 to June 1945). Commissars: Lieutenant General F. E. Bokov (February–April 1944); Lieutenant General L. Z. Mekhlis (April–July 1944); and Lieutenant General N. E. Subbotin (July 1944 to June 1945). Chiefs of Staff: Lieutenant General V. Ia. Kolpakchi (February–April 1944); Lieutenant General S. I. Liubarsky (April–May 1944); and Lieutenant General (Colonel General in February 1945) A. N. Bogoliubov (May 1944 to June 1945).

3rd Belorussian

Formed from the Western Front on 24 April 1944, disbanded on 15 August 1945. Commanders: Colonel General (Army General in 26 June 1944) I. D. Cherniakhovsky (April 1944 to February 1945); Marshal of the Soviet Union A. M. Vasilevsky (February–April 1945); and Army General I. Kh. Bagramian (April–August 1945). Commissar: Army General V. E. Makarov. Chief of Staff: Lieutenant General (Colonel General) A. P. Pokrovsky.

Southwestern

Formed from the Kiev Special Military District on 22 June 1941, encircled and destroyed at Kiev in September 1941 but immediately reestablished, disbanded on 12 July 1942, its headquarters forming the Stalingrad Front and its armies joining the Stalingrad and Southern Fronts, reformed from RVGK armies on 22 October 1942, renamed the 3rd Ukrainian Front on 20 October 1943. Commanders: Colonel General M. P. Kirponos (June–September 1941) (KIA); Marshal of the Soviet Union S. K. Timoshenko (September–December 1941 and April–July 1942); Lieutenant General F. Ia. Kostenko (December 1941 to April 1942); Lieutenant General (Colonel General in December 1942) N. F. Vatutin (October 1942 to March 1943); and Colonel General (Army General in April 1943) R. Ia. Malinovsky (March–October 1943). Commissars: Division Commissar E. P. Rykov (June–August 1941); Secretary of the Ukrainian Communist Party M. A. Burmistenko (August–September 1941); Secretary of the Ukrainian Communist Party N. S. Khrushchev (September 1941 to July 1942); Division Commissar K. A. Gurov (January–July 1942); and Corps Commissar (Lieutenant General in December 1942) A. S. Zheltov (October 1942 to October 1943). Chiefs of Staff: Lieutenant General M. A. Purkaev (June–July 1941); Major General V. I. Tupikov (July–September 1941) (KIA); Major General A. P. Pokrovsky (September–October 1941); Major General (Lieutenant General in November 1941) P. I. Boldin (October 1941 to March 1942 and June–July 1942); Lieutenant General I. Kh. Bagramian (April–June 1942); Major General G. D. Stelmakh (October–December 1942) (KIA); Major General (Lieutenant General in January 1943) S. P. Ivanov (December 1942 to May 1943); and Major General (Lieutenant General in September 1943) F. K. Korzhenevich (May–October 1943).

3rd Ukrainian

Formed from the Southwestern Front on 20 October 1943, disbanded on 15 June 1945, its headquarters forming the Southern Group of Forces (SGF). Commanders: Army General R. Ia. Malinovsky (October 1943 to May 1944) and Army General (Marshal of the Soviet Union in September 1944) F. I. Tolbukhin (May 1944 to June 1945). Commissar: Lieutenant General A. S. Zheltov. Chiefs of Staff: Lieutenant General F. K. Korzhenevich (October 1943 to May 1944); Lieutenant General (Colonel General in May 1944) S. S. Biriuzov (May–October 1944); and Lieutenant General (Colonel General in April 1945) S. P. Ivanov (October 1944 to June 1945).

Southeastern

Formed from the 1st Tank Army's and Southern Front's headquarters and armies on the Stalingrad Front's left wing on 7 August 1942, renamed the Stalingrad Front on 28 September 1942. Commander: Colonel General A. I. Eremenko. Commissar: Brigade Commissar V. M. Laiok (August 1942) and

Secretary of the Ukrainian Communist Party Central Committee N. S. Khrushchev. Chief of Staff: Major General F. G. Zakharov.

Stalingrad

Formed from the Southwestern Front's headquarters and armies and RVGK armies on 12 July 1942, divided into the Stalingrad and Southeastern Fronts on 7 August 1942, renamed the Don Front on 28 September 1942 and the Southern Front on 1 January 1943. Commanders: Marshal of the Soviet Union S. K. Timoshenko (July 1942); Lieutenant General V. N. Gordov (July–August 1942); and Colonel General A. I. Eremenko (August–December 1942). Commissar: Secretary of the Ukrainian Communist Party N. S. Khrushchev. Chiefs of Staff: Lieutenant General P. I. Boldin (July 1942); Major General D. N. Nikishev (July–September 1942); Major General K. A. Kovalenko (September 1942); Major General G. F. Zakharov (September–October 1942); and Major General I. S. Varennikov (October–December 1942).

Southern

Formed from the Moscow Military District and the Odessa Military District's armies on 25 June 1941, disbanded on 28 July 1942, its headquarters and armies forming the North Caucasus Front, second formation from the Stalingrad Front on 1 January 1943, renamed the 4th Ukrainian Front on 20 October 1943. Commanders: Army General I. V. Tiulenev (June–August 1941); Lieutenant General D. I. Riabyshev (August–October 1941); Colonel General Ia. T. Cherevichenko (October–December 1941); Lieutenant General (Colonel General in February 1943) R. Ia. Malinovsky (December 1941 to July 1942 and February–March 1943); Colonel General A. I. Eremenko (January–February 1943); and Lieutenant General (Colonel General in April 1943) F. I. Tolbukhin (March–October 1943). Commissars: Army Commissar 1st Rank A. I. Zaporozhets (July–December 1941); Division Commissar I. I. Larin (December 1941 to July 1942); Secretary of the Ukrainian Communist Party (Lieutenant General in February 1943) N. S. Khrushchev (January–February 1943); Lieutenant General K. A. Gurov (March–September 1943); and Colonel General E. A. Shchadenko (September–October 1943). Chiefs of Staff: Major General G. D. Shishenin (June 1941); Colonel F. K. Korzhenevich (July 1941); Major General F. N. Romanov (July–August 1941); Major General (Lieutenant General in December 1941) A. I. Antonov (August 1941 to July 1942); Major General I. S. Varennikov (January–April 1943); and Major General (Lieutenant General in August 1943) S. S. Biriuzov (April–October 1943).

4th Ukrainian

Formed from the Southern Front on 20 October 1943, disbanded and assigned to the RVGK on 16 May 1944, reestablished on 6 August 1944 to conduct operations in the Carpathian Mountains, reorganized as the Carpathian Military District in July 1945. Commanders: Army General F. I. Tolbukhin (October 1943 to May 1944); Colonel General (Army General in October 1944) I. E. Petrov (August 1944 to March 1945); and Army General A. I. Eremenko (March–July 1945). Commissars: Colonel General E. A. Shchadenko (October 1943 to January 1944); Lieutenant General N. E. Subbotin (January–May 1944); and Colonel General L. Z. Mekhlis (August 1944 to July 1945). Chiefs of Staff: Lieutenant General S. S. Biriuzov (October 1943 to May 1944); Lieutenant General F. K. Korzhenevich (May 1944 and August 1944 to April 1945); and Colonel General L. M. Sandalov (April–July 1945).

Caucasus

Formed from the Trans-Caucasus Front on 30 December 1941, divided into the Crimean Front and Trans-Caucasus Military District on 28 January 1942. Commander: Lieutenant General D. T. Kozlov. Commissar: Division Commissar F. A. Shamanin. Chief of Staff: Major General F. I. Tolbukhin.

Crimean

Formed from the Caucasus Front and the Sevastopol' Defense Region on 28 January 1942, disbanded on 19 May 1942, its forces transferred to the North Caucasus Front. Commander: Lieutenant General D. T. Kozlov (demoted to Major General). Commissar: Division Commissar F. A. Shamanin. Chiefs of Staff: Major General F. I. Tolbukhin (January–March 1942) and Major General P. P. Vechnyi (March–May 1942).

North Caucasus

Formed from the Crimean Front and the disbanded North Caucasus Main Direction's headquarters on 20 May 1942, assigned forces from the disbanded Southern Front on 28 July 1942, subdivided into the Coastal and Don Groups of Forces, reorganized as the Trans-Caucasus Front's Black Sea Group of Forces on 1 September 1942, reestablished from the Trans-Caucasus Front's Northern Group of Forces on 24 January 1943, incorporated the Trans-Caucasus Front's Black Sea Group of Forces on 5 February 1943, reorganized into the Separate Coastal Army under RVGK control on 20 November

1943. Commanders: Marshal of the Soviet Union S. M. Budenny (May–August 1942); Lieutenant General (Colonel General in January 1943) I. I. Maslennikov (January–May 1943); and Lieutenant General (Colonel General in August 1943) I. E. Petrov (May–November 1943). Commissars: Secretary of the Krasnodar District Communist Party Committee P. I. Seleznev (May–June 1942); Secretary of the Communist Party Central Committee L. M. Kaganovich (July–August 1942); and Major General A. Ia. Fominykh (January–November 1943). Chiefs of Staff: Major General G. F. Zakharov (May–June 1942); Lieutenant General A. I. Antonov (July–August 1942); Major General A. A. Zabaluev (January–March 1943); Lieutenant General I. E. Petrov (March–May 1943); and Major General I. A. Laskin (May–November 1943).

Trans-Caucasus

Formed from the Trans-Caucasus Military District on 23 August 1941, renamed the Caucasus Front on 30 December 1941, disbanded and divided into the Crimean Front and Trans-Caucasus Military District in early May 1942, re-established from the Trans-Caucasus Military District on 15 May 1942, reorganized as the Tbilisi Military District on 25 August 1945. Commanders: Lieutenant General D. T. Kozlov (August–December 1941) and Army General I. V. Tiulenev (May 1942 to July 1945). Commissars: Division Commissar F. A. Shamanin (August–December 1941); Brigade Commissar (Major General in December 1942) P. I. Efimov (March–November 1942 and February–May 1945); and L. M. Kaganovich (November 1942 to February 1943). Chiefs of Staff: Major General F. I. Tolbukhin (August–December 1941); Major General A. I. Subbotin (May–August 1942); Lieutenant General P. I. Bodin (August–October 1942); Colonel (Major General in November 1942) S. E. Rozhdestvensky (October–November 1942 and December 1942 to November 1943); and Lieutenant General S. P. Ivanov (November 1943 to June 1944).

Front of the Mozhaisk Defense Line

Formed to defend the approaches to Moscow on 18 July 1941, disbanded on 30 July 1941, its forces transferred to the Reserve Front. Commander: Lieutenant General P. A. Artem'ev. Commissar: Moscow Party Secretary I. M. Sokolov. Chief of Staff: Major General A. I. Kudriashev.

Front of Reserve Armies

Formed to defend the approaches to Moscow on 14 July 1941, reorganized as the Reserve Front on 30 July 1941. Commander: Lieutenant General of

NKVD I. A. Bogdanov. Commissar: Commissar for State Security 3rd Rank S. N. Kruglov. Chief of Staff: Major General P. I. Liapin.

Reserve

Formed from the Front of Reserve Armies and the Moscow Defense Zone on 30 July 1941, encircled and destroyed at Viaz'ma, its remnants joining the Western Front on 10 October 1941, reestablished from the 41st Army's headquarters and RVGK forces on 6 April 1943, reorganized as the Steppe Military District on 15 April 1943. Commanders: Army General G. K. Zhukov (August–September 1941); Marshal of the Soviet Union S. M. Budenny (September–October 1941); and Lieutenant General M. M. Popov (April 1943). Commissars: State Security Commissar 3rd Rank S. N. Kruglov (August–October 1941) and Lieutenant General L. Z. Mekhlis (April 1943). Chiefs of Staff: Major General P. I. Liadin (August 1941); Major General A. F. Anisov (August–October 1941) (KIA); and Lieutenant General M. V. Zakharov (April 1943).

Kursk

Formed from the Central Front's 60th Army, the Voronezh Front's 38th Army, and one army (never assigned) from the RVGK on 23 March 1943, disbanded on 24 March 1943, its headquarters forming the Orel Front. Commander: Colonel General M. A. Reiter. Commissar: Major General of Tank Forces I. Z. Suzaikov. Chief of Staff: Lieutenant General L. M. Sandalov.

Orel

Formed from the Western Front's 61st and 3rd Armies and one army (never assigned) from the RVGK on 27 March 1943, renamed the Briansk Front on 28 March 1943. Commander: Colonel General M. A. Reiter. Commissar: Major General of Tank Forces I. Z. Suzaikov. Chief of Staff: Lieutenant General L. M. Sandalov.

Steppe

Formed in the RVGK from the Steppe Military District on 9 July 1943, renamed the 2nd Ukrainian Front on 20 October 1943. Commander: Army General I. S. Konev. Commissar: Lieutenant General of Tank Forces I. Z. Susaikov. Chief of Staff: Lieutenant General M. V. Zakharov.

2nd Ukrainian

Formed from the Steppe Front on 20 October 1943, disbanded on 10 June 1945, its headquarters forming the Odessa Military District. Commanders: Army General I. S. Konev (October 1943 to May 1944) and Army General (Marshal of the Soviet Union in September 1944) R. Ia. Malinovsky (May 1944 to June 1945). Commissars: Lieutenant General of Tank Forces I. Z. Susaikov (October 1943 to March 1945) and Lieutenant General A. N. Tevchenkov (March–June 1945). Chief of Staff: Colonel General (Army General in May 1945) M. V. Zakharov.

Trans-Baikal

Formed from the Trans-Baikal Military District on 15 September 1941. Commanders: Lieutenant General (Colonel General in May 1943) M. P. Kovalev (September 1941 to July 1945) and Marshal of the Soviet Union R. Ia. Malinovsky (July–October 1945). Commissars: Corps Commissar (Lieutenant General in December 1942) K. N. Zimin (September 1941 to July 1944); Major General K. L. Sorokin (July 1944 to July 1945); and Lieutenant General A. N. Tevchenkov (July–October 1945). Chiefs of Staff: Lieutenant General E. G. Trotsenko (September 1941 to July 1945) and Army General M. V. Zakharov (July–September 1945).

Far Eastern

Formed from the Special Red Banner Far Eastern Army on 28 June 1938, reorganized as the 2nd Far Eastern Front on 5 August 1945. Commanders: Colonel General (Army General in February 1941 I. P. Apanisenko (January 1941 to April 1943) and Colonel General (Army General in October 1944) M. A. Purkaev (April 1943 to August 1945). Commissars: Corps Commissar A. S. Zheltov (February–August 1941); Division Commissar (Corps Commissar in December 1941, Major General in December 1942, and Lieutenant General in January 1944) F. P. Iakovlev (August 1941 to May 1945); and Lieutenant General D. S. Leonov (May–August 1945). Chiefs of Staff: Lieutenant General (Colonel General in October 1941) I. V. Smorodinov (January 1941 to August 1943) and Major General (Lieutenant General in September 1944) F. I. Shevchenko (August 1943 to August 1945).

1st Far Eastern

Formed from the Coastal Army Group on 5 August 1945. Commander: Marshal of the Soviet Union K. A. Meretskov (August–September 1945).

Commissar: Colonel General T. F. Shtykov (August–September 1945). Chief of Staff: Lieutenant General A. N. Krutikov (August–September 1945).

2nd Far Eastern

Formed from the Far Eastern Front on 5 August 1945. Commander: Army General M. A. Purkaev (August–September 1945). Commissar: Lieutenant General D. S. Leonov (August–September 1945). Chief of Staff: Lieutenant General F. I. Shevchenko (August–September 1945).[2]

DEFENSE LINES AND DEFENSE ZONES

Mozhaisk Defense Line

Formed from the 32nd, 33rd, and 34th Armies, NKVD railroad and internal security forces on 18 July 1941 to protect the approaches to Moscow, included in the Moscow Defense Zone on 12 October 1941. Commander: Lieutenant General of NKVD P. A. Artem'ev. Commissar: I. M. Sokolov.

Moscow Defense Zone

Formed as the Directorate for the Defense of Moscow on 12 October 1941, converted into an operational headquarters on 2 December 1942 to defend Moscow, controlled the 24th and 60th Armies and other forces within the region, functioned as a reserve *front* after early 1942 to provide individual and unit replacements for operating *fronts*, disbanded on 15 October 1943. Commander: Lieutenant General of NKVD Forces (Colonel General of NKVD Forces in December 1942) P. A. Artem'ev. Commissars: Division Commissar (Major General in December 1942) K. F. Telegin (December 1941 to December 1942) and Major General D. A. Gapanovich (December 1942 to October 1943). Chiefs of Staff: Major General A. I. Kudriashev (December 1941 to July 1943) and Major General A. I. Subbotin (July–October 1943).[3]

FIELD (COMBINED-ARMS) ARMIES

1st Red Banner

Formed as the Red Banner Far Eastern Front's 1st Coastal Army in July 1938, renamed the 1st Red Banner Army in September 1938. Lieutenant General V. P. Vasil'ev (June 1941 to October 1942) and Major General (Lieutenant General in October 1942) M. S. Savvushkin (October 1942 to June 1945).

2nd Red Banner

Formed in the Far East in July 1938. Lieutenant General of Tank Forces M. F. Terekhin (April 1941 to August 1945).

3rd

Formed in the Special Belorussian Military District from the Vitebsk Army Group of Forces in 1939, encircled and destroyed at Belostok in June 1941, reformed in the RVGK, assigned to the Central Front in August 1941. Lieutenant General V. I. Kuznetsov (June–August 1941); Major General Ia. G. Kreizer (August–December 1941); Lieutenant General P. S. Pshenninkov (December 1941); Lieutenant General P. I. Batov (January–February 1942); Major General F. F. Zhmachenko (February–May 1942); Lieutenant General P. P. Korzun (May 1942 to June 1943); and Lieutenant General (Colonel General in June 1944) A. V. Gorbatov (June 1943 to May 1945).

4th

Formed in the Belorussian Military District from the Bobruisk Army Group in August 1939, encircled and partially destroyed in the Minsk region in June–July 1941, disbanded in late July 1941, its headquarters formed the Central Front, reformed in late September 1941 in the Volkhov region, disbanded in November 1943. Major General A. A. Korobkov (June–July 1941) (executed for treason); Colonel L. M. Sandalov (July 1941); Lieutenant General V. F. Iakovlev (September–November 1941); Army General K. A. Meretskov (November–December 1941); Major General P. A. Ivanov (December 1941 to February 1942); Major General P. I. Liapin (February–June 1942); and Major General (Lieutenant General in September 1943) N. I. Gusev (June 1942 to November 1943).

5th

Formed in the Kiev Special Military District in 1939, encircled and destroyed at Kiev and disbanded in September 1941, reformed from the Mozhaisk Defense Sector (former Mozhaisk Fortified Region) in October 1941. Major General of Tank Forces M. I. Potapov (June–September 1941) (POW); Major General D. D. Leliushenko (October 1941); Major General of Artillery (Lieutenant General of Artillery in November 1941) L. A. Govorov (October 1941 to April 1942); Major General (Lieutenant General in June 1942) I. I. Fediuninsky (April–October 1942); Colonel General Ia. T. Cherevichenko (October 1942 to February 1943); Lieutenant General V. S. Polenov (February–

October 1943); Lieutenant General N. I. Krylov (October 1943 to October 1944 and December 1944–September 1945); and Lieutenant General P. G. Shafronov (October–December 1944).

6th

Formed in the Kiev Special Military District in August 1939, encircled and destroyed at Uman' and disbanded on 10 August 1941, reformed in the Southern Front from the 48th Rifle Corps in late August 1941, encircled and destroyed near Barvenkovo in May 1942 and disbanded in early June 1942, reformed from the 6th Reserve Army in early July 1942, encircled and partially destroyed near Krasnograd in February 1943, its forces transferred to the 37th and 46th Armies in June 1944, headquarters reverted to RVGK on 18 July, reformed and assigned to the 1st Ukrainian Front in December 1944. Lieutenant General I. N. Muzychenko (June–August 1941) (POW); Major General (Lieutenant General in November 1941) R. Ia. Malinovsky (August–December 1941); Major General (Lieutenant General in March 1942) A. M. Gorodniansky (January–May 1942); Major General (Lieutenant General in December 1942) F. M. Kharitonov (July 1942 to May 1943); Lieutenant General I. T. Shlemin (May 1943 to May 1944); Major General F. D. Kuznetsov (June–August and September–December 1944); Colonel General V. D. Tsvetaev (September 1944); and Lieutenant General V. A. Gluzdovsky (December 1944 to May 1945).

7th (Separate)

Formed in the Leningrad Military District in 1940, renamed the 7th Separate Army on 24 September 1941, disbanded in early January 1945, its headquarters forming the 9th Guards Army's headquarters. Lieutenant General F. D. Gorelenko (June–September 1941 and November 1941 to June 1942); Army General K. A. Meretskov (September–November 1941); Lieutenant General S. G. Trofimenko (July 1942 to January 1943); Major General (Lieutenant General in April 1943); A. N. Krutikov (January 1943 to August 1944); and Lieutenant General V. A. Gluzdovsky (August–November 1944).

8th

Formed in the Leningrad Military District from the Novgorod Army Operational Group in October 1939. Major General P. P. Sobennikov (March–June 1941); Lieutenant General F. S. Ivanov (June–July 1941) (repressed); Major General I. M. Liubovtsev (July–August 1941); Lieutenant General P. S. Pshennikov (August–September 1941); Major General V. I. Shcherbakov

(September 1941); Lieutenant General T. I. Shevaldin (September–November 1941); Major General A. L. Bondarev (November 1941 to January 1942); Major General A. V. Sukhomlin (January–April 1942); and Major General (Lieutenant General in November 1942) F. I. Starikov (April 1942 to May 1945).

9th

Formed in the Odessa Military District in June 1941, disbanded in November 1943. Colonel General Ia. T. Cherevichenko (June–September 1941); Major General F. M. Kharitonov (September 1941 to May 1942); Major General P. M. Kozlov (May–June 1942 and May–June 1943); Lieutenant General A. I. Lopatin (June 1942 and June 1943); Major General F. A. Parkhomenko (July–August 1942); Major General K. A. Koroteev (September 1942 to February 1943 and March–May 1943); Major General V. V. Glagolev (February–March 1943); and Major General (Lieutenant General in October 1943) A. A. Grechko (June–October 1943).

10th

Formed in the Belorussian Special Military District in 1939, encircled and destroyed at Belostok and disbanded in July 1941, reformed in the Southern Front in early October 1941, disbanded on 17 October 1941, reformed in the Volga Military District in November 1941, headquarters formed the 2nd Belorussian Front's headquarters in April 1944, its forces transferred to the 49th Army. Major General K. D. Golubev (June–July 1941); Lieutenant General M. G. Efremov (October 1941); Lieutenant General F. I. Golikov (October 1941 to February 1942); and Major General (Lieutenant General in June 1942) V. S. Popov (February 1942 to April 1944).

11th

Formed in the Belorussian Special Military District in 1939, disbanded in December 1943. Lieutenant General V. I. Morozov (June 1941 to 1941 to 1941–November 1942); Lieutenant General P. A. Kurochkin (November 1942 to March 1943); Lieutenant General A. I. Lopatkin (March–July 1943); and Lieutenant General I. I. Fediuninsky (July–December 1943).

12th

Formed in the Kiev Special Military District in 1939, encircled and destroyed at Uman' and disbanded in August 1941, reformed in the Southern Front from the 17th Rifle Corps in August 1941, reorganized as the Tuapse Defense Region in September 1942, its forces transferred to the 18th Army, reformed in the Southwestern Front from the 5th Tank Army in April 1943, disbanded in November 1943. Major General P. G. Ponedelin (June–August 1941); Major General I. V. Galanin (August–October 1941); Major General K. A. Koroteev (October 1941 to April 1942); Major General A. A. Grechko (April–September 1942); Lieutenant General I. T. Shlemin (April–May 1943); and Lieutenant General A. I. Danilov (May–October 1943).

13th

Headquarters formed in the Western Special Military District in May–June 1941, forces assigned in late June and July 1941, partially destroyed near Chernigov in September 1941. Lieutenant General P. M. Filatov (June–July 1941) (KIA); Lieutenant General F. N. Remezov (July 1941); Lieutenant General V. F. Gerasimenko (July 1941); Major General K. D. Golubev (July–August 1941); Major General A. M. Gorodniansky (August 1941 to January 1942); and Major General (Lieutenant General in February 1943 and Colonel General in August 1944) N. P. Pukhov (January 1942 to May 1945).

14th

Formed in the Leningrad Military District in October 1939. Lieutenant General V. A. Frolov (June–August 1941); Major General R. I. Panin (August 1941 to March 1942); and Major General (Lieutenant General in April 1943) V. I. Shcherbakov (March 1942 to May 1945).

15th

Formed in the Far Eastern Front in July 1940. Major General L. G. Cheremisov (July 1940 to November 1941); Major General M. S. Savvushkin (November 1941 to October 1942); and Major General (Lieutenant General in September 1944) S. K. Mamonov (October 1942 to September 1945).

16th

Formed in the Trans-Baikal Military District in July 1940, transferred West in June 1941, encircled and partially destroyed at Smolensk in August 1941, reformed in September 1941, encircled and destroyed at Viaz'ma in October 1941, reestablished in the Mozhaisk Defense Line in late October 1941, reorganized as the 11th Guards Army on 16 April 1943, reestablished in the Far Eastern Front in July 1943. Lieutenant General M. F. Lukin (June–

August 1941); Major General (Lieutenant General in September 1941) K. K. Rokossovsky (August 1941 to July 1942); Lieutenant General I. Kh. Bagramian (July 1942 to April 1943); Major General M. G. Dubkov (July–September 1943); and Major General L. G. Cheremisov (September 1943 to September 1945).

17th

Formed in the Trans-Baikal Military District in July 1940. Lieutenant General P. L. Romanenko (June 1941 to May 1942); Major General A. I. Gastilovich (May 1942 to November 1943); and Lieutenant General A. I. Danilov (November 1943 to September 1945).

18th

Formed from the Khar'kov Military District's headquarters and forces from the Kiev Special Military District in June 1941. Lieutenant General A. K. Smirnov (June–October 1941); Major General V. Ia. Kolpakchi (October–November 1941); Major General F. V. Kamkov (November 1941 to February 1942 and April–October 1942); Lieutenant General I. K. Smirnov (February–April 1942); Major General A. A. Grechko (October 1942 to January 1943); Major General A. I. Ryzhov (January–February 1943); Major General K. A. Koroteev (February–March 1943); Lieutenant General (Colonel General in October 1943) K. N. Leselidze (March 1943 to February 1944); Lieutenant General E. P. Zhuravlev (February–November 1944); and Major General (Lieutenant General in January 1945) A. I. Gastilovich (November 1944 to May 1945).

19th

Formed in the North Caucasus Military District in June 1941, encircled and partially destroyed at Smolensk in July–August 1941, reformed in September 1941, encircled and destroyed at Viaz'ma in October 1941, reformed in the Moscow Military District in November 1941, reorganized into the 1st Shock Army in November 1941, reestablished in the Karelian Front from the Kandalaska Operational Group in April 1942. Lieutenant General I. S. Konev (June–September 1941); Lieutenant General M. F. Lukin (September–October 1941) (POW); Lieutenant General I. V. Boldin (October–November 1941); Major General I. S. Morozov (April 1942 to May 1943); Major General (Lieutenant General in February 1944) G. K. Kozlov (May 1943 to March 1945); and Lieutenant General V. Z. Romanovsky (March–May 1945).

20th

Formed in the Orel Military District in June 1941, encircled and destroyed at Viaz'ma and disbanded in October 1941, reestablished from Operational Group Liziukov in November 1941, in the RVGK from July 1943 to April 1944, disbanded, its headquarters formed the 3rd Baltic Front in April 1944. Lieutenant General F. N. Remezov (June–July 1941); Lieutenant General P. A. Kurochkin (July–August 1941); Lieutenant General M. F. Lukin (August–September 1941); Lieutenant General F. A. Ershakov (September–October 1941) (POW); Lieutenant General A. A. Vlasov (November 1941 to March 1942); Lieutenant General M. A. Reiter (March–September 1942); Major General N. I. Kiriukhin (October–December 1942); Lieutenant General M. S. Khozin (December 1942 to January 1943); Lieutenant General N. E. Berzarin (January–March and August–September 1943); Major General A. N. Ermakov (March–August and September 1943); Lieutenant General A. I. Lopatin (September–October 1943); and Lieutenant General N. I. Gusev (November 1943 to April 1944).

21st

Formed in the Volga Military District in June 1941, encircled and partially destroyed near Chernigov in August–September 1941, reorganized as the 6th Guards Army in April 1943, reestablished from the 3rd Reserve Army in July 1943, headquarters reverted to RVGK in late October 1943, its forces transferred to the 33rd Army, reestablished and assigned to the Leningrad Front in December 1943. Lieutenant General V. F. Gerasimenko (June–July 1941); Colonel General F. I. Kuznetsov (July and October 1941); Lieutenant General M. G. Efremov (July–August 1941); Major General V. N. Gordov (August 1941 and October 1941 to June 1942); Lieutenant General V. I. Kuznetsov (August–September 1941); Major General A. I. Danilov (June–October 1942); Lieutenant General I. M. Chistiakov (October 1942 to April 1943); Lieutenant General N. I. Krylov (July–October 1943); Lieutenant General E. P. Zhuravlev (October 1943 to February 1944); Lieutenant General V. I. Shvetsov (February–April 1944); and Colonel General D. N. Gusev (April 1944 to May 1945).

22nd

Formed in the Ural Military District in June 1941, encircled and partially destroyed near Rzhev in October 1941, reestablished in the Kalinin Front in March 1942. Lieutenant General F. A. Ershakov (June–August 1941); Major

General (Colonel General in March 1943); V. A. Iushkevich (August–October 1941, April–December 1942, and March 1943 to April 1944); Major General V. I. Vostrukhov (October 1941 to March 1942); Major General D. M. Seleznev (December 1942 to March 1943); and Lieutenant General G. P. Korotkov (April 1944 to May 1945).

23rd

Formed in the Leningrad Military District in May 1941. Lieutenant General P. S. Pshennikov (May–August 1941); Lieutenant General M. N. Gerasimov (August–September 1941); Major General (Lieutenant General in September 1943) A. I. Cherepanov (September 1941 to July 1944); and Lieutenant General V. A. Shvetsov (July 1944 to May 1945).

24th

Formed in the Siberian Military District in June 1941, encircled and destroyed at Viaz'ma and disbanded in October 1941, reestablished in the Moscow Military District in December 1941, renamed the 1st Reserve Army on 1 May 1942, reestablished in the Southern Front from the *front's* operational group in May 1942, headquarters formed the 58th Army on 28 August 1942, its forces transferred to the 12th and 37th Armies, reestablished from the 9th Reserve Army in August 1942, reorganized as the 4th Guards Army on 16 April 1943. Lieutenant General S. A. Kalinin (June–July 1941) (repressed in 1944); Major General of NKVD Forces K. I. Rakutin (July–October 1941) (KIA); Major General M. M. Ivanov (December 1941 to March 1942); Major General Ia. I. Broud (March–May 1942); Lieutenant General I. K. Smirnov (May–July 1942); Major General V. N. Martsenkevich (July–August 1942); Major General D. T. Kozlov (August–September 1942); and Major General (Lieutenant General in January 1943) I. V. Galanin (October 1942 to April 1943).

25th

Formed in the Far Eastern Front in June 1941. Lieutenant General F. A. Parusinov (June 1941 to June 1943); Major General A. M. Maksimov (June 1943 to June 1945); and Colonel General I. M. Chistiakov (June–September 1945).

26th

Formed in the Kiev Special Military District in June 40, encircled and destroyed at Kiev and disbanded in September 1941, reestablished in the Moscow Military District from the 1st Guards Rifle Corps in October 1941, disbanded in late October 1941, its forces transferred to the Briansk Front's 50th Army, reestablished in the Volga Military District in November 1941, reorganized as the 2nd Shock Army in December 1941, reestablished in the Karelian Front from the Kemsk Operational Group in March–April 1942. Lieutenant General F. Ia. Kostenko (June–September 1941); Lieutenant General G. G. Sokolov (October 1941 and November–December 1941); Major General N. N. Nikishin (March 1942 to May 1943); Major General (Lieutenant General in August 1944) L. S. Skvirsky (May 1943 to January 1945); and Lieutenant General N. A. Gagen (January–May 1945).

27th

Formed in the Baltic Special Military District in May 1941, reorganized as the 4th Shock Army in December 1941, reestablished in the Northwestern Front in May 1942. Major General N. E. Berzarin (May–December 1941); Major General F. P. Oserov (May 1942 to January 1943); and Lieutenant General (Colonel General in September 1944) S. G. Trofimenko (January 1943 to May 1945).

28th

Formed in the Arkhangel'sk Military District in June 1941, encircled and destroyed at Viaz'ma and disbanded in August 1941, reestablished in the Moscow Military District in November 1941, headquarters formed the 4th Tank Army in July 1942, its forces transferred to the 21st Army, reestablished in the Stalingrad Military District in September 1942. Lieutenant General V. Ia. Kachalov (June–August 1941) (KIA); Army General I. V. Tiulenev (November 1941 to March 1942); Lieutenant General D. I. Riabyshev (May–July 1942); Major General V. D. Kriuchenkin (July 1942); Lieutenant General V. F. Gerasimenko (September 1942 to November 1943); Lieutenant General A. A. Grechkin (November 1943 to May 1944); and Lieutenant General A. A. Luchinsky (May 1944 to May 1945).

29th

Formed in the Moscow Military District from the 30th Rifle Corps in July 1941, encircled and partially destroyed near Rzhev in October 1941 and February 1942, headquarters formed the 1st Tank Army in February 1943, its forces transferred to the 5th and 20th Armies. Lieutenant General of NKVD I. I. Maslennikov (July–December 1941); Major General V. I. Shvetsov (December 1941 to September 1942); and Major General E. P. Zhuravlev (September 1942 to January 1943).

30th

Formed in the VGK in July 1941, reorganized as the 10th Guards Army on 16 April 1943. Major General of NKVD V. A. Khomenko (July–November 1941); Major General (Lieutenant General in January 1942) D. D. Leliushenko (November 1941 to November 1942); and Major General (Lieutenant General in February 1943) V. Ia. Kolpakchi (November 1942 to April 1943).

31st

Formed in the Moscow Military District in July 1941, severely damaged at Viaz'ma in October 1941, headquarters reverted to RVGK in October 1941, its forces transferred to the 29th Army, reestablished in the Kalinin Front on 21 October 1941. Major General of NKVD Forces K. I. Rakutin (July 1941); Major General of NKVD Forces V. N. Dalmatov (July–October 1941) (repressed); Major General V. A. Iushkevich (October 1941 to March 1942); Major General V. I. Vostrukhov (March–April 1942); Major General V. S. Polenov (April 1942 to February 1943); Major General (Lieutenant General in September 1943) V. A. Gluzdovsky (February 1943 to May 1944); Lieutenant General (Colonel General in July 1944) V. V. Glagolev (May–December 1944); and Lieutenant General P. G. Shafranov (December 1944 to May 1945).

32nd

Formed in the Moscow Military District in July 1941, encircled and destroyed at Viaz'ma in October 1941, disbanded on 13 October 1941, its remnants transferred to the 16th and 19th Armies, reestablished in the Karelian Front from the Medvezh'egorsk and Masel'sk Operational Groups in early March 1942. Lieutenant General N. K. Krykov (July–August 1941); Major General I. I. Fediuninsky (August–September 1941); Major General S. V. Vyshnevsky (September–October 1941) (POW); Major General (Lieutenant General in June 1942) S. G. Trofimenko (March–June 1942); and Lieutenant General F. D. Gorelenko (June 1942 to May 1945).

33rd

Formed in the Moscow Military District in July 1941, encircled and partially destroyed near Viaz'ma in March–April 1942. Kombrig D. P. Onuprienko (July–October 1941); Lieutenant General M. G. Efremov (October 1941 to April 1942) (KIA); Army General K. A. Meretskov (May–June 1942); Lieutenant General M. S. Khozin (June–October 1942); Lieutenant General

(Colonel General in September 1943) V. N. Gordov (October 1942 to March 1944); Colonel General I. E. Petrov (March–April 1944); Lieutenant General V. D. Kriuchenkin (April–July 1944); Lieutenant General S. I. Morozov (July–September 1944); and Colonel General V. D. Tsvetaev (October 1944 to May 1945).

34th

Formed in the Moscow Military District in July 1941, encircled and partially destroyed at Staraia Russa in August 1941, forces transferred to the 1st Shock Army in November 1943, headquarters renamed the 4th Army in mid-January 1944. Kombrig N. I. Pronin (July–August 1941); Major General K. M. Kachanov (August–September 1941) (executed for dereliction of duty); Major General P. F. Alfer'ev (September–December 1941); Major General N. E. Berzarin (December 1941 to October 1942); Lieutenant General A. I. Lopatin (October 1942 to March 1943); Lieutenant General P. A. Kurochkin (March–June 1943); and Lieutenant General I. G. Sovetnikov (June 1943 to January 1944).

35th

Formed in the Far East from the 18th Rifle Corps in July 1941. Major General V. A. Zaitsev (July 1941 to June 1945); and Lieutenant General N. D. Zakhvataev (June–September 1945).

36th

Formed in the Trans-Baikal Military District in July 1941. Major General (Lieutenant General in October 1943) S. S. Fomenko (July 1941 to June 1945); and Lieutenant General A. A. Luchinsky (June–September 1945).

37th

Formed in the Southwestern Front from the Kiev Fortified Region and RVGK forces on 8 August 1941, encircled and destroyed at Kiev in September 1941, reestablished in the Southern Front in November 1941, headquarters reverted to the RVGK in July 1943, its forces transferred to the 9th and 56th Armies, reestablished in the Steppe Front in September 1943. Lieutenant General A. A. Vlasov (August–September 1941); Major General (Lieutenant General in March 1942) A. I. Lopatin (October 1941 to June 1942); Major General P. M. Kozlov (June 1942 to May 1943); Lieutenant General K. A. Koroteev (May–July 1943); Major General A. A. Filatov (July–August

1943); Lieutenant General M. N. Sharokhin (August 1943 to October 1944); and Colonel General S. S. Biriuzov (October 1944 to May 1945).

38th

Formed in the Southwestern Front in late July and early August 1941, encircled and partially destroyed in the Donbas in July 1942, formed the headquarters of the 1st Tank Army in July 1942, its forces transferred to the 21st Army, reestablished in the Briansk Front from General Chibisov's Operational Group and the 4th Reserve Army in early August 1942. Lieutenant General D. I. Riabyshev (July–August 1941); Major General of Tank Forces N. V. Feklenko (August–September 1941); Major General V. V. Tsiganov (September–December 1941); Major General of Technical Forces A. G. Maslov (December 1941 to February 1942); Major General G. I. Sherstiuk (February–March 1942); Major General of Artillery (Colonel General in September 1943) K. S. Moskalenko (March–July 1942 and October 1943 to May 1945); and Lieutenant General N. E. Chibisov (August 1942 to October 1943).

39th

Formed in the Arkhangel'sk Military District in November 1941, encircled and destroyed near Belyi in July 1942 and disbanded, reestablished in the Kalinin Front from the 58th Army (2nd formation) in August 1942. Lieutenant General I. A. Bogdanov (November–December 1941); Lieutenant General I. I. Maslennikov (December 1941 to July 1942); Major General (Lieutenant General in January 1943) A. I. Zygin (August 1942 to September 1943); Lieutenant General N. E. Berzarin (September 1943 to May 1944); and Lieutenant General (Colonel General in May 1945) I. I. Liudnikov (May–September 1945).

40th

Formed in the Southwestern Front in August 1941. Major General (Lieutenant General in November 1941) K. P. Podlas (August 1941 to February 1942); Lieutenant General of Artillery M. A. Parsegov (March–July 1942); Lieutenant General M. M. Popov (July–October 1942); Major General (Lieutenant General in January 1943) K. S. Moskalenko (October 1942 to October 1943); and Lieutenant General F. F. Zhmachenko (October 1943 to May 1945).

41st

Formed in the Kalinin Front in May 1942, disbanded in April 1943, its headquarters forming the Reserve Front. Major General of NKVD Forces G. F.

Tarasov (May–December 1942); and Major General I. M. Managarov (December 1942 to March 1943).

42nd

Formed in the Leningrad Front from the Krasnogvardeisk Fortified Region in August 1941. Major General V. I. Shcherbakov (August–September 1941); Lieutenant General F. S. Ivanov (September 1941) (repressed); Major General I. I. Fediuninsky (September–October 1941); Major General (Lieutenant General in May 1942) I. F. Nikolaev (November 1941 to December 1943); Colonel General I. I. Maslennikov (December 1943 to March 1944); Lieutenant General V. Z. Romanovsky (March 1944); and Lieutenant General V. P. Sviridov (March 1944 to May 1945).

43rd

Formed in the VGK from the 33rd Rifle Corps in July 1941. Lieutenant General P. A. Kurochkin (August 1941); Major General D. M. Seleznev (August–September 1941); Major General P. P. Sobennikov (September–October 1941) (repressed); Lieutenant General S. D. Akimov (October 1941); Major General (Lieutenant General in June 1942) K. D. Golubev (October 1941 to May 1944); and Lieutenant General A. P. Beloborodov (May 1944 to May 1945).

44th

Formed in the Trans-Caucasus Military District from the 40th Rifle Corps in July 41, disbanded in November 1943. Major General A. A. Khadeev (August–December 1941); Major General A. N. Pervushin (December 1941 to January 1942); Major General I. F. Dashichev (January 1942) (repressed); Colonel S. E. Rozhdestvensky (January–February 1942); Lieutenant General S. I. Cherniak (February–May 1942) (demoted to colonel in June 1942); Major General A. A. Khriashchev (May–August 1942); Major General I. E. Petrov (August–October 1942); Major General K. S. Mel'nik (October–November 1942); and Major General (Lieutenant General in May 1943) V. A. Khomenko (November 1942 to November 1943) (POW).

45th

Formed in the Trans-Caucasus Military District from the 23rd Rifle Corps in July 1941. Major General K. F. Baronov (July–October 1941); Colonel A. A. Kharitonov (October–December 1941); Major General V. V. Novikov

(December 1941 to April 1942); and Lieutenant General F. N. Remezov (April 1942 to May 1945).

46th

Formed in the Trans-Caucasus Military District from the 3rd Rifle Corps in July 1941. Lieutenant General S. I. Cherniak (July–December 1941); Major General A. A. Khadeev (December 1941 to April 1942); Major General V. F. Sergatskov (April–August 1942); Lieutenant General K. N. Leselidze (August 1942 to January 1943); Major General I. P. Roslyi (January–February 1943); Major General A. I. Ryzhov (February–March 1943); Major General (Lieutenant General in October 1943) V. V. Glagolev (March 1943 to May 1944); Lieutenant General I. T. Shlemin (May 1944 to January 1945); Major General M. S. Filippovsky (January–March 1945); and Lieutenant General A. V. Petrushevsky (March–May 1945).

47th

Formed in the Trans-Caucasus Military District from the 28th Mechanized Corps in July 1941. Major General V. V. Novikov (July–October 1941); Major General K. F. Baronov (October 1941 to February 1942); Lieutenant General S. I. Cherniak (February 1942); Major General K. S. Kolganov (February–May 1942) (demoted to colonel in June 1942); Major General G. P. Kotov (May–September 1942); Major General A. A. Grechko (September–October 1942); Lieutenant General F. V. Kamkov (October 1942 to January 1943); Lieutenant General K. N. Leselidze (January–March 1943); Major General A. I. Ryshov (March–July 1943); Major General P. M. Kozlov (July–August 1943); Lieutenant General P. P. Korzun (August–September 1943); Lieutenant General F. F. Zhmachenko (September–October 1943); Lieutenant General V. S. Polenov (October 1943 to May 1944); Lieutenant General I. I. Gusev (May–November 1944); and Major General (Lieutenant General in January 1945) F. I. Perkhorovich (November 1944 to May 1945).

48th

Formed in the Northwestern Front from the Novgorod Army Operational Group in early August 1941, disbanded on 14 September 1941, its forces transferred to the 54th Army, reestablished in the Briansk Front from the 28th Mechanized Corps in late April 1942. Lieutenant General S. D. Akimov (August 1941); Lieutenant General M.A. Antoniuk (September 1941); Major General G. A. Khaliuzin (May 1942 to February 1943); Lieutenant General (Colonel General in July 1944) P. L. Romanenko (February 1943 to December 1944); and Lieutenant General (Colonel General in May 1945) N. I. Gusev (December 1944 to May 1945).

49th

Formed in the Moscow Military District in early August 1941. Lieutenant General I. G. Zakharkin (August 1941 to June 1943); and Major General (Lieutenant General in September 1943 and Colonel General in March 1945) I. T. Grishin (June 1943 to May 1945).

50th

Formed from the Briansk Front's 2nd Rifle Corps in August 1941. Major General M. P. Petrov (August–October 1941) (KIA); Major General A. N. Ermakov (October–November 1941) (repressed); Lieutenant General (Colonel General in July 1944) I. V. Boldin (November 1941 to February 1945); and Lieutenant General F. P. Ozerov (February–May 1945).

51st

Formed as a separate army in the Crimea in August 1941. Colonel General F. I. Kuznetsov (August–November 1941); Lieutenant General P. I. Batov (November–December 1941); Lieutenant General V. N. L'vov (December 1941 to May 1942) (KIA); Major General N. Ia. Kirpichenko (May–June 1942); Colonel A. M. Kuznetsov (June–July and September 1942); Major General N. I. Trufanov (July 1942 and October 1942 to February 1943); Major General T. K. Kolomiets (July–September and October 1942); Lieutenant General G. F. Zakharov (February–July 1943); and Lieutenant General Ia. G. Kreizer (August 1943 to May 1945).

52nd

Formed in the Northwestern Front from the 25th Rifle Corps in August 1941 as a separate army under RVGK control. Lieutenant General N. K. Klykov (August 1941 to January 1942); Lieutenant General V. F. Iakovlev (January 1942 to July 1943); and Lieutenant General (Colonel General in September 1944) K. A. Koroteev (July 1943 to May 1945).

53rd

Formed in the Central Asian Military District in August 1941, disbanded in December 1941, in the Crimea in the Northwestern Front from the 34th Army's

Southern Group in April 1942. Major General A. S. Ksenofontov (April–October 1942); Major General G. P. Korotkov (October 1942 to January 1943); Major General E. P. Zhuravlev (January–March 1943); Lieutenant General (Colonel General in May 1945) I. M. Managarov (March–December 1943 and March 1944 to May 1945); Major General G. F. Tarasov (December 1943 to January 1944); and Lieutenant General I. V. Galanin (January–February 1944).

54th

Formed in the Moscow Military District from the 44th Rifle Corps in late August and early September 1941, its forces transferred to other armies in October 1944, disbanded in December 1944. Marshal of the Soviet Union G. I. Kulik (August–September 1941); Lieutenant General M. S. Khozin (September–October 1941); Major General I. I. Fediuninsky (October 1941 to April 1942); Major General (Lieutenant General in November 1942) A. V. Sukhomlin (April 1942 to March 1943); and Major General (Lieutenant General in September 1943) S. V. Roginsky (March 1943 to December 1944).

55th

Formed from the Leningrad Front's Slutsk-Kolpino Fortified Region in late August 1941, combined with the 67th Army in late December 1943. Major General of Tank Forces I. G. Lazarov (September–November 1941); and Major General of Artillery (Lieutenant General of Artillery in August 1943) V. P. Sviridov (November 1941 to December 1943).

56th

Formed in the North Caucasus Military District in October 1941, converted into the Separate Coastal Army in November 1943. Lieutenant General F. N. Remezov (October–December 1941); Major General V. V. Tsyganov (December 1941 to July 1942); Major General A. I. Ryzhov (July 1942 to January 1943); Major General (Lieutenant General in April 1943) A. A. Grechko (January–October 1943); and Lieutenant General K. S. Mel'nik (October–November 1943).

57th

Formed in the North Caucasus Military District under RVGK control in October 1941, formed the 68th Army headquarters in February 1943, its forces distributed to other armies, reestablished in the Southwestern Front from the 3rd Tank Army in late April 1943. Lieutenant General D. I. Riabyshev (October 1941 to February 1942); Lieutenant General K. P. Podlas (February–May 1942) (KIA); Major General A. G. Batiunia (May–June 1942); Major General D. N. Nikishev (June–July 1942); Major General (Lieutenant General in January 1943) F. I. Tolbukhin (July 1942 to January 1943); Lieutenant General N. A. Gagen (May 1943 to October 1944); and Lieutenant General (Colonel General in April 1945) M.N. Sharokhin (October 1944 to May 1945).

58th

Formed in the Siberian Military District in November 1941, reorganized as the 3rd Tank Army in May 1942, reestablished in the Kalinin Front in June 1942, renamed the 39th Army in August 1942, reestablished in the Trans-Caucasus Front from the 24th Army in August–September 1942, headquarters converted into the Volga Military District and its forces distributed to other armies in October 1943. Lieutenant General V. I. Kuznetsov (November 1941); Colonel (Major General in March 1942) N. A. Moskvin (November 1941 to May 1942); Major General A. I. Zygin (June–August 1942); Major General V. A. Khomenko (September–November 1942); and Major General (Lieutenant General in April 1943) K. S. Mel'nik (November 1942 to October 1943).

59th

Formed in the Siberian Military District in November 1941. Major General I. V. Galanin (November 1941 to April 1942); and Major General (Lieutenant General in November 1942) I. T. Korovnikov (April 1942 to May 1945).

60th

Formed in the Moscow Military District in November 1941, reorganized as the 3rd Shock Army in December 1941, reestablished from the 3rd Reserve Army in early July 1942. Lieutenant General M. A. Purkaev (November–December 1941); Lieutenant General M. A. Antoniuk (July 1942); Lieutenant General (Colonel General in March 1944) I. D. Cherniakhovsky (July 1942 to April 1944); and Colonel General P. A. Kurochkin (April 1944 to May 1945).

61st

Formed in the Volga Military District in November 1941. Colonel General F. I. Kuznetsov (November 1941); Lieutenant General M. M. Popov (November 1941 to June 1942); and Lieutenant General (Colonel General in July 1944) P. A. Belov (June 1942 to May 1945).

62nd

Formed from the 7th Reserve Army in July 1942, reorganized as the 8th Guards Army in April 1943. Major General V. Ia. Kolpakchi (July–August 1942); Lieutenant General A. I. Lopatin (August–September 1942); and Lieutenant General V. I. Chuikov (September 1942 to April 1943).

63rd

Formed from the 5th Reserve Army on 10 July 1942, renamed the 1st Guards Army on 4 November 1942, reestablished from the 5th Reserve Army in March–April 1943, disbanded in February 1944. Lieutenant General V. I. Kuznetsov (July–November 1942); Lieutenant General V. I. Morozov (March–May 1943); and Lieutenant General V. Ia. Kolpakchi (May 1943 to February 1944).

64th

Formed from the 1st Reserve Army on 10 July 1942, reorganized as the 7th Guards Army on 16 April 1943. Lieutenant General V. I. Chuikov (July–August 1942); and Major General (Lieutenant General in December 1942) M. S. Shumilov (August 1942 to April 1943).

65th

Formed in the Don Front from the 4th Tank Army in October 1942. Lieutenant General (Colonel General in June 1944) P. I. Batov (October 1942 to May 1945).

66th

Formed from the 8th Reserve Army in August 1942, reorganized as the 5th Guards Army on 16 April 1943. Lieutenant General V. N. Kurdiumov (August 1942); Lieutenant General S. A. Kalinin (August 1942); Lieutenant General R. Ia. Malinovsky (August–October 1942); and Major General (Lieutenant General in January 1943) A. S. Zhadov (October 1942 to April 1943).

67th

Formed in the Leningrad Front from the Neva Operational Group in October 1942, combined with the 55th Army in late December 1943, the 55th Army's headquarters became the 67th Army's headquarters. Lieutenant General M. P. Dukhanov (October 1942 to December 1943): Lieutenant General V. P. Sviridov (December 1943 to March 1944); Lieutenant General V. S. Romanovsky (March 1944 to February 1945); and Lieutenant General N. P. Simoniak (March–May 1945).

68th

Formed in the Northwestern Front from the 57th Army in early February 1943, disbanded in early November 1943. Lieutenant General F. I. Tolbukhin (February–March 1943); and Major General (Lieutenant General in September 1943) E. P. Zhuravlev (March–October 1943).

69th

Formed in the Voronezh Front from the 18th Separate Rifle Corps in February 1943. Lieutenant General M. I. Kazakov (February–March 1943); Major General (Lieutenant General in June 1943) V. D. Kriuchenkin (March 1943 to April 1944); and Lieutenant General (Colonel General in November 1944) V. Ia. Kolpakchi (April 1944 to May 1945).

70th

Formed in the RVGK from the Separate NKVD Army from October 1942 to February 1943. Major General G. F. Tarasov (December 1942 to April 1943); Lieutenant General I. V. Galanin (April–September 1943); Major General V. M. Sharopov (September–October 1943); Lieutenant General A. A. Grechkin (October–November 1943); Lieutenant General I. F. Nikolaev (January–March 1944); Major General A. I. Ryshov (March–May 1944); and Colonel General V. S. Popov (May 1944 to May 1945).

1st Shock

Formed in the RVGK from the 19th Army in November 1941. Lieutenant General V. I. Kuznetsov (November 1941 to May 1942); Lieutenant General V. Z. Romanovsky (May–November 1942); Lieutenant General V. I. Morozov (November 1942 to February 1943); Major General (Lieutenant General in October 1943) G. P. Korotkov (February 1943 to April 1944); Colonel General N. E. Chibisov (April–May 1944); Lieutenant General N. D. Zakhvataev (May 1944 to January 1945); and Lieutenant General V. N. Razuvaev (February–May 1945).

2nd Shock

Formed in the Volkhov Front from the 26th Army in December 1941, destroyed at Liuban' in July and Siniavino in September 1942 (twice) but reestablished. Lieutenant General G. G. Sokolov (December 1941 to January 1942); Lieutenant General N. K. Klykov (January–April 1942 and July–December 1942); Lieutenant General A. A. Vlasov (April–July 1942) (POW); Lieutenant General V. Z. Romanovsky (December 1942 to December 1943); and Lieutenant General (Colonel General in October 1944) I. I. Fediuninsky (December 1943 to May 1945).

3rd Shock

Formed in the RVGK from the 60th Army in December 1941. Lieutenant General M. A. Purkaev (December 1941 to August 1942); Major General (Lieutenant General in January 1943) K. N. Galitsky (September 1942 to November 1943); Colonel General N. E. Chibisov (November 1943 to April 1944); Lieutenant General V. A. Iushkevich (April–August 1944); Lieutenant General M. N. Gerasimov (August–October 1944); Major General N. P. Simoniak (October 1944 to March 1945); and Colonel General V. I. Kuznetsov (March–May 1945).

4th Shock

Formed in the Northwestern Front from the 27th Army in December 1941. Colonel General A. I. Eremenko (December 1941 to February 1942); Lieutenant General F. I. Golikov (February–March 1942); Major General (Lieutenant General in May 1942); V. V. Kurasov (March 1942 to April 1943); Major General D. M. Seleznev (April–May 1943); Major General (Lieutenant General in October 1943) V. I. Shvetsov (May–December 1943); and Lieutenant General P. F. Malyshev (December 1943 to May 1945).

5th Shock

Formed in the RVGK from the 10th Reserve Army in December 1942. Lieutenant General M. M. Popov (December 1942); Lieutenant General (Colonel General in September 1943) V. D. Tsvetaev (December 1942 to May 1944); and Lieutenant General (Colonel General in April 1945) N. E. Berzarin (May 1944 to May 1945).

1st Guards

Formed from the 2nd Reserve Army in August 1942, formed the Southeastern Front in October 1942, its forces transferred to the 24th Army, reestablished from the 63rd Army in November 1942, renamed the 3rd Guards Army in December 1942, reestablished from the 4th Reserve Army's headquarters and the Southwestern Front's operational group in December 1942. Lieutenant General F. I. Golikov (August 1942); Major General of Artillery K. S. Moskalenko (August–October 1942); Major General I. M. Chistiakov (October 1942); Lieutenant General V. I. Kuznetsov (November 1942); Lieutenant General D. D. Leliushenko (November–December 1942); Lieutenant General (Colonel General in May 1943) V. I. Kuznetsov (December 1942 to December 1943); and Colonel General A. A. Grechko (December 1943 to May 1945).

2nd Guards

Formed in the RVGK in October 1942. Major General (Lieutenant General in February 1943) Ia. G. Kreizer (October–November 1942 and February–July 1943); Lieutenant General R. Ia. Malinovsky (November 1942 to February 1943); Lieutenant General G. F. Zakharov (July 1943 to June 1944); and Lieutenant General P. G. Chanchibadze (June 1944 to May 1945).

3rd Guards

Formed in the Southwestern Front from the 1st Guards Army (2nd formation) in December 1942. Lieutenant General D. D. Leliushenko (December 1942 to March 1943 and August 1943 to February 1944); Major General of Artillery G. I. Khetagurov (March–August 1943); Lieutenant General D. I. Riabyshev (February–March 1944); and Colonel General V. N. Gordov (April 1944 to May 1945).

4th Guards

Formed from the 24th Army on 16 April 1943. Lieutenant General G. I. Kulik (April–September 1943); Lieutenant General A. I. Zygin (September 1943) (KIA); Lieutenant General I. V. Galanin (September 1943 to January 1944 and February–November 1944); Major General A. I. Ryzhov (January–February 1944); Lieutenant General I. K. Smirnov (February 1944); Army General G. F. Zakharov (November 1944 to March 1945); and Lieutenant General N. D. Zakhvateev (March–May 1945).

5th Guards

Formed from the 66th Army on 16 April 1943. Lieutenant General (Colonel General in September 1944) A. S. Zhadov (April 1943 to May 1945).

6th Guards

Formed from the 21st Army on 16 April 1943. Lieutenant General (Colonel General in June 1944) I. M. Chistiakov (April 1943 to May 1945).

7th Guards

Formed from the 64th Army on 16 April 1943. Lieutenant General (Colonel General in October 1943) M. S. Shumilov (April 1943 to May 1945).

8th Guards

Formed from the 62nd Army on 16 April 1943. Lieutenant General V. I. Chuikov (October 1942 to May 1945).

9th Guards

Formed from the 7th Army and the Separate Airborne Army in January 1945. Colonel General V. V. Glagolev (January–May 1945).

10th Guards

Formed from the 30th Army on 16 April 1943. Lieutenant General V. Ia. Kolpakchi (April–May 1943); Lieutenant General K. P. Trubnikov (May–September 1943); Lieutenant General A. V. Sukhomlin (September 1943 to January 1944); and Lieutenant General M. I. Kazakov (January–May 1945).

11th Guards

Formed from the 16th Army on 16 April 1943. Lieutenant General (Colonel General in 1943) I. Kh. Bagramian (April–November 1943); Major General A. S. Ksenefontov (November 1943); and Lieutenant General (Colonel General in June 1944) K. N. Galitsky (November 1943 to May 1945).

Coastal (Separate)

Formed in the Southern Front from the Coastal Group of Forces in July 1941, designated Separate until 19 August 1941, defended Odessa, Sevastopol', and the Crimea, largely destroyed in May 1942, disbanded in June 1942, reestablished as a separate army from the headquarters of the North Caucasus Front and the 56th Army in November 1943, joined the 4th Ukrainian Front as a field army on 18 April 1944. Lieutenant General G. P. Sofronov (July–October 1941); Major General I. E. Petrov (October 1941 to July 1942 and November 1943 to

February 1944); Army General A. I. Eremenko (February–April 1944); and Lieutenant General K. S. Mel'nik (April 1944 to May 1945).[4]

TANK ARMIES

1st (1st Guards)

Formed from the 38th Army in July 1942, encircled and partially destroyed west of the Don River in July–August 1942, disbanded in early August 1942, its headquarters forming the Southeastern Front, reestablished in the Northwestern Front in January–February 1943, awarded guards title in April 1944. Major General K. S. Moskalenko (July–August 1942); and Lieutenant General of Tank Forces (Colonel General of Tank Forces in April 1944) M. E. Katukov (January 1943 to May 1945).

2nd (2nd Guards)

Formed from the Briansk Front's 3rd Reserve Army in January–February 1943, awarded guards title in November 1944. Lieutenant General P. L. Romanenko (January–February 1943); Lieutenant General of Tank Forces A. G. Rodin (February–September 1943); Lieutenant General of Tank Forces S. I. Bogdanov (September 1943 to July 1944 and January–May 1945); and Major General A. I. Radzievsky (July 1944 to January 1945).

3rd

Formed in the Moscow Military District from the 58th Army in May 1942, encircled and largely destroyed south of Khar'kov in March 1943, reorganized as the 57th Army in April 1943. Lieutenant General P. L. Romanenko (May–September 1942); and Major General (Lieutenant General in January 1943) P. S. Rybalko (October 1942 to April 1943).

4th

Formed in the Stalingrad Front in July 1942, partially encircled and destroyed in July–August 1942, reorganized into the 65th Army in October 1942. Major General V. D. Kriuchenkin (August–October 1942).

5th

Formed in the Moscow Military District under RVGK control in June 1942, headquarters assigned to the RVGK, its forces distributed to the Briansk and

Voronezh Fronts in late July 1942, assigned new forces in early September 1942, converted into the 12th Army in April 1943. Major General A. I. Liziukov (June–July 1942); Major General P. S. Rybalko (July–October 1942); Major General P. L. Romanenko (November–December 1942); Lieutenant General M. M. Popov (December 1942 to January 1943); and Major General (Lieutenant General in March 1943) I. T. Shlemin (January–April 1943).

6th (6th Guards)

Formed in the 1st Ukrainian Front from the 5th Guards Tank and 5th Guards Mechanized Corps in January 1944, awarded guards title in September 1944. Lieutenant General of Tank Forces (Colonel General of Tank Forces in September 1944) A. G. Kravchenko (January 1944 to September 1945).

3rd Guards

Formed in the RVGK in May 1943. Lieutenant General (Colonel General in December 1943) P. S. Rybalko (May 1943 to May 1945).

4th Guards

Formed in the RVGK between late February 1942 and March 1943, reestablished in the Moscow Military District in July 1943. Lieutenant General of Tank Forces V. M. Badanov (July 1943 to March 1944), and Lieutenant General (Colonel General in May 1944) D. D. Leliushenko (March 1944 to May 1945).

5th Guards

Formed in the RVGK in January–February 1943. Lieutenant General of Tank Forces (Colonel General of Tank Forces in October 1943) P. A. Rotmistrov (February 1943 to August 1944); Lieutenant General of Tank Forces M. D. Solomatin (August 1944); Lieutenant General of Tank Forces (Colonel General of Tank Forces in October 1944) V. T. Vol'sky (April 1944 to March 1945); and Major General of Tank Forces M. D. Sinenko (March–May 1945).

6th (6th Guards)

Formed in the 1st Ukrainian Front from the 5th Guards Tank and 5th Mechanized Corps in January 1944. Lieutenant General of Tank Forces (Colonel General of Tank Forces in September 1944) A. G. Kravchenko (January 1944 to September 1945).[5]

SAPPER ARMIES

1st

Formed in the Western Front on 25 December 1941, disbanded on 1 September 1942. Major General of Engineer Forces M. P. Vorob'ev (December 1941 to March 1942); Colonel V. V. Kosarev (March–May 1942); and Major General of Engineer Forces N. P. Baranov (June–August 1942).

2nd

Formed in the Arkhangel'sk Military District on 27 October 1941, disbanded on 27 February 1942. NKVD Major M. M. Tsarevsky.

3rd

Formed in the Moscow Military District and Moscow Defense Zone on 29 October 1942, disbanded on 12 September 1942. NKVD Senior Major Ia. D. Rapoport (November 1941 to February 1942); Major General of Engineer Forces I. A. Petrov (February–April 1942); Colonel I. N. Bryznov (April–August 1942); and Colonel S. P. Grechkin (August–September 1942).

4th

Formed in the Volga Military District in October 1941, disbanded on 18 May 1942. NKVD 3rd Rank S. N. Kruglov (November 1941 to January 1942); NKVD Major G. D. Afanas'ev (January–March 1942); and Colonel M. A. Kovin (March–May 1942).

5th

Formed in the North Caucasus and Stalingrad Military Districts on 15 October 1941, disbanded on 1 March 1942. Brigade Engineer A. N. Komarovsky (November 1941 to January 1942); and Colonel I. E. Pruss (January–March 1942).

6th

Formed in the Volga Military District in October 1941, disbanded on 13 September 1942. Engineer 1st Rank A. S. Kornev (October 1941 to March 1942); Colonel M. I. Chernykh (March–May 1942); Engineer 1st Rank A. G. Andreev (May–June 1942); and Lieutenant General of Engineer Forces A. S. Gundorov (June–September 1942).

7th

Formed in the North Caucasus and Stalingrad Military Districts on 15 October 1941, disbanded on 15 September 1942. Colonel I. E. Kosarev (November 1941 to March 1942); Colonel I. E. Pruss (March–June 1942); and Major General of Technical Forces V. S. Kosenko (June–September 1942).

8th

Formed in the North Caucasus Military District on 30 October 1941, disbanded on 15 October 1942. D. G. Onika (October 1941 to January 1942); Major General K. S. Nazarov (January–March 1942); Lieutenant General of Engineer Forces A. S. Gundorov (March–May 1942); Colonel D. I. Suslin (May–July 1942); and Colonel I. E. Salashchenko (July–October 1942).

9th

Formed in the North Caucasus Military District in October 1941, disbanded on 1 March 1942. NKVD Senior Major I. E. Vladzimirsky (November 1941 to March 1942); and Engineer 1st Rank M. I. Chernykh (January–March 1942).

10th

Formed in the North Caucasus Military District on 26 October 1941, disbanded on 5 March 1942. NKVD Senior Major M. M. Mal'tsev.[6]

AIR ARMIES

1st

Formed in the Western Front in May 1942. Lieutenant General of Aviation T. F. Kutsevalov (May–June 1942); Major General of Aviation (Lieutenant General of Aviation in March 1943) S. A. Khudiakov (July 1942 to May 1943); Lieutenant General of Aviation M. M. Gromov (May 1943 to June 1944); and Colonel General of Aviation T. T. Khriukin (July 1944 to May 1945).

2nd

Formed in the Briansk Front in May 1942. Major General of Aviation (Lieutenant General of Aviation in December 1942 and Colonel General of Aviation in February 1944) S. A. Krasovsky (May–July 1943 and March 1943 to May 1945); and Colonel (Major General of Aviation in October 1942) K. N. Smirnov (July 1942 to March 1943).

3rd

Formed in the Kalinin Front in May 1942. Major General of Aviation (Lieutenant General of Aviation in April 1943) M. M. Gromov (May 1942 to May 1943); and Major General of Aviation (Lieutenant General of Aviation in September 1943 and Colonel General of Aviation in August 1944) N. F. Papivin (May 1943 to May 1945).

4th

Formed in the Southern Front in May 1942. Major General of Aviation (Lieutenant General of Aviation in March 1943 and Colonel General of Aviation in October 1943) K. A. Vershinin (May–September 1942 and May 1943 to May 1945); and Major General of Aviation N. F. Naumenko (September 1942 to April 1943).

5th

Formed in the North Caucasus Front in June 1942. Lieutenant General of Aviation (Colonel General of Aviation in March 1944) S. K. Goriunov (June 1942 to May 1945).

6th

Formed in the Northwestern Front in June 1942, reverted to RVGK in September 1944, its headquarters forming the headquarters of the Polish Air Force in October 1944. Major General of Aviation D. F. Kondratiuk (June 1942 to January 1943); and Major General of Aviation (Lieutenant General of Aviation in March 1943) F. P. Polynin (January 1943 to September 1944).

7th

Formed in the Karelian Front in November 1942, reverted to RVGK in December 1944. Major General of Aviation (Lieutenant General of Aviation in May 1943 and Colonel General of Aviation in November 1944) I. M. Sokolov (November 1942 to December 1944).

8th

Formed in the Southwestern Front in June 1942. Major General of Aviation (Lieutenant General of Aviation in March 1943 and Colonel General of Aviation in May 1944) T. T. Khriukhin (June 1942 to July 1944); and Lieutenant General of Aviation V. N. Zhdanov (August 1944 to May 1945).

9th

Formed in the Far Eastern Front in August 1942. Major General of Aviation A. S. Senatorov (August 1942 to September 1944); Major General of Aviation V. A. Vinogradov (September 1944 to June 1945); and Colonel General of Aviation I. M. Sokolov (June–September 1945).

10th

Formed in the Far Eastern Front in August 1942. Colonel (Major General of Aviation in October 1942) V. A. Vinogradov (August 1942 to September 1944); Colonel D. Ia. Slobozhan (September 1944 to May 1945); and Colonel General of Aviation P. F. Zhigarev (May–September 1945).

11th

Formed in the Far East in August 1942. Colonel (Major General of Aviation in October 1942) V. N. Bibikov (October 1942 to August 1945).

12th

Formed in the Trans-Baikal Front in August 1942. Lieutenant General of Aviation T. F. Kutsevalov (August 1942 to June 1945); and Marshal of Aviation S. A. Khudiakov (June–September 1945).

13th

Formed in the Leningrad Front in November 1942. Lieutenant General of Aviation (Colonel General of Aviation in November 1944) S. D. Rybal'chenko (November 1942 to May 1945).

14th

Formed in the Volkhov Front in June 1942, reverted to RVGK in November 1944. Major General of Aviation (Lieutenant General of Aviation in April 1943) I. P. Zhuravlev (June 1942 to November 1944).

15th

Formed in the Briansk Front in July 1942. Major General of Aviation I. G. Piatykhin (July 1942 to May 1943); and Lieutenant General of Aviation (Colonel General of Aviation in August 1944) N. F. Naumenko (May 1943 to May 1945).

16th

Formed from the 8th Air Army and RVGK forces in August 1942. Major General of Aviation P. S. Stepanov (August–September 1942); and Major General of Aviation (Lieutenant General of Aviation in January 1943 and Colonel General of Aviation in May 1944) S. I. Rudenko (October 1942 to May 1945).

17th

Formed in the Southwestern Front in November 1942. Major General of Aviation (Lieutenant General of Aviation in December 1942) S. A. Krasovsky (November 1942 to March 1943); and Lieutenant General of Aviation (Colonel General of Aviation in March 1944) V. A. Sudets (March 1943 to May 1945).[7]

MILITARY DISTRICTS

Arkhangel'sk

Organized in March 1940, raised the 29th and 39th Armies in 1941, reorganized as the White Sea Military District on 1 January 1945. Lieutenant General A. Z. Romanovsky (1941–42); and Lieutenant General T. I. Shevaldin (1942–45).

White Sea

Organized on 1 January 1945 from the Arkhangel'sk Military District. Colonel General V. A. Frolov (1945).

Baltic

Formed from the Kalinin Military District on 11 July 1940, renamed the Baltic Special Military District on 17 August 1940, consisted of the 8th, 11th, and 27th Armies, reorganized as the Northwestern Front on 22 June 1941, reestablished on 9 July 1945 from the headquarters, 1st Baltic Front. Colonel General F. I. Kuznetsov (1940–41); and Army General I. Kh. Bagramian (1945).

Western (Belorussian)

Formed as the Belorussian Special Military District in July 38, renamed the Western Special Military District on 11 July 1940, consisted of the 3rd, 4th, 10th, 11th, and 13th Armies, reorganized as the Western Front on 22 June 1941, reestablished as the Belorussian Military District from the headquarters, Moscow Defense Zone in October 1943, renamed the Belorussian-Lithuanian Military District in January 1945, divided into the Minsk and Baranovichi Military Districts in July 1945. Army General D. G. Pavlov (1941) (shot for dereliction of duty); Lieutenant General V. F. Iakovlev (1943–45); and Lieutenant General T. I. Shevaldin (1945).

Trans-Baikal

Organized in November 1921, disbanded in May 1922, reestablished in May 1935 from the Special Far Eastern Army's Trans-Baikal Group of Forces, raised the 16th Army in 1941, reorganized as the Trans-Baikal Front on 15 September 1941. Lieutenant General M. P. Kovalev (1941).

Trans-Caucasus

Formed from the Caucasus Red Banner Army in June 1935, raised the 44th, 45th, 46th, and 47th Armies in 1941, reorganized as the Trans-Caucasus Front on 23 August 1941, reestablished on 28 August 1942, and reorganized as the Trans-Caucasus Front on 15 May 1942. Lieutenant General D. T. Kozlov (1941); and Army General I. V. Tiulenev (1942–45).

Kiev

Formed in May 1935, reorganized as the Kiev Special Military District on 26 July 1938, consisted of the 5th, 6th, 26th, and 12th Armies in 1941, reorganized as the Southwestern Front on 22 June 1941, raised the 37th, 38th, and 40th Armies in 1941, disbanded on 10 September 1941, reestablished from the headquarters, Stalingrad Military District on 15 October 1943. Lieutenant General V. F. Iakovlev (1941); Lieutenant General V. V. Kosiakin (1943–44); and Lieutenant General V. F. Gerasimenko (1944–45).

Leningrad

Organized from the Petrograd Military District in February 1924, renamed the Northwestern Front on 7 January 1940, reestablished from the Northwestern Front on 26 March 1940, reorganized as the Northwestern Front on 24 June 1941, consisted of the 14th, 7th, and 23rd Armies. Lieutenant General M. M. Popov (1941).

L'vov

Organized in May 1944. Lieutenant General I. K. Smirnov (1944–45).

Moscow

Organized in May 1918. Colonel General of NKVD Forces P. A. Artem'ev (1941–45).

Odessa

Organized in October 1939, raised the 9th Separate and 51st Armies in 1941, provided forces for the Southern Front's Coastal Army and the Southern Front's Reserve Army, abolished in September 1941, reestablished on 23 March 1944. Lieutenant General N. E. Chibisov (1941); Lieutenant General I. I. Ivanov (1941); Colonel General I. G. Zakharkin (1944); and Lieutenant General V. A. Iushkevich (1944–45).

Orel

Organized in July 1938, raised the 20th Army in 1941, disbanded in October 1941, its headquarters formed the Southern Ural Military District, reestablished in August 1943, renamed the Voronezh Military District in July 1945. Lieutenant General P. A. Kurochkin (1941); Lieutenant General A. A. Tiurin (1941); and Lieutenant General M. T. Popov (1943–45).

North Caucasus

Organized in May 1921, raised the 19th and 56th Armies in 1941, abolished on 21 August 1942, reestablished on 2 July 1943. Lieutenant General V. N. Sergeev (1941); Lieutenant General F. N. Remezov (1941); Lieutenant General V. N. Kurdiumov (1942 and 1943–44); and Lieutenant General N. K. Klykov (1944–45).

Siberian

Formed in December 1919, raised the 24th and 59th Armies in 1941, renamed the Western Siberian Military District on 9 July 1945. Lieutenant General S. A. Kalinin (1941); Lieutenant General N. V. Medvedev (1942–44); Lieutenant General V. N. Kurdiumov (1944–45).

Central Asian

Formed in June 1926, raised the 53rd Army in 1941, divided into the Turkestan and Steppe Military Districts on 9 July 1945. Major General S. G. Trofimenko (1941); Major General P. S. Kurbatkin (1941–44); and Major General M. F. Lipatov (1944–45).

Stalingrad

Formed from the headquarters, Khar'kov Military District in November 1941, subordinate to the Southeastern Front in August 1942, abolished in September 1942, its headquarters formed the 28th Army, reestablished in July 1943, absorbed into the North Caucasus Military District in October 1943, its headquarters formed the Kiev Military District. Major General of Tank Forces N. V. Feklenko (1941); Lieutenant General V. F. Gerasimenko (1941–42); and Lieutenant General V. V. Kosiakin (1943).

Steppe

Formed from the Reserve Front on 15 April 1943, assigned the 24th, 27th, 46th, 47th, 53rd, 66th, 5th Guards Tank, and 5th Air Armies, renamed the Steppe Front on 9 July 1943, reestablished in July 1945. Colonel General M. M. Popov (April–May 1943); Colonel General M. A. Reiter (June 1943); and Colonel General I. S. Konev (June–July 1943).

Ural

Formed in May 1935, raised the 22nd Army in 1941. Major General (Lieutenant General in September 1943) A. V. Katkov (1941–45); and Colonel General F. I. Kuznetsov (1945).

Volga

Formed in May 1918, raised the 21st, 8th, and 10th Armies in 1941. Major General M. T. Popov (1941); Lieutenant General S. A. Kalinin (1941–44); and Colonel General M. S. Khozin (1944–45).

Khar'kov

Formed in 1935, abolished on 26 November 1941, its headquarters formed the headquarters, 28th Army, reestablished in September 1943. Major General A. N. Chernikov (1941); Lieutenant General V. I. Kuznetsov (1941); Colonel General Ia. T. Cherevichenko (1943); Lieutenant General V. F. Gerasimenko (1943); Lieutenant General S. A. Kalinin (1944); and Major General (Lieutenant General in November 1944) P. S. Kurbatkin (1944–45).

Southern Ural

Formed from the headquarters, Orel Military District on 26 November 1941. Lieutenant General V. N. Kurdiumov (1941); Lieutenant General F. N. Remezov (1942); Major General M.T. Popov (1942–43); Colonel General M. A. Reiter (1943–45).[8]

OPERATIONAL GROUPS

Coastal

Formed in the North Caucasus Front on 28 July 1942, disbanded on 17 August 1942. Colonel General Ia. T. Cherevichenko.

Luga

Formed to defend the Luga Defense Line in July 1941, reorganized as the Kingisepp, Luga, and Eastern Defense Sectors on 23 July 1941. Lieutenant General K. P. Piadyshev (purged).

Northern

Formed in the Trans-Caucasus Front on 10 August 1942, reorganized as the North Caucasus Front on 24 January 1943. Lieutenant General I. I. Maslennikov.

DEFENSE ZONES AND REGIONS

Moscow

Formed on 12 October 1941 as a two-belt defense line protecting Moscow, reorganized as a defense zone from the Headquarters for the Defense of Moscow on 2 December 1941, reorganized as a reserve *front* in 1942, its 60th (3rd Shock) and 24th (1st Reserve) Armies transferred to operating *fronts,* disbanded on 15 October 1943. Lieutenant General of NKVD Forces (Colonel General on 22 January 1942) P. A. Artem'ev (October 1941 to October 1943).

Odessa

Organized from part of the Separate Coastal Army and the Odessa Naval Base on 19 August 1941, evacuated and disbanded 16 October 1941. Vice-Admiral G. V. Zhukov (1941).

Sevastopol'

Organized from part of the Separate Coastal Army and the Sevastopol' Naval Base on 4 November 1941, destroyed on 4 July 1942. Vice-Admiral F. S. Oktiabr'sky (November 1941 to June 1942); and Major General P. G. Novikov (July 1942) (POW).

Tuapse

Organized from part of the Trans-Caucasus Front's Black Sea Group of Forces and the Tuapse Naval Base on 22 August 1942, disbanded on 26 January 1943.Vice-Admiral G. V. Zhukov (1942–43).

Novorossiisk

Organized from part of the Trans-Caucasus Front and the Novorossiisk Naval Base on 17 August 1942, disbanded on 12 April 1943. Major General G. P. Kotov (August–September 1942); Major General A. A. Grechko (September–October 1942); and Lieutenant General F. V. Kamkov (October 1942 to April 1943).

Northern

Organized from the 23rd Fortified Region and part of the Northern Fleet on 31 July 1942, disbanded on 5 January 1945. Lieutenant General S. I. Kabanov (August 1942 to September 1943); and Major General (Lieutenant General in November 1944) E. T. Dubovtsev (September 1943 to January 1945).[9]

MECHANIZED CORPS (1ST FORMATION)

1st

Formed on 21 January 1941, disbanded on 23 August. Major General of Tank Forces M. L. Cherniavsky.

2nd

Formed on 4 June 1940, encircled and destroyed at Uman', disbanded on 10 August 1941. Lieutenant General Iu. V. Novosel'sky.

3rd

Formed on 27 January 1941, disbanded on 16 August 1941. Major General of Tank Forces A. V. Kurkin.

4th

Formed on 17 January 1941, disbanded on 15 August 1941. Major General A. A. Vlasov.

5th

Formed on 11 March 1941, encircled and destroyed at Smolensk, disbanded on 2 August 1941. Major General of Tank Forces I. P. Alekseenko (fatally wounded).

6th

Formed on 4 June 1940, encircled and destroyed at Belostok, disbanded on 27 June 1941. Major General M. G. Khatskilevich (KIA).

7th

Formed on 6 June 1940, encircled and destroyed at Smolensk, disbanded on 6 August 1941. Major General V. I. Vinogradov.

8th

Formed on 4 June 1940, disbanded on 30 August 1941. Lieutenant General D. I. Riabyshev.

9th

Formed on 28 November 1940, disbanded on 9 August 1941. Major General K. K. Rokossovsky (28 November 1940 to 11 July 1941) and Major General of Technical Forces A. G. Maslov (19 July to 9 August 1941).

10th

Formed on 11 March 1941, renamed the Luga Operational Group's Right Combat Sector on 20 July 1941. Major General of Tank Forces I. G. Lazarov.

11th

Formed on 11 March 1941, encircled and destroyed west of Minsk, disbanded on 9 August 1941. Major General of Tank Forces D. K. Mostovenko.

12th

Formed on 11 March 1941, disbanded on 25 August 1941. Major General N. M. Shestapalov (11 March to 27 June) (KIA); Colonel V. Ia. Grinberg (1–13 July); and *Komdiv* I. T. Koronikov (14 July to 25 August).

13th

Formed on 27 February 1941, encircled and partially destroyed at Belostok, disbanded on 28 July 1941. Major General P. N. Akliustin (KIA).

14th

Formed on 11 March 1941, encircled and destroyed at Belostok, disbanded on 30 June 1941. Major General S. O. Oborin (repressed).

15th

Formed on 11 March 1941, encircled and partially destroyed near Vladimir-Volynsk, disbanded on 26 June 1941. Major General I. I. Karpezo.

16th

Formed on 11 March 1941, disbanded on 1 July 1941. *Komdiv* A. D. Sokolov.

17th

Formed on 11 March 1941, disbanded on 11 August 1941. Major General M. P. Petrov.

18th

Formed on 11 March 1941, disbanded on 28 August 1941. Major General of Tank Forces P. V. Volokh.

19th

Formed on 11 March 1941, disbanded on 30 August 1941. Major General of Tank Forces N. V. Feklenko.

20th

Formed on 11 March 1941, disbanded on 21 July 1941. Major General A. G. Nikitin.

21st

Formed on 11 March 1941, disbanded on 23 August 1941. Major General D. D. Leliushenko.

22nd

Formed on 11 March 1941, disbanded on 3 September 1941. Major General S. M. Kondrusov (11 March to 24 June) (KIA); Major General of Tank Forces V. S. Tamruchi (25 June to 28 July) (repressed); and Major General V. N. Simvolokov (29 July to 3 September).

23rd

Formed on 11 March 1941, reorganized as the 23rd Rifle Corps on 20 July 1941. Major General M. A. Miasnikov.

24th

Formed on 11 March 1941, disbanded on 1 July 1941. Major General V. I. Chistiakov.

25th

Formed on 11 March 1941, disbanded on 20 August 1941. Major General S. M. Krivoshein.

26th

Formed on 11 March 1941, disbanded on 28 July 1941. Major General N. Ia. Kirichenko.

27th

Formed on 11 March 1941, disbanded on 20 August 1941. Major General I. E. Petrov.

28th

Formed on 11 March 1941, disbanded on 9 August 1941. Major General V. V. Novikov.

29th

Formed on 11 March 1941, disbanded on 7 May 1941. Major General of Tank Forces M. I. Pavelkin.

30th

Formed on 11 March 1941, disbanded on 19 July 1941. Lieutenant General V. S. Golubovsky.[10]

CAVALRY CORPS

Separate

Formed on 16 December 1941, reorganized as the 1st Cavalry Corps on 14 January 1942. Major General F. A. Parkhomenko.

1st

Formed from the Separate Cavalry Corps on 14 January 1942, disbanded on 26 March 1942. Major General F. A. Parkhomenko.

2nd

Formed on 14 March 1941, reorganized as the 1st Guards Cavalry Corps on 26 November 1941, reestablished on 12 December 1941, disbanded on 9 June 1942, reestablished on 1 January 1942, renamed the 9th Cavalry Corps on 3 February 1942. Major General P. A. Belov (14 March to 26 November 1941); Major General M. A. Usenko (23 December 1941 to 9 March 1942); Colonel G. A. Kovalev (10 March to 27 May 1942); Colonel S. T. Shumilo (28 May to 9 June 1942); and Colonel V. A. Gaigukov (1 January to 3 February 1942).

3rd

Formed on 20 November 1941, reorganized as the 2nd Guards Cavalry Corps on 26 November. Major General L. M. Dovator.

4th

Formed on 17 January 1941, disbanded on 30 May 1943. Lieutenant General T. T. Shapkin (17 January 1941 to 22 March 1943) and Major General M. F. Maleev (25 March to 30 May 1943).

5th

Formed on 14 March 1941, reorganized as the 3rd Guards Cavalry Corps on 25 December, reestablished on 18 January 1941, disbanded on 15 July 1942. Major General F. V. Kamkov (14 March to 20 November 1941); Major General V. D. Kriuchenkin (21 November to 25 December 1941); Major General A. A. Grechko (18 January to 15 April 1942); Major General I. A. Pliev (16 April to 7 June 1942); and Major General F. A. Parkhomenko (8 June to 15 July 1942).

6th

Formed on 11 March 1940, encircled and destroyed at Belostok, disbanded on 6 July 1941, reestablished on 4 January 1942, encircled and destroyed south of Khar'kov, disbanded on 25 May 1942. Kombrig (Major General on 5 June 1940) I. S. Nikitin (11 March 1940 to 6 July 1941) (POW); Major General A. F. Bychkovsky (4–15 January 1942); Major General of Artillery K. S. Moskalenko (16 January to 5 March 1942); and Major General A. A. Noskov (6 March to 25 May 1942) (POW).

7th

Formed on 26 December 1941, reorganized as the 6th Guards Cavalry Corps on 19 January 1943. Major General B. A. Pogrebov (26 December 1941 to 27 March 1942); Major General I. M. Managarov (28 March to 27 December 1942); and Major General S. V. Sokolov (28 December 1942 to 19 January 1943).

8th

Formed on 15 January 1942, encircled and partially destroyed at Debal'tsevo in February 1943, remnants reorganized as the 7th Guards Cavalry Corps on 14 February 1943. Major General (Lieutenant General on 3 March 1942)

P. P. Korzun (15 January to 11 May 1942); Major General A. S. Zhadov (12–27 May and 10 September to 16 October 1942); Colonel I. F. Lunev (28 May–9 September 1942); and Major General M. D. Borisov (17 October 1942 to 14 February 1943) (POW).

9th

Formed from the 2nd Cavalry Corps on 3 February 1942, disbanded on 11 April 1942. Colonel M. D. Borisov.

10th

Formed on 12 January 1942, disbanded on 3 February 1942. Major General V. V. Kriukov.

11th

Formed on 17 January 1942, disbanded on 8 August 1942. Major General G. T. Timofeev (17 January to 18 May 1942) and Colonel (Major General on 21 July 1942) S. V. Sokolov (19 May to 8 August 1942).

12th

Formed on 17 January 1942, disbanded on 3 February 1942. Colonel S. V. Sokolov.

13th

Formed on 20 January 1942, disbanded on 28 July 1942. Major General N. I. Gusev (20 January to 26 June 1942) and Major General V. F. Trantin (30 June to 28 July 1942).

14th

Formed on 23 January 1942, disbanded on 5 April 1942. Colonel A. I. Dudkin (23 January to 3 February 1942) and Major General N. Ia. Kirichenko (4 February to 5 April 1942).

15th

Formed on 1 January 1942. Colonel A. G. Selivanov (1 January to 18 March 1942); Major General K. S. Mel'nik (19 March to 15 October 1942); Colonel

V. F. Damberg (16 October 1942 to 11 January 1943); Major General V. A. Gaidukov (12 January 1943 to 28 January 1944); and Major General (Lieutenant General on 20 April 1945) M. I. Glinsky (2 February 1944 to 9 May 1945).

16th

Formed on 4 January 1942, disbanded on 30 March 1942. Major General I. M. Managarov.

17th

Formed on 1 January 1942, reorganized as the 4th Guards Cavalry Corps on 27 August 1942. Major General M. F. Maleev (1 January to 9 June 1942) and Major General N. Ia. Kirichenko (10 June to 28 August 1942).

18th

Formed on 22 April 1942, disbanded on 14 August 1943. Colonel A. Ia. Khvostov (22 April to 1 May 1942); Major General L. D. Il'in (2 May to 20 December 1942); and Major General F. A. Parkhomenko (21 December 1942 to 14 August 1943).

19th

Formed on 22 February 1943, disbanded on 5 July 1943. Major General M. P. Konstantinov.

1st Guards

Formed from the 2nd Cavalry Corps on 26 November 1941. Major General (Lieutenant General on 2 January 1942) P. A. Belov (26 November 1941 to 28 June 1942) and Major General (Lieutenant General on 15 September 1943) V. K. Baranov (10 July 1942 to 11 May 1945).

2nd Guards

Formed from the 3rd Cavalry Corps on 26 November 1941. Major General L. M. Dovator (26 November to 11 December 1941) (KIA); Major General I. A. Pliev (12 December 1941 to 5 March 1942); and Major General (Lieutenant General on 16 October 1943) V. V. Kriukov (6 March 1942 to 9 May 1945).

3rd Guards

Formed from the 5th Cavalry Corps on 25 December 1941. Major General V. D. Kriuchenkin (25 December 1941 to 3 July 1942); Major General I. A. Pliev (4 July to 27 December 1942); and Major General (Lieutenant General on 13 June 1943) N. S. Oslikovsky (28 December 1942 to 9 May 1945).

4th Guards

Formed from the 17th Cavalry Corps on 27 August 1942. Lieutenant General N. Ia. Kirichenko (27 August 1942 to 3 November 1943); Lieutenant General I. A. Pliev (4 November 1943 to 8 November 1944); Major General V. S. Golovsky (15 November 1944 to 8 April 1945); and Lieutenant General F. V. Kamkov (12 April to 11 May 1945).

5th Guards

Formed on 15 November 1942. Major General (Lieutenant General on 18 February 1944); and A. G. Selivanov (15 November 1942 to 4 May 1945); and Major General (Lieutenant General on 13 September 1944) S. I. Gorshkov (5 May 1944 to 9 May 1945).

6th Guards

Formed from the 7th Cavalry Corps on 19 January 1943. Major General (Lieutenant General on 20 December 1943) S. V. Sokolov (19 January 1943 to 9 April 1945) and Major General I. F. Kuts (10 April to 11 May 1945).

7th Guards

Formed from the 8th Cavalry Corps on 14 February 1943. Colonel R. I. Golovanovsky (25 February to 20 March 1943); Major General Ia. S. Sharaburko (21 March to 6 June 1943); Major General M. F. Maleev (7 June to 6 October 1943); and Major General (Lieutenant General on 26 July 1944) M. P. Konstantinov (7 October 1943 to 9 May 1945).[11]

TANK CORPS

1st

Formed on 31 March 1942. Major General of Tank Forces M. E. Katukov (31 March to 18 September 1942) and Major General of Tank Forces V. V. Butkov (19 September 1942 to 11 May 1945).

2nd

Formed on 15 April 1942, reorganized as the 8th Guards Tank Corps on 19 September 1943. Major General of Tank Forces A. I. Liziukov (15 April to 28 May 1942); Colonel S. P. Maltsev (28 May to 9 June 1942); Major General of Tank Forces I. G. Lazarov (10 June to 1 July 1942); Colonel (Major General of Tank Forces on 21 July 1942) A. G. Kravchenko (2 July to 13 September 1942); Major General of Tank Forces A. M. Khasin (14 September to 15 October 1942); and Major General of Tank Forces (Lieutenant General of Tank Forces on 21 August 1943) A. F. Popov (16 October 1942 to 19 September 1943).

3rd

Formed on 31 March 1942, reorganized as the 9th Guards Tank Corps on 20 November 1944. Major General of Tank Forces D. K. Mostovenko (31 March to 3 September 1942); Colonel (Major General of Tank Forces on 10 November 1942) M. D. Sinenko (4 September 1942 to 4 November 1943); Major General of Tank Forces N. M. Teliakov (5 November to 16 December 1943, 1–29 March 1944, and 5–13 July 1944); Major General of Tank Forces A. A. Shamshin (17 December 1943 to 28 February 1944); Lieutenant General of Tank Forces V. A. Mishulin (1 April to 4 July 1944); and Major General of Tank Forces N. D. Vedennev (14 July to 20 November 1944).

4th

Formed on 31 March 1942, reorganized as the 5th Guards Tank Corps on 7 February 1943. Major General of Tank Forces V. A. Mishulin (21 March to 18 September 1942) and Major General of Tank Forces A. G. Kravechenko (18 September 1942 to 7 February 1943).

5th

Formed on 19 April 1942. Major General of Tank Forces K. A. Semenchenko (19 April to 30 December 1942); Colonel (Major General of Tank Forces in 7 February 1943) M. G. Sakhno (1 January 1943 to 1 October 1944); Colonel Ia. I. Babitsky (2 October 1944 to 20 January 1945); and Colonel I. M. Kolesnikov (21 January to 9 May 1945).

6th

Formed on 19 April 1942, reorganized as the 11th Guards Tank Corps on 23 October 1943. Major General of Tank Forces (Lieutenant General of

Tank Forces on 21 August 1943) A. L. Getman (19 April 1942 to 23 October 1943).

7th

Formed on 17 April 1942, reorganized as the 3rd Guards Tank Corps on 29 December 1942. Major General of Tank Forces P. A. Rotmistrov.

8th

Formed on 19 April 1942, reorganized as the 3rd Mechanized Corps on 14 September 1942. Major General of Tank Forces M. D. Solomatin (19 April to 8 September 1942) and Major General of Tank Forces V. V. Butkov (8–14 September 1942).

9th

Formed on 12 May 1942. Major General of Tank Forces A. V. Kurkin (12 May to 18 October 1942); Major General of Tank Forces A. A. Shamshin (19 October 1942 to 10 March 1943); Major General of Tank Forces (Lieutenant General of Tank Forces on 7 June 1943) S. I. Bogdanov (11 March to 28 August 1943); Major General of Tank Forces G. S. Rudenko (25 August to 1 September 1943); Major General of Tank Forces B. S. Bakharov (2 September 1943 to 16 July 1944); Major General of Tank Forces N. I. Voeikov (17 July to 7 December 1944); and Lieutenant General of Tank Forces I. F. Kirichenko (8 December 1944 to 9 May 1945).

10th

Formed on 19 April 1942. Colonel (Major General of Tank Forces on 3 May 1942 and Lieutenant General of Tank Forces on 7 June 1943) V. G. Burkov (19 April 1942 to 16 July 1943); Major General of Tank Forces V. M. Alekseev (17 July to 5 October 1943); Major General of Tank Forces (Lieutenant General of Tank Forces on 11 March 1944) A. P. Panfilov (5 October 1943 to 25 April 1944); Colonel (Major General of Tank Forces on 2 August 1944) M. K. Shaposhnikov (26 April to 9 November 1944); and Major General of Tank Forces M. G. Sakhno (10 November 1944 to 9 May 1945).

11th

Formed on 19 May 1942. Major General of Tank Forces A. F. Popov (19 May to 21 July 1942); Major General of Tank Forces I. G. Lazarov (22 July 1942 to 7 June 1943); Major General of Tank Forces N. N. Parkevich (8 June to 21 October 1943); Major General of Tank Forces D. M. Gritsenko (22 October 1943 to 11 January 1944); Major General of Tank Forces F. N. Rudkin (12 January to 14 July 1944); and Major General of Tank Forces I. I. Iushuk (15 July 1944 to 9 May 1945).

12th

Formed on 19 May 1942, reorganized as the 6th Guards Tank Corps on 26 July 1943. Colonel (Major General of Tank Forces on 21 July 1942) S. I. Bogdanov (12 May to 7 September 1942); Colonel M. I. Chesnokov (8 September to 29 December 1942); Colonel V. A. Mitrofanov (30 December 1942 to 16 January 1943); and Major General of Tank Forces M. I. Zin'kovich (17 January to 26 July 1943).

13th

Formed on 23 May 1942, reorganized as the 4th Guards Mechanized Corps on 9 January 1943. Major General of Tank Forces P. E. Shurov (23 May to 2 July 1942) and Major General of Tank Forces T. I. Tanaschishin (17 July 1942 to 9 January 1943).

14th

Formed on 19 May 1942, reorganized as the 6th Mechanized Corps on 30 September 1942. Major General of Tank Forces N. N. Radkevich.

15th

Formed on 21 May 1942, reorganized as the 7th Guards Tank Corps on 27 July 1943. Major General of Tank Forces V. A. Koptsov (21 May 1942 to 5 March 1943) (KIA); Lieutenant Colonel A. V. Lozovsky (6 March to 10 June 1943); and Major General of Tank Forces F. N. Rudkin (11 June to 27 July 1943).

16th

Formed on 1 June 1942, reorganized as the 12th Guards Tank Corps on 20 November 1944. Major General of Tank Forces M. I. Pavelkin (1 June to 14 September 1942); Major General of Technical Forces A. G. Maslov (15 September 1942 to 24 February 1943); Colonel (Major General of Tank Forces on 7 June 1943) V. E. Grigor'ev (8 March to 18 October 1943); Major

General of Tank Forces K. V. Skorniakov (19 October to 3 December 1943); Major General of Tank Forces I. V. Dubovoi (4 December 1943 to 10 August 1944); and Major General of Tank Forces N. M. Teliakov (11 August to 21 November 1944).

17th

Formed on 22 June 1942, reorganized as the 4th Guards Tank Corps on 3 January 1943. Major General of Tank Forces N. V. Feklenko (22 June to 1 July 1942); Major General of Tank Forces I. P. Korchagin (2–20 July 1942); Colonel B. S. Bakharov (21 July to 6 August 1942); and Colonel (Major General of Tank Forces on 10 November 1942) P. P. Poluboiarov (7 August 1942 to 3 January 1943).

18th

Formed on 15 June 1942. Major General of Tank Forces I. D. Cherniakhovsky (15 June to 25 July 1942); Major General of Tank Forces I. P. Korchagin (26 July to 10 September 1942); Colonel (Major General of Tank Forces on 14 October 1942) B. S. Bakharov (11 September 1942 to 25 July 1943); Colonel A. V. Egorov (26 July to 10 September 1943); Major General of Tank Forces K. G. Trufanov (11 September to 16 October 1943); Colonel (Major General of Tank Forces on 17 January 1944) A. N. Fursovich (17 October to 23 December 1943); Major General of Tank Forces V. I. Polozkov (24 December 1943 to 28 August 1944); Colonel I. M. Kolesnikov (29 August to 23 September 1944); and Major General of Tank Forces (Lieutenant General of Tank Forces on 19 April 1945) P. D. Goborudenko (24 September 1944 to 9 May 1945).

19th

Formed on 31 December 1942. Lieutenant Colonel S. A. Vershkovich (31 December 1942 to 24 January 1943); Colonel N. A. Iuplin (25 January to 2 February 1943); and Major General of Tank Forces (Lieutenant General of Tank Forces on 27 October 1943) I. D. Vasil'ev (3 February 1943 to 9 May 1945).

20th

Formed on 28 December 1942. Colonel D. M. Gritsenko (28 December 1942 to 9 February 1943); Colonel A. K. Pogosov (10 February to 18 April 1943); Colonel N. A. Iuplin (19 April to 25 May 1943); and Lieutenant General of Tank Forces I. G. Lazarev (26 May 1943 to 9 May 1945).

21st

Formed on 19 April 1942, destroyed south of Khar'kov in May, disbanded on 10 June. Major General of Tank Forces G. I. Kuz'min (KIA).

22nd

Formed on 3 April 1942, reorganized as the 5th Mechanized Corps on 30 August 1942. Colonel (Major General of Tank Forces on 13 May 1942) A. A. Shamshin.

23rd

Formed on 12 April 1942. Major General of Tank Forces (Lieutenant General of Tank Forces on 18 January 1943) E. G. Pushkin (12 April to 4 June 1942 and 29 November 1942 to 11 March 1944) (KIA); Colonel (Major General of Tank Forces on 21 July 1942) A. M. Khasin (5 June to 25 August 1942); Major General of Tank Forces A. F. Popov (30 August to 15 October 1942); Lieutenant Colonel V. V. Koshelev (16 October to 28 November 1942); and Major General of Tank Forces (Lieutenant General of Tank Forces on 13 September 1944) A. O. Akhmanov (12 March 1944 to 9 May 1945).

24th

Formed on 19 April 1942, reorganized as the 2nd Guards Tank Corps on 26 December 1942. Major General of Tank Forces (Lieutenant General of Tank Forces on 26 December 1942) V. M. Badanov.

25th

Formed on 13 July 1942. Major General of Tank Forces P. P. Pavlov (13 July 1942 to 25 March 1943); Major General of Tank Forces F. G. Anikushkin (25 March 1943 to 4 October 1944); Colonel V. G. Petrovsky (5 October to 9 November 1944); and Major General of Tank Forces E. I. Fominykh (10 November 1944 to 11 May 1945).

26th

Formed on 8 July 1942, reorganized as the 1st Guards Tank Corps on 8 December 1942. Major General of Tank Forces A. G. Rodin.

27th

Formed on 3 June 1942, reorganized as the 1st Mechanized Corps on 8 September 1942. Major General of Tank Forces F. T. Remizov.

28th

Formed on 13 July 1942, reorganized as the 4th Mechanized Corps on 10 September 1942. Major General of Tank Forces G. S. Rodin.

29th

Formed on 18 February 1943. Major General of Tank Forces F. G. Anikushkin (18 February to 20 March 1943); Major General of Tank Forces (Lieutenant General of Tank Forces on 18 February 1944) I. F. Kirichenko (27 April 1943 to 18 April 1944); Major General of Tank Forces E. I. Fominykh (19 April to 27 July 1944); and Major General of Tank Forces E. I. Malakhov (9 August 1944 to 9 May 1945).

30th

Formed on 26 February 1943, reorganized as the 10th Guards Tank Corps on 23 October 1943. Colonel V. I. Sokolov (26 February to 27 March 1943) and Major General of Tank Forces (Lieutenant General of Tank Forces on 7 June 1943) G. S. Rodin (28 March to 23 October 1943).

31st

Formed on 29 May 1943. Major General of Tank Forces D. Kh. Chernienko (29 May to 18 August 1943); Colonel P. K. Zhidkov (19 August to 21 October 1943); Major General of Tank Forces V. E. Grigor'ev (2 October 1943 to 7 January 1945); and Major General of Tank Forces G. G. Kuznetsov (8 January to 11 May 1945).

1st Guards

Formed from the 26th Tank Corps on 8 December 1942. Major General of Tank Forces (Lieutenant General of Tank Forces on 4 February 1943) A. G. Rodin (8 December 1942 to 5 February 1943); Major General of Tank Forces A. V. Kukushkin (6 February to 25 April 1943); and Major General of Tank Forces (Lieutenant General of Tank Forces on 19 April 1945) M. F. Panov (28 April 1943 to 9 May 1945).

2nd Guards

Formed from the 24th Tank Corps on 26 December 1942. Lieutenant General of Tank Forces V. M. Badanov (26 December 1942 to 25 June 1943) and Colonel (Major General of Tank Forces on 31 August 1943 and Lieutenant General of Tank Forces on 2 November 1944) A. S. Burdeinyi (26 June 1943 to 9 May 1945).

3rd Guards

Formed from the 7th Tank Corps on 29 December 1942. Lieutenant General of Tank Forces P. A. Rotmistrov (29 December 1942 to 22 February 1943); Major General of Tank Forces I. A. Vovchenko (2 March 1943 to 10 August 1944); and Lieutenant General of Tank Forces A. P. Panfilov (11 August 1944 to 9 May 1945).

4th Guards

Formed from the 17th Tank Corps on 3 January 1943. Major General of Tank Forces (Lieutenant General of Tank Forces on 19 March 1943) P. P. Poluboiarov (3 January 1943 to 11 May 1945).

5th Guards

Formed from the 4th Tank Corps on 7 February 1943. Major General of Tank Forces (Lieutenant General of Tank Forces on 7 June 1943) A. G. Kravchenko (7 February 1943 to 24 January 1944); Lieutenant General of Tank Forces V. M. Alekseev (25 January to 25 August 1944) (KIA); and Major General of Tank Forces (Lieutenant General of Tank Forces on 19 April 1945) M. I. Savel'ev (26 August 1944 to 3 September 1945).

6th Guards

Formed from the 12th Tank Corps on 26 July 1943. Major General of Tank Forces M. I. Zin'kovich (26 July to 23 September 1943); Major General of Tank Forces I. P. Sukhov (24 September to 7 October 1943); Major General of Tank Forces (Lieutenant General of Tank Forces on 11 March 1944) A. P. Panfilov (8 October 1943 to 25 April 1944); Major General V. V. Novikov (29 April 1944 to 9 April 1945); and Colonel (Major General of Tank Forces on 7 June 1943) V. A. Mitrofanov (10–11 April 1945).

7th Guards

Formed from the 15th Tank Corps on 27 July 1943. Major General of Tank Forces F. N. Rudkin (27 July to 6 August 1943); Major General of Tank Forces K. F. Suleikov (7 August to 13 December 1943); Major General of Tank Forces S. A. Ivanov (14 December 1943 to 20 July 1944 and 8 October 1944 to April 1945); Major General of Tank Forces V. A. Mitrofanov (21 July to 7 October 1944); and Major General V. V. Novikov (13 April to 11 May 1945).

8th Guards

Formed from the 2nd Tank Corps on 19 September 1943. Lieutenant General of Tank Forces A. F. Popov (19 September 1943 to 9 May 1945).

9th Guards

Formed from the 3rd Tank Corps on 20 November 1944. Major General of Tank Forces N. D. Vedeneev (20 November 1944 to 9 May 1945).

10th Guards

Formed from the 30th Tank Corps on 23 October 1943. Lieutenant General of Tank Forces G. S. Rodin (23 October 1943 to 15 March 1944); Major General of Tank Forces (Lieutenant General of Tank Forces on 2 August 1944) E. E. Belov (16 March to 21 October 1944 and 11 February to 11 May 1945); and Colonel N. D. Chuprov (22 October 1944 to 10 February 1945).

11th Guards

Formed from the 6th Tank Corps on 23 October 1943. Lieutenant General of Tank Forces A. A. Getman (23 October 1943 to 25 August 1944) and Colonel A. Kh. Babadzhanian (25 August 1944 to 9 May 1945).

12th Guards

Formed from the 16th Tank Corps on 20 October 1944. Major General of Tank Forces N. M. Teliakov (20 November 1944 to 26 April 1945) and Major General of Tank Forces M. F. Salminov (26 April to 9 May 1945).[12]

MECHANIZED CORPS (2ND FORMATION)

1st

Formed from the 27th Tank Corps on 8 September 1942. Major General of Tank Forces (Lieutenant General of Tank Forces on 18 January 1943) M. D. Solomatin (8 September 1942 to 9 February 1944) and Lieutenant General of Tank Forces S. M. Krivoshein (10 February 1944 to 9 May 1945).

2nd

Formed on 8 September 1942, reorganized as the 7th Guards Mechanized Corps on 25 July 1943. Major General of Tank Forces (Lieutenant General of Tank Forces on 18 January 1943) I. P. Korchagin.

3rd

Formed from the 8th Tank Corps on 18 September 1942, reorganized as the 8th Guards Mechanized Corps on 23 October 1943. Major General of Tank Forces (Lieutenant General of Tank Forces on 18 January 1943) M. E. Katukov (18 September 1942 to 30 January 1943) and Major General of Tank Forces (Lieutenant General of Tank Forces on 21 August 1943) S. M. Krivoshein (7 February to 23 October 1943).

4th

Formed from the 28th Tank Corps on 10 September 1942, reorganized as the 3rd Guards Mechanized Corps on 18 December 1942. Major General of Tank Forces G. S. Rodin (10 September to 10 October 1942) and Major General of Tank Forces V. T. Vol'sky (11 October to 18 December 1942).

5th

Formed from the 22nd Tank Corps on 2 November 1942, reorganized as the 9th Guards Mechanized Corps on 12 September 1944. Major General of Tank Forces (Lieutenant General of Tank Forces on 5 November 1943) M. V. Volkov.

6th

Formed from the 14th Tank Corps on 26 September 1942, reorganized as the 5th Guards Mechanized Corps on 9 January 1943. Major General of Tank Forces S. I. Bogdanov.

7th

Formed on 1 August 1943. Major General of Tank Forces I. V. Dubovoi (1 August to 5 November 1943) and Major General of Tank Forces (Lieutenant General of Tank Forces on 29 May 1945) F. G. Katkov (6 November 1943 to 3 September 1945).

8th

Formed on 9 August 1943. Major General of Tank Forces A. M. Khasin (9 August 43 to 10 January 1944) and Major General of Tank Forces A. N. Fursovich (11 January 1944 to 9 May 1945).

9th

Formed on 1 August 1943. Major General of Tank Forces K. A. Malygin (1 August 1943 to 7 April 1944) and Lieutenant General of Tank Forces I. P. Sukhov (7 April 1944 to 11 May 1945).

10th

Formed on 1 December 1944. Major General of Tank Forces P. S. Ziabrev (1 December 1944 to 1 June 1945) and Lieutenant General of Tank Forces I. D. Vasil'ev (5 July to 3 September 1945).

1st Guards

Formed on 2 November 1942. Major General (Lieutenant General on 7 June 1943) I. N. Russiianov (2 November 1942 to 9 May 1945).

2nd Guards

Formed on 15 October 1942. Major General (Lieutenant General on 7 June 1943) K. Z. Sviridov (15 October 1942 to 11 May 1945).

3rd Guards

Formed from the 4th Mechanized Corps on 18 December 1942. Major General of Tank Forces V. T. Vol'sky (18 December 1942 to 3 January 1943); Major General A. P. Sharogin (4 January to 3 May 1943); and Major General of Tank Forces (Lieutenant General of Tank Forces on 5 November 1943) V. T. Obukhov (4 May 1943 to 11 May 1945).

4th Guards

Formed from the 13th Tank Corps on 9 January 1943. Major General of Tank Forces (Lieutenant General of Tank Forces on 30 August 1943) T. I. Tanaschishin (9 January 1943 to 31 March 1944) (KIA) and Major General of Tank Forces (Lieutenant General of Tank Forces on 13 September 1944) V. I. Zhadov (31 March 1944 to 9 May 1945).

5th Guards

Formed from the 6th Mechanized Corps on 9 January 1943. Major General of Tank Forces S. I. Bogdanov (9 January to 25 February 1943); Colonel (Major General of Tank Forces on 7 February 1943) B. M. Skvortsov (26 February 1943 to 13 April 1944); and Major General of Tank Forces I. P. Ermakov (14 April 1944 to 11 May 1945).

6th Guards

Formed on 26 June 1943. Major General (Lieutenant General on 15 December 1943); A. I. Akimov (26 June 1943 to 6 December 1944); Colonel V. F. Orlov (7 December 1944 to 18 March 1945); Colonel V. I. Koretsky (19 March to 30 April 1945); and Colonel S. F. Pushkarev (31 April to 11 May 1945).

7th Guards

Formed from the 2nd Mechanized Corps on 25 July 1943. Lieutenant General of Tank Forces I. P. Korchagin (25 July 1943 to 11 May 1945).

8th Guards

Formed from the 3rd Mechanized Corps on 23 October 1943. Lieutenant General of Tank Forces S. M. Krivoshein (23 October 1943 to 2 January 1944) and Major General I. F. Dremov (3 January 1944 to 9 May 1945).

9th Guards

Formed from the 5th Mechanized Corps on 12 September 1944. Lieutenant General of Tank Forces M. V. Volkov (12 September 1944 to 20 June 1945).[13]

ARTILLERY PENETRATION CORPS

1st

Formed on 30 December 1944. Major General of Artillery B. A. Frolov (30 December 1944 to 9 May 1945).

2nd

Formed on 24 April 1943, disbanded on 10 April 1944, second formation on 27 October 44. Major General of Artillery (Lieutenant General of Artillery on 7 June 1943) M. M. Barsukov (24 April to 10 April 1944); Major General of Artillery P. M. Rozhanovich (27 October to 9 November 1944); Colonel G. K. D'iachan (10 November 1944 to 27 January 1944); and Lieutenant General of Artillery V. S. Nesteruk (28 January to 9 May 1945).

3rd

Formed on 15 March 1943. Major General of Artillery (Lieutenant General of Artillery on 18 November 1944) N. N. Zhdanov (15 March 1943 to 12 December 1944) and Major General of Artillery V. M. Likhachev (13 December 1944 to 9 May 1945).

4th

Formed on 24 April 1943. Major General of Artillery V. N. Mazur (24 April to 19 May 1943) and Major General of Artillery (Lieutenant General of Artillery on 2 November 1944) N. V. Ignatov (2 June 1943 to 9 May 1945).

5th

Formed on 24 April 1943. Major General of Artillery P. M. Korol'kov (24 April to 18 May 1943); Colonel P. G. Chipkov (19–29 May 1943); Major General of Artillery M. I. Nedelin (30 May to 10 June 1943); Major General of Artillery M. P. Kuteinikov (11 June 1943 to 8 June 1944); Lieutenant General of Artillery N. F. Salichko (9 June 1944 to 5 April 1945); and Major General of Artillery L. N. Alekseev (6 April to 3 September 1945).

6th

Formed on 20 November 1944. Major General of Artillery (Lieutenant General of Artillery on 20 April 1945) P. M. Rozhanovich (20 November 1944 to 9 May 1945).

7th

Formed on 24 April 1943. Major General of Artillery N. V. Ignatov (24 April to 7 May 1943) and Major General of Artillery (Lieutenant General of Artillery on 16 November 1943) P. M. Korol'kov (8 May 1943 to 11 May 1945).

8th

Formed on 24 April 1943. Major General of Artillery (Lieutenant General of Artillery on 7 June 1943) N. F. Salichko (24 April 1943 to 4 March 1944); Colonel I. G. Maliarov (5 May 1943 to 18 July 1944); and Major General of Artillery I. M. Piadusov (19 July 1943 to 9 May 1945).

9th

Formed on 10 October 1944. Major General of Artillery A. F. Pavlov (10 October 1944 to 11 May 1945).

10th

Formed on 20 September 1944. Major General of Artillery (Lieutenant General of Artillery on 18 November 1944) L. I. Kozhukhov (20 September 1944 to 11 May 1945).[14]

PVO FRONTS, ARMIES, CORPS

Moscow Front PVO

Formed from the Moscow Corps Region PVO on 5 April 1942, reorganized as the Western Fronts PVO's Special Moscow Army PVO in July 1943. Lieutenant General of Artillery D. A. Zhuravlev.

Western Front PVO

Formed on 29 June 1943, disbanded on 29 March 1944, reestablished from the Northern Front PVO on 24 December 1944. Colonel General M. S. Gromadin (August 1943 to 29 March 1944) and Colonel General of Artillery D. A. Zhuravlev (24 December 1944 to 9 May 1945).

Eastern Front PVO

Formed in 29 June 1943, disbanded on 29 March 1944. Lieutenant General of Artillery G. S. Zashikhin.

98   Appendix 2

Northern Front PVO

Formed on 29 March 1944, reorganized as the Western Front PVO (2nd formation) on 24 December 1944. Colonel General M. S. Gromadin.

Southern Front PVO

Formed from the Eastern and Western Fronts PVO on 29 March 1944, reorganized as the Southwestern Front PVO on 24 December 1944. Lieutenant General of Artillery (Colonel General of Artillery in November 1944) G. S. Zashikhin.

Trans-Caucasus Front PVO

Formed from the Trans-Caucasus PVO Zone in March 1944. Lieutenant General of Artillery P. E. Gudymenko (March 1944 to May 1945).

Southwestern Front PVO

Formed from the Southern Front PVO on 24 December 1944. Colonel General of Artillery G. S. Zashikhin (24 December 1944 to 9 May 1945).

Central Front PVO

Formed from the Special Moscow Army PVO on 24 December 1944. Colonel General M. S. Gromadin (24 December 1944 to 9 May 1945).

Leningrad Army PVO

Formed from the Leningrad Corps PVO Region in April 1942. Major General of Coastal Services G. S. Zashikhin (April 1942 to July 1943); Major General of Artillery P. F. Rozhkov (August 1943 to November 1944); and Lieutenant General of Artillery S. I. Makeev (November 1944 to May 1945).

Special Moscow Army PVO

Formed from the Moscow PVO Front in July 1943, reorganized as the Central Front PVO on 24 December 1944. Lieutenant General of Artillery D. A. Zhuravlev.

1st Corps PVO (Moscow)

Formed on 23 May 1942, reorganized as Moscow PVO Corps Region on 19 November 1941. Major General of Artillery (Lieutenant General of Artillery on 28 October 1941) D. A. Zhuravlev.

1st Corps PVO (Murmansk)

Formed on 21 April 1944. Major General of Artillery F. A. Ivanov (21 April to 29 May 1944) and Colonel (Major General of Artillery on 18 November 1944) I. F. Korolenko (30 May 1944 to 9 May 1945).

2nd Corps PVO

Formed on 4 June 40, reorganized as the Leningrad PVO Army on 7 April 1942, reestablished on 18 April 1944. Major General of Artillery M. M. Protsvetkin (4 June 1940 to 18 November 1941); Major General of Coastal Services G. S. Zashikhin (19 November 1941 to 7 April 1942); Colonel (Major General of Artillery on 17 May 1944) V. M. Dobriansky (18 April to 14 October 1944); and Major General of Artillery A. I. Kupcha (15 October 1944 to 9 May 1945).

3rd Corps PVO

Formed on 4 January 1941, reorganized as Baku PVO Army on 4 May 1942, reestablished on 24 April 1944. Major General of Artillery P. E. Gudymenko (4 January to 26 December 1941); Colonel (Major General of Artillery on 3 May 1942) P. M. Beskrovnov (30 December 1941 to 4 May 1942); Major General of Artillery (Lieutenant General of Artillery on 18 November 1944) N. V. Markov (24 April 1944 to 24 February 1945); and Major General G. M. Koblents (26 February to 13 April 1945).

4th Corps PVO

Formed on 10 April 1944. Major General of Artillery V. A. Gerasimov (10 April 1944 to 9 May 1945).

5th PVO Corps

Formed on 21 April 1944. Major General of Artillery M. V. Antonenko (21 April 1944 to 9 May 1945).

6th PVO Corps

Formed on 22 April 1944. Major General P. A. Krivko (22 April 1944 to 9 May 1945).

7th PVO Corps

Formed on 18 April 1944. Major General of Artillery N. K. Vasil'kov (18 April 1944 to 9 May 1945).

8th PVO Corps

Formed on 20 April 1944. Major General of Artillery I. S. Smirnov (20 April 1944 to 26 March 1945) and Major General of Artillery P. M. Beskrovnov (27 March to 9 May 1945).

9th PVO Corps

Formed on 21 April 1944. Major General of Artillery E. A. Rainin (21 April 1944 to 9 May 1945).

10th PVO Corps

Formed on 22 April 1944. Major General of Artillery P. E. Khoroshilov (22 April to 3 August 1944); Colonel A. N. Kurochkin (4 August to 29 November 1944); and Major General of Artillery A. E. Kravtsov (30 November 1944 to 9 May 1945).

11th PVO Corps

Formed on 22 April 1944. Major General of Artillery P. S. Alymov (22 April to 9 December 1944); Major General P. E. Khoroshilov (10 December 1944 to 18 January 1945); and Colonel I. F. Morozov (19 January to 9 May 1945).

12th PVO Corps

Formed on 10 April 1944. Major General of Artillery F. G. Iankovsky (10 April 1944 to 9 May 1945).

13th PVO Corps

Formed on 18 August 1944. Colonel Major General of Artillery on 22 August 1944) A. I. Kupcha (18 August to 10 October 1944); Lieutenant Colonel I. A. Kiselev (12–28 October 1944); Major General of Artillery V. M. Dobriansky (29 October to 15 November 1944); Major General of Artillery P. G. Slepchenko (16 November to 28 December 1944); Colonel I. A. Kiselev (5 January to 2 February 1945); and Major General of Artillery M. M. Protsvetkin (3 February to 9 May 1945).

14th PVO Corps

Formed on 25 September 1944. Major General of Artillery V. A. Martyniuk-Maksimchuk (25 September 1944 to 9 May 1945).

15th PVO Corps

Formed on 15 April 1945. Major General of Artillery G. P. Mezhinsky (15 April to 9 May 1945).[15]

AVIATION CORPS

1st Long-Range Bomber

Formed on 11 January 1941, disbanded on 25 August 1941. Major General of Aviation V. I. Izotov.

2nd Long-Range Bomber

Formed on 14 November 1940, disbanded on 18 August 1941. Colonel K. N. Smirnov.

3rd Long-Range Bomber

Formed on 15 August 1940, disbanded on 18 August 1941. Colonel N. S. Skripko.

4th Long-Range Bomber

Formed on 14 November 1940, disbanded on 15 August 1941. Colonel V. A. Sudets.

1st Guards Long-Range Action

Formed on 22 May 1943, reorganized as 1st Guards Bomber Aviation Corps on 31 December 1944. Major General of Aviation (Lieutenant General of Aviation on 19 August 1944) D. P. Iukhanov (22 May 1943 to 19 December 1944) and Lieutenant General of Aviation G. N. Tupikov (20–31 December 1944).

2nd Guards Long-Range Action

Formed on 18 May 1943, reorganized as 2nd Guards Bomber Aviation Corps on 17 January 1945. Major General of Aviation (Lieutenant General of Aviation on 13 March 1944) E. F. Loginov.

3rd Guards Long-Range Action

Formed on 15 May 1943, disbanded on 23 December 1944. Major General of Aviation (Lieutenant General of Aviation on 19 August 4) N. A. Volkov.

4th Guards Long-Range Action

Formed on 3 July 1943, reorganized as 4th Guards Bomber Aviation Corps on 29 December 1944. Colonel S. P. Kovalev (3 July 1943 to 25 April 1944) and Major General of Aviation (Lieutenant General of Aviation on 5 November 1944) G. S. Schetchikov (26 April to 29 December 1944).

5th Long-Range Action

Formed on 27 May 1943, reorganized as 11th Bomber Aviation Corps on 1 January 1945. Major General of Aviation (Lieutenant General of Aviation on 18 September 1943) I. V. Georgiev.

6th Long-Range Action

Formed on 20 May 1943, reorganized as 6th Bomber Aviation Corps on 20 December 1944. Major General of Aviation (Lieutenant General of Aviation on 13 March 1944) G. N. Tupikov.

7th Long-Range Action

Formed on 1 May 1943, reorganized as 3rd Guards Bomber Aviation Corps on 22 December 1944. Major General of Aviation (Lieutenant General of Aviation on 13 March 1944) V. E. Nestertsev.

8th Long-Range Action

Formed on 10 July 1943, disbanded on 31 December 1944, forces transferred to the 19th Bomber Aviation Corps. Major General of Aviation (Lieutenant General of Aviation on 19 August 1944) N. N. Buiansky.

1st Guards Bomber Long-Range Action

Formed from the 1st Guards Long-Range Action Aviation Corps on 31 December 1944. Lieutenant General of Aviation G. N. Tupikov (1 January to 9 May 1945).

2nd Guards Bomber Long-Range Action

Formed from the 2nd Guards Long-Range Action Aviation Corps on 17 January 1945. Lieutenant General of Aviation E. F. Loginov (17 January to 9 May 1945).

3rd Guards Bomber Long-Range Action

Formed on 22 December 1944. Lieutenant General of Aviation V. E. Nestertsev (22 January to 9 May 1945).

4th Guards Bomber Long-Range Action

Formed from the 4th Guards Long-Range Aviation Corps on 29 December 1944. Lieutenant General of Aviation G. S. Schetchikov (29 December 1944 to 9 May 1945).

6th Bomber Long-Range Action

Formed from the 6th Long-Range Aviation Corps on 20 December 1944. Colonel G. S. Zotin (25 December 1944 to 27 March 1945) and Colonel (Major General of Aviation on 20 April 1945) I. P. Skok (28 March to 3 September 1945).

19th Bomber

Formed from the 8th Long-Range Aviation Corps on 31 December 1944. Colonel M. N. Kalinushkin (16 December 1944 to 1 February 1945) and Lieutenant General of Aviation N. A. Volkov (2 February to 3 September 1945).

1st Bomber

Formed on 10 September 1942, reorganized as 2nd Guards Bomber Aviation Corps on 5 February 1944. Lieutenant General of Aviation V. A. Sudets (10 September 1942 to 31 March 1943) and Colonel (Major General of Aviation on 20 October 1943) I. S. Polbin (1 April 1943 to 5 February 1944).

2nd Bomber

Formed on 10 October 1942, reorganized as 1st Guards Bomber Aviation Corps on 3 September 1943. Major General of Aviation I. L. Turkel' (10 October 1942 to 6 February 1943) and Major General of Aviation V. A. Ushakov (7 February to 3 September 1943).

3rd Bomber

Formed on 9 November 1942. Major General of Aviation A. Z. Karavatsky (9 November 1943 to 9 May 1945).

4th Bomber

Formed from the 7th Mixed Aviation Corps on 31 December 1943. Major General of Aviation (Lieutenant General of Aviation on 27 June 1943) P. P. Arkhangel'sky (31 December 1943 to 11 May 1945).

5th Bomber

Formed from the 6th Mixed Aviation Corps on 28 September 1944. Major General of Aviation M. Kh. Borisenko (28 September 1944 to 9 May 1945).

6th Bomber

Formed on 1 May 1943. Major General of Aviation (Lieutenant General of Aviation on 14 March 1944) G. N. Tupikov (1 May 1943 to 15 March 1945) and Colonel (Major General of Aviation on 20 April 1945) I. P. Skok (16 March to 9 May 1945).

7th Bomber

Formed on 16 April 1945. Lieutenant General of Aviation V. A. Ushakov (16 April to 3 September 1945).

1st Guards Bomber

Formed on 3 September 1943, reorganized as the 5th Guards Bomber Aviation Corps on 26 December 1944. Major General of Aviation (Lieutenant General of Aviation on 28 September 1943) V. A. Ushakov.

2nd Guards Bomber

Formed on 5 February 1944, reorganized as the 6th Guards Bomber Aviation Corps on 26 December 1944. Major General of Aviation I. S. Polbin.

5th Guards Bomber

Formed from the 1st Guards Bomber Aviation Corps on 26 December 1944. Lieutenant General of Aviation V. A. Ushakov (26 December 1944 to 9 May 1945).

6th Guards Bomber

Formed from the 2nd Guards Bomber Aviation Corps on 26 December 1944. Major General of Aviation I. S. Polbin (26 December 1944 to 11 February

1945); Major General of Aviation F. I. Kachev (12 February to 13 March 1945); and Colonel D. T. Nikishin (14 March to 9 May 1945).

9th Guards Bomber

Formed on 13 October 1944. Major General of Aviation (Lieutenant General of Aviation on 5 November 1944) I. T. Spirin (13 October 1944 to 8 February 1945) and Lieutenant General of Aviation I. V. Georgiev (9 February to 9 May 1945).

1st Mixed

Formed on 23 October 1942, reorganized as the 9th Assault Aviation Corps on 28 September 1944. Major General of Aviation V. I. Shevchenko (23 October 1942 to 12 May 1944); Major General of Aviation A. E. Zlatotsvetov (13 May to 12 June 1944); Major General of Aviation S. U. Rubanov (13 June to 4 July 1944); Colonel V. I. Ivolgin (5–22 July 1944); Major General of Aviation V. A. Vinogradov (23 July to 11 August 1944); and Major General of Aviation I. V. Krupsky (12 August to 28 September 1944).

2nd Mixed

Formed on 1 November 1942, reorganized as the 10th Fighter Aviation Corps on 13 July 1943. Major General of Aviation I. T. Eremenko.

3rd Mixed

Formed on 10 October 1942, reorganized as the 1st Guards Mixed Aviation Corps on 24 August 1943. Colonel (Major General of Aviation on 10 November 1942) V. I. Aladinsky.

4th Mixed

Formed on 19 February 1943, reorganized as the 8th Fighter Aviation Corps on 22 June 1943. Major General of Aviation F. F. Zherebchenko.

5th Mixed

Formed on 8 March 1943, reorganized as the 7th Fighter Aviation Corps on 23 June 1943. Major General of Aviation S. V. Sliusarev.

6th Mixed

Formed on 5 March 1943, reorganized as the 5th Bomber Aviation Corps on 28 September 1944. Major General of Aviation I. D. Antoshkin (5 March 1943 to 2 May 1944) and Colonel (Major General of Aviation on 19 August 1944) M. Kh. Borisenko (3 May to 28 September 1944).

7th Mixed

Formed on 15 February 1943, reorganized as the 4th Bomber Aviation Corps on 31 December 1943. Colonel (Major General of Aviation on 17 March 1943) P. P. Arkhangel'sky.

8th Mixed

Formed on 15 February 1943, reorganized as the 5th Assault Aviation Corps on 21 July 1943. Major General of Aviation N. P. Kaminin.

9th Mixed

Formed on 15 February 1943, reorganized as the 10th Assault Aviation Corps on 29 September 1944. Major General of Aviation (Lieutenant General of Aviation on 2 August 1944) O. V. Tolstikov.

10th Mixed

Formed on 9 March 1943, reorganized as the 7th Assault Aviation Corps on 21 July 1943. Major General of Aviation V. M. Filin.

11th Mixed

Formed on 24 July 1943, reorganized as the 1st Fighter Aviation Corps on 28 September 1944. Major General of Aviation S. P. Danilov.

18th Mixed

Formed on 18 December 1944. Colonel V. F. Niukhtilin (18 December 1944 to 9 May 1945).

1st Guards Mixed

Formed from the 3rd Mixed Aviation Corps on 24 August 1943, reorganized as the 2nd Guards Assault Aviation Corps on 28 September 1944. Major

General of Aviation (Lieutenant General of Aviation on 4 February 1944) V. I. Aladinsky (24 August 1943 to 29 June 1944); Lieutenant General of Aviation A. E. Zlatotsvetov (30 June to 26 August 1944); and Major General of Aviation S. V. Sliusarev (27 August to 28 September 1944).

1st Assault

Formed on 10 September 1942, reorganized as the 1st Guards Assault Aviation Corps on 5 February 1944. Major General of Aviation (Lieutenant General of Aviation on 17 March 1943) V. G. Riazanov.

2nd Assault

Formed on 10 October 1942, reorganized as the 3rd Guards Assault Aviation Corps on 27 October 1944. Colonel (Major General of Aviation on 17 March 1943 and Lieutenant General of Aviation on 11 May 1944) V. V. Stepichev.

3rd Assault

Formed on 6 December 1942. Colonel (Major General of Aviation on 17 March 1943) M. I. Gorlachenko (6 December 1942 to 11 May 1945).

4th Assault

Formed on 1 January 1944. Major General of Aviation (Lieutenant General of Aviation on 19 August 1944) G. F. Baidukov (1 January 1944 to 9 May 1945).

5th Assault

Formed from the 8th Mixed Aviation Corps on 21 July 1943. Major General of Aviation (Lieutenant General of Aviation on 20 April 1945) N. P. Kamanin (21 July 1943 to 11 May 1945).

6th Assault

Formed on 31 December 1943. Major General of Aviation B. K. Tokarev (31 December 1943 to 9 May 1945).

7th Assault

Formed from the 10th Mixed Aviation Corps on 21 July 1943. Major General of Aviation (Lieutenant General of Aviation on 16 May 1944) V. M. Filin (21 July 1943 to 9 May 1945).

8th Assault

Formed on 15 April 1944. Major General of Aviation (Lieutenant General of Aviation on 11 May 1944) V. V. Naneishvili (15 April 1944 to 6 January 1945 and 30 April to 9 May 1945); Major General of Aviation M. V. Kotel'nikov (7 January to 3 April 1945); and Major General of Aviation S. U. Rubanov (4–29 April 1945).

9th Assault

Formed from the 1st Mixed Aviation Corps on 28 September 1944. Major General of Aviation I. V. Krupsky (28 September 1944 to 9 May 1945).

10th Assault

Formed from the 9th Mixed Aviation Corps on 29 September 1944. Lieutenant General of Aviation O. V. Tolstikov (29 September 1944 to 9 May 1945).

1st Guards Assault

Formed from the 1st Assault Aviation Corps on 5 February 1944. Lieutenant General of Aviation V. G. Riazanov (5 February 1944 to 11 May 1945).

2nd Guards Assault

Formed from the 1st Guards Mixed Aviation Corps on 28 September 1944. Major General of Aviation S. V. Sliusarev (28 September to 12 October 1944 and 4 November 1944 to 11 May 1945) and Major General of Aviation A. A. Ivanov (13–22 October 1944).

3rd Guards Assault

Formed from the 2nd Assault Aviation Corps on 27 October 1944. Lieutenant General of Aviation V. V. Stepichev (27 October 1944 to 11 May 1945).

1st Fighter

Formed on 10 September 1942, reorganized as the 1st Guards Fighter Aviation Corps on 18 March 1943. Major General of Aviation (Lieutenant General of Aviation on 17 March 1943) E. M. Beletsky.

2nd Fighter

Formed on 10 October 1942. Major General of Aviation (Lieutenant General of Aviation on 30 April 1943) A. S. Blagoveshchensky (10 October 1942 to 10 February 1945) and Major General of Aviation V. M. Zabaluev (11 February to 11 May 1945).

3rd Fighter

Formed on 10 December 1942. Major General of Aviation (Lieutenant General of Aviation on 11 May 1944) E. Ia. Savitsky (10 December 1942 to 9 May 1945).

4th Fighter

Formed on 6 December 1942, reorganized as the 3rd Guards Fighter Aviation Corps on 2 July 1944. Major General of Aviation I. D. Podgornyi.

5th Fighter

Formed on 15 February 1943. Major General of Aviation I. D. Klimov (15 February to 26 June 1943); Major General of Aviation D. P. Galunov (27 June 1943 to 27 August 1944); and Colonel (Major General of Aviation on 20 April 1945) M. G. Machin (28 August 1944 to 11 May 1945).

6th Fighter

Formed on 19 February 1943. Major General of Aviation A. B. Iumashev (19 February to 29 June 1943); Major General of Aviation E. E. Erlykin (10 July 1943 to 28 May 1944); and Major General of Aviation I. M. Dzusov (29 May 1944 to 9 May 1945).

6th Fighter PVO

Formed on 20 June 1941. Colonel A. I. Mitenkov (20 June 1941 to 26 September 1942) and Major General of Aviation A. A. Demidov (27 September 1942 to 15 June 1943).

7th Fighter

Formed from the 5th Mixed Aviation Corps on 23 June 1943, reorganized as the 6th Guards Fighter Aviation Corps on 27 October 1944. Major General of Aviation A. V. Utin.

7th Fighter PVO

Formed on 7 January 1941, reorganized as the 2nd Guards Fighter Aviation Corps on 7 July 1943. Colonel S. P. Lavrilov (7 January to 25 September 1941); Colonel (Major General of Aviation on 10 November 1942) E. E. Erlykin (26 September 1941 to 23 June 1943); and Colonel I. D. Antonov (30 June to 7 July 1943).

8th Fighter

Formed from the 4th Mixed Aviation Corps on 24 June 1943. Major General of Aviation F. F. Zherebchenko (24 June 1943 to 13 September 1944) and Lieutenant General of Aviation A. S. Osipenko (16 September 1944 to 9 May 1945).

8th Fighter PVO

Formed on 6 July 1941. Lieutenant Colonel I. G. Puntus (6 July 1941 to 29 September 1942); Major General of Aviation I. I. Evsev'ev (30 September 1942 to 4 August 1944 and 23 April to 11 May 1945); and Colonel I. K. Starostenkov (5 August 1944 to 22 April 1945).

9th Fighter Voronezh PVO

Formed on 15 June 1943. Major General of Aviation (Lieutenant General of Aviation on 16 May 1944) S. G. Korol' (15 June 1943 to 11 May 1945).

10th Fighter

Formed from the 2nd Mixed Aviation Corps on 13 July 1943. Colonel (Major General of Aviation on 7 August 34) M. M. Glovnia (13 July 1943 to 11 May 1945).

10th Fighter PVO

Formed on 5 July 1943. Colonel (Major General of Aviation on 10 October 1943) L. G. Rybkin (5 July 1943 to 5 September 1944) and Colonel I. A. Skvorchevsky (6 September 1944 to 5 May 1945).

11th Fighter

Formed on 1 February 1944. Major General of Aviation G. A. Ivanov (1 February 1944 to 9 May 1945).

13th Fighter

Formed on 29 December 1943. Major General of Aviation B. A. Sidnev (29 December 1943 to 9 May 1945).

14th Fighter

Formed from the 11th Mixed Aviation Corps on 28 September 1944. Major General of Aviation S. P. Danilov (28 September 1944 to 9 May 1945).

1st Guards Fighter

Formed from the 1st Fighter Aviation Corps on 18 March 1943. Lieutenant General of Aviation E. M. Beletsky (18 March 1943 to 9 May 1945).

2nd Guards Fighter

Formed from the 7th Fighter Aviation Corps PVO on 7 July 1943. Major General of Aviation N. D. Antonov (7 July 1943 to 9 May 1945).

3rd Guards Fighter

Formed from the 4th Fighter Aviation Corps on 2 July 1944. Major General of Aviation (Lieutenant General of Aviation on 13 September 1944) I. D. Podgornyi (2 July 1944 to 11 May 1945).

6th Guards Fighter

Formed from the 7th Fighter Aviation Corps on 27 October 1944. Major General of Aviation A. V. Utin (27 October 1944 to 11 May 1945).[16]

SPECIAL CORPS OF RAILROAD FORCES

Special Corps of Railroad Forces

Formed on 1 January 39, disbanded on 7 January 1942. *Kombrig* (Major General of Technical Forces on 5 June 40) N. A. Prosvirov.[17]

Notes

1. M. M. Kozlov, ed., *Velikaia Otechestvennaia voina 1941–1945: Entsiklopediia* [The Great Patriotic War 1941–1945: An encyclopedia] (Moscow: Sovetskaia Entsiklopediia, 1985), 418–19.

2. Ibid., 88–89, 115, 172–73, 177, 229, 251, 274–75, 278, 312, 316–17, 322–23, 385, 405–6, 580, 607, 642–44, 686, 688, 743–45, 776, 821–23.

3. Ibid.

4. Ibid.

5. Ibid.

6. G. V. Malinovsky, "Sapernye armii i ikh rol' v pervyi period Velikoi otechestvennoi voiny" [Sapper armies and their role in the initial period of the Great Patriotic War], in *Voenno-istoricheskii arkhiv* [Military-historical archives], vol. 2 (17), pp. 146–79 (Moscow: Tserera, 2001), 152–56.

7. Kozlov, *Velikaia Otechestvennaia voina 1941–1945*.

8. Ibid., 88–89.

9. Ibid.

10. *Komandovanie korpusnogo i divizionnogo zvena Sovetskikh vooruzhennykh sil perioda Velikoi Otechestvennoi voiny 1941–1945 gg.* [Corps- and division-level commanders of the Soviet Armed Forces during the Great Patriotic War 1941–1945] (Moscow: Frunze Academy, 1964), 61–66. Prepared by the Main Cadre Directorate of the USSR's Ministry of Defense.

11. Ibid., 65–61.

12. Ibid., 69–80.

13. Ibid., 61–68.

14. Ibid., 81–82.

15. Kozlov, *Velikaia Otechestvennaia voina 1941–1945,* and *Komandovanie korpusnogo i divizionnogo zvena Sovetskikh vooruzhennykh*, 83–85.

16. *Komandovanie korpusnogo i divizionnogo zvena Sovetskikh vooruzhennykh*, 85–99.

17. Ibid., 99.

APPENDIX 3

NKVD Forces and Other Specialized Red Army Forces in Wartime

IDENTIFIED WARTIME NKVD DIVISIONS

1st NKVD Rifle Division (1st, 2nd, 3rd, and 7th Rifle Regiments)

Formed August and September 1941 at Mga near Leningrad). Fought in the Northwestern and Leningrad Fronts from August 1941 through July 1942. Converted into the 46th Rifle Division (3rd formation) on 9 August 1942 and transferred to the Red Army.

Separate NKVD Order of Lenin Motorized Rifle Division Special Designation in the name of F. E. Dzerzhinsky (1st, 2nd, 3rd, and 10th Motorized Rifle Regiments, 1st Artillery Battalion, and 1st Tank Battalion)

Formed on 23 June 1938 in Moscow and in June 1941 employed on the Western Front. Renamed the 1st Order of Lenin Motorized Rifle Division Special Designation in the name of F. E. Dzerzhinsky on 14 February 1943.

1st NKVD Order of Lenin Motorized Rifle Division Special Designation in the name of F. E. Dzerzhinsky (3rd Motorized Rifle Regiment, 26th, 145th, 169th, 290th, and 308th Rifle Regiments, and 1 separate rifle battalion)

Formed on 14 February 1943 at Krasnodar in the North Caucasus Military District from the above. Fought with the 56th Army through June 1943 and later stationed in Moscow. Currently assigned to MVD as 1st Separate Division Special Designation.

2nd NKVD Railroad Security Division (51st, 52nd, 80th, and 82nd Railroad Regiments)

Formed on 8 March 1939 in Leningrad. Served in the Leningrad and Special Baltic Military Districts after June 1941. Reorganized as the 23rd NKVD Railroad Security Division on 11 February 1942.

2nd NKVD Separate Motorized Rifle Division (7th, 9th, and 20th Motorized Rifle Regiments, 2nd Artillery Battalion, and four separate NKVD rifle battalions

Formed in July 1941 in Moscow on the basis of cadre from the Dzerzhinsky division. Provided rear-area security in the Leningrad and Baltic region. Disbanded in October 1945.

3rd NKVD Railroad Security Division (53rd, 58th, 60th, and 84th Railroad Security Regiments)

Formed on 8 March 1939 at Mogilev in the Special Western Military District from the 24th Railroad Security Brigade. Destroyed in July 1941 but reformed in August with the 53rd, 73rd, 76th, 79th, 83rd, 188th, and 252nd Railroad Regiments. Supported the Western and Briansk Fronts but destroyed in October 1941. Reformed as the 24th Railroad Security Division on 11 February 1942.

3rd NKVD Rifle Division

Formed in January 1942 at Leningrad but disbanded in August 1942.

3rd Rifle Division of NKVD Internal Forces (26th, 44th, and 289th Rifle Regiments, and 20th Separate Rifle Battalion)

Formed in June 1944 at Alma-Ata in the Central Asian Military District from cadre from the Tbilisi Division of Internal Forces. Transferred to Khabarovsk in the Far Eastern Front in mid-1945. Supported the 2nd Far Eastern Front in the Manchurian offensive but disbanded in January 1946.

4th NKVD Railroad Security Division (Cavalry) (55th, 56th, 57th, and 64th Railroad Regiments and the 227th Convoy Regiment)

Formed on 8 March 1939 in Kiev. Stationed in Odessa Military District in June 1941 but reorganized in late June with the (55th, 56th, 57th, 114th, and 64th Railroad, 227th Convoy, the 81st Separate NKVD Rifle Battalion and later the 34th Separate NKVD Rifle Battalion). Supported the Southern Front until converted into the 25th NKVD Railroad Division on 11 February 1942.

4th NKVD Rifle Division (Crimean Militia) (3rd, 6th, and 9th NKVD Rifle Regiments)

Formed in the Crimea in August and September 1941. Served in the 51st Army and Coastal Army in October 1941. Converted into the 184th Rifle Division (2nd formation) in October 1941.

4th NKVD Motorized Rifle Division (6th, 15th, 16th, and 28th Motorized Rifle Regiments)

Formed in Leningrad in January 1942 but disbanded in August 1942.

4th Rifle Division of NKVD Internal Forces (298th, and other unknown rifle regiments)

Formed on 10 October 1943 in Moscow. Later served in the Baltic region. Disbanded on 12 August 1951.

5th NKVD Railroad Security Division (54th, 81st, 113th, and 125th Railroad Regiments).

Formed on 8 March 1939 in Khar'kov from the 6th Railroad Security Brigade. Elements split between the Khar'kov and Volga Military Districts in June 1941. Later supported the Southwestern Front. Renumbered as the 26th Railroad Security Division on 11 February 1942.

5th NKVD Rifle Division (10th, 137th, 138th 140th, 260th, and 261st Rifle Regiments and associated 3rd NKVD Motorized Rifle Regiment)

Formed on 11 January 1942 at Tikhvin in the Leningrad Front. Served in the Leningrad and Baltic region until redesignated as the 5th Rifle Division of NKVD Internal Forces in 1944. Disbanded on 15 September 1951.

6th NKVD Railroad Security Division

Formed on 8 March 1939 in Khabarovsk in the Far East from the 1st Railroad Security Brigade. Redesignated as the 37th Railroad Security Division on 11 February 1942.

6th NKVD Motorized Rifle Division (6th, 16th, and 28th NKVD Motorized Rifle Regiments)

Formed in November 1941 in the rear area of the Southwestern Front. Renumbered as the 8th NKVD Motorized Rifle Division on 11 February 1942.

6th NKVD Rifle Division (135th, 136th, 139th, 145th [removed in late 1942], 262nd, and 297th Rifle Regiments)

Formed at Kalinin in the Moscow Military District in January 1942. Supported the Kalinin and 2nd Baltic Fronts in 1943 and 1944 and provided security in the Belorussian Military District. Redesignated as the 6th Rifle Division of NKVD Internal Forces in the summer of 1944. Disbanded in October 1945.

7th NKVD Railroad Security Division

Formed on 8 March 1939 at Svobodnyi in the Far East Front from the 3rd Railroad Security Brigade. Renumbered as the 28th Railroad Security Division on 11 February 1942.

7th NKVD Motorized Rifle Division (12th, 32nd, 34th [removed in late 1942], and 164th Motorized Rifle Regiments and 143rd [removed in early 1943], 264th, 265th, and 267th Rifle Regiments)

Formed at Orel and Tula between January and April 1942. Supported the Western, Briansk, Central, Belorussian, and 1st Belorussian Fronts from 1942 through early summer 1944. Redesignated as the 7th Motorized Division of NKVD Internal Forces in the summer of 1944 and served in the Belorussian Military District until war's end. Disbanded on 13 September 1951.

8th NKVD Railroad Security Division

Formed on 8 March 1939 in Chita, Trans-Baikal Military District from the 2nd Railroad Security Brigade. Renumbered as the 29th Railroad Security Division on 11 February 1942.

8th NKVD Motorized Rifle Division (4th, 41st, and 89th Motorized Rifle Regiments—the former 6th, 16th, and 28th NKVD Motorized Rifle Regiments)

Formed at Voronezh in the Southwestern Front in January 1942 from the 6th NKVD Motorized Rifle Division. Renumbered as the 63rd Rifle Division in July 1942 and reassigned to the Red Army. Redesignated as the 52nd Guards Rifle Division in November 1943.

8th NKVD Motorized Rifle Division

Formed at Voronezh in January 1942 but redesignated as the 13th NKVD Motorized Rifle Division in May 1942.

9th NKVD Railroad Security Division (58th, 60th, and 84th Railroad Regiments)

Formed on 8 March 1939 at Vilnius in the Baltic Special Military District from an unknown railroad security brigade. Supported the Special Baltic and Special Western Military Districts in June 1941. Destroyed by advancing German forces and disbanded on 25 September 1941.

9th NKVD Motorized Rifle Division (19th, 21st, 30th, and 33rd Motorized Rifle Regiment, and 267th Rifle Regiment [after August 1942])

Formed in Rostov in the North Caucasus Military District in January 1942 from the 76th Motorized Rifle Brigade. Converted into the 31st Rifle Division in August 1942 and assigned to the Red Army.

9th Rifle Division of NKVD Internal Forces (25th, 263rd, and other unknown rifle regiments)

Formed on 9 May 1944 in Krasnodar from the Ordzhonikidze Division. Provided security in the North Caucasus Military District. Disbanded in October 1944.

10th NKVD Railroad Security Division (64th, 66th, 75th, and 77th Railroad Regiments)

Formed on 14 November 1939 at L'vov in the Special Kiev Military District from an unknown railroad security brigade. Supported the Southwestern Front but destroyed in the August and September Uman' and Kiev encirclements and officially disbanded in October 1941.

10th "Stalingrad" NKVD Rifle Division (269th, 270th, 271st, 272nd, 273rd, 274th, and 282nd Rifle Regiments)

Formed between January and July 1942 at Saratov and Stalingrad in the Volga Military District. Supported the Southeastern and Stalingrad Front during the German advance toward Stalingrad and fought at Stalingrad. Converted into the 181st Rifle Division (3rd formation) and assigned to the NKVD Army in October 1942, which was redesignated as the 70th Army and assigned to the Central Front in February 1943.

10th Rifle Division of NKVD Internal Forces (34th Motorized Rifle, 284th Rifle, and later the 266th, 267th, 268th, 273rd, and 274th Rifle Regiments)

Formed in April 1944 in Sarny from the Sukhumi NKVD Division. Supported the Central, Belorussian, and 1st Belorussian Fronts in 1943 and 1944 and the Belorussian Military District from late summer 1944 through 1945. Disbanded in June 1946.

11th NKVD Rifle Division (initially the 26th and 276th Rifle Regiments, 95th Border Guards Regiment, and 25th Border Guards Command, and, after 8 August 1942, the 275th, 276th, 277th, 278th, and 279th Rifle Regiments and the 11th and 17th Cavalry Regiments)

Formed at Nal'chik and Krasnodar in the North Caucasus Military District in January 1942. Supported the Crimean and Trans-Caucasus Fronts (37th Army) from September through December 1942. Disbanded in December 1942 with its remnants assigned to the 2nd NKVD Taman Guards Rifle Division.

11th NKVD Special Installation Security Division (160th, 173rd, and 207th Rifle Regiments)

Formed on 6 November 1939 from the 26th NKVD Security Brigade. Reorganized and consolidated with the 12th Special Installation Security Division into the 15th NKVD Special Installation Security Division on 31 January 1942. Stationed in the Moscow region with the mission of protecting key political and economic objectives throughout the war.

12th NKVD Special Installation Security Division (189th and unknown security regiments)

Formed in the Moscow region on 25 August 1941. Operated in the Moscow region to protect key political and economic objectives and support the Western Front until consolidated with the 11th Special Installation Security Division into the 15th NKVD Special Installation Security Division on 31 January 1942.

12th NKVD Mountain Rifle Division (280th, 283rd, 284th, 285th, and 334th Rifle Regiments)

Formed at Saratov in the Volga Military District on 29 June 1941. Converted into the 268th Rifle Division (1st formation) in July 1941 and assigned to the Red Army.

12th NKVD Rifle Division

Formed at Moscow in January 1942. Reorganized into the 22nd NKVD Separate Rifle Brigade in September 1942.

13th NKVD Convoy Forces Security Division (227th and 233rd Convoy Regiments, 237th Garrison Regiment, and 249th Convoy Regiment)

Formed in November 1939 in Kiev from the 1st and 2nd Convoy Forces Security Brigades. Stationed in the Special Kiev, Khar'kov, and Odessa Military Districts in June 1941. Supported the Southwestern and Southern Fronts until major portions of the division were broken up and destroyed during the Uman', Kiev, and Odessa encirclements in September 1941. Its remnants were renumbered as the 35th NKVD Convoy Forces Security Division in February 1942.

13th NKVD Motorized Rifle Division (regiments unknown)

Formed in the Moscow Military District in May 1942 from the 8th NKVD Motorized Rifle Division. Supported the Voronezh Front in 1942 and was redesignated as the 95th Rifle Division (2nd formation) in August 1942 and assigned to the Red Army.

14th NKVD Convoy Forces Security Division (regiments unknown)

Formed in the Moscow Military District in September 1940 from the 11th NKVD Convoy Forces Security Brigade. Stationed in the Moscow Military District in June 1941. Performed convoy duty until redesignated as the 36th NKVD Convoy Forces Security Division in February 1942.

14th NKVD Special Installation Security Division

Formed on 3 August 1944 in Vil'nius to provide security for key political and economic objectives in Lithuania. Disbanded on 15 May 1951.

15th NKVD Mountain Rifle Division (47th and other unknown rifle regiments)

Formed in Moscow on 29 June 1941 from existing NKVD rifle regiments. Assigned to the Southern Front in July 1941. Fought with the Southern Front throughout 1941 and 1942 and converted into the 257th Rifle Division (1st formation) in July 1942.

15th NKVD Special Installation Security Division

Formed in Moscow on 31 January 1942 by a consolidation of the 11th and 12th Special Installation Security Divisions. Disbanded on 15 May 1951.

16th NKVD Mountain Rifle Division (159th, 165th, and 197th Rifle Regiments)

Formed in Moscow on 29 June 1941. Reassigned to the Red Army in July 1941 and renumbered as the 262nd Rifle Division (1st formation) in July 1942.

16th NKVD Special Installation Security Division

Formed in Moscow on 31 January 1942. Disbanded on 30 May 1950.

17th NKVD Special Installation Security Division (regiments unknown)

Formed at Gor'kii in the Moscow Military District on 31 January 1942. Provided security for Soviet industrial complexes throughout the war. Disbanded on 15 May 1951.

18th NKVD Railroad Security Division

Formed on 24 June 1941 in Tbilisi in the Trans-Caucasus Military District from an unknown railroad security brigade. Renumbered the 30th Railroad Security Division on 11 February 1942.

18th NKVD Special Installation Security Division

Formed on 31 January 1942 in Sverdlovsk in the Ural Military District by renaming the 25th NKVD Special Installation Security Division. Provided security for industrial objectives in the Ural region. Disbanded on 15 May 1951.

19th NKVD Special Installation Security Division (172nd, 175th, and 176th Rifle Regiments and 85th, 89th, 113th Separate Rifle Battalions)

Formed at Voroshilovgrad in the Donbas region in January 1942 from the 71st NKVD Security Brigade. Supported the Southern and Trans-Caucasus Front (Northern Group) in 1942. Converted into the 8th NKVD Special Installation Security Brigade on 10 November 1942.

19th NKVD Special Installation and Railroad Security Division

Formed in Gor'kii on 24 June 1941 from the 28th Special Installation Security Brigade. Renumbered as the 31st Special Installation and Railroad Security Division on 26 March 1942.

19th NKVD Rifle Division (24th, 66th, and 308th Rifle Regiments)

Formed in August 1942 in the Trans-Caucasus Front's Northern Group. Defended Groznyi from August through October 1942 but reverted to NKVD control in January 1943, after which it performed security missions and detached units to form the 58th NKVD Rifle Division at the front.

20th NKVD Special Installation and Railroad Security Division (1st and 56th Security Brigades, 151st, 152nd, 154th, and 155th Rifle Regiments, at times the 225th Rifle Regiment, and the 111th, 166th, and 167th Separate Rifle Battalions)

Formed in Leningrad on 24 June 1941 from the 56th Special Installation Security Brigade. Protected economic objectives in the Leningrad Military District and Karelia. Reorganized as the 20th NKVD Rifle Division on 5 September 1941.

20th NKVD Rifle Division (with the 7th, 8th, 9th, and 151st Security Regiments)

Formed at Tikhvin in the Leningrad Front on 5 September 1941 from the 20th Special Installation and Railroad Security Division. Supported the Neva Operational Group and the 8th and 23rd Armies. Converted into the 92nd Rifle Division in August 1942 and assigned to the Red Army.

20th NKVD Special Installation Security Division (regiments unknown)

Formed at Novosibirsk and Kuibyshev in the Volga Military District on 10 November 1942 from the 4th NKVD Security Brigade. Thereafter, provided security for the Kuibyshev industrial region. Disbanded on 15 May 1951.

21st NKVD Motorized Rifle Division (13th, 14th, 15th, and 35th Motorized Rifle Regiments)

Formed at Leningrad in late June 1941. Supported the 42nd Army until converted into the 21st NKVD Rifle Division on 1 September 1941. Its 35th Motorized Rifle Regiment joined the 44th Rifle Division.

21st NKVD Rifle Division (6th, 8th, and 14th Rifle Regiments)

Formed from the 21st NKVD Motorized Rifle Division on 1 September 1941. Transferred its 8th Rifle Regiment to the 20th NKVD Rifle Division on 15 September 1941. Supported the 42nd Army until converted into the 109th Rifle Division in August 1942.

21st NKVD Special Installation Security Division

Formed on 28 July 1943 in Novosibiirsk from the 6th NKVD Security Brigade. Reorganized as the 54th NKVD Security Brigade on 22 November 1945.

22nd NKVD Motorized Rifle Division (1st, 3rd, and 5th Motorized Rifle Regiments, and 83rd Railroad Regiment)

Formed in the Northwestern Front on 23 June 1941. Supported the 8th Army's 10th Rifle Corps and severely damaged in fighting along the border and at Riga. Largely destroyed in August 1941 and disbanded in January 1942.

22nd NKVD Railroad Security Division (regiments unknown)

Formed on 29 February 1944 in Kuibyshev from the 29th NKVD Special Installation Security Brigade. Disbanded on 25 May 1946.

23rd NKVD Motorized Rifle Division (6th, 16th, and 28th Motorized Rifle Regiments)

Formed in the Special Kiev Military District in late June 1941. Supported the Southwestern Front until converted into the 8th NKVD Motorized Rifle Division in December 1941 and January 1942.

23rd NKVD Railroad Security Division (51st, 52nd, 53rd, 80th, 82nd, 87th, 109th, 110th, 115th, and 152nd Railroad Regiments and 2nd and 32nd Separate Reserve Railroad Battalions)

Formed at Leningrad on 11 February 1942 from the 2nd NKVD Railroad Security Division. Defended railroad lines from to Leningrad to Moscow, Murmansk, Arkhangel'sk, and Vologda as well as the "ice road" across Lake Ladoga until war's end. Disbanded on 15 May 1951.

24th NKVD Railroad Security Division (53rd and other unknown railroad regiments)

Formed in Moscow on 11 February 1942 from the renamed 3rd Railroad Security Division. Disbanded on 21 December 1946.

25th NKVD Railroad Security Division (55th, 56th, 57th, 78th, 114th, and 119th Railroad Regiments)

Formed on 11 February 1942 at Saratov in the Volga Military District from the renamed 4th Railroad Security Division. Supported the Southwestern and 2nd and 3rd Ukrainian Fronts. Disbanded on 15 May 1951.

25th NKVD Special Installation Security Division

Formed on 22 June 1941 in Sverdlovsk from the 58th NKVD Security Brigade. Redesignated as the 18th NKVD Special Installation Security Division on 31 January 1942.

26th NKVD Railroad Security Division (56th, 90th, 115th, and 151st Railroad Regiments)

Formed in Liski on 11 February 1942 from the renamed 5th NKVD Railroad Security Division. Disbanded on 21 December 1946.

26th NKVD Mountain Rifle Division

Formed in Moscow on 29 June 1941. Assigned to the Red Army (as an unknown division) in July 1941.

27th NKVD Railroad Security Division (73rd, 103rd, and other unknown railroad regiments)

Formed in Khabarovsk on 11 February 1942 from the renamed 6th NKVD Railroad Security Division. Disbanded on 15 May 1951.

28th NKVD Railroad Security Division (60th, 70th, and other unknown railroad regiments)

Formed on 11 February 1942 at Svobodnyi in the Far East Front from the renamed 7th NKVD Railroad Security Division. Reorganized on 29 February 1944 into the 32nd NKVD Railroad Security Brigade.

29th NKVD Railroad Security Division (68th, 69th, and other unknown railroad regiments)

Formed on 11 February 1942 at Chita in the Trans-Baikal Military District from the renamed 8th NKVD Railroad Security Division. Disbanded on 21 December 1946.

30th NKVD Railroad Security Division (64th, 66th, 116th, and 119th Railroad Regiments)

Formed at Tbilisi in the Trans-Caucasus Military District on 11 February 1942 from the renamed 18th NKVD Railroad Security Division. Disbanded on 16 December 1946.

31st NKVD Railroad Security Division (64th, 91st, other unknown railroad regiments, and the 31st Armored Train Battalion)

Formed at Gor'kii on 26 March 1942 from the renamed 19th NKVD Railroad Security Division. Disbanded on 25 May 1946.

32nd NKVD Railroad Security Division (62nd, 117th, 154th, and other unknown railroad regiments)

Formed on 26 March 1942 in Voroshilov. Supported the Voronezh, Central, Belorussian, and 1st Ukrainian Fronts until war's end. Disbanded on 15 May 1951.

33rd NKVD Railroad Security Division (regiments unknown)

Formed on 26 March 1942 in Kuibyshev in the Central Asian Military District to construct and protect railroads. Disbanded on 8 January 1947.

34th NKVD Railroad Security Division (regiments unknown)

Formed at Sverdlovsk on 26 March 1942. Disbanded on 21 December 1946.

35th NKVD Convoy Forces Security Division (249th, and other convoy regiments)

Formed in Borisoglebsk near Voronezh in February 1942 from the renamed 13th NKVD Convoy Forces Security Division. Assigned to the Stalingrad and Central Asian Military Districts to convoy and secure prisoners of war and convicts. Disbanded in July 1951.

36th NKVD Convoy Forces Security Division (256th Convoy and other unknown regiments)

Formed at Minusinsk near Krasnoiarsk in February 1942 from the renamed 14th NKVD Convoy Forces Security Division. Served in the Ukrainian Military District from August 1944 through 1945. Disbanded in January 1948.

37th NKVD Convoy Forces Security Division (226th, 230th, 236th, and 251st Convoy Regiments)

Formed at Marfino near Volodarsk in March 1942 from the reorganized 42nd NKVD Convoy Forces Security Brigade. Assigned to the Western Front and combined with the 42nd NKVD Convoy Forces Security Brigade. Supported the Western and 1st Belorussian Fronts until war's end. Disbanded in July 1951.

38th NKVD Convoy Forces Security Division (regiments unknown)

Formed at Novosibirsk and Irkutsk in March 1942 from the reorganized 46th NKVD Convoy Forces Security Brigade. Disbanded in July 1951.

39th NKVD Convoy Forces Security Division (regiments unknown)

Formed in August 1943 in Sverdlovsk from the reorganized 45th NKVD Convoy Forces Security Brigade. Disbanded in January 1951.

41st NKVD Railroad Security Division (91st and other unknown regiments)

Formed on 26 March 1942 in Rostov. Renamed the Sukhumi Division on 24 September 1942.

45th NKVD Convoy Forces Security Division

Formed at Bel'tsy in the Ukraine in August 1944. Supported the 2nd Ukrainian Front to war's end. Disbanded in September 1955.

46th NKVD Convoy Forces Security Division

Formed at Moscow in August 1944. Disbanded in September 1955.

47th NKVD Convoy Forces Security Division
Formed at Leningrad in May 1945.

48th NKVD Convoy Forces Security Division
Formed at Riga in May 1945.

49th NKVD Convoy Forces Security Division
Formed at Odessa in May 1945.

50th NKVD Convoy Forces Security Division
Formed at Voronezh in May 1945.

51st NKVD Convoy Forces Security Division
Formed at Khar'kov in May 1945

52nd NKVD Convoy Forces Security Division
Formed at Voroshilovgrad in May 1945

53rd NKVD Convoy Forces Security Division
Formed at Rostov in May 1945

56th Rifle Division of NKVD Internal Forces
Formed in May 1945 at Alma-Ata in the Central Asian Military District.

57th Rifle Division of NKVD Internal Forces (369th, 370th, and 371st Rifle Regiments)
Formed on 18 January 1945 in Gaizhunai. Supported the 3d Belorussian Front. Disbanded in October 1945.

58th Rifle Division of NKVD Internal Forces (372nd, 373rd, and 374th Rifle Regiments)
Formed in January 1945 in Slonim, Belorussia, from elements of the 19th NKVD Rifle Division. Support the 1st Belorussian Front to war's end. Disbanded in June 1945.

59th Rifle Division of NKVD Internal Forces (regiments unknown)

Formed in January 1945 in L'vov, Ukraine. Supported the 1st Ukrainian Front to war's end. Disbanded in October 1945.

60th Rifle Division of NKVD Internal Forces (regiments unknown)

Formed on 22 February 1945 in Vinnitsa. Supported the 2nd Ukrainian Front to war's end. Disbanded on 4 October 1946.

61st Rifle Division of NKVD Internal Forces (regiments unknown)

Formed in February 1945 in Bel'tsy. Supported the Ukrainian *fronts* to war's end. Disbanded in December 1945.

62nd Rifle Division of NKVD Internal Forces (regiments unknown)

Formed in December 1944 in Belgrade. Supported the 3rd Ukrainian Front to war's end. Disbanded in September 1951.

63rd Rifle Division of NKVD Internal Forces (32nd, 108th, and 273rd Rifle Regiments)

Formed in January 1945 in Belostok, Belorussia. Supported the 2nd Belorussian Front until war's end. Disbanded in December 1946.

64th Rifle Division of NKVD Internal Forces (145th Rifle Regiment, 2nd, 11th, 18th, and 98th and 104th Border Guards Regiments, 771st Artillery Regiment, and 198th Separate Motorized Rifle Battalion)

Formed in December 1944 at L'vov in the western Ukraine from the Mixed [*Svodnaia*] Division of NKVD Internal Forces. Supported the 1st Ukrainian Front and provided security in the western Ukraine until war's end. Disbanded in June 1948.

65th Rifle Division of NKVD Internal Forces (387th Rifle Regiment, 336th Border Guards Regiment, and other unknown units)

Formed on 23 January 1945 in Stanislaw, southern Poland. Supported the 2nd and 3rd Ukrainian Fronts in Hungary, and thereafter, performed security missions in Hungary. Disbanded on 18 July 1946.

66th Rifle Division of NKVD Internal Forces (201st Rifle Regiment and other unknown regiments)

Formed in January 1945 in Sibiu. Supported the 3rd Ukrainian Front in Romania. Remained in Romania to perform security missions. Disbanded in October 1945.

Groznyi Rifle Division of NKVD Internal Forces (44th, 66th, and 308th Rifle Regiments and, later, 24th NKVD Border Guards Regiment)

Formed on 15 August 1942 at Groznyi as a part of the Trans-Caucasus Front's Northern Group of Forces. Participated in defensive and offensive operations through December 1942. Thereafter, performed security missions until being used in the creation of higher-numbered NKVD rifle divisions in 1944. Disbanded on 18 April 1944.

Ordzhonikidze (9th) Rifle Division of NKVD Internal Forces (34th Motorized Rifle Regiment, 169th and 273rd Rifle Regiments, 26th Red Banner Border Guards Regiment, 19th Separate Ordzhonikidze Rifle Regiment, and 29th Artillery Regiment)

Formed on 22 August 1942 in Ordzhonikidze, North Caucasus Military District, to protect the city and the vital Georgian military highway. Operated defensively and offensively with the Trans-Caucasus Front's Northern Group from September through December 1942. Provided security in the region after December 1942 and reorganized into a numbered NKVD rifle division in late 1943 and early 1944. Renamed the 9th Rifle Division of NKVD Internal Forces on 9 May 1944.

Sukhumi (10th) Rifle Division of NKVD Internal Forces (initially the 34th Motorized Rifle Regiment, and 263rd, 266th, 267th, 268th, 273rd, and 274th Rifle Regiments)

Formed in September 1942 at Sukhumi in the Trans-Caucasus Front. Subordinate to the 46th Army of the Trans-Caucasus Front's Black Sea Group in combat from October through December 1942, when it also controlled the 8th NKVD Motorized Rifle Regiment and the 23rd, 25th, and 33rd Border Guards Regiments. Thereafter, performed security missions in the region until some of its forces were assigned to other NKVD divisions after March 1943. Renamed the 10th Rifle Division of NKVD Internal Forces in April 1944.

Makhachkala Rifle Division of NKVD Internal Forces (237th, 284th, and other unknown rifle regiments and the 18th Cavalry Regiment)

Formed in August 1942 at Makhachkala in the Trans-Caucasus Front. Fought under Red Army control from August through November 1942. Thereafter, performed security missions until January 1943, when it was disbanded and its forces were assigned to higher-numbered NKVD rifle divisions operating in the West.

Tbilisi Rifle Division of NKVD Internal Forces

Formed in September 1942 in Tbilisi in the Trans-Caucasus Front. Performed internal security missions through early 1944. Reorganized into the 3rd Rifle Division of NKVD Internal Forces in April 1944.

Separate NKVD Army

Headquarters formed at Sverdlovsk on 26 October 1942. Converted into the Red Army's 70th Army on 1 February 1943. Consisted of:

- Siberian Rifle Division of NKVD Internal Forces: formed in the Siberian Military District in October 1942; reassigned to the Red Army as the 140th Rifle Division on 1 February 1943
- Central Asian Rifle Division of NKVD Internal Forces: formed in the Siberian Military District in October 1942; reassigned to the Red Army as the 161st Rifle Division on 1 February 1943
- Far Eastern Rifle Division of NKVD Internal Forces: formed in the Siberian Military District in October 1942; reassigned to the Red Army as the 102nd Rifle Division on 1 February 1943
- Trans-Baikal Rifle Division of NKVD Internal Forces: formed in the Siberian Military District in October 1942; reassigned to the Red Army as the 106th Rifle Division on 1 February 1943
- Ural Rifle Division of NKVD Internal Forces: formed in the Siberian Military District in October 1942; reassigned to the Red Army as the 175th Rifle Division on 1 February 1943
- Stalingrad (10th) Rifle Division of NKVD Internal Forces (see above); reassigned to the Red Army as the 181st Rifle Division on 1 February 1943

Separate Rifle Division of NKVD Internal Forces

Formed in Krasnodar in March 1943 to provide internal security in the North Caucasus Front. Disbanded in April 1943.

Composite [*Svodnaia*] Rifle Division of NKVD Internal Forces

Formed in Lublin in October 1944 to provide security in eastern Poland and the western Ukraine. Renamed the 64th Rifle Division of NKVD Internal Forces in December 1944.

NKVD Militia Division for Rear-Area Security

Formed in September 1941 to provide for rear-area security in the Southern and North Caucasus Fronts. Renamed Headquarters of NKVD Forces for Rear-Area Security in the Southern and North Caucasus Fronts in August 1942. Fielded four security regiments. Probably used to fill out other NKVD divisions in late 1942 and early 1943.[1]

Note

1. V. V. Dushen'kin, ed., *Vnutrennie voiska v Velikoi Otechestvennoi voine 1941–1945 gg.: Dokumenty i materialy* [Internal forces in the Great Patriotic War 1941–1945: Documents and materials] (Moscow: Iuridicheskaia Literatura, 1975); N. P. Patrushev, ed., *Organy gosudarstvennoi bezopasnosti SSSR v Velikoi Otechestvennoi voine, Sbornik dokumentov, Tom vtoroi, Kniga I: Nachalo 22 iiunia–31 avgusta 1941 goda* [Organs of state security of the USSR in the Great Patriotic War, collection of documents, vol. 2, book I: The Beginning, 22 June–31 August 1941] and *Kniga II: Nachalo, 1 sentiabria–31 dekabria 1941 goda* [Book II: The Beginning, 1 September–31 December 1941] (Moscow: Rus', 2000); G. P. Sechkin, *Pogranichnye voiska v Velikoi Otechestvennoi voine* [Border guards troops in the Great Patriotic War] (Moscow: Order of Lenin and Red Banner Higher Command Courses of the KGB USSR, 1990); A. G. Lensky, *Sukhoputnye sily RKKA v predvoennye gody* [The RKKA's ground forces in the prewar years] (Saint Petersburg: N.p., 2000); *Truppen-Ubersicht und Kriegsgliederungen Rote Armee, Stand August 1944*, Fremde Heere Ost Ic Unterlagen Ost, Merkblatt geh. 11/6, Pruf.-Nr. 0157, in National Archives Microfilm Series T-78, Roll 459.

IDENTIFIED WARTIME NKVD BRIGADES

Brigade (Composition)	Location and Date
1st NKVD Rifle (61st, 62nd, 63rd, 64th, 95th, 110th Sep RBns)	Leningrad Front (Jan 42)
1st NKVD Rifle (unknown)	4th Ukr Front (1944)
2nd NKVD Rifle (156th, 180th Sep RBns)	Moscow MD (Jan 42 from 69th NKVD Brigade), 1st Belo Front (1944)
3rd NKVD Rifle (141st RR)	Moscow MD (Jan 42)
5th NKVD Rifle (unknown)	Trans-Caucasus MD (Baku)
5th NKVD Railroad (unknown)	Central Asian MD (Tashkent)
8th NKVD Rifle (unknown)	Trans-Caucasus Front (Dec 42)
10th NKVD Rifle (unknown)	Trans-Caucasus Front
12th NKVD Railroad (unknown)	Dnepropetrovsk
16th NKVD Rifle (202nd, 203rd, 204th Sep RBns)	SW, 2nd Ukr Fronts
17th NKVD Rifle (206th, 207th, 208th, 209th, 210th, 225th Sep RBns)	Vor, 1st Ukr Fronts
18th NKVD Rifle (185th, 186th, 187th, 188th, 189th Sep RBns)	Vor, 1st Ukr Fronts
19th NKVD "Kursk" (unknown)	Briansk, Central, 1st Ukr Fronts
20th NKVD Rifle (298th and 299th Sep RBns)	Vor, 1st Ukr Fronts
21st NKVD Rifle (226th, 227th, 228th, 229th, 230th Sep RBns)	Don, Central, Belo, 1st Ukr Fronts
22nd NKVD Rifle (281st Sep RBn)	Unknown
23rd NKVD Rifle (236th, 237th, 238th, and 239th, Sep RBns)	SW, 2nd Ukr Fronts
24th NKVD Rifle (216th, 217th 218th, 219th, 220th Sep RBns)	Vor, 1st Ukr Fronts
25th NKVD Rifle (223rd, 226th Sep RBns)	Southern, 4th Ukr Fronts
25th NKVD Security (unknown)	Penza
26th NKVD Railroad (80th Railroad Bn)	Vologda
28th NKVD Railroad (3rd Railroad Bn)	Unknown
29th NKVD Railroad (124th, 209th Railroad Bns)	Trans-Caucasus Front
30th NKVD Railroad (unknown)	Central Asian MD
41st NKVD Convoy (250th Sep Convoy Bn)	Vologda, Western Front
42nd NKVD Convoy (226th, 236th, 240th, 251st Convoy Bns)	Moscow (Western Front) converted into the 37th NKVD Convoy Division)
43rd NKVD Convoy (230th, 231st Convoy Bns)	Piatigorsk (Stavropol'), Southern Front
44th NKVD Convoy (unknown)	Kuibyshev, Trans-Caucasus Front
45th NKVD Convoy (unknown)	Sverdlovsk (Siberian MD)
47th NKVD Convoy (unknown)	Tashkent, Tiflis (Trans-Caucasus MD)
56th NKVD Security (155th Security Bn)	Northern Front (to 20th NKVD RD (Sep 41)
57th NKVD Rifle (157th, 169th, 170th RRs, 120th Sep RBn)	Odessa MD, SW, Briansk Fronts (destroyed May 42, remnants to 1st NKVD RD)
69th NDVK Rifle (115th, 156th, 180th Rifle RRs, 80th Sep RBn)	Briansk, Western Fronts (renamed 2nd NKVD RB (Jan 42)

—continued

Appendix 3

Brigade (Composition)	Location and Date
71st NKVD Rifle (172nd, 175th, 176th RRs, 85th, 89th Sep RBns)	Khar'kov, North Caucasus MDs (converted into the 19th NKVD RD (Jan 42)
243rd NKVD Rifle (230th Sep RBn)	Southern Front (destroyed Dec 41)

Sources: V. V. Dushen'kin, ed., *Vnutrennie voiska v Velikoi Otechestvennoi voine 1941–1945 gg.: Dokumenty i materialy* [Internal forces in the Great Patriotic War 1941–1945: Documents and materials] (Moscow: Iuridicheskaia Literatura, 1975); N. P. Patrushev, ed., *Organy gosudarstvennoi bezopasnosti SSSR v Velikoi Otechestvennoi voine, Sbornik dokumentov, Tom vtoroi, Kniga I: Nachalo 22 iiunia–31 avgusta 1941 goda* [Organs of state security of the USSR in the Great Patriotic War, collection of documents, vol. 2, book I: The Beginning, 22 June–31 August 1941] and *Kniga II: Nachalo, 1 sentiabria–31 dekabria 1941 goda* [Book II: The Beginning, 1 September–31 December 1941] (Moscow: Rus', 2000); G. P. Sechkin, *Pogranichnye voiska v Velikoi Otechestvennoi voine* [Border guards troops in the Great Patriotic War] (Moscow: Order of Lenin and Red Banner Higher Command Courses of the KGB USSR, 1990); A. G. Lensky, *Sukhoputnye sily RKKA v predvoennye gody* [The RKKA's ground forces in the prewar years] (Saint Petersburg, N.p., 2000); *Truppen-Ubersicht und Kriegsgliederungen Rote Armee, Stand August 1944*, Fremde Heere Ost Ic Unterlagen Ost, Merkblatt geh. 11/6, Pruf.-Nr. 0157, in National Archives Microfilm Series T-78, Roll 459.

IDENTIFIED WARTIME SEPARATE NKVD REGIMENTS

Regiment	Location
1st Belostok NKVD Mot Rifle	29th Army, Western Front (Jul–Aug 41)
1st NKVD Partisan	Belorussia
2nd NKVD Border Guards	Stalingrad, Voronezh, 1st Ukr Fronts, Ukr MD
2nd NKVD Mot (Internal)	Moscow (to MVD)
2nd NKVD Border Guards	1st Belo in 64th NKVD RD (Oct 44)
2nd NKVD Partisan	Ukraine
3rd NKVD Mot Rifle	Sp Western MD, NW Front, in 22nd NKVD MRD (Jun 41)
5th NKVD Mot Rifle	NW Front, in 22nd NKVD MRD (Jun 41)
6th NKVD Border Guards	Leningrad Front
6th L'vov NKVD Mot Rifle	SW Front, in 8th NKVD MRD (Dec 41)
7th NKVD Border Guards	Karelian Front
8th NKVD Mot Rifle	Trans-Caucasus Front, Georgia
9th NKVD Border Guards	NW Front
10th NKVD Border Guards	NW, 2nd Ukr Fronts
11th NKVD Border Guards	NW, 1st Belo Fronts, in 64th NKVD RD (Oct 44)
12th NKVD Border Guards	2nd Baltic Front (1944–1945)
13th NKVD Mot Rifle	Northern Front (1941), in 21st NKVD MRD (Jun 41)
13th NKVD Border Guards	Kalinin, Western, 3rd Belo Fronts
14th NKVD Mot Rifle	Northern Front (1941), in 21st NKVD MRD (Jun 41)
15th NKVD Mot Rifle	Northern Front, 37th RD (Sep 41)
16th NKVD Cavalry	Sp. Western MD, Western, 1st Ukr Fronts
16th NKVD Mot Rifle	SW Front, in 8th NKVD MRD (Dec 41)
16th NKVD Border Guards	Western, Kalinin, 1st Baltic Fronts
17th NKVD Border Guards	Briansk, Steppe, Southern, 3rd Ukr Fronts
18th NKVD Border Guards	SW, Western, Briansk, Central, 1st Belo Fronts, in 64th NKVD RD (Oct 44)
21st NKVD Cavalry	Sp. Kiev MD, SW Front
23rd NKVD Border Guards	Southern Front, converted to 3rd NVKD RR, 4th NKVD RD (Aug 41)
23rd NKVD Border Guards	Coastal Army, SW, 4th Ukr Fronts

NKVD Forces and Other Specialized Red Army Forces in Wartime   133

Regiment	Location
23rd NKVD Mot Rifle	Sp Baltic MD
24th NKVD Border Guards	Southern Front, converted to 6th NKVD RR, 4th NKVD RD (Aug 41)
24th NKVD Border Guards	Southern, North Caucasus, 2nd Ukr Fronts
25th NKVD Border Guards	Southern Front, converted to 9th NKVD RR, 4th NKVD RD (Aug 41)
25th NKVD Border Guards	SW, 3rd Ukr Fronts
26th NKVD Border Guards	Odessa MD, Southern Front, in 4th NKVD RD (Aug 41)
26th NKVD Rifle	Ukraine
28th NKVD Mot Rifle	SW Front, in 8th NKVD MRD (Dec 41)
30th NKVD Railroad	Kalinin Front, disbanded in Oct 41
31st NKVD Border Guards	Kalinin, 1st Baltic Fronts, Carpathian MD
32nd NKVD Mot Rifle	Leningrad Front
32nd NKVD Border Guards	North Caucasus, 3rd Belo Fronts
33rd NKVD Border Guards	Trans-Caucasus MD, NW, 1st Baltic, 3rd Belo Fronts
33rd NKVD Mot Rifle	56th Army Southern Front (Rostov)
34th NKVD Mot Rifle	50th Army, Briansk, Western Fronts
35th NKVD Mot Rifle	Northern Front, in 21st NKVD MRD (Jun 41)
37th NKVD Border Guards	27th Army, NW, Kalinin, 2nd Ukr Fronts
38th NKVD Border Guards	Western, Briansk, 1st Belo Fronts
42nd NKVD Reserve Border Guards	SW Front, destroyed at Kiev (Sep 41)
43rd NKVD Reserve Border Guards	SW Front, destroyed at Kiev (Sep 41)
47th NKVD Rifle	6th Army, Southern Front, to 15th NKVD RD
72nd NKVD Border Guards	26th Army, Northern, Karelian Fronts
73rd NKVD Border Guards	Northern, Karelian Fronts
79th NKVD Border Guards	SW, Stalingrad, Vor, Southern, 4th Ukr Fronts
80th NKVD Border Guards	32nd Army, Northern, Karelian Fronts
82nd NVKD Border Guards	Northern, Karelian Fronts
83rd NKVD Border Guards	Western, Kalinin, 1st Baltic Fronts
84th NKVD Railroad	Western Front (1941)
86th NKVD Border Guards	Western, 3rd Belo Fronts
87th NKVD Border Guards	Western, 2nd Belo Fronts
88th NKVD Border Guards	Kalinin, 1st Baltic Fronts, Ukr MD
90th NKVD Border Guards	Briansk, SW, 1st Ukr Fronts
91st NKVD Border Guards	SW, Southern, 3rd Ukr Fronts
92nd NKVD Border Guards	SW, Stalingrad, 1st, 4th Ukr Fronts
95th NKVD Border Guards	Southern, Crimean, North Caucasus Fronts, Crimea
98th NKVD Border Guards	SW, 1st Belo Fronts, in 64th NKVD RD (Oct 44)
99th NKVD Border Guards	Leningrad Front
100th NKVD Border Guards	14th Army, Karelian Front
101st NKVD Border Guards	Karelian Front
103rd NKVD Border Guards	Leningrad, 2nd Belo Fronts
104th NKVD Border Guards	Leningrad, 1st Belo Fronts, in 64th NKVD RD (Oct 44)
105th NKVD Border Guards	Leningrad, 2nd Baltic, 1st Belo Fronts
106th NKVD Border Guards	Leningrad Front
108th NKVD Border Guards	Leningrad Front
109th NKVD Railroad	NW Front, disbanded in Aug 41
109th NKVD Border Guards Maneuver Group	2nd, 3rd Ukr Fronts
112th NKVD Border Guards Maneuver Group	4th Ukr Front

—continued

Appendix 3

Regiment	Location
113th NKVD Sep Rifle	37th Army, Trans-Caucasus Front
123rd NKVD Border Guards	SW, 2nd Ukr Fronts
124th NKVD Border Guards	SW, 2nd Ukr Fronts
127th NKVD Border Guards	2nd Belo Front
128th NKVD Border Guards	2nd Ukr Front
130th NKVD Border Guards	2nd Baltic Front
132nd NKVD Border Guards	Western, 3rd Belo Fronts
134th NKVD Border Guards	3rd Ukr Front
143rd NKVD Railroad	SW Front
145th NKVD Rifle Rgt	6th NKVD RD (1942), Baku NKVD Brigade (Jan 43), Separate NKVD Division (Apr 43), 1st Belo Front's 64th NKVD RD (Oct 44)
156th Separate NKVD Rifle	50th Army, Briansk Front, 3rd Baltic Front
157th NKVD Border Guards	Belo, 1st Belo Fronts
173rd NKVD Reserve	SW Front
177th NKVD Border Guards (Rifle)	Belo MD (1944–1945)
180th NKVD Rifle	50th Army, Western Front
215th NKVD Border Guards	4th Ukr Front
216th NKVD Border Guards	1st Baltic Front
217th NKVD Border Guards	3rd Belo Front
218th NKVD Border Guards	2nd Belo Front (former 99th NKVD Border Guards Rgt)
219th NKVD Border Guards	2nd Belo Front
220th NKVD Border Guards	3rd Baltic Front
225th NKVD Security	Leningrad Front
230th NKVD Rifle	Southern Front
232nd NKVD Convoy	Siberian MD
251st NKVD Convoy	Leningrad Front
252nd NKVD Border Guards	Western Front
263rd NKVD Rifle	Trans-Caucasus MD
272nd NKVD Rifle	Stalingrad Front
287th NKVD Rifle	Belo MD (1944–1945)
290th Sep Novorossiisk NKVD	Southern Front
308th NKVD Rifle	Moscow, from NKVD Destroyer MRR (Jul 42), in 23rd NKVD Brigade (Jul 42), in Groznyi NKVD Division (Aug 42), disbanded in July 43
337th NKVD Rifle	(1945)
NKVD Destroyer Mot Rifle	Moscow (Oct 41)
Mixed NKVD Rifle Rgt	Sevastopol', destroyed in 1942

Sources: V. V. Dushen'kin, ed., *Vnutrennie voiska v Velikoi Otechestvennoi voine 1941–1945 gg.: Dokumenty i materialy* [Internal forces in the Great Patriotic War 1941–1945: Documents and materials] (Moscow: Iuridicheskaia Literatura, 1975); N. P. Patrushev, ed., *Organy gosudarstvennoi bezopasnosti SSSR v Velikoi Otechestvennoi voine, Sbornik dokumentov, Tom vtoroi, Kniga I: Nachalo 22 iiunia–31 avgusta 1941 goda* [Organs of state security of the USSR in the Great Patriotic War, collection of documents, vol. 2, Book I: The Beginning, 22 June–31 August 1941] and *Kniga II: Nachalo, 1 sentiabria–31 dekabria 1941 goda* [Book II: The Beginning, 1 September–31 December 1941] (Moscow: Rus', 2000); G. P. Sechkin, *Pogranichnye voiska v Velikoi Otechestvennoi voine* [Border guards troops in the Great Patriotic War] (Moscow: Order of Lenin and Red Banner Higher Command Courses of the KGB USSR, 1990); A. G. Lensky, *Sukhoputnye sily RKKA v predvoennye gody* [The RKKA's ground forces in the prewar years] (Saint Petersburg, N.p., 2000); *Truppen-Ubersicht und Kriegsgliederungen Rote Armee, Stand August 1944,* Fremde Heere Ost Ic Unterlagen Ost, Merkblatt geh. 11/6, Pruf.-Nr. 0157, in National Archives Microfilm Series T-78, Roll 459.

IDENTIFIED WARTIME RED ARMY (NKPS) RAILROAD BRIGADES

Brigade	Subordination
1st	Sp. NKPS Corps (SW Direction)
2nd	Sp NKPS Corps
3rd	Sp NKPS Corps
4th	Sp NKPS Corps (SW Direction)
5th	Sp NKPS Corps (SW Direction)
1st	Moscow, Western, 3rd Belo Fronts, Siberian MD (1945)
3rd	Central, Belo, 1st Belo, 1st Far Eastern Fronts
4th	SW, Western, 2nd Belo Fronts
5th	SW, Vor, 1st Belo Fronts
6th	Western, Kalinin, 1st Baltic, Trans-Baikal Fronts
7th	Vor, 1st Ukr, Trans-Baikal Fronts
8th	Central, 2nd Belo Fronts
9th	Karelian, Western, Leningrad, Trans-Baikal Fronts
10th	1st Baltic Front
11th	Leningrad Front, Ural MD, Manchuria
12th	Vor Front
13th	Southern, SW, Vor Fronts
14th	Vor, 1st Ukr Fronts
15th	NW, Kalinin, Stalingrad, 2nd Belo Fronts
17th	Western, Briansk Fronts
19th	Southern, Vor, 1st Ukr Fronts
21st	Leningrad MD (1944)
23rd	Central, 3rd Belo Fronts
24th	Stalingrad Front
25th	SW, 1st Belo, 2nd Far Eastern Fronts
26th	Moscow MD, Western, 3rd Belo Fronts
27th	SW, Don, Vor Fronts, Southern Ural MD, Manchuria
28th (1st Gds. Apr 42)	Southern, North Caucasus, Stalingrad, Southern, 4th Ukr, 1st Belo Fronts
29th	Southern, North Caucasus, 3rd Ukr, 1st Belo Fronts
30th	NW Front
36th	North Caucasus Front
44th	North Caucasus Front
45th	1st Belo Front
46th	Stalingrad Front
47th	Stalingrad Front, Southern Ural MD
49th	Trans-Baikal Front
Plus numerous separate regiments and battalions.	

Sources: M. K. Makartsev, "Sovershenstvovanie organizatsii zheleznodorozhnykh voisk v gody Velikoi Otechestvennoi voiny" [Improvement of the organization of railroad forces in the Great Patriotic War], VIZh, no. 9 (September 1985): 80–85; F. F. Gusarev and L. A. Butakov, "Tekhnicheskoe prikrytie zheleznykh dorog" [Technical protection of the railroads], VIZh, no. 4 (April 1988): 51–58; A. Ia. Ponomarov and B. G. Smirnov, "Zagrazhdenie zheleznykh dorog v pervom perioda voiny" [The obstruction of railroads in the first period of the war], VIZh, no. 3 (March 1986): 77–81; G. A. Kumanov, Voina i zheleznodorozhnyi transport SSSR [War and railroad transport of the USSR] (Moscow: Nauka, 1988); and I. V. Kovalev, Transport v Velikoi Otechestvennoi voine [Transport in the Great Patriotic War] (Moscow: Nauka, 1981).

136   Appendix 3

SELECTED RED ARMY WARTIME MILITARY ROAD, AUTO-TRANSPORT, AND ROAD SERVICE FORCES

Force	Subordination (Date)
1st Military Road Directorate	Kalinin Front (Oct 41)
2nd Military Road Directorate	Western Front (Oct 41)
3rd Military Road Directorate	Western Front (Oct 41), 1st Belo Front (Feb 45)
4th Military Road Directorate	SW Front (Oct 41), Vor Front (Jun 43), 1st Belo Front (Feb 45)
6th Military Road Directorate	Southern Front (Oct 41), SW Front (Feb 43), 3rd Ukr Front (Aug 44)
22nd Military Road Directorate	Minsk (Jun 44)
1st Military-Automobile Road (VAD) (Minsk-Mozhaisk-Gzhatsk)	Western Front (Oct 41)
2nd Military-Automobile Road (Moscow-Iukhnov)	Western Front (Oct 41)
5th Military-Automobile Road (Moscow-Tula)	Western Front (Oct 41)
1st Military-Automobile Road (El'ton-St Akhtuba)	Stalingrad Front (Nov 43)
2nd Military-Automobile Road (Verkh Baskuchak-Solodovka)	Stalingrad Front (Nov 43)
7th Military-Automobile Road (Liski-Okunevka)	Central Front (Feb 43), Steppe Front (Aug 43)
9th Military-Automobile Road (Moscow-Kalinin-Torzhok)	Western Front (Oct 41)
13th Military-Automobile Road (Tuapse-Maikop)	Trans-Caucasus Front (Jan 43)
15th Military-Automobile Road (Gureev-Astrakhan)	Stalingrad Front (Nov 42)
16th Military-Automobile Road (Ubakh-Astrakhan)	Stalingrad Front (Nov 42)
21st Military-Automobile Road (St Oskol-Kursk)	Vor Front (Aug 43)
22nd Military-Automobile Road (Serefimovich-Millerovo)	SW Front (Jan 43)
23rd Military-Automobile Road (Serafimovich-Millerovo)	SW Front (Jan 43)
24th Military-Automobile Road (Kalich-Kupiansk)	SW Front (Feb 43)
101st Military-Automobile Road (Leningrad-Lake Ladoga)	Leningrad Front (Oct 41)
102nd Military-Automobile Road (Kobony-Novaia Ladoga-Volkhov)	Leningrad Front (Oct 41) (temporarily cut in Nov 41, combined with 101st VAD)
5th Auto Rgt	SE Front (Aug 42), Stalingrad Front (Dec 42), Central Front (Feb 43)
10th Auto Rgt	Western Front (Oct 41), SE Front (Aug 42), SW Front (Jan 43)
15th Auto Rgt	Western Front (Sep 41), SW Front (Jan 43)
35th Auto Rgt	1st Gds Tank Army (Jul 44)
21st Road Exploitation Rgt	Leningrad Front (Nov 41)
22nd Road Exploitation Rgt	Leningrad Front (Nov 41)
41st Road Exploitation Rgt	Western Front (Oct 41)
76th Road Exploitation Rgt	Leningrad Front (Nov 41)
3rd Auto Bn	Stalingrad Front (Nov 42)
32nd Auto Bn	Western Front (Jul 41)
37th Auto Bn	Stalingrad Front (Oct 42)
65th Auto Bn	Western Front (Sep 41)
106th Auto Bn	Western Front (Sep 41)

Force	Subordination (Date)
226th Sep Auto Bn	Western Front (Oct 41)
272nd Auto Bn	14th Army, Karelian Front (Oct 44)
282nd Auto Bn	1st Gds Tank Army (Jul 44)
390th Auto Bn	Leningrad Front (Sep 41)
396th Auto Bn	Stalingrad Front (Nov 42)
400th Automobile Bn	Stalingrad Front (Nov 42)
425th Auto Bn	14th Army, Karelian Front (Oct 44)
431st Auto Bn	North Caucasus Front (Oct 43)
634th Auto Bn	14th Army, Karelian Front (1944)
784th Auto Bn	Stalingrad Front (Oct 42)
21st Sep Road Construction Bn	Trans-Caucasus Front (Jan 43)
24th Sep Road Construction Bn	Southern Front (Jan 42)
25th Sep Road Construction Bn	Trans-Caucasus Front (Jan 42)
112th Sep Road Construction Bn	3rd Ukr Front (Oct 44)
132nd Sep Road Construction Bn	Western Front (Jan 43)
187th Sep Road Construction Bn	2nd Ukr Front (Oct 43)
22nd Sep Bridge Construction Bn	Western Front (Jan 43)
24th Sep Bridge Construction Bn	North Caucasus Front (Oct 43)
87th Sep Bridge Construction Bn	Western Front (Jan 43)
88th Sep Bridge Construction Bn	Leningrad Front (Nov 41)
90th Sep Bridge Construction Bn	3rd Belo Front (Jun 44)
91st Sep Bridge Construction Bn	Southern Front (Jan 42)
96th Sep Bridge Construction Bn	North Caucasus Front (Oct 43)
126th Sep Bridge Construction Bn	3rd Ukrainian Front (Oct 44)
146th Sep Bridge Construction Bn	1st Gds Tank Army (Jul 44)
152nd Sep Bridge Construction Bn	North Caucasus Front (Oct 43)
2nd Sep Road Exploitation Bn	1st Gds Tank Army (Jul 44)
31st Sep Road Exploitation Bn	North Caucasus Front (Oct 43)
43rd Sep Road Exploitation Bn	Western Front (Jan 43)
82nd Sep Road Exploitation Bn	Kalinin Front (Oct 43)
88th Sep Road Exploitation Bn	SE Front (Aug 42)
138th Sep Road Exploitation Bn	Southern Front (Jan 42)
124th Sep Road Exploitation Bn	SW Front (Feb 43)
140th Sep Road Exploitation Bn	SW Front (Feb 43)
125th Sep Bridge Construction Bn	Stalingrad Front (Dec 42)
126th Sep Bridge Construction Bn	SW (Feb 43)
25th Sep Road Exploitation Rgt	Trans-Caucasus Front (Jan 43)
10th Auto-Transport Rgt	SW (Jan 43), 3rd Belo Front (Jun 44)
15th Auto-Transport Rgt	SW Front (Jan 43)
14th Auto-Transport Brigade	Western Front (Oct 41)
17th Auto-Transport Brigade	Leningrad Front (Oct 41)
22nd Auto-Transport Brigade (15th, 65th, 66th Auto-Transport Rgts)	SW Front (June 43)
12th Reserve Auto Training Rgt	SW Front (June 43)
18th Auto-Transport Brigade (56th, 57th, 58th Auto-Transport Rgts)	1st Belo Front (Jun 44)

Sources: N. Maliugin, "Avtomobil'nyi transport frontov i armii v gody voiny" [Automobile transport of *fronts* and armies in the war years], *VIZh*, no. 2 (February 1971): 87–91; N. Strakhov, "Na avtomobil'nykh dorogakh" [Along automobile roads], *VIZh*, no. 11 (November 1964): 63–64, no. 8 (August 1965): 45–57; Z. I. Kondrat'ev, *Dorogi voiny* [The roads of war] (Moscow: Voenizdat, 1968); and N. Maliugin, "Nekotorye voprosy tylovogo obespecheniia stalingradskogo fronta v kontranastuplenii" [Some questions about the rear support of the Stalingrad Front during the counteroffensive], *VIZh*, no. 8 (August 1977): 98–104.

REPRESENTATIVE RED ARMY WARTIME CONSTRUCTION FORCES

Force	Subordination (Date)
3rd Directorate of Military-Field Construction (UVPS)	Odessa MD (Sep 41), Sevastopol' (1941), Stalingrad (Dec 41)
4th Directorate of Military-Field Construction	Odessa MD (Sep 41)
5th Directorate of Military-Field Construction	Odessa MD (Jun 41), Sevastopol' (1941–1942)
10th Directorate of Military-Field Construction	NW (Aug 41)
20th Directorate of Military-Field Construction	Western Front (Mozhaisk) (Nov 41)
82nd Directorate of Military-Field Construction	Odessa MD (Sep 41), Sevastopol' (1941), Stalingrad (Dec 41)
83rd Directorate of Military-Field Construction	Odessa MD (Sep 41)
3rd *Front* Defensive Construction Directorate	2nd Ukr Front (Jan 44)
12th Defensive Construction Directorate	Trans-Baikal Front (Aug 45)
14th Defensive Construction Directorate	2nd Ukr Front (Jan 44)
20th Defensive Construction Directorate	2nd Belo Front (Jun 44)
21st Defensive Construction Directorate	1st Baltic Front (Jun 44)
4th *Front* Defensive Construction Directorate	1st Baltic Front (Jun 44)
23rd Defensive Construction Directorate	1st Ukr Front (Jul 44)
24th Defensive Construction Directorate	Stalingrad Front (Jun 42), 2nd Ukr Front (Aug 44)
25th Defensive Construction Directorate	2nd Ukr Front (Aug 44)
26th Defensive Construction Directorate	Western Front (Jan 42), Stalingrad Front (Jun 42), 3rd Ukr Front (Aug 44)
27th Defensive Construction Directorate	1st Belo Front (Jun 44)
36th Defensive Construction Directorate	2nd Ukr Front (Dec 44)
52nd Defensive Construction Directorate	3rd Belo Front (Jun 44)
5th *Front* Defensive Construction Directorate	3rd Belo Front (Jun 44)

Sources: A. A. Soskov, "Sovershenstvovanie organizatsionnoi struktury inzhenernykh voisk v gody Velikoi Otechestvennoi voiny" [Improvement in the organizational structure of engineer forces in the Great Patriotic War], *VIZh*, no. 12 (December 1985): 66–70; and A. D. Tsirlin, et al., eds., *Inzhenernye voiska v boiakh za sovetskuiu rodinu* [Engineer forces in combat for the Soviet homeland] (Moscow: Voenizdat, 1970).

APPENDIX 4

Characteristics of Red Army Wartime Weaponry and Equipment (Including Lend-Lease)

PISTOLS

Weapon	Caliber (mm)	Weight (kg)	Magazine Capacity (rds)	Rate of Fire (per min)	Range (m)
Tokarov TT-2 Model 1930/1933 automatic pistol	7.62	0.940	8	NA	NA
Nagant Model 1895 revolver	7.62	0.880	7	NA	NA

NA indicates data not available.
Source: Iu. P. Babich and A. G. Baier, *Razvitie vooruzheniia i organizatsii sovetskikh sukhoputnykh voisk v gody Velikoi Otechestvennoi voiny* [The development of arms and the organization of Soviet ground forces in the Great Patriotic War] (Moscow: Izdanie Akademii, 1990), 84.

RIFLES

Model	Caliber (mm)	Length with Bayonet / w/o Bayonet (mm)	Barrel Length (mm)	Weight with Bayonet / w/o Bayonet (kg)	Magazine Capacity (rds)	Range (m)
Moisin/Nagant, 1891/1930	7.62	1232/1660	729	4.0/4.5	5	2000
Moisin/Nagant, 1938 carbine	7.62	1020	512	3.5	5	1000
Moisin, 1944 carbine	7.62	1020/1330	517	3.9°	5	1000
Moisin/Nagant, 1891/1930 sniper rifle	7.62	1232/1660	729	4.3	5	1500
Tokarev, SVT-38	7.62	1266/1583	635	4.15/4.55	10	1500
Tokarev, SVT-40	7.62	1266/1470	625	3.85/4.13	10	1500

°Bayonet permanently attached.
Source: A. B. Zhuk, *Strelkovoe oruzhie* [Rifle weapons] (Moscow: Voenizdat, 1992), 506, 544.

SUBMACHINE GUNS

Model	Caliber (mm)	Length with Butt-stock / w/o Butt-stock (mm)	Barrel Length (mm)	Weight w/o Bullets / w/ Bullets (kg)	Magazine Capacity (rds)	Rate of Fire (per min)
Degtiarev, PPD-34/38	7.62	777	273	3.75/4.54	25 or 71	800
Degtiarev, PPD-40	7.62	788	267	3.63/5.45	71	800
Shpagin, PPSh-41	7.62	843	269	3.63/5.45	35 or 71	900
Sudaev, PPS-42	7.62	907/641	273	2.95/3.63	35	700
Sudaev, PPS-43	7.62	820/615	255	3.04/3.67	35	700
Thompson 1928A1	.45 cal.	852	267	4.78/5.35	20, 30, 50, or 100	700

Source: A. B. Zhuk, *Strelkovoe oruzhie* [Rifle weapons] (Moscow: Voenizdat, 1992), 576.

MACHINE GUNS, 1941–1943

Weapon	Caliber (mm)	Weight (kg)	Magazine Capacity (rds)	Rate of Fire (per min)	Range (m)
Degtarev DP light machine gun	7.62	8.9	47	600	1,500
Maksim Model 1910 machine gun	7.62	66.0	250	600	2,700
Degtarev DShK AA machine gun	12.7	170.0	50	NA	3,500
AA model 1931 machine gun	7.62	460.0	500	600	2,700
DS Model 1939 heavy machine gun	7.62	NA	NA	NA	NA
DT tank machine gun	7.62	10.25	63	600	1,500
Goruniov Model SG-1943 machine gun	7.62	40.4	250	600–700	2,000

NA indicates data not available.
Source: Iu. P. Babich and A. G. Baier, *Razvitie vooruzheniia i organizatsii sovetskikh sukhoputnykh voisk v gody Velikoi Otechestvennoi voiny* [The development of arms and the organization of Soviet ground forces in the Great Patriotic War] (Moscow: Izdanie Akademii, 1990), 85.

ANTITANK RIFLES, 1941–1943

Weapon	Caliber (mm)	Weight (kg)	Magazine Capacity (rds)	Rate of Fire (per min.)	Range (m)
Degtarev PTRD Model 1941 antitank rifle	14.5	17.3	1	NA	1,500
Simonov PTRS Model 1941 antitank rifle	14.5	20.33	5	NA	1,500

NA indicates data not available.
Source: Iu. P. Babich and A. G. Baier, *Razvitie vooruzheniia i organizatsii sovetskikh sukhoputnykh voisk v gody Velikoi Otechestvennoi voiny* [The development of arms and the organization of Soviet ground forces in the Great Patriotic War] (Moscow: Izdanie Akademii, 1990), 87.

TANKS

Weapon	Weight (T)	Crew	Guns Caliber	MGs	Combat Load (Shells/Bullets)	Armor Turret/Body (mm)	Speed (km/hr)	Road Range (km)
Prewar								
T-26 light Model 1931	10.5	3	45	2	165/3,654	15/15	30	200
BT light Model 1931	13.8	3	45	1	132/2,334	15-20/13	52-73	350-500
BT 7 light Model 1937	13.8	3	45	1	NA	15-20/13	55-73	375-500
BT-7M Model 1939	14.7	3	45	2	NA	15-20/13	60-86	600-700
T-28 medium Model 1931	28.0	6	76	4	70/7,938	20/30	37	220
T-34 medium model 1939	28.6	4	76.2	2	100/1,953	45-52/45	55	300
KV-1 heavy Model 1939	47.6	5	76	3	114/3,000	95-100/75	35	250
T-50 light Model 1941	14.0	4	45	2	150/4,000	37/0	45	344
Wartime								
T-60 light Model 1941	6.4	2	20	1	780/945	15/35	45	450
T-70 light Model 1942	9.8	2	45	1	90/945	15/45	45	250
T-34 medium Model 1940	30.9	4	76	2	100/3,600	45/52	55	300
T-34 medium Model 1943	30.9	4	76	2	100/3,600	52/70	55	300
T-34-85 medium Model 1943	32.0	5	85	2	55/1,953	45/90	55	300
T-44 medium Model 1944	31.5	4	85	2	58/0	75/120	51	0
KV-1 heavy Model 1941	47.5	5	76.2	3	114/3,000	75/100	35	250
KV-1S heavy Model 1942	42.5	5	76.2	3	102/3,000	82/75	42	250
KV-85 heavy Model 1943	46.0	4	85	3	70/0	100/75	42	250
IS-1 heavy Model 1943	44.0	4	85	3	59/0	100/120	37	240
IS-2 heavy Model 1943	46.0	4	122	4	28/2,331	90/120	37	240
IS-3 heavy Model 1945	47.0	4	122	2	28/956	90/120	40	190

—continued

TANKS *Continued*

Weapon	Weight (T)	Crew	Guns Caliber	MGs	Combat Load (Shells/Bullets)	Armor Turret/ Body (mm)	Speed (km/hr)	Road Range (km)
Wartime Lend-Lease								
Mk-VII Tetrarch light (A17), 20 (1942)	7.6	3	40	1	50/unknown	4/14	65 road, 45 off road	225
Mk-III Valentine light, 3,782 (1942–43)	16.3	4	40(2)	1	79/3,150	8/65	24 road, 13 off road	144
Mk-II Matilda heavy (A12), 1,084 (1942–43)	26.9	4	40	1	93/3,150	13/78	24 road, 13 off road	256
Mk-III, Mk-IV Churchill medium (A22), 301 (1942–43)	39.5	5	42	2	NA	16/102	24.8 road, 12.8 off road	144
M3A1 Stuart light, 1,676 (1941–43)	12.4	4	37	5	103/8,270	10/45	48	113
M3 General Lee medium, 1,152 (1942–43)	27.2	6	75	4	NA	12/37	42 road, 26 off road	190
M4A2 Sherman medium, 4,063 (1,990 75mm, 2,073 76mm) (1942–43), +300 (1945 Manchuria)	31.5	5	75 or 76, 12.7	2	NA	15/100	42	160
M-10 (SAU) Wolvereen, 52 (1943)	29.9	5	75, 12.7	NA	NA	12.7/50.8	48	320

NA indicates data not available.
Source: Iu. P. Babich and A. G. Baier, *Razvitie vooruzheniia i organizatsii sovetskikh sukhoputnykh voisk v gody Velikoi Otechestvennoi voiny* [The development of arms and the organization of Soviet ground forces in the Great Patriotic War] (Moscow: Izdanie Akademii, 1990), 93; V. A. Zolotarev et al., eds., *Velikaia Otechestvennaia voina 1941–1945. Kn. 1* [The Great Patriotic War 1941–1945, book 1] (Moscow: Nauka, 1998), 511; O. A. Losik, *Stroitel'stvo i boevoe primenenie sovetskikh tankovykh voisk v gody Velikoi Otechestvennoi voiny* [The formation and combat employment of Soviet tank forces in the Great Patriotic War] (Moscow: Voenizdat, 1979), 24; and G. L. Kholiavsky, ed., *Entsiklopediia tankov: Polnaia entsiklopediia tankov mira 1915–2000 g.g.* [An encyclopedia of tanks: A complete encyclopedia of the world's tanks, 1915–2000] (Moscow: N.p., 1998), 182–201, 252–81, 294–310.

FIELD ARTILLERY AND MORTAR SYSTEMS

Weapon	System Weight (kg)	Shell Weight (kg)	Range (m)	Rate of Fire (rds per min)
Through 22 June 1941				
76mm regimental gun Model 1927	900	6.2	8,500	10–12
76mm mountain gun Model 1938	785	6.2	10,100	10–15
76mm regimental gun Model 1936	1,600	6.2	13,700	15–20
76mm divisional gun USV Model 1939	1,480	6.2	13,290	15
107mm gun M-60 Model 1940	4,000	17.2	NA	NA
122mm howitzer M-30 Model 1938	2,500	21.7	11,800	5–6
122mm gun A-19 Model 1931/1937	7,120	25.0	19,750	3–4
152mm howitzer M-10 Model 1938	4,150	40.0	12,390	2–4
152mm gun-howitzer ML-20 Model 1937	7,129	43.5	17,230	3–4
152mm gun BR-2 Model 1935	18,200	48.8	25,070	0.75–1.0
203mm howitzer B-4 Model 1931	17,700	100.0	18,020	1.0–0.5
210mm gun BR-17 Model 1939	440,000	133.0	28,650	0.5
305mm howitzer BR-18 Model 1939	45,700	330.0	16,580	0.63
50mm company mortar Model 1940	95	0.9	800	30.0
82mm mortar BM-82 Model 1937	56	3.1	3,040	to 25
107mm mountain mortar Model 1938	170	8.0	5,000	to 16
120mm mortar PM-120 Model 1938	275	16.0	5,700	to 15
280mm mortar BR-5 Model 1939	18,400	246.0	10,410	0.3
1941–1945				
45mm gun M-42 Model 1942°	570	1.43	6,600/1,000	to 20
57mm gun ZIS-2 Model 1943°	1,150	3.14	6,600/1,100	to 25
76mm gun ZIS-3 Model 1942°	1,116	6.5	13,200/900	to 25
100mm gun BS-3 Model 1944°	3,650	15.9	20,100/1,100	5–7
152mm howitzer D-1 Model 1943	3,650	40.0	12,400/600	2–5
160mm mortar Model MT-13 1943	1,130	41.1	5,050	3

°Employed as both a field and an antitank system. Ranges in both roles shown.
Sources: Iu. P. Babich and A. G. Baier, *Razvitie vooruzheniia i organizatsii sovetskikh sukhoputnykh voisk v gody Velikoi Otechestvennoi voiny* [The development of arms and the organization of Soviet ground forces in the Great Patriotic War] (Moscow: Izdanie Akademii, 1990), 84–85; V. A. Zolotarev et al., eds., *Velikaia Otechestvennaia voina 1941–1945, Kn. 1* [The Great Patriotic War 1941–1945, book 1] (Moscow: Nauka, 1998), 512; Steven J. Zaloga and Leland S. Ness, *Red Army Handbook 1939–1945* (Gloucester, UK: Sutton, 1998), 210–11; and A. B. Shirokorad, *Entsiklopediia Otechestvennoi artillerii* [An encyclopedia of national artillery] (Minsk: Kharvest, 2000).

ANTITANK GUNS

Weapon	Type of Shell	Muzzle Velocity (m/sec)	Rate of Fire (min)	Armor-Piercing Capability (mm) at Ranges of:		
				500m	1,000m	1,500m
45mm gun Model 1937	AP	760	20	45–75	35–23	28–23
	SC			70–45		
45mm gun Model 1942	AP	870	20	70–35	55–45	45–3u
	SC			80–55	50–35	
76mm gun ZIS-1 Model 1942	HC	325	25	90	NA	75
	AP	680		69–57	61–50	52–43
	SC	950			NA	
57mm gun ZIS-2 Model 1943	AP	990	25	102–85	89–72	73–63
	SC	1,270		146–101	105–73	
100mm BS-3 Model 1944	AP	900	5–7	162–130	150–120	110

Key: AP = armored piercing; SC = sub-caliber; HC = hollow charge. Strike angle from the horizontal (in degrees): 45mm, 60; 76mm, 54; 57mm, 54; and 100mm, 58.
NA indicates data not available.
Source: Iu. P. Babich and A. G. Baier, *Razvitie vooruzheniia i organizatsii sovetskikh sukhoputnykh voisk v gody Velikoi Otechestvennoi voiny* [The development of arms and the organization of Soviet ground forces in the Great Patriotic War] (Moscow: Izdanie Akademii, 1990), 87, 90; and A. B. Shirokorad, *Entsiklopediia Otechestvennoi artillerii* [An encyclopedia of national artillery] (Minsk: Kharvest, 2000).

ANTIAIRCRAFT GUNS

Weapon	Weight (kg)	Project. Weight (kg)	Muzzle Velocity (m/sec)	Range (m)	Angle of Fire (degrees)	Rate of Fire (rds/min)	Movement Speed (km/hr)
25mm auto. gun 72-K Model 1940	1,060	0.28	910	2,000/ 2,400	–20/+85	250	60
37mm auto. gun 61-K Model 1939	2,100	0.78	880	3,000/ 4,000	–5/+85	180	60
76mm gun Model 1931	3,750	6.61	813	9,500/ 14,000	–3/+82	20	35
76mm gun Model 1938	4,300	6.61	813	9,500/ 14,000	–3/+82	20	50
85mm gun KS-12 Model 1939	4,300	9.2	700	10,500/ 15,600	–3/+82	20	50
85mm gun KS-12A Model 1944	5,000	9.2	700	11,600/ 15,600	–3+82	20	50

Note: Ranges given are both vertical and horizontal.
Sources: Iu. P. Babich and A. G. Baier, *Razvitie vooruzheniia i organizatsii sovetskikh sukhoputnykh voisk v gody Velikoi Otechestvennoi voiny* [The development of arms and the organization of Soviet ground forces in the Great Patriotic War] (Moscow: Izdanie Akademii, 1990), 92; Steven J. Zaloga and Leland S. Ness, *Red Army Handbook 1939–1945* (Gloucester, UK: Sutton, 1998), 217–20; and A. B. Shirokorad, *Entsiklopediia Otechestvennoi artillerii* [An encyclopedia of national artillery] (Minsk: Kharvest, 2000), 798–809.

MULTIPLE ROCKET LAUNCHER (GUARDS-MORTAR) SYSTEMS

Weapon	Shell System	Shell Caliber (mm)	Shell* Weight (kg)	Range (m)
M-8 Model 1939	BM-8	82	0.64	5,000
M-13 Model 1939	BM-13	132	4.9	8,470
M-13 DD (long-range)	BM-13	132	4.9	11,800
M-20 Model 1942	M-20	132	18.4	5,050
M-28	M-28	280	60.0	1,950
M-30 Model 1942	M-30	300	28.9	2,800
M-31 Model 1942/1944	M-31	300	28.8	4,325
M-13 uk Model 1944	M-13uk	132	4.9	7,900
M-31 uk Model 1944	M-31uk	300	28.9	4,000
BM-31-12 Model 1944	BM-31-12	300	28.9	4,000

*Denotes the weight of the explosive charge.
Source: Iu. P. Babich and A. G. Baier, *Razvitie vooruzheniia i organizatsii sovetskikh sukhoputnykh voisk v gody Velikoi Otechestvennoi voiny* [The development of arms and the organization of Soviet ground forces in the Great Patriotic War] (Moscow: Izdanie Akademii, 1990), 90.

SELF-PROPELLED GUNS

Weapon	Crew	Weight (T)	Speed (km/hr)	Frontal Armor (mm)/ Angle of Fire (degrees)	Stored Rounds	Armor Penetration at 500/1,000 m	Mount	Road Range (km)
57mm ZIS-30 gun Model 1938	NA	4.5	NA	NA/55	NA	103/91	Komsomol semi-arm'd tractor	NA
122mm M-30 how. SU-122 Model 1938	NA	30.3	NA	45/10	40	140	T-34	400–600
76mm ZIS 3 gun SU-76M Model 1943	4	10.5	45	35/32	60	71/63	T-70	290–320
85mm D-5S gun SU-85 Model 1943	4	29.6	55	45/11	48	NA	T-34	250–350
122mm M-30S gun SU-122 Model 1931	5	30.9	55	70/12	40	155-120, 145-120	KV-1S	165–330
152mm ML-20S gun how. SU-152 Model 1937	5	45.5	43	60/12	20	135-110, 125-100	KV-1S	165–330
100mm D-10S gun SU-100 Model 1944	4	31.6	48	75/16	33	162-130, 150-120	T-34	160–250
122mm D-25 gun ISU-122S	5	45.5	37	90/11	30	155-120, 145-120	IS	145–220
152mm ML-20S gun how. ISU-152	5	46.0	37	90/10	20	135-110, 125-100	IS	145–220

NA indicates data not available.
Sources: Iu. P. Babich and A. G. Baier, *Razvitie vooruzheniia i organizatsii sovetskikh sukhoputnykh voisk v gody Velikoi Otechestvennoi voiny* [The development of arms and the organization of Soviet ground forces in the Great Patriotic War] (Moscow: Izdanie Akademii, 1990). 91; Steven J. Zaloga and Leland S. Ness, *Red Army Handbook 1939–1945* (Gloucester, UK: Sutton, 1998), 92–93; O. A. Losik, *Stroitel'stvo i boevoe primenenie sovetskikh tankovykh voisk v gody Velikoi Otechestvennoi voiny* [The formation and combat employment of Soviet tank forces in the Great Patriotic War] (Moscow: Voenizdat, 1979): 30; and G. L. Kholiavsky, ed., *Entsiklopediia tankov: Polnaia entsiklopediia tankov mira 1915–2000 g.g.* [An encyclopedia of tanks: A complete encyclopedia of the world's tanks, 1915–2000] (Moscow: N.p, 1998), 282–87.

AIRCRAFT (SOVIET-PRODUCED)

Model (year)	Maximum Speed (km/hr)	Range (km)/ Ceiling (m)	Bomb Load (kg)	Armament Machine Guns/ Guns (mm)
Bombers				
TB-3 (1931–34)	288	4,000/7,740	2–4	8 × 7.62
DB-3F (1937–40)	440	2,700/9,700	1–2.5	3 × 7.62/2 × 20
Pe-2 (1940)	540	1,100/8,800	0.6–1.0	4 × 7.62
Pe-8 (TB-7) (1939)	440	4,700/9,300	2–4	2 × 7.62/2 × 12.7/2 × 20
SB-2 (1935)	445	980/9,560	0.6–1.5	4 × 7.62
SB-2bis (1939)	450	1.200/10,000	0.6	4 × 7.62
Su-2 (1940)	485	1,100/8,400	0.4	NA
Tu-2 (1942)	547	2,100/9,500	1–2.0	3 × 12.7/2 × 20
Assault				
Il-2 (1941) (*Shturmovik*)	412	510/7,500	0.4–0.6	2 × 7.62/2 × 20/8 rockets
Il-2 M3 (1942)	420	675/3,500	0	2 × 7.62/1 × 12.7/2 × 23
Il-10 (1944)	507	1,000/7,500	0.4	2 × 7.62/1 × 12.7/2 × 23
Fighters				
I-15 (1933)	363	725/9,800	0.1	4 × 7.62
I-15bis (1935)	367	770/9,800	0.15	4 × 7.62
I-16 (1934)	462	625/9,200	0.1	4 × 7.62
I-16 (24) (1939)	489	600/9,470	0	2 × 7.62/2 × 20
I-153 (1938)	427	690/10,700	0.2	4 × 7.62
MiG-3 (1940)	620	1,000/10,600	0.2	2 × 7.62/1 × 12.7
Iak-1 (1941)	480–577	700/9,500	0.2	2 × 7.62/1 × 20
LaGG-3 (1941)	549	556/9,300	0	2 × 7.62/ 1 × 12.7/1 × 20
Iak-7b (1942)	593	820/10,000	0	2 × 12.7/1 × 20
Iak-9 (1943)	597	900/10,000	0	1 × 12.7/1 × 37
Iak-9D (1943)	602	1,410/10,600	0	2 × 12.7/1 × 37
Iak-3 (1943)	610–720	900/11,800	0	2 × 20
La-5FN (1942)	648	765/9,500	0	2 × 20
La-7 (1944)	665	635/9,900	0.1	2 × 20
Others				
Po-2 (U-2) (1927)	145	470/1,500	0.25	Light night bomber
MBR-2 (1932)	195	1,500 range	0.3	3 × 7.62 Reconnaissance
MBR-2bis (1935)	243	1,500/5,000	0	2 × 7.62 Reconnaissance

Sources: Iu. P. Babich and A. G. Baier, *Razvitie vooruzheniia i organizatsii sovetskikh sukhoputnykh voisk v gody Velikoi Otechestvennoi voiny* [The development of arms and the organization of Soviet ground forces in the Great Patriotic War] (Moscow: Izdanie Akademii, 1990), 95–96; V. A. Zolotarev et al., eds., *Velikaia Otechestvennaia voina 1941–1945, Kn. 1* [The Great Patriotic War 1941–1945, Book 1] (Moscow: Nauka, 1998), 513; M. P. Pevnevets, *Boevoe primenenie sovetskikh voenno-vozdushnykh sil v gody Velikoi Otechestvennoi voiny* [The combat employment of the Soviet Air Force in the Great Patriotic War] (Moscow: Frunze Academy, 1984), 40–42; and Von Hardesty, *Red Phoenix: The Rise of Soviet Air Power 1941–1945* (Washington, DC: Smithsonian Institution Press, 1982), 250–51. Where discrepancies exist in these data, the chart lists figures from the most recent Russian sources.

AIRCRAFT (LEND-LEASE)

United States

	Sent	Delivered
Fighters		
P-39Ds, Ks, Ls, Ms, Ns, Qs (Bell Aircobras)	4,924	4,719
P-40C and E (Curtiss Tomahawks) and Ks, Ms, and Ns (Kittyhawks)	2,430	2,097
P-47D (Thunderbolts)	203	195
P-63 (Bell Kingcobras)	2,421	2,400
Total	9,978	9,411
Bombers		
A-20 (Douglas Boston)	3,125	2,908
B-25B (Mitchell)	870	862
B-24A (Liberator)	1	1
Total	3,996	3,771
Others		
C-46 (Douglas)	1	1
C-47 (Douglas)	709	707
O-52 (Curtiss observation)	30	19
AT-6Cs, Fs (trainers)	84	82
Total	824	809
Grand total	14,798	13,991
Plus:		
PBN Flying boats		138
PBY-6A (Catalina)		48

Shipments:
1 October 1941–30 June 1942	1,311
1 July 1942–30 June 1943	3,816
1 July 1943–30 June 1944	5,735
1 July 1944–12 May 1945	2,983
13 May 1945–2 August 1945	744
Total	14,589*

Great Britain

	Allocated
Hurricane II fighters	2,952
Spitfire VB fighters	143
Spitfire IX fighters	1,188
Others	30
Total	4,313

*The differences in these figures are due to aircraft shipped prior to 1 October 1941.
Sources: Ray Wagner, ed., Leland Fetzer, trans., *The Soviet Air Forces in World War II: The Official History* (Garden City, NY: Doubleday, 1973), 397–99, a translation of the official Soviet history with editorial comments; and Von Hardesty, *Red Phoenix: The Rise of Soviet Air Power 1941–1945* (Washington, DC: Smithsonian Institution Press, 1982), 253.

MINES

	Casing	Weight (kg) Total	Weight (kg) Explosive	Interval (m)	Density per km
Prewar					
Antitank TM-35m	Metal	7.0	4.0	6–10	1,000
Antitank TM-39	Metal	5.2	3.6	6–10	1,000
Antitank TMD-40	Wooden	NA	3.6	6–10	1,000
Antipersonnel PMZ-40	Metal	7.0	3.5	6–10	1,000
Antipersonnel PMK-40	Cardboard	0.9	0.05	6–10	1,000
Wartime					
Antitank IaM-5m	Wooden	7–8	5	6–10	1,000
Antitank IaM-10	Wooden	10–12	10	6–10	1,000
Antitank TMD-B	Wooden	7–8	5	6–10	1,000
Antitank TMB	Cardboard	7–8	5	6–10	1,000
Antitank LMG	Cardboard	10	2.8	20	200
Antitank TM-41	Metal	5.5	4	6–10	1,000
Antitank TM-44	Metal	7–8	5	6–10	1,000
Antipersonnel PMD-6	Wooden	0.6	0.2	1–2	Up to 3,000
Antipersonnel PMD-7	Wooden	0.325	0.07	1–2	Up to 3,000
Antipersonnel PMD-7ts	Wooden	0.3	0.07	1–2	Up to 3,000
Antipersonnel POMZ-2	Wooden	2	0.07	5–7	Up to 500

NA indicates data not available.
Notes: Early in the war the Red Army fielded the MZD-1 delayed-action mine, which exploded after a delay of up to 120 days, and, in 1942–43, the MZD-60 mine with a 60-day delay mechanism. In 1944 the Red Army began fielding the KZ-1 hollow-charge shell. Finally, at the end of 1941, the Army fielded the electrification station model AE-2 with 15 kilowatts of power, which was able to electrify up to 2 kilometers of barely visible barbed-wire obstacles contained in the special P-5 wire set.
Source: Iu. P. Babich and A. G. Baier, *Razvitie vooruzheniia i organizatsii sovetskikh sukhoputnykh voisk v gody Velikoi Otechestvennoi voiny* [The development of arms and the organization of Soviet ground forces in the Great Patriotic War] (Moscow: Izdanie Akademii, 1990), 97.

MINE-CLEARING EQUIPMENT

	Weight (kg)	Work Duration (continuous hrs)	Sensitivity (depth-cm)
Mine-sweeper VIM-203	NA	Up to 35	Up to 60
Mine-sweeper VIM-625	6.5	Up to 70	Up to 60
Mine-sweeper DIM-186	10.5	NA	Up to 75

	Sweeper Weight (T)	Sweep Width (m)	Interval (m)	Movement Speed Road (km/hr)	Movement Speed Open	Obstacles Snow	Obstacles Climb	Obstacles Slope
T-34 tank with PT-3 minesweeper	5.3	3.6	1.2	25	10–12	0.4 m	25°	30°

NA indicates data not available.
Source: Iu. P. Babich and A. G. Baier, *Razvitie vooruzheniia i organizatsii sovetskikh sukhoputnykh voisk v gody Velikoi Otechestvennoi voiny* [The development of arms and the organization of Soviet ground forces in the Great Patriotic War] (Moscow: Izdanie Akademii, 1990), 98.

RIVER-CROSSING EQUIPMENT (TACTICAL BRIDGING)

	Desant [Assault] Crossing			Barge Crossing				Bridges		
	No. of Men	No. of Bridges	Time (min)	Weight (T)	No. of Pontoons	No. of Ferries	Time (min)	Weight (T)	Length (m)	Time (min)
Light pontoon park NLP	25	28	5	5–16	2–6	4–14	30–50	5–16	77–140	80
Light wood pontoon park DLP	32–48	20–30	5–10	6–34	2–5	6–15	30–60	12–34	60–190	90–120
Pontoon park H2P-41	50–75	15–24	10–15	16–60	5–6	2–3	30–60	16–75	55–185	3–4 hrs
Heavy pontoon park TMP	0	0	0	16–100	2–5	3–18	40–80	16–100	110–450	3–5 hrs
Heavy pontoon park MdPA-3	0	0	0	5–14	0	3–11	35–45	5–14	46–111	65–75
Heavy pontoon park UVS-A 3	0	0	0	6–14	0	4–10	0	6–14	80–114	0

	Ferry Crossing			Bridge	
	Total Weight (T)	No. of Ferries	Time (min)	Weight (T)	Length (m)	Time (min)
N2P	16–60	2–5	35–55	16–60	64–160	115–180
DPM-42	16–50	5–20	30–40	5–50	71–620	180–240
DPM-41	9–30	5–20	20–35	16–30	64–129	NA

Source: Iu. P. Babich and A. G. Baier, *Razvitie vooruzheniia i organizatsii sovetskikh sukhoputnykh voisk v gody Velikoi Otechestvennoi voiny* [The development of arms and the organization of Soviet ground forces in the Great Patriotic War] (Moscow: Izdanie Akademii, 1990), 100–101.

RADIOS

	Range (km)		Wave		Means of Transport	Communications Nets
	Telegraph	Telephone	Power (kw)	Length (m)		
On the Eve of War						
RAT	2,000	600	1,000	25–120	3 vehicles	General Staff
RAF	600	300	400	25–125	2 vehicles	*Front*, army, corps
RSB	60	30	40–50	25–125	1 vehicle	Army, corps, division
RSMK	200	100	50	25–125	1 armored vehicle	Army, mechanized corps
71-TK	50/15	15–30	5–8	53.3–75	1 armored vehicle	Army, mechanized corps, tank brigade
9-P	NA	25/18	5–8	NA	1 armored vehicle	Tank battalion
10-P	NA	40/25	8–10	53.3–75	1 heavy tank	Tank brigade
RB	10	7	0.5	50–200	Man-packed	Rifle regiment, artillery regiment, artillery battalion
RBS	NA	3–6	NA	66–124	Man-packed	Artillery regiment, artillery battery
RRU	NA	2.5–3	0.1	7.42–9.05	Man-packed	Battalion
Wartime						
RAF-KV	600	300	500	25–125	2 vehicles	*Front*, army
RSB-F	160	80/30	40/50	25–125	1 vehicle	Army, corps
RB	50	25	0.5	50–200	Man-packed	Division, rifle regiment, artillery regiment
RBM	20–30	10–30	1.0	50–200	Man-packed	Rifle corps, rifle division, tank corps, tank brigade
Sever	700	300	50	700–300	Man-packed	Army, corps
A-7/A-7a/A-7b	15–50	3–14–20	1.5	UHF	Man-packed	Rifle corps, rifle division, rifle regiment, rifle battalion
13-R	17–25	12–18	NA	70–170	Man-packed	Rifle regiment, rifle battalion, artillery regiment
13-RA	NA	8–12	NA	12–220	Man-packed	Rifle regiment, rifle battalion, artillery regiment
Ural-m	Receiver	NA	NA	60–240	Man-packed	
Aviation						
RSB-3 bis	To 1,500	To 350	50	25–120	Aircraft	
RSI-4	NA	To 150	5	60–85.71	Aircraft	
RSR-M	To 300	To 100	To 30	25–120	Aircraft	
Tank						
9P	NA	25 static; 18 march	5–8	53.3–75	Armored vehicle	
10R	NA	40 static; 25 march	8–10	50–80	Armored vehicle	
RSMK	200 static; 60 march	100 static; 40 march	50	25–125	Armored vehicle	

NA indicates data not available.
Sources: Iu. P. Babich and A. G. Baier, *Razvitie vooruzheniia i organizatsii sovetskikh sukhoputnykh voisk v gody Velikoi Otechestvennoi voiny* [The development of arms and the organization of Soviet ground forces in the Great Patriotic War] (Moscow: Izdanie Akademii, 1990), 102; and I. P. Grishin, ed., *Voennye sviazisty v dni voiny i mira* [Military signalmen in war and peace] (Moscow: Voenizdat, 1968), 123.

MILITARY-FIELD TELEPHONES

	Range (km)				
	Field Telephone Line	PGT-19 Cable Line	Continuous 3mm Steel Line	Continuous 4mm Copper Line	Weight (kg)
UNA-F-41	20	30–40	120	500	4.7
UNA-F-42	20	30–40	120	500	5.0
UNI-FI	25	40–50	175	600	7.6
TAI-43	40–50	40–50	Up to 200	600	3.9

Source: Iu. P. Babich and A. G. Baier, *Razvitie vooruzheniia i organizatsii sovetskikh sukhoputnykh voisk v gody Velikoi Otechestvennoi voiny* [The development of arms and the organization of Soviet ground forces in the Great Patriotic War] (Moscow Izdanie Akademii, 1990), 103.

FIELD TELEPHONE SWITCHBOARDS

	Weight (kg)	Capacity	Notes
KOF	2.4	6	Used at battalion, regiment, and division level
R-20	60.0	22, 20 mb, 1 tsb, 1 atc	Used at division and corps
R-60	126.0	50–60	Used at corps and army
PK-10	12.5	3 tsb, 2 atc, 5 ind, 5 phones	Used at division and regiment
PK-30	80.0	30, incl. 25 ind., 3 phones, and 2 tsb.	Used at division and higher

Source: Iu. P. Babich and A. G. Baier, *Razvitie vooruzheniia i organizatsii sovetskikh sukhoputnykh voisk v gody Velikoi Otechestvennoi voiny* [The development of arms and the organization of Soviet ground forces in the Great Patriotic War] (Moscow: Izdanie Akademii, 1990), 104.

RADIO-TELEGRAPH APPARATUSES

		Range (km) via			
	Words (per hr)	Cable Line	"Sixth" Line	Continuous Line	Employed by:
MORSE	400	75	150	800	Division, corps
ST-35	1,250	35	100	250	Army, corps, division
BODO	2,000–3,500	NA	NA	600	*Stavka, front*, army

NA indicates data not available.
Source: Iu. P. Babich and A. G. Baier, *Razvitie vooruzheniia i organizatsii sovetskikh sukhoputnykh voisk v gody Velikoi Otechestvennoi voiny* [The development of arms and the organization of Soviet ground forces in the Great Patriotic War] (Moscow: Izdanie Akademii, 1990), 104.

OTHER MOBILE COMMUNICATION MEANS

	Where Employed	Speed (km/hr)	Range (km)	Distance between Means (km)	Duration (hr)
Foot messenger	Platoon to regiment	1 km/ 8–10 min	1–5	0.1–0.15	4–5
Horseback messenger	Battalion and above	8–10	20–25	6–8	6–7
Ski messenger	Platoon and above	8–10	20	6–8	5–6
Bicycle messenger	Battalion and above	10	25	8–10	5–6
Liaison dog	Company to regiment	1 km/ 3–5 min	Up to 3	NA	4–5
Motorcycle messengers	Regiment and above	20–40	60	20–30	6–8
Communications vehicles	Regiment and above	35–40	150–200	40–50	8–10
BA-10/BA-64 armored car	Regiment and above	35–40	150–200	40–50	8–10
PO-2/U-2 aircraft	Division and above	125–150	300	NA	2.5–3

NA indicates data not available.
Source: Iu. P. Babich and A. G. Baier, *Razvitie vooruzheniia i organizatsii sovetskikh sukhoputnykh voisk v gody Velikoi Otechestvennoi voiny* [The development of arms and the organization of Soviet ground forces in the Great Patriotic War] (Moscow: Izdanie Akademii, 1990), 103.

"FLAME BOTTLES" ("MOLOTOV COCKTAILS")

Fuel Mixture	Burn Temperature (degrees)	Burn Time (sec)	Bottle Volume (l)	Throw Range (m)
Liquid kerosene	800–1,000	90–120	0.5–0.75	15–20
Mixture no. 1	700–800	Up to 50	0.5–0.75	15–20

Source: Iu. P. Babich and A. G. Baier, *Razvitie vooruzheniia i organizatsii sovetskikh sukhoputnykh voisk v gody Velikoi Otechestvennoi voiny* [The development of arms and the organization of Soviet ground forces in the Great Patriotic War] (Moscow: Izdanie Akademii, 1990), 105.

BACKPACKED FLAMETHROWERS

Prewar

	Weight (kg)	Liquid Volume (l)	Shots per Load	Range (m)
Backpack ROKS-2	21	10	6–8	30–35
Fugasse FOG-1	55	25	1	60–140

Wartime

	Weight (kg)		Liquid Volume (l)	Reservoir Pressure	Shots per Load	Range (m)	
	Unfilled	Filled				Overall	Aimed
Backpack ROKS-3	14.7	23.2	10	15–17	6–8	30–35	NA
Fugasse FOG-2	35.0	55.0	25	45–50	1	up to 100	NA
Amplemet (ampule mortar)	25.0	26.5	10 per ampule	NA	6–8 per min.	250–350	150

NA indicates data not available.
Note: The weight of one ampule for the ampulemet was 1.5 kilograms (3.3 pounds).
Source: Iu. P. Babich and A. G. Baier, *Razvitie vooruzheniia i organizatsii sovetskikh sukhoputnykh voisk v gody Velikoi Otechestvennoi voiny* [The development of arms and the organization of Soviet ground forces in the Great Patriotic War] (Moscow: Izdanie Akademii, 1990), 105.

TANK-MOUNTED FLAMETHROWERS

	Base	Gun	Machine Gun	Liquid Volume (l)	Number of Shots	Range (m)	Nozzle-Turning Angle	
							Horizontal	Vertical
Prewar								
OT-26	T-26	None	1	360	50–60	30–35	270	10
OT-130	T-26	None	1	360	40	53	360	10
OT-133	T-26	None	1	360	40	53	360	10
T-O34 w/ ATO-41	T-34	76mm	1	100	10	100	15	−2 to +10
Wartime								
T-34-85 w/ATO-42	T-34	85mm	1	200	20	120	15	−2 to +10
KV-8 w/ ATO-42	KV	45mm	3	570	57	100–200	360	−8 to +25

Source: Iu. P. Babich and A. G. Baier, *Razvitie vooruzheniia i organizatsii sovetskikh sukhoputnykh voisk v gody Velikoi Otechestvennoi voiny* [The development of arms and the organization of Soviet ground forces in the Great Patriotic War] (Moscow: Izdanie Akademii, 1990), 106.

SMOKE GENERATORS

	Weight (kg)	Volume (l)	Duration (min)
Prewar			
Smoke charge DM-II	2	NA	5–6
Naval smoke charge MDSh-I	40	NA	10–12
Smoke machine ARS	2-ton smoke mixture	NA	Up to 180
Aviation smoke bomb DAB-100F	80	NA	20–30
Universal chemical aviation apparatus	NA	NA	4 km for 10–15
Wartime			
Smoke grenade PDG	0.5	NA	Up to 1.5
Smoke trailer DP	1–1.2-ton smoke mixture	NA	Up to 150
Smoke apparatus/5 barrel*	0.8–2.1 tons	NA	150–300
Smoke apparatus DAP (aviation)	Unknown	95–155	3–5 sec

*A barrel [*kochka*] measure equals about 108 gallons.
NA indicates data not available.
Source: Iu. P. Babich and A. G. Baier, *Razvitie vooruzheniia i organizatsii sovetskikh sukhoputnykh voisk v gody Velikoi Otechestvennoi voiny* [The development of arms and the organization of Soviet ground forces in the Great Patriotic War] (Moscow: Izdanie Akademii, 1990), 107.

APPENDIX 5

Red Army Orders of Battle, 1941–1943

22 JUNE 1941

Fronts and Armies	Rifle, Airborne, and Cavalry	Artillery	Tank and Mechanized	Air	Engineers
Field Forces					
Northern					
7th Army	54, 71,168, 237 RD, 26 (Sortavala) FR	208 AAABn		55 MAD	184 SBn
14th Army	42 RC (104, 122 RD), 14 52 RD, 23 (Murmansk) FR	104 GunAR (RGK)	1 TD	1 MAD, 42 CAS	31 SBn
23rd Army	19 RC (115, 142 RD), 50 RC (43, 70, 123 RD), 27 (Keksholm), 28 (Vyborg) FR	24, 28, 43 CAR, 573 GunAR, 101 HowAR, 108, 519 HowARhp (RGK), 20 MtrBn, 27, 241 AAABn	10 MC (21, 24 TD, 198 MD, 7 MtcR)	5 MAD, 41 BAD, 15, 19 CAS	109 MotEBn, 153 EBn
Front	177, 191 RD, 8 RB, 21 22 (Karelia), 25 (Pskov), 29 FR	541, 577 HowAR (RGK) 2 PVOC (115, 169, 189, 192, 194, 351 AAR), Vyborg, Pskov, Luga, Svir, Petrozavodsk, Murmansk PVOBR	1 MC (3 TD, 163 MD, 5 MtcR)	2 MAD, 39 FAD, 3, 54 PVOFAD, 311 RAR, 103 CAS	12, 29 ER, 6 PBR
Total (3 armies)	3 RCs, 15 RDs, 1 RB, 8 FRs	10 ARs, 1 MtrBn, 1 PVOC, 5 PVOBRs, 3 AAABns	2 MCs, 4 TDs, 2 MDs, 2 MtcRs	2 PVOFADs, 1 FAD, 4 MADs, 1 BAD, 1 RAR	3 ERs, 2 EBns, 2 SBns
Northwestern					
8th Army	10 RC (10, 48, 90 RD), 11 RC (48, 125 RD), 44 (Kaunas), 48 (Alytus) FR	9 ATB, 47, 51, 73 CAR, 39, 242 AAABn	12 MC (23, 28 TD, 202 MD, 10 MtcR)		25 ER
11th Army	16 RC (5, 33, 188 RD), 29 RC (179, 184 RD), 23, 126, 128 RD, 42 (Siauliai), 45, 46 (Telshiai) FR	10 ATB, 270, 448, 615 CAR, 110 HowARhp (RGK), 429 HowAR (RGK), 19, 247 AAABn	3 MC (2, 5 TD, 84 MD, 1 MtcR)		38 SBn
27th Army	22 RC (180, 182 RD) 24 RC (181, 183 RD), 16, 67 RD, 3 RB	613, 614 CAR, 111 AAABn			

—*continued*

22 JUNE 1941 Continued

Fronts and Armies	Rifle, Airborne, and Cavalry	Artillery	Tank and Mechanized	Air	Engineers
Front	65 RC (hq), 5 AbnC (9, 10, 201 AbnB), 41 (Libava) FR	402 HowARhp (RGK), 11 AAABn, 10, 12, 14 PVOB, Riga, Estonian, Kaunas PVOBR		57 FAD, 4, 6, 7, 8 MAD, 21 PVOFAD, 312 RAR	4, 30 PBR
Total (3 armies)	7 RCs, 19 RDs, 1 RB, 1 AbnC, 3 AbnBs, 6 FRs	2 ATBs, 11 ARs, 3 PVOBs, 3 PVOBRs, 7 AAABns	2 MCs, 4 TDs, 2 MDs, 2 MtcRs	1 FAD, 4 MADs, 1 PVOFAD, 1 RAR	3 ERs, 1 EBn
Western					
3rd Army	4 RC (27, 56, 85 RD), 68 (Grodno) FR	7 ATB, 152, 444 CAR, 16 AAABn	11 MC (29, 33 TD, 204 MD, 16 MtcR)		
4th Army	28 RC (6, 49, 42, 75 RD), 62 (Brest-Litovsk) FR	447, 455, 462 CAR, 120 HowARhp (RGK), 12 AAABn	14 MC (22, 30 TD, 205 MD, 20 MtcR)		
10th Army	1 RC (2, 8 RD), 5 RC (13, 86, 113 RD), 6 CC (6, 36 CD, 155 RD, 66 (Osovets) FR	6 ATB, 130, 156, 262, 315 CAR, 311 GunAR, 124, 375 HowAR (RGK), 38, 71 AAABn	6 MC (4, 7 TD, 29 MD, 4 MtcR), 13 MC (25, 31 TD, 208 MD, 18 MtcR)		
13th Army	Hq only				
Front	2 RC (100, 161 RD), 21 RC (17, 24, 37 RD), 44 RC (64, 108 RD), 47 RC (55, 121, 143 RD), 50 RD, 4 AbnC (7, 8, 214 AbnB), 58 (Sebezh), 61 (Polotsk), 63 (Minsk-Slutsk), 64 (Zambrov), 65 (Mozyr') FR	8 ATB, 293, 611 GunAR, 360 HowAR, 5, 318, 612 HowARhp (RGK), 29, 49, 56, 151, 467, 587 CAR, 32 ABnsp (RGK), 24 MtrBn, 4, 7 PVOB, Baranovichi, Kobrin, Gomel, Vitebsk, Smolensk PVOBR	17 MC (27, 36 TD, 209 MD, 22 MtcR), 20 MC (26, 38 TD, 210 MD, 24 MtcR)	43 FAD, 12, 13 BAD, 9, 10, 11 MAD, 184 PVOFAD, 313, 314 RAR, 59, 60 FAD (forming)	10, 23, 33 ER, 34, 35 PBR, 275 EBn
Total (4 armies)	8 RCs, 24 RDs, 1 CC, 2 CDs, 1 AbnC, 3 AbnBs, 8 FRs	3 ATBs, 25 ARs, 1 ABn, 1 MtrBn, 2 PVOBs, 5 PVO BRs, 5 AAABns	6 MCs, 12 TDs, 6 MDs, 6 MtcRs	3 FADs, 3 MADs, 2 BADs, 1 PVOFAD, 2 RARs	5 ERs, 1 EBn

Southwestern				
5th Army	15 RC (45, 62 RD), 27 RC (87, 124, 135 RD), 2 (Vladimir-Volynskii) FR	1 ATB, 21, 231, 264, 460 CAR, 23, 243 AAABn	9 MC (20, 35 TD, 131 MD, 32 MtcR), 22 MC (19, 41 TD, 215 MD, 23 MtcR)		5 PBR
6th Army	6 RC (41, 97, 159 RD), 37 RC (80, 139, 141 RD), 5 CC (3, 14 CD), 4 (Strumilov), 6 (Rava-Russkaia) FR	3 ATB, 209, 229, 441, 445 CAR, 135 GunAR (RGK), 17, 307 AAABn	4 MC (8, 32 TD, 81 MD, 3 MtcR), 15 MC (10, 37 TD, 212 MD, 25 MtcR)		9 ER
12th Army	13 RC (44, 58, 192 MtnRD), 17 RC (60, 96 MtnRD, 164 RD), 10 (Kamenets-Podol'sk) 11 and 12 (Mogilev-Podol'sk) FR	4 ATB, 269, 274, 283, 468 CAR, 20, 30 AAABn, Mogilev-Podol'sk PVOBR	16 MC (15, 39 TD, 240 MD, 19 MtcR)		37 ER, 19 PBR
26th Army	8 RC (99, 173 RD, 72 MtnRD), 8 FR	2 ATB, 233, 236 CAR, 28 AAABn	8 MC (12, 34 TD, 7 MD, 2 MtcR)		17 PBR
Front	31 RC (193, 195, 200 RD), 36 RC (140, 146, 228 RD), 49 RC (190, 197, 199 RD), 55 RC (130, 169, 189 RD), 1 AbnC (1, 204, 211 AbnB), 1 (Kiev), 3 (Letichev), 5 (Korosten'), 7 (Novograd-Volynskii), 13 (Shepetovka), 15 (Ostropol'), 17 (Iziaslav) FR	5 CAR, 205, 207, 368, 437, 458, 507, 543, 646 CAR, 305, 555 GunAR (RGK), 4, 168, 324, 330, 526 HowARhp (RGK), 331, 376, 529, 536, 589 HowAR (RGK), 34, 245, 315, 316 ABnsp (RGK), 263 AAABn, 3, 4 PVOD, 11 PVOB, Stanislav, Rovno, Zhitomir, Tarnopol', Vinnitsa PVOBR	19 MC (40, 43 TD, 213 MD, 21 MtcR), 24 MC (45, 49 TD, 216 MD, 17 MtcR), 1 AtrBn	44, 64 FAD, 19, 62 BAD, 14, 15, 16, 17, 63 MAD, 36 PVOFAD, 315, 316 RAR	45 ER, 1 PBR
Total (4 armies)	11 RCs, 32 RDs, 1 CC, 2 CDs, 1 AbnC, 3 AbnBs, 14 FRs	5 ATBs, 35 ARs, 4 ABns, 2 PVODs, 1 PVOB, 6 PVOBRs, 8 AAABns	8 MCs, 16 TDs, 8 MDs, 8 MtcRs, 1 AtrBn	1 PVOFAD, 2 FADs, 5 MADs, 2 BADs, 2 RARs	7 ERs

—*continued*

22 JUNE 1941 *Continued*

Fronts and Armies	Rifle, Airborne, and Cavalry	Artillery	Tank and Mechanized	Air	Engineers
9th Separate Army	14 RC (25, 51 RD), 35 RC (95, 176 RD), 48 RC (30 MtnRD, 74 RD), 150 RD, 2 CC (5, 9 CD), 80 (Rybinsk), 81 (Danube), 82 (Tiraspol'), 84 (Verkhne Prut), 86 (Nizhne Prut) FR	320 GumAR (RGK), 430 HowARhp (RGK), 265, 266, 374, 648 CAR, 317 ABnsp (RGK), 26, 268 AAABn, Kishinev PVOBR	2 MC (11, 16 TD, 15 MD, 6 MtcR), 18 MC (44, 47 TD, 218 MD, 26 MtcR)	20, 21, 45 MAD, 131 PVOFAR, 317 RAR, 65, 66 FAD (forming)	8, 16 EBn, 121 MotEBn
Total	3 RCs, 7 RDs, 1 CC, 2 CDs, 5 FRs	6 ARs, 1 ABn, 1 PVOBR, 2 AAABns	2 MCs, 4 TDs, 2 MDs, 2 MtcRs	2 FADs, 3 MADs, 1 PVOFAR, 1 RAR	3 EBns
Long-Range Bomber Aviation				1 BAC (40, 51 BAD), 2 BAC (35, 48 BAD), 3 BAC (42, 52 BAD), 4 BAC (22, 50 BAD), 56, 61 BAD, 18 BAD	
Total				4 BACs, 9 BADs, 2 FADs	
Grand total (3 fronts, 15 armies)	32 RCs, 97 RDs, 3 CCs, 6 CDs, 3 AbnCs, 9 AbnBs, 2 RBs, 41 FRs	10 ATBs, 87 ARs, 6 ABns, 2 MtrBns, 1 PVOC, 2 PVODs, 6 PVOBs, 20 PVOBRs, 25 AAABns	20 MCs, 40 TDs, 20 MDs, 20 MtcRs, 1 AtrBn	4 BACs, 3 PVOFADs, 11 FADs, 19 MADs, 14 BADs, 3 PVO FARs, 7 RARs	18 ERs, 7 EBns, 2 SBns
Stavka GK Reserve					
16th Army	32 RC (46, 152 RD)	126 CAR, 112 AAABn	5 MC (13, 13 TD, 109 MD, 8 MtcR)		
19th Army	25 RC (127, 134, 162 RD), 34 RC (129, 158, 171 RD), 38 RD	442, 471 CAR	26 MC (52, 56 TD, 103 MD, 27 MtcR)		111 MotEBn, 238, 321 SBn

20th Army	61 RC (110, 144, 172 RD), 69 RC (73, 229, 233 RD), 18 RD	301 HowAR (RGK), 537 HowARhp (RGK), 438 CAR	7 MC (14, 18 TD, 1 MD, 9 MtcR)			60 PBBn
21st Army	63 RC (53, 148, 167 RD), 66 RC (61, 117, 154 RD), 51 RC (98, 119, 153 RD), 62 RC (170, 174, 186 RD)	387 HowAR (RGK), 420, 546 CAR 336, 545 CAR	25 MC (50, 55 TD, 219 MD, 12 MtcR)			
22nd Army						
24th Army	52 RC (91, 119, 166 RD), 53 RC (107, 133, 178 RD)	524 HGunAR (RGK), 392, 542, 685 CAR				
Separate	20 RC (137, 160 RD), 45 RC (187, 227, 232 RD), 67 RC (102, 132, 151 RD)	267, 390 CAR	21 MC (42, 46 TD, 185 MD, 11 MtcR)			
Grand total (6 armies)	14 RCs, 42 RDs	17 ARs, 1 AAABn	5 MCs, 10 TDs, 5 MDs, 5 MtcRs			2 EBns, 2 SBns

The *Stavka* Reserve included the 20th, 61st, and 69th RC, 7th and 21st MC, 524th HHowAR (RGK), and 438th CAR from the Moscow MD, the 45th and 67th RC and 442nd CAR from the Khar'kov MD, the 16th Army and 126th CAR from the Trans-Baikal MD, the 19th Army and 471st CAR from the North Caucasus MD, the 21st Army, 18th RD, and 387th HowAR (RGK) from the Volga MD, the 22nd Army and 336th CAR from the Ural MD, the 24th Army and 392nd and 542nd CAR from the Siberian MD, and the field headquarters of the 20th Army from the Orel MD.

Military Districts and Nonoperating Fronts

Moscow MD	41 RC (118, 235 RD)	275, 396, 649 CAR, 403, 590 HowARhp (RGK), 594 GunAR (RGK), 40, 226, 228, 233 ABnsp (RGK), 1 PVOC (176, 193, 250, 251, 329, 745 AAR), Gor'kii, Tula, Kalinin, Iaroslavl' PVOBR	51 TBn	24 FAD, 23, 46 MAD, 77 MAD, 78 FAD (forming)	28 ER, 40 EBn	
Total	1 RC, 2 RDs	6 ARs, 4 ABns, 1 PVOC, 4 PVOBRs	1 TBn	2 FADs, 3 MADs	1 ER, 1 EBn	
Volga MD Total		637 CAR, 592 GunAR (RGK) 2 ARs		58 FAD (forming) 1 BAD		

—*continued*

22 JUNE 1941 *Continued*

Fronts and Armies	Rifle, Airborne, and Cavalry	Artillery	Tank and Mechanized	Air	Engineers
Orel MD	30 RC (19, 149, 217 RD), 33 RC (89, 120, 145 RD), 222 RD	281 HowARsp (RGK), 399 HowAR (RGK), 364, 488, 643, 644 CAR, Voronezh PVOBR, 733 AAAR, 46, 123 AAABn	23 MC (48, 51 TD), 220 MD, 27 MtcR), 4 AtrBn	47, 67 FAD, 68 BAD, 1 Res. AB (-)	
Total	2 RCs, 7 RDs	6 ARs, 1 PVOBR, 1 AAR, 2 AAABns	1 MC, 2 TDs, 1 MD, 1 MtcR, 1 AtrBn	2 FADs, 1 BAD, 1 MAB	
Ural MD					22 ER
Total					1 ER
Siberian MD	681 RR	486, 544 HowARhp (RKG), 11 MtrBn		30 BAR	27 ER
Total	1 RR	2 ARs, 1 MtrBn		1 BAR	1 ER
Khar'kov MD	18th Army (hq), 2 AbnC (2, 3, 4 AbnB), 214 RD	435, 645 CAR, 191 HowARhp (RGK), Donbas, Konotop PVOBR		75, 76 FAD, 49 BAD	
Total	1 RD, 1 AbnC, 3 AbnBs	3 ARs, 2 PVOBRs		2 FADs, 1 BAD	
Odessa MD	7 RC (116, 196, 206 RD), 9 RC (106, 156 RD, 32 CD), 47 RD, 3 AbnC (5, 6, 212 AbnB), 83 FR	137, 515, 522, 527 HowARhp (RGK), 268, 272, 377 CAR, 296, 391 AAABn, 15 PVOB, Zaporozh'e, Pervomaisk PVOBR			7 PBR, 8 ER
Total	2 RCs, 6 RDs, 1 CD, 1 AbnC, 3 AbnBs, 1 FR	7 ARs, 1 PVOB, 2 PVOBRs, 2 AAABns			2 ERs
Arkhangel'sk MD	88, 111 RD	310 GunAR (RGK), 1, 2 HMGBtry (RGK), Arkhangel'sk PVOBR		1 MAB	
Total	2 RDs	1 AR, 1 PVOBR		1 MAB	

North Caucasus MD	64 RC (165, 175 RD), 28 MtnRD, 157 RD	394, 596 CAR, 138, 302 HowAR, 440 HowARhp, 5 MtrBn, Novorossiisk PVOBR	8 AtrBn	73 FAD, 74 BAD	
Total	1 RC, 4 RDs	5 ARs, 1 MtrBn, 1 PVOBR	1 AtrBn	1 FAD, 1 BAD	
Trans-Caucasus MD	3 RC (4 RD, 20, 47 MtnRD), 23 RC (136 RD, 138 MtnRD), 40 RC (9 MtnRD, 31 RD), 63, 76, 77 MtnRD, 17 MtnCD, 24 CD, 51 (Batumi), 55 (Leninakin) FR, Erevan Fortified Position	25, 456, 457, 647 CAR, 116, 337, 547 HowAR (RGK), 136, 350 HowARhp (RGK), 31 AAABn, 3 PVOC (180, 190, 195, 252, 335, 339, 513 AAAR), 8 PVOB, Tbilisi PVOBR, 443 AAAR, 45, 151, 365, 380, 381 AAABn	28 MC (6, 54 TD, 236 MD, 13 MtcR), 7 AtrBn	27, 71 PVOFAD, 25, 72 MAD, 26 LRBAD, 68 FAR, 320 RAR, 3, 23 CAS	21 ER
Total	3 RCs, 10 RDs, 2 CDs, 2 FRs	9 ARs, 1 PVOC, 1 PVOB, 1 AAAR, 1 PVOBR, 6 AAABns	1 MC, 2 TDs, 1 MD, 1 MtcR, 1 AtrBn	2 PVOFADs, 2 MADs, 1 BAD, 1 FAR, 1 RAR	1 ER
Central Asian MD	58 RC (68, 83, 194 MtnRD), 238 RD, 4 CC (18, 20, 21 MtnCD)	123, 450 CAR, 9 MtrBn, 143, 187, 189 AAABn	27 MC (9, 53 TD, 221 MD, 31 MtcR), 10, 11 LtAtr	4 MAB (116 FAR, 34 BAR)	20 ER
Total	1 RC, 4 RDs, 1 CC, 3 CDs	2 ARs, 1 MtrBn, 3 AAABns	1 MC, 2 TDs, 1 MD, 1 MtcR	1 MAB	1 ER
Trans-Baikal MD					
17th Army	36, 57 MRD	185 GunAR (RGK), 2 (Bain-Tumen) PVOBR	57, 61 TD, 82 MD, 9 MB		17 PBBn
MD forces	12 RC (65, 94 RD), 93, 114 RD, Trans-Baikal FR	106 HowARhp (RGK), 216, 413 HowAR (RGK), 13 MtrBn, 68 AAABn, 1 (79th Station), 3 (Chita) PVOBR		38 FAD, 30 LRBAD, 28, 37 MAD, 2 MAB, 9 PVOFAR, 51 FAR, 64 MAR, 318 RAR	31 ER, 15 PBR, 39 SBn
Total (1 army)	1 RC, 6 RDs, 1 FR	4 ARs, 1 MtrBn, 3 PVOBRs, 1 AAABn	2 TDs, 1 MD, 1 MB	1 FAD, 2 MADs, 1 BAD, 1 MAB, 1 FAR, 1 PVOFAR, 1 MAR, 1 RAR	2 ERs, 1 EBn, 1 SBn

—continued

22 JUNE 1941 Continued

Fronts and Armies	Rifle, Airborne, and Cavalry	Artillery	Tank and Mechanized	Air	Engineers
Far Eastern Front					
1st Army	26 RC (21, 22, 26 RD), 59 RC (39, 59 RD), 1, 4, 5 RB, 8 CD, 105 FR	50, 273 CAR, 165 HowAR (RGK), 199, 549 HowARhp (RGK), 115, 129 AAABn, 4 (Spassk-Ussuriisk) PVOBR	30 MC (58, 60 TD, 239 MD, 29 MtcR), 3 AtrBn	32, 34 MAD, 79 FAD (forming)	29 EBn
2nd Army	3, 12 RD, Ust'-Bureisk, 101 FR	42 CAR, 114 HowAR and 550 HowARhp (RGK), 1 (Kuibyshev) PVOBR	59 TD, 69 MD, 2, 5 AtrBn	31 MAD, 391 RAR	2 HPBR, 36 PBR
15th Army	18 RC (34 RD, 202 AbnB), 102 FR	52, 76 CAR, 110 AAABn, 2 (Birobidzhan) PVOBR		69 MAD, 18 CAS	3 HPBR, 11, 16 PBR, 129 SBn
25th Army	39 RC (32, 40, 92 RD), 105 RD, 106, 107, 108, 110, 111 FR	282, 548 CAR, 215, 386 HowAR, 59 AAABn, 5 (Voroshilov-Ussuriisk) PVOBR	9 AtrBn	70 MAD, 39, 59 CAS	32 ER, 69 SBn
Front forces	Special RC (79 RD, 101 MtnRD), 35, 66, 78 RD, 103, 104, 109 FR	181, 372, 411 HowAR (RGK), 187 CAR, 362, 367 ABn, 21, 22 MtrBn, 70 AAABn, 5 PVOB, 3 (Komsomol'sk-on-Amur) PVOBR	66 Atr	5 BAC (33, 53 BAD), 29 FAD, 5 MAB, 71 MAR, 168 RAR, 18 PVOFAR	26 ER, 60 SBn
Total (4 armies)	5 RCs, 17 RDs, 3 RBs, 1 CD, 1 AbnB, 12 FRs	18 ARs, 2 ABns, 1 PVOB, 2 MtrBns, 5 PVOBRs, 5 AAABns	1 MC, 3 TDs, 2 MDs, 1 MtcR, 3 AtrBns, 1 Atr	1 BAC, 2 FADs, 5 MADs, 2 BADs, 1 MAB, 1 PVOFAR, 1 MAR, 2 RARs	7 ERs, 1 EBn, 3 SBns
Grand total (1 *front* 6 armies)	16 RCs, 59 RDs, 3 RBs, 1 CC, 7 CDs, 2 AbnCs, 7 AbnBs, 16 FRs, 1 RR	65 ARs, 6 ABns, 6 MtrBns, 2 PVOCs, 3 PVOBs, 20 PVOBRs, 2 AAARs, 19 AAABns	4 MCs, 11 TDs, 6 MDs, 1 MB, 4 MtcRs, 1 TBn, 6 AtrBns, 1 Atr	1 BAC, 10 FADs, 2 PVOFADS, 12 MADs, 8 BADs, 5 MABs, 2 FARs, 2 PVOFARs, 2 MARs, 1 BAR, 4 RARs	16 ERs, 3 EBns, 4 SBns

1 JANUARY 1942

Fronts and Armies	Rifle, Airborne, and Cavalry	Artillery	Tank and Mechanized	Air	Engineers
Field Forces					
Karelian					
14th Army	10G, 104, 122 RD, 72 NRB, 12 NIB, 135 RR (14 RD), 23 FR	73 AR, 104 GumAR, 487 AAABn	107 TBn, 73 AtrBn	1 MAD	31, 279 SBn
Kemsk Op Gp	14 RD (-135 RR), 27, 54, 88 RD				
Medvezhegorsk Op Gp	71, 313 RD, SkiB (Bn)	17 MtrBn	4 TBn		1 SB
Masel'sk Op Gp	186, 289, 367 RD, 61 NRB	208, 261, 298 AAABn	227 TCo		19 EBn
Front forces	37, 263 RD, 65, 66 NRB	15, 16 MtrBn, 15, 32 AAABn	2 TBns	103 MAD, 118 RAS	1 SB, 1 EBn, 2 SBns
Total (1 army, 3 op gps)	14 RDs, 5 RBs, 1 SkiB, 1 FR	2 ARs, 3 MtrBns, 6 AAABns		2 ADs	
Leningrad					
8th Army	10, 86 RD, 1 RD (NKVD), 11 RB, 4 NIB	101 HowAR, 7 ATR, 20 MtrBn, 486 AAABn	28 AtrBn, AcBn	439 FAR	2, 112 SBn
23rd Army	123, 142, 291 RD, 22 FR	260, 577 HowAR, 27, 241 AAABn	48, 106 TBn, 30 Atr	5 MAD, 117 RAS	234 SBn
42nd Army	13, 189 RD, 21 RD (NKVD), 247, 291, 292 MGABn	14 ATB, 47, 73 AR, 541 HowAR, 1, 2, 3, 4, 5 ATR, 3 ABnsp, 72, 89 AAABn	51 TBn		29, 54, 106 EBn
54th Army	3G, 80, 115, 128, 198, 281, 285, 286, 294, 311 RD, 1 MtnRB, 6 NIB, 2 SkiR, 4, 5 SkiBn	882, 883 AR, Akkuks HowAR, 2/5 GMR, 4/4 GMR	21 TD, 16, 122 TB, 60 Atr	18 BAR, 46, 563 FAR, 116 RAS	5, 109, 135, 136, 262 EBn, 12 SBn
55th Army	11, 43, 56, 70, 72, 85, 90, 125, 177, 268 RD, 261, 267, 283, 289, 290 MGABn	24, 28 CAR, 690 ATR, 2 ABnsp, 47 MtrBn, 198 AAABn	84, 86 TBn, "Narodnyi Mstitel" Atr		2, 53 EBn, 325, 367 SBn
Coastal Op Gp	48 RD, 2, 5 NIB, 3 RR, 50 NIBn	519 HowAR, MtrBn, 39 AAABn	287 TBn		295 SBn

—*continued*

1 JANUARY 1942 Continued

Fronts and Armies	Rifle, Airborne, and Cavalry	Artillery	Tank and Mechanized	Air	Engineers
Front forces	168, 265 RD, 8, 9 RB, 20 RD (NKVD), 13 MRR (NKVD), 1 SkiBn	GMR	123, 124 TB, 107 TBn, "Baltiets," "Za Rodinu," 26 Atr	2 MAD, 39, 92 FAD, 127, 286 FAR, 90 and 91 MAD (hqs)	21, 41, 42 PBBn
Total (5 armies, 1 op gp)	33 RDs, 8 RBs, 2 RRs, 1 SkiR, 3 SkiBns, 1 FR	1 ATB, 12 ARs, 8 ATRs, 2 ABns, 1 GMR, 2 GMBns, 3 MtrBns, 7 AAABns	1 TD, 5 TBs, 7 TBns, 1 AcBn	6 ADs, 6 ARs	10 EBns, 7 SBns, 3 PBBns
Volkhov					
2nd Shock Army	327 RD, 22, 23, 24, 25, 53, 57, 58, 59 RB, 39, 40, 41, 42, 43, 44 SkiBn	18 AR, 839 HowAR	160, 162 TBn	121 BAR, 522 FAR, 704 LBAR	1741, 1756 SBn
4th Army	4G, 44, 65, 92, 191, 310, 377 RD, 1 GrenRB, 27, 80 CD, 84, 85, 86, 88, 89, 90 SkiBn	881 AR, 6, 9 GMBn	46 TB, 119, 120, 128 TBn	3 Res AvGp (160, 185, 239 FAR, 218 AAR, 225 BAR)	159 PBBn, 248 SBn
52nd Army	46, 111, 225, 259, 267, 288, 305 RD, 25 CD	442, 448, 561 AR, 884 ATR, 44 GMBn		2G, 513 FAR, 313 AAR, 673 LBAR	3, 4, 770 EBn, 771 SBn 55 PBBn
59th Army	366, 372, 374, 376, 378, 382 RD, 45, 46, 47, 48, 49, 50 SkiBn	104, 105, 203 GMBn	163, 166 TBn		
Front forces	87 CD	137, 430 HowARhp, 216 AAABn	60 TD	2 Res AvGp (138 BAR, 283, 434, 515 FAR, 504 AAR), 520 FAR	539 MSBn
Total (4 armies)	21 RDs, 9 RBs, 4 CDs, 18 SkiBns	8 ARs, 1 ATR, 6 GMBns, 1 AAABn	1 TD, 1 TB, 7 TBns	2 Res AvGps, 18 ARs	3 EBns, 4 SBns, 2 PBBns, 1 MSBn

Northwestern					
3rd Shock Army	23, 33, 257 RD, 20, 27, 31, 42, 45, 54 RB, 63, 65, 67, 78, 79, 80 SkiBn, 1 DR	429 HowAR, 613 AR, 106, 107 GMBn	170 TBn		110 EBn, 299, 469, 690, 1334 SBn
4th Shock Army	249, 332, 334, 358, 360 RD, 21 RB, 62, 64 SkiBn	270 GunAR, 109 GMBn	171 TBn		56 MotPBBn, 210, 491, 1333 SBn
11th Army	84, 180, 182, 188, 254 RD	264, 614 AR, 46 GMBn	103, 150, 161 TBn		25 EBn, 202, 1390, 1391 SBn
34th Army	26, 163, 202, 241, 245 RD	698 ATR	85 TBn		28, 38, 134 EBn, 238, 492 SBn
Front forces	39, 48, 51 RB	171, 759 ATR, 8, 29, 239, 242, 246, 250, 306 AAABn		4, 6, 7, 57 MAD, 670 LBAR, 240 RAS	50, 67 EBn, 50, 57 MPBBn
Total (4 armies)	18 RDs, 10 RBs, 8 SkiBns, 1 DR	5 ARs, 3 ATRs, 4 MGBns, 7 AAABns	6 TBns	4 ADs, 1 AR	7 EBns, 12 SBns, 3 PBBns
Kalinin					
22nd Army	178, 179, 186, 357 RD, 653 RR (220 RD)	301, 390 HowAR, 43, 545 AR, 11 MtrBn, 183, 397 AAABn	129 TBn		115 EBn, 251 SBn
29th Army	174, 243, 246, 252, 375 RD, 29 CR, 16, 17, 18 Spetsnaz Det	432 HowAR, 644 GunAR, 873 ATR, 213 ATBn			63 PBBn, 71, 267 EBn
30th Army	107 MRD, 185, 251, 348, 363, 365, 371, 379 RD, 18, 24, 82 CD, 75, 76 SkiBn, 307 MGABn	392, 542 GunAR, 13, 24, 29, 43 GMBn, 12 MtrBn, 61, 651 AAABn	8, 21, 35, 58 TB, 2, 46 MtcR, 145 TBn, 21 AeroSBn	593 LBAR	60 PBBn, 133 EBn, 263 SBn
31st Army	5, 119, 247, 250, 262, 359 RD, 46, 54 CD, 3, 21 SkiBn	56 AR, 510 HowAR, 39, 47 GMBn, 30 GMtrBtry	143, 159 TBn		72, 114 EBn, 537 MSBn
39th Army	183, 220 (-653 RR), 355, 361, 369, 373, 381 RD, 73, 74, 81, 82, 83 SkiBn	336, 646 AR, 360 HowAR, 102, 103, 202 GMBn	148, 165 TBn		39 EBn

—continued

1 JANUARY 1942 Continued

Fronts and Armies	Rifle, Airborne, and Cavalry	Artillery	Tank and Mechanized	Air	Engineers
Front forces	256 RD	108 AR, 12, 64, 221 AAABn		31, 38, 46 MAD, 5G, 10, 193 FAR, 132, 617 BAR, 6G, 569 AAR	22, 69 EBn
Total (5 armies)	31 RDs, 5 CDs, 1 CR, 9 SkiBns	14 ARs, 1 ATR, 1 ABn, 9 GMBns, 2 MtrBns, 7 AAABns	4 TBs, 2 MtrRs, 6 TBns, 1 AeroSBn	3 ADs, 8 ARs	9 EBns, 2 SBns, 1 MSBn, 2 PBBns
Western					
1st Shock Army	29, 41, 44, 46, 47, 50, 55, 56 RB, 62, 71, 84 NRB, 17, 44 CD, 1, 4, 5, 6, 7, 8, 17, 18, 19, 20 SkiBn, 310 MGABn	701 GunAR, 641 ATR, 1, 3, 38 GMBn	123 TBn, 23 AeroSBn	23 HBAD, 710 LBAR	2 EBn, 214, 244, 381 SBn
5th Army	19, 32, 50, 108, 144, 329, 336 RD, 82 MRD, 37, 43, 60 RB, 2 CR, 457 RR (222 RD), 1310 RR (18 RD), 300 MGABn	537, 552, 554, 572, 995 AR, 509, 703 ATR, 2, 5, 27, 28, 37 GMBn	20 TB, 36 MtcR, 7 AeroSBn	611, 692 LBAR, 705 BAR	129 EBn, 467 SBn
10th Army	239, 322, 323, 324, 325, 326, 328, 330 RD	10 GMBn		706 BAR	694, 695 SBn
16th Army	9G, 18, 354 RD, 18, 36, 40, 49 RB, 2 GCC (3, 4G, 20 CD)	138, 471, 523 GunAR, 289, 296, 610, 694, 768, 863, 871 ATR, 17, 26, 30, 31 GMBn, 172 AAABn	22, 146 TB, 140 TBn, 21 AtrBn		42 EBn. 243, 499 SBn
20th Army	331, 352 RD, 17, 28, 35 RB, 64 NRB	517 GunAR, 483 ATR, 7, 15, 35 GMBn	1G, 17, 24, 31, 145 TB, 53 Atr	601 LBAR	226 EBn, 127, 291 SBn

33rd Army	1 GMRD, 93, 110, 113, 201, 222, 338 RD, MixedRR (Bn), 23, 24 SkiBn		246, 321 SBn
43rd Army	17, 53, 415 RD, RBn, 5 AbnC (10, 201 AbnB), 298 MGABn	109, 364, 486 HowAR, 320, 403, 557 AR, 551, 60 ATR, 18, 25, 42 GMBn, 3/590 HowAR	37, 38 SB, 273, 312 SBn, 538 MSBn
49th Army	5G, 60, 133, 173, 194, 238 RD, 19, 26, 30, 34 RB, 299 MGABn	590 HowARhp (-3 ABn), 998 HowAR, 868, 869 ATR, 275 ATBn, 24 MtrBn, 22, 41 GMBn, 64, 71, 164, 230, 304 AAABn	26 TB, "Podol'sk rabochii" Atr, AtrBn
		440, 564, 570 AR, 304, 593, 992 ATR, 4, 20, 33 GMBn	18, 23 TB
50th Army	154, 217, 258, 290, 340, 413 RD, 31 CD	447 GunAR, 21, 23, 34, 36 GMBn, 112, 168 AAABn	686 LBAR
Front forces	160 RD, 4, 41, 57, 75 CD, 1 GCC (1, 2 GCD)	39, 528 GunAR, 544 HowARhp, 316, 533, 540, 766, 989 ATR, 8, 11, 12, 16, 19, 32 GMBn, 4, 21, 86, 111, 152, 210, 525 AAABn	112 TD, 32 TB, 131 TBn, 22 AtrBn	698 LBAR

(Entries aligned by row:)

50th Army	154, 217, 258, 290, 340, 413 RD, 31 CD	447 GunAR, 21, 23, 34, 36 GMBn, 112, 168 AAABn	112 TD, 32 TB, 131 TBn, 22 AtrBn	698 LBAR	5, 70 EBn, 451, 466 SBn
Front forces	160 RD, 4, 41, 57, 75 CD, 1 GCC (1, 2 GCD)	39, 528 GunAR, 544 HowARhp, 316, 533, 540, 766, 989 ATR, 8, 11, 12, 16, 19, 32 GMBn, 4, 21, 86, 111, 152, 210, 525 AAABn	5, 9 TB, 35 TBn, 6 AtrBn	28, 43, 47, 77, 146 MAD, AvGp Nikolaenko (10, 60 MAD), 700, 701, 703 LBAR	6, 111, 113, 122 EBn, 9, 51, 61, 62, 64 PBBn, 136, 145, 290 SBn
Total (9 armies)	44 RDs, 26 RBs, 2 CCs, 12 CDs, 1 CR, 1 AbnC, 2 AbnBs, 2 RRs, 12 SkiBns	25 ARs, 23 ATRs, 1 ABn, 34 GMBns, 1 MtrBn, 15 AAABns	1 TD, 14 TBs, 1 MtcR, 5 TBns, 2 AeroSBns, 3 AtrBns	1 AvGp, 8 ADs, 11 ARs	2 SBs, 12 EBns, 21 SBns, 1 MSBn, 5 PBBns

Briansk

3rd Army	6G, 137, 212, 269, 283 RD 6, 132, 143, 148, 307 RD	569 ATR, 6 GMR, 42 AAABn 455, 462 AR		11 MAD	511, 512 SBn
13th Army				61 MAD	27, 275 EBn, 533 SBn
61st Army	342, 346, 350, 356, 387 RD, 91 CD	207 AR, 40, 201 GMBn	142 TBn	12 MAD	
Op Gp Gen. Kostenko	1 GRD, 52, 55 CD, 3 GCC (5, 6G, 32 CD)	642 GunAR	34 MRB, 129 TB		

—*continued*

1 JANUARY 1942 Continued

Fronts and Armies	Rifle, Airborne, and Cavalry	Artillery	Tank and Mechanized	Air	Engineers
Front forces	121, 287 RD, 21 MtnCD, 29, 83 CD, 100, 101 SkiBn	420 AR, 1002 ATR, 49 GMBn, 46, 386 AAABn	150 TB		50 PBBn, 513, 532, 535 SBn
Total (3 armies, 1 op gp)	18 RDs, 1 CC, 9 CDs, 2 SkiBns	5 ARs, 2 ATRs, 1 GMR, 3 GMBns, 3 AAABns		3 ADs	2 EBns, 6 SBns, 1 PBBn
Southwestern					
6th Army	255, 270, 275, 393, 411 RD, 34 CD	229, 671 HowAR, 274 GunAR, 582, 591 ATR, 20, 23, 27, 29 AAABn		44 FAD	1, 2, 520, 523 EBn
21st Army	81, 169, 226, 227, 297 RD, 8 RD (NKVD)	445 HowAR, 21, 126, 158 AAABn		16 MAD	1, 2, 540 EBn, 526 SBn
38th Army	47, 76, 199, 300, 304 RD	555 GunAR, 764 ATR, 47, 505 AAABn	12 TB, 3 AtrBn	75 MAD	45, 56 EBn, 516 SBn
40th Army	2G, 45, 62, 87, 160, 293 RD	21, 594, 602 GunAR, 595, 738, 760 ATR, 205, 332, 576 AAABn	1, 14 TB, 1 AtrBn, 4 TBn	63 MAD	14 EBn
Front forces	124 RD, Special CR	209 GunAR, 338, 651 ATR, 4, 5 GMR, 25, 31, 75, 146, 215, 227, 307 AAABn	21 MRB, 7, 13, 121, 133 TB, 71, 132 TBn, 2, 377 AtrBn, 9, 13, 14 Atr	19, 64 MAD, 6, 186 FAR, 4 Res. AvGp (99 BAR, 148, 273 FAR, 431 AAR)	12, 48, 119, 120 EBn, 19, 26, 28, 37 MotPBBn, 525, 530, 534, 536 SBn, 377, 531 MSBn
Total (4 armies)	23 RDs, 1 CD, 1 CR	9 ARs, 8 ATRs, 2 GMRs, 19 AAABns	1 MRB, 8 TBs, 3 TBns, 4 AtrBns	1 AvGp, 6 ADs, 6 ARs	14 EBns, 6 SBns, 4 PBBns, 2 MSBns

Southern				
9th Army	30, 51, 317, 339 RD, 23 MRR (NKVD)	8 HowAR, 268 GunAR, 186, 754 ATR, 203, 268 AAABn	6 TB	20 MAD	121 EBn, 522 SBn
12th Army	4, 15, 74, 159, 176, 218, 230, 261 RD, 11, 78 RB, 71 RB (NKVD), 38, 39 CD, 6 CC (26, 28, 30 CD)	266, 374, 648 AR, 521 ATR, 2/8 GMR, 11, 14, 504 AAABn	3 TB, 92 TBn, 1, 2, 6, 8, 10 Atr		50, 524 SBn, 8 EBn
18th Army	136, 296, 353, 383, 395 RD, 1 CC (35, 56, 68 CD), 73 CR	870 HowAR, 530, 558, 727 ATR, 2 GMR, 30 AAABn	2 TB	14, 21, 45 MAD	247, 517 SBn, 68 EBn
37th Army	96, 99, 216, 253, 295 RD, 66 CD	269, 437 AR, 756 ATR, 48 GMBn, 508 AAABn	142 TB	76 MAD	
56th Army	31, 106, 343, 347 RD, 13, 16 RB, Rostov RR, 62, 64, 70 CD	116, 574 HowAR, 526 HowARhp, 476 GunAR, 124, 593 AAABn	54 TB, 7 AtrBn	73 MAD, 277 BAR	9, 16 EBn
Front forces	MRR, 2 SkiBn	665 ATR, 8 GMR (-2, 3 Bn), 17 AAABn	15, 132 TB, 62, 75 TBn	22, 50, 66 BAD, 74 MAD, 654, 655 LBAR, 2, 246 FAR, 5 Res. AvGp (4 AAR, 8, 40, 183 FAR, 242 BAR)	38 ER, 7, 19, 21, 22, 35, 37, 85 PBBn, MSBn
Total (5 armies)	26 RDs, 5 RBs, 3 RRs, 1 SkiBn, 2 CC, 12 CDs, 1 CR	12 ARs, 8 ATRs, 2 GMRs, 10 AAABns, 1 GMBn	7 TBs, 3 TBns, 1 AtrBn	1 AvGp, 10 ADs, 10 ARs	1 ER, 5 EBns, EBns, 5 SBns, 7 PBBns, 1 MSBn
Caucasus					
44th Army	9 RC (63, 236 MtnRD, 157, 404 RD), 251 MtnRR (9 MtnRD), 105 MtnRR (77 MtnRD)	547 GunAR, 31, 339, 513 AAABn	79, 126 TBn, 24 TR	25, 27, 135 FAD, 40 CAS, 152 RAS	61 EBn, 19 SBn
46th Army	9 (-251 RR), 20 MtnRD, 392, 394 RD, 51 FR	647 HowAR	125 TBn, 55 Atr	132, 134 BAD, 133 FAR	51 SBn
47th Army	77 MtnRD (-105 MtnRR), 138 MtnRD	136 HowARhp, 335 AAABn	56 Atr		256 EBn

—*continued*

1 JANUARY 1942 Continued

Fronts and Armies	Rifle, Airborne, and Cavalry	Artillery	Tank and Mechanized	Air	Engineers
51st Army	224, 390, 396 RD, 302 MtnRD, 12 RB, 83 NRB	25, 53, 456 AR, 457 Gun AR, 1/7 GMR, 180, 220 AAABn	124 TBn	71 MAD, 72 FAD, 2 AAR, 23 CAS, 151, 507 RAS	75, 132 EBn, 6, 54 PBBn, 205, 275 SBn
Coastal Army	2, 25, 95, 172, 345, 386, 388 RD, 79 NRB, 7, 8 NIB, 40 CD	52, 265 AR, 51 MtrBn, 3/8 GMR, 2 AAAR, 3, 19, 26 AABn, 61 AAAR	81 TBn, "Zhelezniakov" Atr		138 EBn, 82 SBn
Front forces	75, 89, 91, 151, 156, 223, 398, 400 RD, 143 RB, 54 MRR, 72 CD	350 HowARhp (-3 Bn)	52 TB, 219, 220, 221, 222, 223, 224, 225, 226, 240, 241 TBn	482 FAR, 41 BAR, 128 CAS, 149, 150 RAS	
Total (5 armies)	1 RC, 29 RDs, 6 RBs, 1 FR, 1 RR, 2 CDs	10 ARs, 1 MtrBn, 2 GMBns, 2 AAARs, 9 AAABns	1 TB, 1 TR, 15 TBns	7 ADs, 4 ARs	5 EBns, 5 SBns, 2 PBBns
Separate Armies					
7th Army	21, 67, 114, 272, 314 RD, 3 NIB	514 ATR, 1 MtrB, 45 GMBn, 48, 54 AAABn		55 MAD	18 EBn, 40 PBBn, 184 SBn
57th Army (SW Direction)	333, 335, 337, 341, 349, 351 RD, 60, 79 CD		130 TB		
Total (2 armies)	11 RDs, 1 RB, 2 CDs	1 MtrB, 1 ATR, 1 GMBn, 2 AAABns	1 TB	1 AD	1 EBn, 1 SBBn, 1 PBBn
Moscow Defense Zone					
24th Army Zone forces	385 RD 2, 3, 4, 5 DNO, 344, 391 RD, 14, 15, 38, 52 RB, 74, 75, 166 NRB, 11 CD, Moscow FR	104 AR, 168, 191, 402, 472, 515, 527 HowAR, 488, 524, 761 GunAR, 261, 262, 267, 276 ABn, ABn, 253 AAABn	ArmorBn, 73 Atr, MtcBn	41, 172 FAR, 65 AAR, 173 BAR	161, 162 EBn, 692, 693 SBn
Total (1 army)	3 RDs, 4 DNOs, 7 RBs, 1 FR, 1 CD	10 ARs, 5 ABns, 1 AAABn	1 MtcBn	4 ARs	2 EBns, 2 SBns

Long-Range Bomber and Reconnaissance Aviation			1 HBAD, 26, 40, 42, 52 LRBAD, 133 AD, 2, 40 RAR
Total			6 ADs, 2 ARs
Grand Total (10 *fronts*, 48 armies, 5 op gps, 1 def zone)	1 RC, 275 RDs, 77 RBs, 10 RRs, 1 SkB, 53 SkiBns, 1 AbnC, 2 AbnB, 5 CCs, 48 CDs, 4 CRs, 4 FRs	1 ATB, 1 MtrB, 112 ARs, 55 ATRs, 10 AbnS, 10 MtrBns, 6 GMRs, 62 GMBns, 2 AAARs, 87 AAABns	3 TDs, 43 TBs, 2 MRBs, 1 TR, 55 TBns, 3 MtcRs, 3 AeroSBns, 1 AcBn, 1 MtcBn, 8 AtrBns	5 AvGps, 56 ADs, 70 ARs	3 SBs, 1 ER, 71 EBns, 73 SBns, 6 MSBns, 39 PBBns

***Stavka* VGK Reserve**				
28th Army	(Hq)			
58th Army	362, 364, 368, 370, 380, 384 RD, 77, 78 CD			
Separate	7, 8G, 158 RD, 67, 69, 70, 73, 77, 80, 85 NRB, 4 AbnC (8, 9, 214 AbnB), 7 AbnB, 73, 74, 76, 94 CD, 25, 26, 27, 28, 29, 30, 31, 32, 61, 68, 69, 70, 71 SkiBn	151, 367 GunAR, 156, 376, 827 HowAR, 396, 421 AR, 702, 765 ATR, 14, 101, 108, 110, 111, 112, 204, 205, 206, 207, 208 GMBn, 245 AAABn	11, 19, 25, 27, 28, 68, 69, 70, 71 TB, 141 TBn	41 MAD, 81, 140, 143 BAD, 3 RAR, 3G, 12, 15, 19, 24, 156, 157, 169, 237, 238, 274, 295, 416, 435, 440, 494, 659, 728 FAR, 61, 299, 502, 504, 525, 765 AAR, 9, 10, 72, 201, 202, 224, 625, 681, 683, 711, 716, 733 BAR, 596, 614, 617, 619, 620, 621, 623, 633, 636, 656, 660, 661, 662, 663, 664, 665, 667, 668, 669, 672, 682, 691, 696, 707, 718, 734 LBAR	160 PBBn
Total (2 armies)	9 RDs, 7 RBs, 1 AbnC, 4 AbnBs, 6 CDs, 13 SkiBns	7 ARs, 2 ATRs, 11 GMBns, 1 AAABn	9 TBs, 1 TBn	4 ADs, 63 ARs	1 PBBn

—continued

1 JANUARY 1942 Continued

Fronts and Armies	Rifle, Airborne, and Cavalry	Artillery	Tank and Mechanized	Air	Engineers
Military Districts and Nonoperating Fronts					
Moscow MD	16, 117, 118, 131, 134, 135, 139, 140, 141, 145, 146, 147, 149, 234 RD, 1, 4, 86, 104, 105, 106, 107, 108, 109, 110, 111, 112, 113 RB, 1 AbnC (1, 204, 211 AbnB), 6 AbnC (11, 12, 13 AbnB), 7 AbnC (14, 15, 16 AbnB), 8 AbnC (17, 18, 19 AbnB), 9 AbnC (20, 21, 22 AbnB), 10 AbnC (23, 24, 25 AbnB), 1, 2, 3 MvrAbnB, 121, 122, 123, 124, 126, 127, 128, 129, 141, 144, 148, 152, 154, 174 SkiBn	4, 110, 318, 324, 330 HowAR, 689, 753 AR, 32, 40, 226, 228, 233, 245 ABnsp, 16, 17 GMR	36, 37, 38, 39, 40, 80, 148 TB, 155, 156, 157, 167, 168, 175, 176, 177, 178, 179, 180, 181, 182, 183, 184, 185, 186, 187, 188 TBn, 8 MtcR, 3 AeroSBn, 24, 30, 31, 32, 43, 45, 50, 51, 53, 54 AtrBn	42, 92, 192, 425 FAR, 57, 96, 261, 275, 279, 616, 634, 678, 679 BAR	8 SB (4 SA), 16, 19 SB (6 SA)
3rd Sapper Army Total (1 sapper army)	14 RDs, 13 RBs, 6 AbnCs, 21 AbnBs, 14 SkiBns	7 ARs, 6 ABns, 2 GMRs	7 TBs, 19 TBns, 1 MtcR, 1 AeroSBn, 10 AtrBns	13 ARs	4, 5, 6, 7 SB 7 SBs
Arkhangel'sk MD	32, 33 RB; 2, 24, 28 RD (forming)	310 GunAR, 385 HowAR	1, 4, 5, 6, 9, 10, 11, 12, 14, 15, 16, 17, 19, 20 AeroSBn	134 MAD	
2nd Sapper Army Total (1 sapper army)	3 RDs, 2 RBs	2 ARs	14 AeroSBns	1 AD	2, 3 SB 2 SBs
Ural MD	152, 159, 162, 164, 165, 166, 167, 170, 171, 175 RD, 125, 126, 127, 128, 129, 130, 131, 132, 133, 151 RB, 336, 337,	387, 643 GunAR	26, 37, 38, 39, 44, 48 AtrBn	1G, 9, 67, 179, 435 FAR	

Total	338, 339, 340, 341, 342, 343, 344, 345 MGABn, 36, 58 SkiBn (all forming) 10 RDs, 10 RBs, 2 SkiBns	2 ARs	6 AtrBns	5 Ars
Southern Ural MD	193, 195, 196, 200, 206, 211, 214, 219 RD, 101, 114, 115, 116, 117, 124, 152 RB, 112, 113 CD (all forming)	322, 328, 329, 330, 331 ABnsp		284, 640 BAR
Total	8 RDs, 7 RBs, 2 CDs	5 ABns		2 ARs
Volga MD	41, 42, 55, 58, 397 RD, 118, 119,120, 121, 122, 123, 134, 136 RB, 236 SkiBn (all forming)	5, 522 HowAR, 317 ABnsp	51, 56 TBn; 41, 50, 51 TB, 33, 34, 35, 52 AtrBn (forming)	518, 581 FAR; 13, 31, 49, 166, 211, 240, 293, 296, 426, 484, 508, 509, 510, 517, 580, 754 FAR, 66, 74, 150, 190, 198, 211a, 214, 217, 235, 237, 245, 505, 565 AAR, 2, 8, 16, 30, 32, 37, 38, 39, 45, 48, 58, 63, 134, 140, 175, 205, 244, 260, 321, 452, 506, 507, 527, 597, 602, 723 BAR, 326, 598, 600, 621a, 637, 638, 641, 642, 644, 645, 647, 648, 750 LBAR, 52a, 54a, 60, 242, 507a, 586 AR (forming)
Total	5 RDs, 8 RBs, 1 SkiBn	2 ARs, 1 ABn	3 TBs, 2 TBns, 4 AtrBns	76 ARs
4th Sapper Army				9, 10, 11 SB
6th Sapper Army				17, 18 SB
7th Sapper Army				12, 20, 21 SB
Total (3 sapper armies)				8 SBs

—continued

1 JANUARY 1942 Continued

Fronts and Armies	Rifle, Airborne, and Cavalry	Artillery	Tank and Mechanized	Air	Engineers
Stalingrad MD	240 RD, 244, 248, 266, 277, 278, 280 RD, 135, 139, 141 RB, 138, 142 NRB, Don Cossack CD, 110, 11 CD, 5 MvrAbnB (forming)		6, 45, 47, 48, 49, 131 TB, 199, 200, 201, 202, 203, 204, 205, 206, 207, 208, 209, 210, 211, 212, 213, 214, 215, 216, 217, 218 TBn (all forming)	4 BAR	
5th Sapper Army					13, 14, 15, 22 SB
Total (1 sapper army)	7 RDs, 5 RBs, 3 CDs, 1 AbnB		8 TBs, 20 TBns	1 AR	4 SBs
North Caucasus MD	73, 242, 271, 276, 320 RD, 68, 76, 81, 102 NRB, 114, 115 CD, 2 AbnC (2, 3, 4 AbnB), 3 AbnC (5, 6, 212 AbnB), 4 MvrAbnB	34, 315, 316 ABnsp	8 AtrBn	8, 35, 50, 213, 650, 763, 764 LBAR	23, 24, 25, 26 SB
8th Sapper Army					27, 28 SB
9th Sapper Army					29, 30 SB
10th Sapper Army Total (3 sapper armies)	5 RDs, 4 RBs, 2 CDs, 2 AbnCs, 7 AbnBs	3 ABns	1 AtrBn	7 ARs	8 SBs
Caucasus Front (nonoperating)					
45th Army	61, 406, 408, 409 RD, 55 FR	337 GunAR, 3/350 HowAR	55, 56 TB	69, 84, 263, 292, 297 FAR	10 SBn
Forces in Iran	15 CC (1, 23 CD), 402 RD		13 MtcR		
Total (1 army)	5 RDs, 1 FR, 1 CC, 2 CDs	1 AR	2 TBs, 1 MtcR	5 ARs	1 SBn

Central Asian MD	389 RD, 4 CC (61, 63, 81 CD); 8, 29, 38, 69, 102, 103, 213 RD, 87, 88, 89, 90, 91, 92, 93, 94, 95, 96, 97, 98, 99, 100, 150 153 RB, 97, 98, 99, 100, 101, 102, 103, 104, 105, 106, 107, 108, 109 CD (forming)	9 MtrBn	10, 11, 61 Atr		136, 137, 138 MAD, 15 RAS, 58, 204 CAS	125, 126 EBn
Forces in Iran	58 RC (68, 83 MtnRD, 72 MtnRR), 39 MtnCD					
Total	1 RC, 10 RDs, 16 RBs, 1 CC, 17 CDs, 1 CR	2 ARs, 1 MtrBn		3 ADs		2 EBns
Siberian MD	228, 229, 232, 235, 237, 282, 284, 298, 310, 303, 309, 312 RD, 137, 140, 144, 145, 146, 147, 148, 194 RB, 235, 237 SkBn (all forming)		27, 29, 40, 41, 42, 47, 49 AtrBn		162, 425, 431 FAR	
Total	12 RDs, 8 RBs, 2 SkBns		7 AtrBns	3 ARs		
Trans-Baikal Front						
17th Army	36, 57 MRD, 1, 3 MRR	185 GunAR, 63, 66, 376, 382 AAABn	61 TD, 9 MotArB, 30 MtcR, 82 TBn, 63 Atr		37, 84 MAD, 85 FAD, 132 BAS	17, 84 PBBn
36th Army	94, 209, 210 RD, 51 CD, 31 (Dauriia), 32 (Borzia) FR	267, 390 CAR, 14 MtrBn, 120, 401, 405, 414 AAABn	111 TD, 33, 35 TBn, 64, 65 Atr		88 FAD, 89 AAD, 135 RAS	39 SBn, 2 PBBn
Front forces	97, 116 RD, AbnBn	106, 216, 413 HowAR, 13 MtrBn, 410 AAABn			30, 86, 87 MAD, 133, 134 RAS	1, 15 PBBn, 51, 102 EBn
Total (2 armies)	7 RDs, 2 FRs, 1 CD, 2 RRs	6 ARs, 2 MtrBns, 9 AAABns	2 TDs, 1 MB, 3 TBns, 1 MtcR		8 ADs	2 EBns, 5 PBBns, 1 SBn
Far Eastern Front						
1st Army	26 RC (22, 59, Grodekova RD), 59 RC (39, Spassk RD), 8 CD, Ussuriisk CR, 105, 112 FR	50, 273 CAR, 165, 199 HowAR, 43, 44, 45, 103 AAABn	2 (Ussuriisk) TD, 75, 77 TB, MRB, 3, 5 AtrBn		32, 33, 34, 98 MAD, 26, 59 CAS, 137 RAS	29 EBn, 58 PBBn

—continued

1 JANUARY 1942 Continued

Fronts and Armies	Rifle, Airborne, and Cavalry	Artillery	Tank and Mechanized	Air	Engineers
2nd Army	3, 12, 204 RD, 101 FR	42, 114, 411 AR, 550 HowAR, 192 ABn, 22 MtrBn, 9, 42 AAABn 52 AR, ABn, 46 AAABn	73, 74 TB, 2 AtrBn	82 BAD, 95, 96 MAD, 140 RAS, 328 CAS	2 HPBR, 10, 29 PBBn
15th Army	34 RD, 102 FR		1 (Amur) TD, "Viaz'ma" Atr	69, 97 MAD, 329 CAS	3 HPBR, 11, 23, 24 PBBn, 120 SBn
25th Army	39 RC (40, 105, 208 RD), Voroshilov and Poltava RD, Coastal CD, 106, 107, 108, 110, 111 FR	215, 282, 386, 548 AR, 549 HowAR, 21 MtrBn, 28, 70 AAABn	72, 76 TB, 9 AtrBn	70, 93 MAD, 83 BAD, 39, 330 CAS	32, 100 EBn, 69 SBn
35th Army	35, 66 RD, Amur RR, 109 FR	76, 187 CAR, 110 AAABn	29 MtcR	79 FAD, 18, 130 CAS	3, 9, 16, 20 PBBn, 60 SBn, 280, 402 EBn
Front forces	Special RC (79, 101 RD, Sakhalin RB), 205 RD, 2 RB, 202 AbnB, 103, 104 FR	181 HowAR, 362, 367 ABn, 102 AAABn	13 Atr	29 FAD, 53 BAD, 5 MAB, 71 MAR, 139 AAR, 168 RAR, 251 BAR	26, 101 EBn
Total (5 armies)	4 RCs, 19 RDs, 2 RBs, 1 RR, 1 AbnB, 1 CD, 2 CRs, 12 FRs	17 ARs, 4 ABns, 2 MtrBns, 11 AAABns	2 TDs, 6 TBs, 1 MRB, 1 MtcR, 4 AtrBns	15 ADs, 1 MAB, 4 ARs	2 ERs, 7 EBns, 10 PBBns, 3 SBns
Grand total (8 armies, 9 sapper armies)	5 RCs, 105 RDs, 75 RBs, 3 RRs, 8 AbnCs, 30 AbnBs, 2 CCs, 28 CDs, 3 CRs, 15 FRs, 19 SkiBns	39 ARs, 19 ABns, 2 GMRs, 5 MtrBns, 20 AAABns	4 TDs, 24 TBs, 1 MB, 1 MRB, 4 MtcRs, 44 TBns, 15 AeroSBns, 32 AtrBns	27 ADs, 1 AB, 116 ARs	29 SBs, 2 ERs, 11 EBns, 5 SBns, 15 PBBns

Note: 186th RD existed in both the Karelian Front's Masel'sk Op Gp and the Kalinin Front's 22nd Army, 160th RD existed in both the Western Front and Southwestern Front's 40th Army, and 2nd RD existed in the Arkhangel'sk MD and the Caucasus Front's Coastal Army.

Supported Formation	PVO Formation	PVO Regions	PVO Separate Units	PVO Aviation
PVO Strany Forces: Protecting Operating Armies				
Karelian Front			33, 48, 426, 446 AAABn	
Leningrad Front	2 PVOC (115, 169, 189, 192, 194, 351 AAAR, 2 AAMGR, 2 ProjR, 20 AAABn)	Svir BR (1, 37, 65, 177, 225, 253, 434, 447 AAABn); Ladoga BR (21, 25, 432 AAABn)	251 AAABn	7 FAC (26, 44, 123, 124 FAR)
Volkhov Front			15 AAABn	
Northwestern Front			248 AAABn	
Southwestern Front	3 PVOD (183, 254 AAAR, 4 AAMGR, 93, 96 AAABn), 4 PVOD (317, 736 AAAR, 7 AAMGR, 68, 79, 86, 267 AAABn)	Voronezh-Borisoglebsk DR (746 AAAR, 256, 296, 308 AAABn)	56, 135, 139, 141, 288, 436 AAABn	101 FAD (487, 573, 581 FAR)
Southern Front		Donbas BR (16 AAAR, 11, 159, 179, 234, 235, 383 AAABn); Rostov DR (734 AAAR, 265, 266 AAABn)	18, 36, 57, 286, 364, 375, 411 AAABn	105 FAD (182, 572, 630 FAR)
Caucasus Front	15 PVOB (638 AAAR)		151, 214, 391, 511, 571 AAABn, one AAABn each from the 190, 195, 339 AAAR (3 PVOC)	268 FAR
PVO Strany Forces Located in Military Districts and Nonoperating Fronts				
Moscow MD		Moscow CR (176, 193, 250, 251, 329, 745, 751, 862, 864 AAAR, 1, 20, 22 AAMGR, 1 ProjR, 41, 198, 205, 207, 215, 232, 237, 240, 241, 244, 247, 257, 270, 324 AAABn); Gor'ki DR (196, 583, 742 AAAR, 45		6 FAC (11, 16, 27, 28, 34, 120, 121, 126, 161, 163, 171, 176, 177, 178, 233, 253, 291, 309, 423, 428, 436, 438, 445, 488, 495, 562, 564, 565, 736 FAR, 95, 208 BAR);

—continued

1 JANUARY 1942 Continued

Supported Formation	PVO Formation	PVO Regions	PVO Separate Units	PVO Aviation
		ProjR, 13, 39, 58, 236, 238, 279, 281, 289 AAABn); Rybinsk-Iaroslavl' DR (201 AAAR, 38, 40, 59, 61, 62, 192, 200, 212, 273, 287, 312, 362, 458 AAABn); Tula BR (732 AAAR, 269, 283, 291, 336, 352 AAABn); Kazan' DR (91,202, 271 AAABn)		142 FAD (33, 249, 632, 722 FAR); 147 FAD (4, 441, 721 FAR);
Arkhangel'sk MD		Arkhangel'sk DR (213 AAABn); Cherepovets-Vologda DR (55, 74, 272 AAABn)		104 FAD (729, 730 FAR); 148 FAD (283, 731 FAR)
Volga MD	5 PVOD (767, 861 AAAR, 14, 40 ProjR)	Riazhsk-Tambov DR (733 AAAR, 16, 290 AAABn); Penza DR (174, 277, 285 AAABn); Kuibyshev DR (90 AAABn); Saratov-Balashov DR (89, 243, 374, 501 AAABn)		36 FAD (234, 591, 785 FAR); 141 FAD (631 FAR); 144 FAD (439, 753 FAR)
Central Asian MD			53, 143, 187, 189, 211, 249 AAABn	
Stalingrad MD		Stalingrad DR (748 AAAR, 6, 23, 80, 81, 82, 84, 85, 169, 188, 191, 194, 275 AAABn)		102 FAD (282, 628, 629, 651, 652 FAR)

North Caucasus MD			738 FAR
Caucasus Front *(nonoperating forces)*	3 PVOC (180, 190, 195, 252, 335, 339, 513 AAAR, 3 AAMGR, 3 ProjR); 8 PVOB (466 AAAR, 76, 365, 510 AAABn)	Groznyi DR (744 AAAR); Krasnodar DR (454, 485 AAAR) Tbilisi BR (415 AAAR, 45, 224, 380, 388, 509 AAABn)	443 AAAR, 381 AAABn	8 FAC (35, 45, 50, 68, 82, 266, 267, 480, 481, 483 FAR)
Trans-Baikal Front		1 BR (10, 132, 162, 390 AAABn); 2 BR (150, 387, 408 AAABn); 3 BR (750 AAAR, 107, 166, 262, 264 AAABn)		3 FAR
Far Eastern Front		1 BR (757 AAAR, 138, 167, 175 AAABn); 2 BR (77, 137, 195 AAABn); 3 BR (749 AAAR, 147, 163, 190 AAABn); 4 BR (4, 155, 298 AAABn); 5 BR (755 AAAR, 78, 152, 186 AAABn); 6 BR (752 AAAR)		18 FAR
Total	2 PVOCs, 3 PVODs, 2 PVOBs	1 CR, 14 DRs, 14 BRs	1 AAAR, 32 AAABns	60 FAR 3 FACs, 10 FADs, 5 FARs

1 JULY 1942

Fronts and Armies	Rifle, Airborne, and Cavalry	Artillery	Tank and Mechanized	Air	Engineers
Field Forces					
Karelian					
14th Army	10G, 14 RD, 72 NRB, 5, 6 SkiB, 9 SkiBn, 23 FR	101, 1236 AAR, 645 LAR, 41 GMR		19, 20G, 197, 837 FAR	31, 90, 259 EBn
19th Army	104, 122 RD, 77 NRB	438 LAR, 53 GMR, 261, 487 AAABn	377, 429 TBn	435, 609, 835 FAR	279 EBn
26th Army	23G, 27, 54, 263 RD, 67, 80, 85 NRB	471 AAR, 441, 444 LAR, 172 MtrR, 52 GMR, 15, 48 AAABn	374, 375 TBn, 73 Atr	17G AAR, 760 FAR	21, 30 EBn
32nd Army	37, 71, 289, 313, 367 RD, 1, 2 RB, 61, 65 NRB	1237 AAR, 173 MtrR, 63 GMR, 208, 298 AAABn	376 TBn	152, 195, 828 FAR, 668 LBAR	31, 261 EBn
Front forces	152, 186 RD, 3 RB	32, 446 AAABn	27, 47 AtrBn	80, 137, 608 BAR, 679 LBAR, 118 RAS; 839, 841 FAR (forming)	1 SDEB, 19, 27 EBn
Total (4 armies)	15 RDs, 10 RBs, 2 SkiBs, 1 SkiBn, 1 FR	4 ARs, 4 LARs, 2 MtrRs, 4 GMRs, 8 AAABns	5 TBns, 2 AtrBns	19 ARs	1 EB, 10 EBns
Leningrad					
23rd Army	123, 136, 142, 291 RD, 10 and 20 RD (NKVD), 22 FR	28 AAR, 260, 577 HowAR, 94, 883 LAR, 184 MtrR, 73, 108 AAABn	152 TB, 30 Atr	14G FAR, 15G AAR	14 PBBn, 106, 234 EBn
42nd Army	13, 21, 72, 85, 189 RD, 34, 247, 291, 292, 339 MGABn	14G, 73 AAR, 541 HowAR, 289, 304, 509, 596, 705, 760, 884 LAR, 72, 89 AAABn	2 AcBn, 72 AtrBn		29, 54, 585 EBn
55th Army	43, 56, 90, 268 RD, 33, 261, 267, 289, 290 MGABn	12G AAR, 690 LAR, 175 MtrR, 70, 71 AAABn	220 TB, 71 AtrBn	7 LBAS, 12 CAS	325, 367 EBn
Neva Op Gp	70, 86 RD, 1 RD (NKVD), 11 RB, 35 MGABn	871, 882 LAR, 174 MtrR	86 TBn		53 EBn, 1325 SBn
Coastal Op Gp	48, 168 RD, 2, 5 NIB, 338 MGABn	519 HowAR, MtrBn	287 TBn		295 EBn

Front forces	125 RD, 13 RB, 55, 56 RR, 79 FR	39 GMR, ABn, ATBn, 92, 116 AAABn	1 TB, 1, 3 AcBn	AvGp Gen. Zhdanov (44 BAR, 154, 159, 196 FAR), 19, 286 FAR, 117 RAS	2 SB, 2 EBn, 8, 12, 18, 21, 41, 42 PBBn, 71, 325 SBn
Total (3 armies, 2 op gps)	21 RDs, 4 RBs, 2 FR, 2 RRs	8 ARs, 12 LARs, 2 ABns, 3 MtrRs, 1 GMR, 1 MtrBn, 8 AAABns	3 TBs, 2 TBns, 3 AcBns, 2 AtrBns	1 AvGp, 8 ARs	1 SB, 10 EBns, 3 SBns, 7 PBBns
Volkhov					
2nd Shock Army	19G, 46, 92, 259, 267, 327, 382 RD, 22, 23, 25, 53, 57, 59 RB	18, 442 AAR, 839 HowAR	166 TBn	696 LBAR, 844 TAR	1234, 1708, 1741, 1746 EBn
4th Army	14, 288, 310 RD	70 HowARhp, 168, 1197 HowARhp, 3/8G AAR, 2/1196 HowARhp, 21, 24 GMR	185, 195 TBn, 32 AtrBn	667, 689 LBAR	159 PBBn, 248 EBn, 1242 SBn
8th Army	128, 265, 286 RD, 1 RB	71G AAR, 445 HowAR (-3 Bn), 884 LAR, 50 GMBn	107 TBn, 2, 124 AcBns, 60 Atr		12, 112 EBn
52nd Army	65, 165, 225, 305 RD, 54 RR, 150 FR	137, 430, 1198 HowARhp, 1225 HowAR, 448, 561 AAR, 30 GMR, 168 AAABn	193 TBn	2G, 10 FAR, 662 LBAR	4, 770 EBn
54th Army	4G RC (3G RD, 32, 33, 137, 140 RB), 11, 80, 115, 177, 198, 281, 285, 294, 311 RD, 6 NIB	13G, 21, 24 AAR, 40G CAR, 3/445 HowAR, 29 GMR, 51, 115 GMBn, 177 AAABn	16, 98, 122, 124 TB	18 BAR, 691 LBAR	5, 109, 136, 262 EBn
59th Army	2, 119, 372, 374, 376, 377 RD, 24 RB, 1269 RR (382 RD)	8G (-3 Bn), 367 AAR, 172, 827 HowAR, 1196 HowARhp (-2 Bn), 20, 28 GMR, 6 GMBn, 213, 216 AAABn	7G, 29 TB, 48 AtrBn	283, 845 FAR, 658, 660 LBAR	3, 771 EBn, 1235, 1247 SBn

—continued

1 JULY 1942 Continued

Fronts and Armies	Rifle, Airborne, and Cavalry	Artillery	Tank and Mechanized	Air	Engineers
Front forces	6G RC (4, 24G RD, 58 RB), 13 CC (25, 80, 87 CD), 378 RD, 1 AbnB	42G CAR, 165 MtrR, 15, 100, 101, 461 AAABn	128 TBn, 23, 50 AtrBn, 123 AAAtr	2 Res AvGp (3G, 41 FAR, 10 BAS), 522 FAR, 116 RAS	2 SB, 32, 34, 36, 38, 55 PBBn, 40 EBn, 539 MSBn
Total (6 armies)	2 RCs, 36 RDs, 14 RBs, 1 AbnB, 1 CC, 3 CDs, 1 FR, 1 RR	24 ARs, 1 LAR, 1 MtrR, 6 GMRs, 4 GMBn, 9 AAABns	8 TBs, 4 TBns, 1 AtrBn, 2 AcBns	1 AvGp, 17 ARs	1 SB, 12 EBns, 1 MSBn, 7 EBns, 6 PBBns
Northwestern					
1st Shock Army	1G RC (7G, 391 RD), 129, 364, 397 RD, 14, 15, 27, 37, 42, 44, 45, 47, 121 RB	37G CAR, 701 AAR, 589, 641 LAR, 230/27 GMR, 16, 33 GMBn, 178 AAABn	103 TBn		2, 244, 1257, 1706, 1745 SBn, 381 EBn, 92, 102 PBBn
11th Army	50, 200, 202, 282, 370 RD, 116, 126, 127, 133, 144, 145, 151, 161 RB, 90 FR	264 AAR, 643, 841 GunAR, 305, 382 HowAR, 467 LAR, 105, 116, 121 MtrR, 22, 39 GMR, 242 AAABn	69 TB, 150, 161, 470, 471, 482 TBn		15, 202 EBn, 54, 101 PBBn, 1391 SBn
27th Army	26, 84, 182, 188, 254, 384 RD, 46 RB, 62, 84 NRB	11G AAR, 191 HowARhp, 719, 759 LAR, 137, 167 MtrR, 27 GMR, (-230 Bn)	85, 238 TBn		25, 38 EBn, 50, 86 PBBn, 1732 SBn
34th Army	163, 170, 171, 245 RD, 146, 147 RB, 91 FR	387 AAR, 515 HowARhp, 458, 698 LAR, 102 MtrR, 23 GMR	35 AtrBn	597 MAR	238 EBn, 1317, 1330, 1701 SBn
53rd Army	22G, 23, 130, 166, 235, 241, 250 RD, 20, 86 RB	151, 1235 GunAR, 231, 429 HowAR, 573, 592 LAR, 110, 111, 115 MtrR, 26, 42 GMR	33, 60, 177 TB, 410, 411 TBn, 29 AtrBn		11, 17 EBn, 492, 1259, 1343 SBn, 58 PBBn

6th Air Army				239, 240 FAD, 241 BAD, 242 NBAD, 243 AAD, 514, 645 LBAR, 642, 644, 649, 677 MAR, 699 TAR, 6 RAS	35 SB, 28, 50, 67, 134 EBn, 56 PBBn, 1277, 1743 SBn
Front forces	28G, 201 RD, 309, 365, 366 MGABn	1199, 1200 HowARhp, 46 GMBn, 29, 239, 246, 250, 443, 444, 445, 467, 468 AAABn	83 TB, 149, 483 TBn, 24 AAATr		
Total (5 armies, 1 air army)	1 RC, 29 RDs, 24 RBs, 2 FRs	17 ARs, 9 LARs, 9 MtrRs, 6 GMRs, 3 GMBns, 11 AAABns	5 TBs, 12 TBns, 2 AtrBns	5 ADs, 8 ARs	1 SB, 16 SBns, 12 EBns, 8 PBBns
Kalinin					
3rd Shock Army	2G RC (8G RD, 4G, 26 RB), 24, 28, 33, 117, 257 RD, 31, 54 RB, 63, 65, 157, 159, 226, 227, 228 SkiBn	38G CAR, 613 AAR, 171, 699 LAR, 603 MtrR, 32, 43, 106, 107, 205 GMBn, 12 AAABn	104, 184 TB, 146, 170 TBn		299, 469, 690, 1296, 1334, 1390 SBn
4th Shock Army	145, 332, 334, 358, 360 RD, 21 RB, 10 DB, 140, 231 SkiBn	270, 421 AAR, 765 LAR, 408 MtrR, 17 GMR	78 TB, 141, 171 TBn, 69 MtcBn, 52 AtrBn		210 EBn, 491, 1276, 1308, 1314, 1333 SBn
22nd Army	155, 185, 186, 355, 362, 380 RD, 117 RB, 296 MGABn	10G, 43 AAR, 440 HowAR, 587 LAR, 170 MtrR, 16 GMR, 183, 397 AAABn	82 TB		115, 251 EBn
29th Army	5, 183, 246, 369 RD, 29 CR	360, 432, 510 HowAR, 644 GunAR, 873 LAR, 135 MtrR, 213 ATBn, 13 GMBn, 492, 493 AAABn			71, 267 EBn
30th Army	158, 178, 243, 348, 359, 371, 379 RD, 130, 132, 136 RB	392, 542, 545 GunAR, 646 AAR, 758 LAR, 171 MtrR, 40 GMR, 47 GMBn, 61, 500 AAABn	28, 143 TB, 2G MtcR		60 PBBn, 133, 263 EBn

—continued

1 JULY 1942 Continued

Fronts and Armies	Rifle, Airborne, and Cavalry	Artillery	Tank and Mechanized	Air	Engineers
31st Army	20G, 247, 251 RD	56, 108 AAR, 680 LAR, 56 GMR	92, 101 TB		72 EBn
39th Army	21G, 252, 256, 262, 357, 373, 381 RD	336 GunAR, 102, 103, 202 GMBn	312 TBn		39, 69 EBn
41st Army	17G, 134, 135, 179, 234 RD, 147 SkiBn	109, 204 GMBn, 491 AAABn	21 TB		1709 SBn
58th Army	16, 27G, 215, 375 RD	61 GMR	35, 81 TB		17, 20 EBn
3rd Air Army				209, 210, 256 FAD, 211 BAD, 212, 264 AAD, 195, 708, 881, 882, 883, 884, 885, 887 MAR, 617, 695 LBAR, 3 RAS	
Front forces	11 CC (18, 24, 46, 82 CD), 2G MRD, 220 RD, 114, 131 RB, 141 SkiBn	163 MtrR, 64, 221, 245, 490 AAABn	71 TB, 148 TBn		5 SDEB, 7 SB, 22, 110, 114, 903 EBn, 57, 63, 93, 94 PBBn
Total (9 armies, 1 air army)	1 RC, 49 RDs, 11 RBs, 1 DB, 1 CC, 4 CDs, 1 CR, 11 SkiBns	18 ARs, 7 LARs, 1 ABn, 6 MtrR, 5 GMRs, 12 MGBns, 12 AAABns	12 TBs, 1 MtcR, 6 TBns, 1 MtcBn, 1 AtrBn	6 ADs, 10 ARs	1 EB, 1 SB, 16 EBns, 12 SBns, 5 PBBns
Western					
5th Army	29G, 19, 50, 108, 144, 352, 354 RD, 1G, 36, 60 RB	2G AAR, 66G, 517, 528, 554, 572 GunAR, 544 HowARhp, 610, 703 LAR, 17, 28, 41 GMBn, 1267, 1272 AAAR	20 TB, 5 TBn, 22 AtrBn	162 MAR	2, 467, 499 EBn
10th Army	239, 290, 323, 326, 330 RD	311, 1091 GunAR, 3G, 637, 649 LAR, 123 MtrR, 10 GMBn, 1268, 1277 AAAR	32 TB, 1 AtrBn	880 MAR	303, 694, 695 EBn

Army	Rifle/Cavalry units	Artillery/Mortar units	Tank units	MAR	Engineer
16th Army	5G RC (11G RD, 4, 19, 115, 123 RB), 31G, 97, 322, 324, 336, 385 RD, 7G CD	41G CAR, 486 AAR, 523, 1093, 1094 GunAR, 1222 HowARhp, 533, 696, 1171 LAR, 112 MtrR, 59 GMR, 5, 31, 240 GMBn, 1279, 1280 AAAR, 50 AAABn	94, 112, 146 TB, 519 TBn, 43 AtrBn	168 MAR	145, 243, 451 EBn
20th Army	8G RC (26G RD, 129, 148, 150, 153 RB), 82, 331 RD, 28, 35, 40, 49 RB	39 GunAR, 56 AR, 537 AAR, 1G, 1170 LAR, 169 MtrR, 20, 37, 319 GMBn, 1265, 1271 AAAR, 64 AAABn	17, 120, 188 TB, 21 AtrBn	431 MAR	127, 214, 291 EBn
33rd Army	110, 113, 160, 222 RD	302 HowAR, 403 AAR, 557 GunAR, 551, 600 LAR, 19, 40 GMBn, 1266, 1270 AAAR, 4 AAABn	145 TB, 520 TBn, 6 AtrBn	172 MAR	136, 246, 321 EBn
43rd Army	17, 53, 338, 415 RD, SkiBn, 129, 186, 188 SkiBn	128 HowAR, 570 GunAR, 998 AAR, 868, 869 LAR, 3, 21 GMBn, 1269, 1278 AAAR	18 TB	627 MAR	211, 273, 312 EBn
49th Army	18, 30G, 42, 194, 217 RD, 51, 121 SkiBn	1G AAR, 564 GunAR, 15G, 173, 511 HowAR, 590 HowARhp, 5G, 593 LAR, 37 GMR, 1273, 1274 AAAR	34 TB, 438 TBn	510 MAR	352, 452, 518 EBn
50th Army	58, 69, 116, 146, 173, 298, 325, 344, 413 RD	16G HowAR, 17G, 447, 761 AAR, 1099 GunAR, 2G, 685 LAR, 113 MtrR, 60 GMR, 1275, 1276 AAAR, 112, 304 AAABn	11, 108 TB	745 MAR	5, 70, 466 EBn
61st Army	9G RC (12G RD, 105, 108, 110, 257 RB), 149, 342, 346, 350, 356, 387 RD, 107 RB	60G CAR, 67G, 207 AAR, 483, 546, 702 LAR, 130 MtrR, 54 GMR, 308 GMBn, 1282 AAAR	3 TC (50, 51, 103 TB, 3 MRB), 68, 192 TB, 10 AtrBn	875 MAR	48 PBBn, 535, 536 EBn

—*continued*

187

1 JULY 1942 Continued

Fronts and Armies	Rifle, Airborne, and Cavalry	Artillery	Tank and Mechanized	Air	Engineers
1st Air Army				201, 202, 203, 234 FAD, 204 BAD, 213 NBAD, 214, 224, 231, 232, 233 AAD, 215 MAD, 10 RAR, 713 TAR	
1st Sapper Army					31, 32, 34, 36, 37, 38, 39, 40 SB
Front forces	7G RC (5G RD, 112, 120, 125, 128 RB), 1 GCC (1, 2 GCD), 1, 3G MRD, 38, 122, 123, 124, 126, 127, 128 SkiBn	49, 364 GunAR, 55 CAR, 296 HowAR, 1221 HowARhp, 995 AAR, 6G, 992 LAR, 150 MtrR, 2 GMBn, 1281 AAAR, 35, 324, 525 AAABn	5 TC (24, 41, 70 TB, 5 MRB), 6 TC (22, 100, 200 TB, 6 MRB), 8 TC (25, 31, 93 TB, 8 MRB), 9 TC (23, 95, 187 TB, 10 MRB), 10 TC (178, 183, 186 TB, 11 MRB), 2, 6G TB, 1 MtcB, Spec TBn, 41 AAATr		33 SDEB, 6, 42, 84, 103, 111, 113, 122, 129, 226, 290, 304 EBn, 9, 51, 61, 62, 64, 87, 88, 89, 90, 91, 99 PBBn, 537, 538 MSBn
Total (9 armies, 1 air army, 1 sapper army	4 RCs, 54 RDs, 24 RBs, 1 CC, 3 CDs, 13 SkiBns	44 ARs, 23 LARs, 6 MtrRs, 4 GMRs, 16 GMBns, 18 AAARs, 8 AAABns	6 TCs, 35 TBs, 6 MRBs, 1 MtcB, 5 TBns, 6 AtrBns	12 ADs, 11 ARs	1 EB, 8 SBs, 37 EBns, 2 MSBns, 12 PBBns
Briansk					
3rd Army	60, 137, 240, 269, 283, 287 RD, 104, 134 RB	420, 455 AAR, 316, 584, 697, 768 LAR, 139 MtrR, 6 GMR, 1283 AAAR	79, 150 TB, 31, 55 AtrBn	876 MAR	53 PBBn, 31, 512 EBn
13th Army	15, 132, 143, 148, 307 RD, 109 RB	642 GunAR, 130, 452, 874 LAR, 106, 142 MtrR, 65 GMR, 1287, 1288 AAAR	129 TB, 45 AtrBn	877 MAR	130, 131 SBn, 275 EBn

40th Army	6, 45, 62, 121, 160, 212 RD, 111, 119, 141 RB	602, 1109 GumAR, 4G, 121, 525, 529, 595 LAR, 119 MtrR, 35 GMR, 1289, 1290 AAAR, 215, 332 AAABn	14, 170 TB, 62 AtrBn	878 MAR	1 SBn, 2, 3, 14 EBn, 531, 1505 MSBn
48th Army	6G, 8, 211, 280 RD, 118, 122 RB, 55 CD	376 HowAR, 753 AAR, 543, 569 LAR, 124, 131 MtrR, 48 GMR, 1285, 1286 AAAR, 386 AAABn	80, 202 TB, 37, 54 AtrBn	879 MAR	1428, 1444 MSBn
5th Tank Army	340 RD	644 LAR, 66 GMR	2 TC (26, 27, 148 TB, 2 MRB), 11 TC (53, 59, 160 TB, 12 MRB), 19 TB		1382 EBn
2nd Air Army				205, 207, 266, FAD, 208 NBAD, 223 BAD, 225, 227, 267 AAD, 13 Av Gp (CAF)	
6th Sapper Army *Front* forces	1G, 284 RD, 106, 135 RB, 2 DD (3, 4, 16 DB), 7 CC (11, 17, 83 CD), 8 CC (21, 112 CD)	19G, 396 AAR, 124 HowAR, 540, 694, 1241, 1242, 1244 LAR, 148, 161 MtrR, 45 GMR, 307, 309 GMBn, 1284 AAAR	1 TC (1G, 49, 89 TB, 1 MRB), 4 TC (45, 47, 102 TB, 4 MRB), 16 TC (107, 109, 164 TB, 15 MRB), 17 TC (66, 67, 174 TB, 31 MRB), 24 TC (4G, 54, 130 TB, 24 MRB), 118, 157, 201 TB, 39 AtrBn, 133, 134 AAAtr		17, 18, 19 SB 8 SDEB, 27, 78, 511, 513, 533 EBn, 1375 SBn, 23, 49, 50 PBBn
Total (4 armies, 1 tank army, 1 air army, 1 sapper army)	24 RDs, 10 RBs, 1 DD, 2 CC, 6 CDs	10 ARs, 20 LARs, 8 MtrRs, 6 GMRs, 2 GMBns, 8 AAARs, 3 AAABns	7 TCs, 32 TBs, 7 MRBs, 7 AtrBns	8 ADs, 1 AvGp, 4 ARs	3 SBs, 1 EB, 4 MSBns, 4 SBns, 12 EBns, 4 PBBns

—continued

1 JULY 1942 Continued

Fronts and Armies	Rifle, Airborne, and Cavalry	Artillery	Tank and Mechanized	Air	Engineers
Southwestern					
9th Army	51, 81, 106, 140, 255, 296, 318, 333 RD, 18, 19 DB, 5 CC (30, 34, 60 CD)	68, 69G AAR, 667 HowAR, 186, 1173, 1174, 1181, 1182 LAR, 2, 73, 78 GMR, 48 GMBn, 1258, 1260 AAAR, 268 AAABn	12 TB, 71, 132 TBn	633 MAR	7 PBBn, 121 EBn, 860, 861, 862 SBn
21st Army	76, 124, 226, 227, 293, 297, 301, 343 RD, 8 MRD (NKVD)	5G, 156, 574 AAR, 135 HowAR, 338, 538, 1240 LAR, 57, 70, 74 GMR, 1263, 1264 AAAR, 158 AAABn	13 TC (85, 167 TB, 20 MRB), 10 TB, 1 MRB, 478 TBn	32 MAR	1 SBn, 2, 526, 540 EBn
28th Army	13, 45G, 38, 169, 175 RD	265, 594 GunAR, 870 HowAR, 1181 LAR, 4, 58 GMR, 110 GMBn, 1257, 1261 AAAR, 126 AAABn	23 TC (6G, 114 TB, 9 MRB), 65, 90, 91 TB	655 MAR	12 EBn, 1361, 1570 SBn, 1504 MSBn
38th Army	162, 199, 242, 277, 278, 304 RD	51, 233, 648 AAR, 236 HowAR, 468, 507, 651, 738, 1175, 1238 LAR, 5, 51 GMR, 1259 AAAR, 47, 505 AAABn	22 TC (3, 13, 36 TB, 51 MtcBn), 133, 156, 159, 168 TB, 22 MRB, 92 TBn, 50 MtcBn	282 MAR	56 EBn, 516, 516a, 516b SBn
57th Army					122, 175 EBn, 525, 871, 872 SBn
8th Air Army				206, 220, 235, 268, 269 FAD, 226, 228 AAD, 221, 270 BAD, 271, 272 NBAD, 13G BAR, 43, 434 FAR, 8 RAR	
7th Sapper Army					12, 14, 15, 20, 21 SB

Front forces	9G, 103, 244, 300 RD, 1 DD (1, 2, 5 DB), 11, 13, 15, 17 DB, 3 GCC (5, 6G, 32 CD), 52, 53, 74, 117, 118 FR	7, 70G, 671 AAR, 205 HowAR, 612, 665, 764, 1239, 1243 LAR, 152 MtrR, 342 GMBn, 1262 AAAR, 27, 31, 52, 67, 75, 139, 141, 146, 227, 288, 307, 354, 355, 436, 462 AAABn	14 TC (138, 139 TB), 57, 58, 84, 88, 158, 176 TB, 21 MRB, TBn, 58, 59, 60, 61, 377 AtrBn	164, 929 FAR, 826 LRBAR	16 SDEB, 48, 119, 120 EBn, 6, 9, 19, 20, 26, 28, 37, 103, 105, 107 PBBn, 530, 532, 534 SBn, 377 MSBn
Total (5 armies, 1 air army, 1 sapper army)	32 RDs, 1 DD, 6 DBs, 2 CCs, 6 CDs, 5 FRs	18 ARs, 20 LARs, 1 MtrR, 10 GMRs, 3 GMBns, 8 AAARs, 20 AAABns	4 TCs, 24 TBs, 5 MRBs, 5 TBns, 2 MtrBns, 5 AtrBns	11 ADs, 11 ARs	5 SBs, 1 EB, 2 MSBns, 15 SBns, 11 EBns, 11 PBBns
Southern					
12th Army	4, 74, 176, 261, 349 RD	81 HowAR, 368 AAR, 374 GunAR, 521 LAR, MtrBn, 8 GMR, 7, 14 AAABn	64, 66 AtrBn		8, 50 EBn, 524, 863, 864 SBn
18th Army	216, 353, 384, 395 RD	377, 880 AAR, 530 LAR, 49 GMR, 101 GMBn, 30, 364 AAABn	64 TB, 65 AtrBn	718 MAR	38 ER, 68, 172 EBn, 247, 517, 865 SBn
24th Army	73, 228, 335, 341 RD	262 AAR, 203 AAABn			1660, 1663 SBn
37th Army	102, 218, 230, 275, 295 RD	4G, 268 AAR, 727 LAR, 43 GMR, 508, 537 AAABn	121 TB	446 MAR	116, 173 EBn, 866, 867, 868 SBn
56th Army	3G RC (2G RD, 68, 76, 81 NRB), 30, 31, 339 RD, 16 RB, 70, 158 FR	39G CAR, 689 AAR, 1195 HowAR, 526, 1223 HowARhp, 756 LAR, 14 GMBn, 57, 593 AAABn	63 TB	750 MAR	16 EBn, 522, 869, 870, 1581, 1602, 1615 SBn, 1593 MSBn

—*continued*

191

1 JULY 1942 Continued

Fronts and Armies	Rifle, Airborne, and Cavalry	Artillery	Tank and Mechanized	Air	Engineers
4th Air Army				216, 217 FAD, 218 NBAD, 219 BAD, 230 AAD, 647, 762, 889 MAR; 229 FAD (forming)	
8th Sapper Army					10, 11, 23, 24, 25, 26, 28, 29, 30 SB
Front forces	347 RD, MRR, 69, 73 FR	67 GMR, 17, 504 AAABn	5G, 15, 140 TB, 62, 75 TBn, 15, 57 AtrBn		27 SDEB, 9, 108, 112, 123, 124, 170, 273 EBn, 97 MSBn, 857, 858, 859 SBn, 19, 21, 22, 35, 37, 85, 96, 160 PBBn
Total (5 armies, 1 air army, 1 sapper army)	1 RC, 23 RDs, 4 RBs, 1 RR, 4 FRs	13 ARs, 4 LARs, 1 MtrR, 4 GMRs, 2 GMBns, 11 AAABns	6 TBs, 2 TBns, 5 AtrBns	6 ADs, 6 ARs	9 SBs, 1 EB, 1 ER, 14 EBns, 20 SBns, 2 MSBns, 8 PBBns

North Caucasus

47th Army	32G, 77 RD, 66 NRB, 103 RB, 32 CR	25, 456, 457, 547, 1167, 1168 GunAR, 53 AR, 1188 LAR, 18, 25 GMR	126 TBn	931 MAR	54 PBBn, 61, 91, 132, 256 EBn
51st Army	91, 138, 156, 157 RD, 110, 115 CD, 255 CR	19 GMR	40 TB, 51 AtrBn	932 MAR	205, 275 SBn

192

Coastal Army	25, 95, 109, 172, 345, 386, 388 RD, 79, 138 NRB, 7, 8 NIB	18G AAR, 47, 101 GunAR, 674, 700 LAR, 53 GMBn, 880 AAAR, 26 AAABn	81, 125 TBn		82, 138 EBn
5th Air Army				132 BAD, 236, 237, 265 FAD, 238 AAD, 742 RAR, 763 LBAR	
Front forces	1 RC (236, 302 RD, 113, 139 RB), 83, 142, 154 NRB, 17 CC (12, 13, 15, 116 CD)	1187 LAR, 149 MtrR, 8, 220, 294, 319, 333, 347, 348, 351, 373, 388 AAABn	136, 137 TB, Special MRB (Bn), 79 TBn, 8, 16, 24, 53 AtrBn	653 FAR	6 PBBn, 3, 75 EBn, 1637, 1677, 1679 SBn
Total (3 armies, 1 air army)	1 RC, 15 RDs, 11 RBs, 1 CC, 6 CDs, 2 CRs	10 ARs, 4 LARs, 1 MtrR, 3 GMRs, 1 GMBn, 1 AAAR, 11 AAABns	3 TBs, 1 MRB, 4 TBns, 5 AtrBns	5 ADs, 5 ARs	8 EBns, 5 SBns, 2 PBBns
Trans-Caucasus					
44th Army	223, 414, 416 RD, 9, 10 RB	136, 1147 HowARhp 647, 1231, 1232 AAR, 1115 LAR, 153 MtrR	17 Atr		19 EBn
46th Army	3 RC (9, 20 MtnRD), 389, 392, 394, 406 RD, 155 RB, 63 CD, 51 FR		11, 12, 36, 41, 42 AtrBn		51 EBn, 11 SBn
Front forces	417 RD	350, 1023, 1150 HowARhp, 1169 GunAR, 44, 50 GMR	52 TB	84, 790, 862, 863, 926, 927 FAR, 859, 870 BAR, 3 CAS, 145, 149 RAS	321 EBn
Total (2 armies)	1 RC, 10 RDs, 3 RBs, 1 CD, 1 FR	9 ARs, 1 LAR, 1 MtrR, 2 GMRs	1 TB, 5 AtrBns	8 ARs	3 EBns, 1 SBn
Separate Armies					
7th Army	4 RC (114, 272, 368 RD), 21, 67, 314 RD, 69, 70, 73 NRB, 3 NIB, 162 FR	109, 480, 1224 HowAR, 460, 514, 712 LAR, 46, 64 GMR, 48, 54 AAABn	363, 431 TBn	4G BAR, 415, 524 FAR, 716 LBAR	1G, 261, 877, 1725 SBn, 18, 35, 36 EBn, 40 PBBn
Total (1 army)	1 RC, 6 RDs, 4 RBs, 1 FR	3 ARs, 3 LARs, 2 GMRs, 2 AAABns	2 TBns	4 ARs	4 SBns, 3 EBns, 1 PBBn

—*continued*

1 JULY 1942 Continued

Fronts and Armies	Rifle, Airborne, and Cavalry	Artillery	Tank and Mechanized	Air	Engineers
Moscow Defense Zone	49, 119, 233, 258, 260, 264, 273 RD, 149, 256 RB, 119, 152, 153, 154, 155, 156, 157, 159, 160, 161 FR	402, 527, 1149, 1152 HowARhp, 472 HowAR, 488 AAR, 1146 AR, 1155 GunAR, 12, 222, 1070, 1071, 1072, 1073, 1074, 1075, 1076, 1141, 1145 LAR, 400, 402, 406, 409 HGunABn, 253 AAABn	MtcBn	173 BAR	161, 162 EBn, 693, 873, 874 SBn
3rd Sapper Army Total (1 sapper army)	7 RDs, 2 RBs, 10 FRs	8 ARs, 11 LARs, 4 ABns, 1 AAABn	1 MtcBn	1 AR	4, 6 SB 2 SBs, 3 SBns, 2 EBns
Stavka Special Aviation 1st Shock AvGp (Volkhov Front) Total				244 BAD (BF) 35, 771 BAR, 815, 823 LRBAR, 92, 160, 293 FAR, 175, 313, 448, 569 AAR 1 AvGp, 1 AD, 11 ARs	
Long-Range and Reconnaissance Aviation Total				3, 17, 24, 36, 45, 50, 53, 62, 113 LRAD, 1 TAD, 2, 4, 40 RAR 10 ADs, 3 ARs	
Grand total (11 *fronts*, 56 armies, 1 tank	12 RCs, 321 RDs, 121 RBs, 4 RRs, 2 SkiBs, 25 SkiBns,	186 ARs, 7 ABns, 39 MtrRs, 1 MtrBn, 119 LARs, 53	17 TCs, 129 TBs, 19 MRBs, 1 MtcB, 47	4 AvGps, 64 ADs, 126 ARs	31 SBs, 6 EBs, 1 ER, 150

194

army, 7 air armies, 5 sapper armies, 1 defense zone, 2 op gps)	27 FRs, 2 DDs, 7 DBs, 1 AbnB, 8 CCs, 29 CDs, 3 CRs	GMRs, 43 GMBns, 35 AAARs, 104 AAABns	TBns, 1 MtcR, 4 MtcBns, 5 AcBns, 44 AtrBns	EBns, 90 SBns, 11 MSBns, 64 PBBns
***Stavka* VGK Reserve**				
1st Res Army	18, 29, 112, 131, 164, 214, 229 RD			1363 SBn
2nd Res Army	25G, 52, 100, 111, 237, 303 RD			1727 SBn
3rd Res Army	107, 159, 161, 167, 193, 195 RD			1305 SBn
4th Res Army	78, 88, 118, 139, 274, 312 RD			
5th Res Army	14G, 1, 127, 153, 197, 203 RD			
6th Res Army	99, 141, 174, 206, 219, 232, 309 RD			
7th Res Army	33G, 147, 181, 184, 192, 196 RD			1523, 1524 SBn
8th Res Army	64, 120, 221, 231, 231, 308, 315 RD			
9th Res Army	32, 93, 238, 279, 316 RD			
10th Res Army	133, 180, 207, 292, 299, 306 RD			
3rd Tank Army	154 RD	1172 LAR, 62 GMR, 470 AAABn	12 TC (30, 86, 97 TB, 13 MRB),15 TC (96, 105, 113 TB, 17 MRB), 2, 99, 166, 179 TB	182 EBn

—continued

1 JULY 1942 Continued

Fronts and Armies	Rifle, Airborne, and Cavalry	Artillery	Tank and Mechanized	Air	Engineers
Separate	2G CC (3, 4G, 20 CD), 6, 7, 8, 10 DB	1180, 1246, 1247 LAR, 151 MtrR, 72, 74 GMR, 68, 69, 77 HGMR, 324, 326 GMBn	7 TC (3G, 62, 87 TB, 7 MRB), 18 TC (110, 180, 181 TB, 18 MRB), 25 TC (111, 162, 175 TB, 16 MRB), 28 AtrBn	222 BAD, 50, 127, 156, 183, 192, 249, 271, 291, 437, 517 FAR, 9, 134, 136, 261, 275, 279, 511, 624, 779, 780, 803 BAR, 622, 671, 766, 893 AAR, 598, 600, 638, 690, 701, 702, 765 LBAR, 1 Res. AB (644 LBAR), 2 Res. AB (32, 205, 507 BAR, 621 AAR), 3 Res. AB (640 BAR)	
Total (10 res armies, 1 tank army	62 RDs, 4 DBs, 1 CC, 3 CDs	4 LARs, 1 MtrR, 6 GMRs, 2 GMBns, 1 AAABn	5 TCs, 19 TBs, 5 MRBs, 1 AtrBn	1 AD, 3 ABs, 38 ARs	1 EBn, 5 SBns

Military Districts and Nonoperating *Fronts*

Moscow MD	16 RD, 124, 152 RB, 73 CD, 71, 72, 75, 78, 116 FR, 1 AbnC (20I, 211 AbnB), 4 AbnC (8, 9, 211 AbnB), 5 AbnC (7, 10, 210 AbnB), 6 AbnC (11, 12, 13 AbnB), 7 AbnC (14, 15, 16 AbnB), 8 AbnC (17, 18, 19 AbnB), 9 AbnC (20, 21, 22 AbnB), 10 AbnC (23, 24, 25 AbnB), 1, 2, 3, 5 MvrAbmB	4, 110, 318, 324, 330, 1016, 1017, 1018, 1019, 1020, 1021, 1022, 1145, 1148, 1153, 1154, 1191 HowARhp, 138, 152, 229, 265, 272, 274, 275, 283, 293, 315, 320, 877 HowAR, 1092, 1110, 1111, 1112, 1156, 1157 GunAR, 210, 269, 301, 437, 462, 1176, 1178, 1179, 1189, 1245, 1248, 1249, 1250, 1251, 1252, 1253, 1254,	115, 117, 119, 134, 135, 153, 154, 155, 161, 163, 169, 189, 193, 196 TB, 14 MRB, 8, 11 MtcR, 51, 160, 163, 180, 181, 184, 186, 187, 454, 455, 472, 473, 474, 475, 476, 488, 489, 490, 491, 492, 500, 501, 502, 503, 506, 507 TBn, 52, 53, 54,	9, 24, 49, 181, 416, 438, 440, 812, 813, 814 FAR, 54, 132, 140, 150, 703 BAR, 783 AAR, 648, 704, 969 LBAR	15, 39, 43, 44, 47, 100, 104, 106, 108 PBBn, 1262, 1286, 1348, 1486, 1720, 1758 SBn

Total	1 RD, 2 RBs, 1 CD, 8 AbnCs, 27 AbnBs, 5 FRs	1255 LAR, 32, 40, 226, 245 ABnsp, 101, 103, 107, 108, 109, 114, 127, 136, 138 MtrR, 34, 36, 47, 75, 76, 79, 81, 82, 83 GMR, 83, 84, 299, 316, 327, 328, 332 GMBn 35 ARs, 18 LARs, 4 ABns, 9 MtrRs, 9 GMRs, 7 GMBns	55, 56, 57, 58, 64, 65, 55, 56, 57, 58, 64, 65, 66, 67, 68 MtcBn, 25, 26, 30, 33, 34, 38, 40, 44, 46, 49, 79 AtrBn 14 TBs, 1 MRB, 2 MtcRs, 26 TBns, 12 MtcBns, 11 AtrBns	19 ARs 6 SBns, 9 PBBns
Arkhangel'sk MD	63 NRB	310 GunAR, 385, 875, 876 HowAR, 1234 AAR, 104 MtrR, 1, 8 Abtrysp		456, 561 BAR
Total	1 RB	5 ARs, 1 MtrR		2 ARs
Volga MD	12, 14 DB, 76, 77 FR	5, 522, 1024, 1025, 1144, 1151 HowARhp, 1000, 1101, 1102, 1103, 1160, 1161, 1162 GunAR, 1177 LAR, 317 ABnsp, 128, 143 MtrR	116 TB, 32, 36 MRB	12, 32, 133, 146, 169, 211, 237, 265, 428, 431, 484, 486, 520, 580, 581, 605, 739, 770, 774, 795, 797, 864, 894, 896, 897, 898, 899, 900 FAR, 66, 214, 225, 232, 243, 245, 502, 567, 568, 614, 618, 637, 657, 672, 673, 685, 686, 687, 688, 724, 735, 806, 807, 808, 810, 811, 820, 825, 843, 873 AAR, 39, 321, 506, 587, 602, 778 BAR, 678 TAR
Total	2 DBs, 2 FRs	13 ARs, 1 LAR, 1 ABn, 2 MtrRs	1 TB, 2 MRBs	65 ARs

—continued

1 JULY 1942 Continued

Fronts and Armies	Rifle, Airborne, and Cavalry	Artillery	Tank and Mechanized	Air	Engineers
Stalingrad MD	5 DD (22, 23, 24 DB), 21, 25 DB, 54 FR	331 HowAR, 1104, 1105, 1158, 1159 GunAR, 508, 552, 555, 614, 881, 1183, 1185, 1186 LAR, 140, 141 MtrR	6, 39, 55, 56, 173, 182, 191 TB, 56 AtrBn	86, 224, 853, 854, 855 BAR	43, 44, 52, 57 EBn
Total	1 DD, 2 DBs, 1 FR	5 ARs, 8 LARs, 2 MtrRs	7 TBs, 1 AtrBn	5 ARs	4 EBns
North Caucasus MD	20 DB, 4 MvrAbnB, 115, 151 FR	34, 315, 316 ABnsp	19 AtrBn, 14 Atr	202, 892 BAR	
Total	1 DB, 1 AbnB, 2 FRs	3 ABns	1 AtrBn	2 ARs	
Trans-Caucasus Front (nonoperating)				48, 63, 242, 244, 277, 449, 452, 454, 745 BAR, 246, 269, 270, 743, 773, 824 FAR	
45th Army	61, 89, 151, 402, 408, 409 RD, 55 FR	337 AAR, 863 LAR, 132 MtrR	151 TB, 55, 56 Atr		10 SBn
Forces in Iran	75 RD, 15 CC (1, 23 CD)	166 MtrR	207 TB		
Total	7 RDs, 1 FR, 1 CC, 2 CDs	1 AR, 1 LAR, 2 MtrRs	2 TBs	15 ARs	1 SBn
Ural MD	7, 249 RD, 9 DB	1106, 1107, 1108, 1163, 1164, 1190 GunAR	106 TB, 19 MRB	694 AAR	
Total	2 RDs, 1 DB	6 ARs	1 TB, 1 MRB	1 AR	
South Ural MD	101 RB	1095, 1096, 1097, 1098, 1165, 1166 GunAR, 322, 328, 329, 330, 331 ABnsp, 117, 118, 120, 122, 129, 134, 144, 145, 146 MtrR		34, 230, 284 BAR, 626 LBAR	
Total	1 RB	6 ARs, 5 ABns, 9 MtrRs		4 ARs	
Siberian MD	6 CR			12, 30 BAR	
Total	1 CR			2 ARs	

Central Asian MD	213 RD, 87, 90, 94, 100 RB, 4 CC (61, 81 CD) 97, 99, 104, 105, 107 CD	179 MtrR		125, 126 EBn
Forces in Iran	58 RC (68, 83 MtnRD, 39 MtnCD, 72 MtnRR)		136 MAD, 106 AAR, 352 FAR, 15 RAS, 204 CAS	253, 319 EBn
Total	1 RC, 3 RDs, 4 RBs, 1 CC, 8 CDs, 1 CR	123 AAR, 450 HowAR	167 FAR, 492 AAR, 58 CAS	4 EBns
		2 ARs, 1 MtrR	1 AD, 4 ARs	
Trans-Baikal Front				
17th Army	36, 57 MRD, 227 RB, 1, 3 MRR	185, 1141 GunAR, 413 HowAR, 63, 66, 376, 382 AAABn	61 TD, 43 TB, 9 MotArmB, 30 MtcR, 70, 82 TBn, 67 Atr	22, 56, 350 FAR, 56, 454 BAR, 291 AAR, 847 LBAR, 132 RAS	84 PBBn, 102, 282 EBn
36th Army	94, 209, 210, 321 RD, 226 RB, 31, 32 FR	259 HowAR, 267, 390, 1233 GunAR, 177 MtrR, 120, 401, 405, 414 AAABn	111 TD, 33, 35 TBn, 64, 65 Atr	64 AAR, 70, 351, 718 FAR, 455, 541 BAR, 135 RAS	39 EBn
Front forces	2 RC (399 RD, 229 RB, 51 CD)	106, 1146 HowARhp, 216 HowAR, 1142, 1143 GunAR, 176, 178 MtrR, 32 GMR, 410 AAABn	44, 205, 206 TB, "Zabaikalets" Atr	30 BAD, 51 FAR, 49, 456, 457 BAR, 133, 134 RAS, 10 BAS; 46, 260, 804 BAR, 846, 848, 849 LBAR (forming)	51, 281, 283 EBn, 1, 2, 17 PBBn
Total (2 armies)	1 RC, 7 RDs, 3 RBs, 1 CD, 2 RRs, 2 FRs	12 ARs, 3 MtrRs, 1 GMR, 9 AAABns	2 TDs, 4 TBs, 1 MB, 1 MtcR, 4 TBns	1 AD, 23 ARs	6 EBns, 4 PBBns
Far Eastern Front					
1st Army	5 RC (246, 248 RB), 26 RC (22, 59, 87 RD), 59 RC (39, 98 RD), 18 CC (7, 8 CD, 246 CR), 187 RD, 105, 112 FR	45, 87, 165, 182, 372, 1132, 1133 HowAR, 199, 1192 HowARhp, 50, 273, 1124, 1125, 1138, 1139 GunAR, 168, 185 MtrR, 33 GMR, 43, 44, 45, 103 AAABn	75, 77, 204, 208, 209, 210 TB, 263 MRB, 442 TBn, 3, 78 AtrBn	32, 33, 34, MAD, 47 FAR, 78, 536 AAR, 776 LBAR, 137 RAS, 26, 59 CAS	29, 278 EBn
2nd Army	3, 12, 96, 204 RD, 258, 259 RB, 101 FR	42, 1120 GunAR, 114, 147, 238, 411, 1129 HowAR, 550 HowARhp, 192 ABn, 181 MtrR, 9, 42 AAABn	73, 74 TB, 2, 5 AtrBn, 24 Atr	82 BAD, 96 FAD, 14, 529 FAR, 319 MBAR, 777 LBAR, 140 RAS, 328 CAS	2 HPBR, 10 PBBn, 277 EBn

—*continued*

1 JULY 1942 Continued

Fronts and Armies	Rifle, Airborne, and Cavalry	Artillery	Tank and Mechanized	Air	Engineers
15th Army	34 RD, 250, 260 RB, 102 FR	52, 1121 GunAR, 145, 1128, 1130 HowAR, 1194 HowARhp, 183 MtrR, 46 AAABn	165, 171 TB, TBn, 14, 59 Atr	76 AAR, 300, 301, 302 FAR, 581 MBAR, 139 RAS, 329 CAS	3 HPBR, 11, 24, 29 PBBn, 69 SBn, 129 EBn
25th Army	39 RC (40, 105, 126, 208 RD, 247, 253 RB), 190 RD 261, 262 RB, 247 CR, 106, 107, 108, 110, 111, 113 FR	107, 148, 215, 386, 1134, 1135 HowAR, 549, 1193 HowARhp, 282, 548, 1126, 1127, 1136 GunAR, 180, 182 MtrR, 28, 59, 70 AAABn	72, 76 TB, 302 TBn, 9 AtrBn, 23, 62 Atr	83 BAD, 5, 305, 582 FAR, 75, 77, 537, 906 AAR, 781 TAR, 39, 330 CAS, 138 RAS	32, 100, 276, 279 EBn
35th Army	35, 66, 422 RD, 109 FR	76, 187, 1122, 1123 GunAR, 177, 181, 263, 1131 HowAR, 110 AAABn	125, 172 TB, 29 MtcR, 13 AtrBn, 53, 61 Atr	48, 308, 530 FAR, 782 BAR, 18 RAS, 130 CAS	60 SBn, 280, 402 EBn, 3, 16, 58 PBBn
Front forces	Special RC (79, 101 RD, Sakhalin RB, 302 RR), 205 RD, 2 RB, 202 AbnB, 103, 104 FR	428, 1137 HowAR, Khabarovsk ABn, 362, 367 ABn, 102 AAABn	203 TB, "Viaz'ma" Atr	29 FAD, 53 BAD, 128 MAD, 5 MAB, 139 AAR, 168 RAR, 251 BAR	26, 101 EBn
Total (5 armies)	5 RCs, 22 RDs, 12 RBs, 1 RR, 1 AbnB, 1 CC, 2 CDs, 2 CRs, 13 FRs	52 ARs, 4 ABns, 6 MtrRs, 1 GMR, 12 AAABns	15 TBs, 1 MRB, 1 MtcR, 5 TBns, 6 AtrBns	9 ADs, 1 AB, 28 ARs	2 PBRs, 12 EBns, 2 SBns, 7 PBBns
Grand Total (8 armies)	7 RCs, 42 RDs, 23 RBs, 4 RRs, 1 DD, 6 DBs, 8 AbnCs, 29 AbnBs, 3 CCs, 14 CDs, 2 CRs, 26 FRs	137 ARs, 28 LARs, 17 ABns, 35 MtrRs, 11 GMRs, 7 GMBns, 21 AAABns	2 TDs, 44 TBs, 1 MB, 5 MRBs, 4 MRRs, 33 TBs, 12 MtcBns, 19 AtrBns	11 ADs, 1 AB, 170 ARs	2 PBRs, 26 EBns, 9 SBns, 20 PBBns

Note: 186th RD existed in the Karelian Front and the Kalinin Front's 22nd Army and 160th RD existed in the Western Front's 33rd Army and the Briansk Front's 40th Army.

PVO Fronts and Armies	PVO Formations	PVO Regions	PVO Separate Units	PVO Aviation
PVO Strany Forces: PVO Fronts and Armies				
Moscow PVO Front			82, 176, 193, 250, 251, 329, 745, 761, 862, 864, 1201, 1202, 1203, 1204, 1205 AAAR, 1, 20, 22 AAMGR, 1, 14, 30, 31 ProjR, 1, 9, 13, 14 AeroObsR, 41, 198, 205, 207, 232, 237, 240, 241, 244, 247, 257, 270, 352 AAABn	6 FAC (12G, 11, 16, 27, 28, 34, 67, 126, 176, 177, 178, 233, 287, 309, 429, 445, 488, 508, 562, 564, 565, 736 FAR)
Leningrad PVO Army			2, 115, 169, 189, 192, 194, 351 AAAR, 2 AAMGR, 2 ProjR, 20 AAABn	7 FAC (11G, 26, 123, 124, 158 FAR)
Baku PVO Army			180, 190, 195, 252, 335, 339, 513 AAAR, 3 AAMGR, 3 ProjR	8 FAC (82, 266, 267, 480, 481, 483, 822 FAR)
PVO Strany Forces: Protecting Operating Armies				
Karelian Front		Murmansk DR (885 AAAR, 33, 135, 417, 426 AAABn)		122 FAD (767, 768, 769 FAR)
Leningrad Front		Svir BR (1, 37, 65, 69, 214, 447 AAABn); Ladoga BR (25, 225, 251, 253, 432, 434 AAABn)		
Northwestern and Kalinin Fronts		Bologoe DR (87, 215, 248, 256, 271, 308 AAAR, 57, 58, 74, 75 AAAtr		106 FAD (33, 253, 441, 630 FAR)
Southwestern Front	3 PVOD (183, 254 AAAR, 4 AAMGR, 93, 96 AAABn), 4 PVOD (317, 736 AAAR, 7 AAMGR, 86 AAABn	Voronezh-Borisoglebsk DR (746 AAAR, 224, 296, 471, 510 AAABn)		101 FAD (487, 573, 826 FAR)

—continued

1 JULY 1942 Continued

PVO Fronts and Armies	PVO Formations	PVO Regions	PVO Separate Units	PVO Aviation
Southern Front		Donbas BR (113, 159, 165, 234, 235, 540 AAABn); Rostov DR (16, 485, 734 AAAR, 11, 18, 23, 36, 106, 265, 266, 286, 344, 375, 383, 411 AAABn)	179 AAABn	105 FAD (182, 234, 572 FAR)
North Caucasus Front				268 FAR

PVO Strany Forces: Located in Military Districts and Nonoperating Fronts

Moscow MD		Gor'kii CR (196, 583, 742, 784 AAAR, 45 ProjR, 13, 39, 58, 91, 202, 236, 238, 279, 281, 289, 310, 379 AAABn); Rybinsk-Iaroslavl' DR (201 AAAR, 38, 40, 59, 61, 62, 192, 200, 212, 273, 287, 312, 362, 458 AAABn); Tula BR (732 AAAR, 269, 283, 291, 511 AAABn, 72, 124, 125, 126, 129 AAAtr)		142 FAD (249, 423, 632, 722, 786 FAR); 147 FAD (4, 721 FAR); 125 FAD (171, 495, 787 FAR)
Arkhangel'sk MD		Arkhangel'sk DR (84, 213, 372, 480 AAAR); Cherepovets-Vologda DR (55, 74, 99, 272, 385, 413 AAABn)		104 FAD (348, 729, 730 FAR), 126 FAD (833 FAR); 148 FAD (731, 740 FAR)
Volga MD		Riazhsk-Tambov DR (733 AAAR, 16, 290, 353 AAABn, 73, 121, 122, 127 AAAtr); Kuibyshev DR (767, 861 AAAR, 40 ProjR, 90, 174, 285 AAABn); Saratov-Balashov DR (56, 89, 243, 343, 374, 380, 501 AAABn);Penza BR (79, 277 AAABn)		36 FAD (591, 785 FAR); 141 FAD (631, 802 FAR); 144 FAD (586, 753 FAR)

Stalingrad MD	Stalingrad CR (748, 1077, 1078, 1079, 1080, 1082, 1083, 1087, 1088 AAAR, 43 ProjR, 80, 82, 85, 188, 267, 284, 416 AAABn)	102 FAD (439, 629, 651, 652, 788 FAR)
North Caucasus MD 15 PVOB (638 AAAR)	Krasnodar DR (454 AAAR, 53, 143, 151, 189, 195, 211, 249, 422, 425, 430, 433 AAABn, 53 AAAtr); Grozny DR (744 AAAR, 509, 571 AAABn)	628 FAR
		738 FAR
Trans-Caucasus Front 8 PVOB (466 AAAR, 76, (*nonoperating forces*) 365, 419 AAABn)	Tbilisi BR (415, 443 AAAR, 3, 381 AAABn)	35, 68 FAR
Central Asian MD		
Trans-Baikal Front	1 BR (10, 132, 162, 390 AAABn); 2 BR (150, 387, 408 AAABn); 3 BR (750 AAAR, 107, 166, 187, 262, 264 AAABn)	611 FAR
Far Eastern Front	1 BR (757 AAAR, 138, 167, 175 AAABn); 2 BR (77, 137, 195 AAABn); 3 BR (749 AAAR, 147, 163, 190, 217 AAABn, 68 AAAtr); 4 BR (4, 155, 398 AAABn); 5 BR (755 AAAR, 78, 152, 186 AAABn); 6 BR (752 AAAR, 463, 465 AAABn)	3 FAR
		18 FAR
		60 FAR
Total (1 PVO *front*, 2 PVODs, 2 PVOBs, 2 PVO armies)	2 CR, 13 DRs, 14 BRs	3 FACs, 14 FADs, 9 FARs
	29 AAAR, 5 AAMGRs, 6 ProjRs, 15 AAABns	

1 FEBRUARY 1943

Fronts and Armies	Rifle, Airborne, and Cavalry	Artillery	Tank and Mechanized	Air	Engineers
Field Forces					
Karelian					
14th Army	10G, 14 RD, 72 NRB, 31 SkiB	1236 AAR, 645 TDR, 275, 297 MtrR, 41 GMR, 325, 487 AAABn		197 MAR	31 EBn
19th Army	104, 122 RD, 77 NRB, MGBn	209 GunAR, 438 TDR, 566 MtrR, 53 GMR, 261 AAABn	377, 429 TBn	835 MAR	279 EBn
26th Army	27, 54, 186 RD, 61, 67, 80, 85 NRB, MGBn	471 AAR, 441, 444 TDR, 172, 278, 565 MtrR, 52 GMR, 297 GMBn (63 GMR), 48, 298, 369 AAABn	374, 375 TBn, 2, 3, 24, 24 AeroSBn, 73 Atr	435 MAR	259 EBn
32nd Army	37, 289, 313, 367 RD, 65 NRB, 33 SkiB, MGBn	1237 AAR, 173, 280, 298 MtrR, 63 GMR (-297 GMBn), 208, 446 AAABn	376 TBn (-KV TCo), 1, 4, 8, 21, 22, 26 AeroSBn	841 MAR	261 EBn
7th Air Army				258, 259 FAD, 260 BAD, 261 AAD, 679 TAR, 42 CRAS, 118 RAS	
Front forces	32 SkiB	32 AAABn	KV TCo (376 TBn), 28 AeroSBn, 27, 47 AtrBn		1 SDEB, 6 GBnM, 19, 27 EBn
Total (4 armies, 1 air army)	11 RDs, 7 RBs, 3 SkiBs	4 ARs, 4 TDRs, 9 MtrRs, 4 GMRs, 9 AAABns	5 TBns, 11 AeroSBns, 2 AtrBns	1 BAD, 1 AAD, 2 FADs, 4 MARs	1 EB, 7 EBns
Leningrad					
23rd Army	10, 92, 291 RD, 27 RB, 22 FR	260 AAR, 336 GunAR, 94, 883 TDR, 104 AMtrR, 73, 618 AAABn	222 TB, 5 AeroSBn	915 MAR	234 EBn

42nd Army	85, 109, 125 RD, 162 RB, 79 FR	14G, 73, 1475 AAR, 289, 304, 384, 509, 705, 760 TDR, 533 AMtrR, 631 AAAR	1, 2 AeroSBn	914 MAR	54, 585 EBn
55th Army	45G, 43, 56, 72 RD, 14 FR	12G AAR, 126 GunAR, 690 TDR, 534 AMtrR, 474 AAAR, 71 AAABn	71 AtrBn	987 MAR	325, 367 EBn
67th Army	13, 46, 90, 142, 189, 224 RD, 11, 55, 56, 102, 123, 138, 142, 250 RB, 34, 35 SkiB, 16 FR	28 AD (79 LAB, 81 GunAB, 80 HowAB, 42 MtrB), 28 AAR, 1106 GunAR, 599, 754 HowAR, HowABn, 882 TDR, 127, 134, 144 AMtrR, 174, 175 MtrR, 5, 6 GMB, 321 GMR, 575, 576, 585 GMBn, 7 AAAD (465, 632, 785, 803 AAAR), 108, 613 AAABn	1, 61, 152, 220 TB, 31, 46G TR, 86, 118 TBn, 42 AerSBn, 3 AcBn	407 MAR	53 EBn
Coastal Op Gp	48, 168 RD, 50 RB, 48, 71 NRB, 73, 338 MGABn	519 HowAR, 184 MtrR	287 TBn, 17 AeroSBn		295 EBn
13th Air Army				273, 275 FAD, 276 BAD, 277 AAD, 5 RAS, 12 CAS	
Front forces	63G, 86, 123, 268 RD, 13 RB, 260 NIB, 6 NIR, 122, 123, 124, 130, 131, 136 MGABn (Leningrad Internal Defense)	38, 320, 322 GMR, 970, 988 AAAR, 72, 89, 92, 116 AAABn	260, 261 TR, 14, 72 AtrBn		2 SDEB, 3 PBB, 52 ESB, 7 GMnM, 21, 41, 42 PBBn, 106, 267 EBn, 447 SBn
Total (4 armies, 1 op gp, 1 air army)	22 RDs, 15 RBs, 2 SkiBs, 5 FRs, 1 RR	1 AD, 12 ARs, 10 TDRs, 1 ABn, 9 MtrRs, 2 GMBs, 4 GMRs, 3 GMBns, 1 AAAD, 4 AAARs, 9 AAABns	5 TBs, 4 TRs, 3 TBns, 3 AeroSBns, 3 AtrBns	1 BAD, 1 AAD, 2 FADs, 4 MARs	2 EBs, 11 EBns, 1 PBB, 3 PBBns

—*continued*

1 FEBRUARY 1943 Continued

Fronts and Armies	Rifle, Airborne, and Cavalry	Artillery	Tank and Mechanized	Air	Engineers
Volkhov					
2nd Shock Army	11, 18, 71, 80, 147, 191, 239, 256, 314, 364, 376, 379 RD, 22 RB, 11 SkiB	13G, 21, 24, 561 AAR, 168, 430 HowARhp, 122, 191, 192, 193, 194, 499, 502, 503, 504 AMtrR, 165 MtrR, 10, 12 GMB, 20 (-211 GMBn), 29, 318 GMR, 509, 512 GMBn, 43 AAAD (464, 635, 1463, 1464 AAAR), 45 AAAD (737, 1465, 1466 AAAR), 15, 213 AAABn	16, 98 TB, 32G TR, 500, 501, 503, 507 TBn, 32, 44 AeroSBn, 22 AAATr	696 MAR	32 PBBn, 734 MSBn, 770 EBn
4th Army	44, 288, 310 RD, 24, 58 RB, 206 MGABn	214 GMBn (20 GMR)	32 AtrBn	689 MAR	365 EBn
8th Army	265, 286 RD, 1, 73 RB	71G, 70 AAR, 1096, 1097 GunAR, 884 TDR, 145 MtrR (5 MtrB), 146, 500, 501 AMtrR, 30 GMR, 41 AAAD (244, 245, 463, 634 AAAR), 177 AAABn	25 TR, 107, 502 TBn, 47, 49 AcBn, 50 AtrBn, 4 Atr	935 MAR	112 EBn
52nd Army	65, 225 RD, 38 SkiB, 150 FR	448 AAR, 506 AMtrR, 231 GMBn (28 GMR)	34, 53 AeroSBn	662 MAR	109, 366 EBn
54th Army	115, 177, 198, 281, 285, 294, 311 RD, 140 RB, 6 NRB	319 GMR, 461 AAABn	124 TB, 48 AcBn	691 MAR	364 EBn
59th Army	2, 377, 378, 382 RD, 37 SkiB, 42, 47, 215 MGABn	367 AAR, 505 AMtrR, 28 GMR (-231 GMBn)	29 TB, 48 AtrBn	660 MAR	539 MSBn, 771 EBn
14th Air Army				1 BAC (263, 293 BAD), 2 FAC (209, 215 FAD), 232, 281	

Front forces	64G, 128, 165, 372, 374 RD, 14, 53 RB, 12, 13 SkiB	2 AD (20 LAB, 7 GunAB, 4 HowAB, 5 MtrB), 8G AAR, 46 AAAD (1467, 1468, 1469, 1470 AAAR), 707 AAAR (45 AAAD), 168, 216 AAABn	7G, 122, 185 TB, 56 AeroSBn, 23 AtrBn, 123 AAAtr	AAD, 279 FAD, 280 BAD, 844 TAR, 8 LRRAS	1 EMB, 39 SDEB, 53 ESB, 2, 8 GBnM, 34, 36, 38, 55, 159 PBBn, 40, 135, 136 EBn
Total (5 armies, 1 air army)	35 RDs, 9 RBs, 1 FR, 5 SkiBs	1 AD, 13 ARs, 1 TDR, 15 MtrRs, 2 GMBs, 6 GMRs, 2 GMBns, 3 AAADs, 6 AAABns	7 TBs, 2 TRs, 6 TBns, 3 AcBns, 5 AeroSBns, 4 AtrBns	1 BAC, 1 FAC, 3 BADs, 2 AADs, 3 FADs, 6 MARs	3 EBs, 14 EBns, 6 PBBns
Northwestern					
1st Shock Army	7, 23, 53G, 129, 380, 391, 397 RD, 44, 45, 47, 86, 121 RB, 43 SkiB	589 LAR (78 LAB), 37G CAR, 701 AAR, 641 TDR, 110 AMtrR, 70 GMR, 230 GMBn (27 GMR), 709, 714 AAAR (42 AAAD)	103 TBn		55 ESB, 2, 28, 67 EBn, 92 PBBn
11th Army	12G RC (26, 202, 282 RD), 28, 43G, 55, 163, 188, 254, 370 RD, 20, 87, 126 RB, 40 SkiB	26 AD (75 LAB, 72 GunAB, 77 HowAB, 24 MtrB), 11G AAR, 1235 GunAR, 191 HowARhp, 481 MtrR, 8 GMB, 22, 26, 39 GMR, 44 AAAD (508, 708, 710, 1274 AAAR)	60 TB, 3G, 56, 227, 239 TR, 514 TBn		13 EMB, 50, 202, 223, 277 EBn, 54 PBBn
27th Army	170, 253 RD, 15, 127, 147 RB	719 LAR (75 LAB), 1199 HowARhp, 26 MtrB (27 AD), 480 MtrR, 27 GMR (-230 GMBn), 246 AAABn	150 TBn, 11, 18, 35 AeroSBn		25, 38 EBn, 50, 86 PBBn

—*continued*

1 FEBRUARY 1943 *Continued*

Fronts and Armies	Rifle, Airborne, and Cavalry	Artillery	Tank and Mechanized	Air	Engineers
34th Army	171, 182, 200, 245 RD, 144, 146, 161 RB, 91 FR	458 LAR (75 LAB), 698 LAR (78 LAB), 387 GunAR (76 GunAB), 575, 1200 HowARhp, 482 MtrR, 9 GMB, 65 GMR	83 TB, 29 AtrBn	597 BAR	238, 1391 EBn
53rd Army	166, 235, 241, 250, 348 RD, 42 SkiB	573 LAR (78 LAB), 151 GunAR, 111 MtrR (26 MtrB), 115 MtrR (24 MtrR), 490 MtrR, 1 GMD (1, 2 GMB, 96, 307, 308, 309 GMR), 42 GMBn	177 TB, 57 TR, 19, 36 AeroSBn, 35 AtrBn		11, 17, 134 EBn, 58 PBBn
6th Air Army				239, 240 FAD, 242 NBAD, 243 AAD, 58 BAR, 72 RAR, 699 TAR	
Front forces	14G RC (hq), 41 SkiB	27 AD (78 LAB, 76 GunAB, 74 HowAB), 42 AAAD (620, 729 AAAR), 29, 239, 242, 250, 467 AAABn	543 TBn		41 SDEB, 9 GBnM, 56 PBBn, 222 EBn
Total (5 armies, 1 air army)	2 RCs, 28 RDs, 14 RBs, 4 SkiBs, 1 FR	2 ADs, 9 ARs, 1 TDR, 5 MtrRs, 1 GMD, 2 GMBs, 7 GMRs, 2 AAADs, 6 AAABns	3 TBs, 5 TRs, 4 TBns, 5 AeroSBns, 2 AtrBns	1 AAD, 2 FADs, 1 NBAD, 2 BARs, 1 RAR	3 EBs, 16 EBns, 6 PBBns
Kalinin					
3rd Shock Army	2G RC (8G, 33, 117 RD), 5GRC (9, 46G RD), 19, 21G, 28, 32, 150, 257, 357, 360, 381 RD, 23, 26, 31, 46, 54, 100, 145 RB, 44 SkiB	38, 41G CAR, 270, 455, 613 AAR, 1094, 1190 GunAR, 385 HowAR, 1198 HowARhp, 141, 171, 316, 389, 483, 699 TDR, 560, 561, 603 AMtrR, 550, 551 MtrR, 11 GMB, 61, 77 GMR, 43, 106, 107, 205,	2 MC (18, 34, 43 MB, 33, 36 TB, 68 MtcBn, 33 AcBn, 79 TDR, 410 GMBn), 78, 184, 236 TB, 46, 47 MB, 13G, 34, 39, 45 TR, 170, 515 TBn, 57,		225, 288, 289, 293 EBn

208

Army	RD/RB	AR/TDR	TB/MC	EBn/MSBn
4th Shock Army	47, 332, 334, 358 RD, 45 SkiB, 26 DB	240 GMBn, 243, 582, 609 AAAR	62 AtrBn	290, 348 EBn, 736 MSBn
22nd Army	155, 185, 362 RD, 114 RB, 296 MGABn	488 AAR, 569, 759, 765 TDR, 408, 552 AMtrR, 17 GMR (-29 GMBn), 617 AAABn	171 TBn	20, 114, 249, 251 EBn 125 PBBn
39th Army	135, 158, 178, 186, 373 RD, 101, 117, 130, 136 RB, 89 MGABn	10G, 43 AAR, 1157 GunAR, 376, 472 HowAR, 144, 610 TDR, 553, 554 MtrR, 34 GMR (-123 MGBn), 109 GMBn, 618, 621 AAAR, 183, 397 AAABn	3 MC (1, 3, 10 MB, 1G, 49 TB, 58 MtcBn, 34 AcBn, 35 TDR, 405 GMBn), 48 MB	54 SB, 17, 228 EBn
41st Army	6 RC (74, 75, 78, 91 RB), 17G, 93, 134, 262 RD	421 AAR, 545 GunAR, 480, 827 HowAR, 269, 587, 712 TDR, 555, 556 AMtrR, 170 MtrR, 99 GMR, 47 GMBn, 601 AAAR	28, 81 TB	
43rd Army	145, 179, 234, 306 RD	83 CAR, 1098 GunAR, 64, 440, 1224 HowAR, 301, 592 TDR, 557, 558 AMtrR, 24 GMR, 225, 717 AAAR, 490 AAABn; 283 HowAR, 232, 437, 452, 478 TDR, 118, 559 AMtrR, 123 GMBn (34 GMR), 219 GMBn (17 GMR), 246 AAAR	1 MC (19, 35, 37 MB, 65, 219 TB, 57 MtcBn, 32 AcBn, 75 TDR), 104 TB, 229 TR; 143 TB	110, 292, 903 EBn, 60 PBBn, 737 MSBn; 273, 312, 353, 354 EBn
3rd Air Army		1 AAC (266, 292 AAD), 2 AAC (231 AAD), 1 FAC (210, 274 FAD), 212 AAD, 211 NBAD, 256 FAD, 6G AAR, 11 RAR, 195, 648, 708, 881, 882, 883 MAR, 887 TAR, 13, 36 CAS		

—*continued*

1 FEBRUARY 1943 Continued

Fronts and Armies	Rifle, Airborne, and Cavalry	Artillery	Tank and Mechanized	Air	Engineers
Front forces					2 EMB, 5 SDEB, 56 ESB, 210, 245, 352 EBn, 57, 63, 93, 94, 106, 122 PBBn
Total (6 armies, 1 air army)	4 RCs, 37 RDs, 16 RBs, 2 SkiBs, 1 DB	26 ARs, 20 TDRs, 18 MtrRs, 1 GMB, 6 GMRs, 7 GMBns, 10 AAARs, 6 AAABns	3 MCs, 3 MBs, 7 TBs, 5 TRs, 3 TBns, 2 AtrBns	2 AAC, 1 FAC, 4 AADs, 3 FADs, 1 NBAD, 1 AAR, 6 MARs, 1 RAR	4 EBs, 24 EBns, 6 PBBns
Western					
5th Army	29G, 108, 144, 352 RD	486 GunAR (10 GunAB), 66G, 554, 572 GunAR, 590 HowARhp, 409 GunABnhp, 5G, 696 TDR, 135 MtrR (2 MtrB), 537 AMtrR, 60 GMR (-35 GMBn), 41 GMBn, 1272 AAAR	153 TB, 7, 40 AeroSBn, 22 AtrBn	162 MAR	296, 297 EBn
10th Army	31G, 290, 323, 330, 385 RD, 9 DB	1091 GunAR, 533, 637 TDR, 123 MtrR (2 MtrB), 543, 544 AMtrR, 36 GMBn, 1268 AAAR	94 TB, 1 AtrBn	880 MAR	303, 345, 368 EBn
16th Army	11G, 97, 217, 324 RD, 4 RB	551 LAR (21 LAB), 523 GunAR, 600, 649 TDR, 545, 546 AMtrR, 10 GMBn, 1280 AAAR, 4 AAABn	6G TB, 43 AtrBn	168 MAR	226, 243, 367 EBn
20th Army	8G RC (26G RD, 150 RB), 30, 42G, 251, 331, 336, 415 RD	3 AD (15 LAB, 5 GunAB, 1 HowAB, 7 MtrB), 56G CAR, 17G, 403 AAR, 49 GunAR, 15G HowAR, 3, 6G TDR,	18 TB, 37, 38 AeroSBn	431 MAR	291, 301, 302 EBn

Army					
29th Army	82, 312 RD, 3G MRD, 28, 35, 40, 49 RB, 307 MGABn	535 AMtrR, 14 GMB, 54, 59 GMR, 14 AAAD (715, 718, 721, 1277 AAAR), 50, 64, 525 AABn	161 TB	627 MAR	71, 267 EBn
30th Army	215, 220, 274, 359, 369 RD, 49 SkiB	537 AAR, 39, 517, 1093 GunAR, 1G, 992 TDR, 536 AMtrR, 35 GMBn (60 GMR), 28 GMBn, 716 AAAR			
		646 AAR, 392, 542 GunAR, 16G HowAR, 544, 1221 HowARhp, 758, 1179 TDR, 171 MtrR (7 MtrB), 13 GMB, 74 GMR (-353 MGBn), 31, 201, 308 GMBn, 240, 341 AAAR, 245, 500 AAABn	10G, 146, 196 TB, 2G MtcR, 52 AtrBn	884 MAR	51 PBBn, 263 EBn
31st Army	88, 118, 133, 371 RD	74, 75G AAR, 644, 1165 GunAR, 128, 360, 364 HowAR, 529, 873 TDR, 549 MtrR, 40 GMR, 13 GMBn, 1269 AAAR, 614 AAABn	120, 145 TB, 519 TBn, 6, 20 AeroSBn, 21 AtrBn	885 MAR	72, 113 EBn, 99 PBBn, 537 MSBn
33rd Army	7G RC (5G RD, 112 RB), 17, 50, 53, 110, 160, 222 RD, 50 SkiB	55G CAR, 2G, 761, 995 AAR, 557, 564, 1099 GunAR, 2G, 868 TDR, 113 MtrR (2 MtrB), 538, 539 AMtrR, 3 GMBn, 1266 AAAR	213, 248, 256 TB, 520 TBn, 6 AtrBn	172 MAR	42, 298, 321 EBn
49th Army	18G, 42, 164, 338 RD	1G GunAR, 593 TDR, 540 AMtrR, 40 GMBn, 1273 AAAR	138 TBn	510 MAR	305, 306, 369 EBn
50th Army	58, 69, 146, 325, 344, 413 RD	447 AAR, 570 GunAR, 685 TDR, 541, 542 AMtrR, 353 GMBn (74 GMR), 1275 AAAR	2G, 108 TB, 12, 41 AeroSBn	745 MAR	307, 309 EBn

—*continued*

1 FEBRUARY 1943 Continued

Fronts and Armies	Rifle, Airborne, and Cavalry	Artillery	Tank and Mechanized	Air	Engineers
61st Army	9G RC (12G RD, 105, 108, 110 RB), 149, 342, 356 RD, 51 SkiB, 12 DB	60G CAR, 67G AAR, 546, 706 TDR, 130 MtrR (2 MtrB), 547, 548 AMtrR, 1282 AAAR	68 TB, 10 AtrBn	875 MAR	310, 344 EBn
1st Air Army				203, 234 FAD, 204 BAD, 213 NBAD, 224, 233 AAD, 1 MedAR, 10 RAR, 179 FAR, 289 AAR, 713 TAR, 20, 21 CRAS	
Front forces	1, 16, 20G, 19, 113, 139, 194, 246, 247, 326, 354, 375 RD, 36, 125, 128, 148, 153 RB	6 AD (21 LAB, 10 GunAB, 18 HowAB, 2 MtrB), 1222 HowARhp, 2, 348 GMBn, 17 AAAD (1267, 1276, 1278, 1279 AAAR), 739, 1265, 1270, 1271, 1281 AAAR, 324 AAABn, 16, 17, 18, 19, 31, 32, 33 AAABtry	5 TC (24, 41, 70 TB, 5 MRB), 6 TC (22, 100, 200 TB, 6 MRB), 9 TC (23, 95, 187 TB, 8 MRB), Special TBn, 145 AAATr		10, 11, 12 EMB, 33 SDEB, 11 GBnM, 6, 84, 122, 129, 133, 229, 230 EBn, 9, 48, 61, 62, 87, 88, 89, 90, 91 PBBn, 738 MSBn
Total (11 armies, 1 air army)	3 RCs, 64 RDs, 1 MRD, 15 RBs, 3 SkiBs, 2 DBs	2 ADs, 41 ARs, 20 TDRs, 1 ABn, 15 MtrRs, 2 GMBs, 5 GMRs, 12 GMBns, 2 AAADs, 16 AAARs, 8 AAABns	3 TCs, 16 TBs, 1 MtcR, 4 TBns, 8 AeroSBns, 7 AtrBns	1 BAD, 2 AADs, 2 FADs, 1 NBAD, 1 AAR, 1 FAR, 11 MARs, 1 RAR	4 EBs, 36 EBns, 11 PBBns
Briansk					
3rd Army	5, 60, 269, 283, 287 RD, 116 NRB	420 AAR, 584, 1242 TDR, 474, 475 MtrR, 6 GMR, 1284 AAAR	20 TC (11, 155 TB, AcBn), 31, 55 AtrBn		348 EBn

13th Army	8, 15, 74, 81, 132, 148, 211, 280, 307 RD	5 AD (16 LAB, 24 GunAB, 9 HowAB, 1 MtrB), 12 AD (46 LAB, 41 GunAB, 32 HowAB), 19G AAR, 130, 543, 874 TDR, 131 AMtrR, 476, 477, 479 MtrR, 65 GMR, 1287 AAAR	79 TB (19 TC), 118, 129 TB, 42, 43, 193 TR, 45, 55 AeroSBn, 49 AtrBn	130 SBn, 233, 275 EBn
48th Army	41, 73, 143, 399 RD	478 MtrR	37, 54 AtrBn	53 PBBn, 131 SBn, 313 EBn
2nd Tank Army	6G, 16 RD	37 GMR	16 TC (107, 109, 164 TB, 15 MRB), 51 MtcBn	357 EBn
15th Air Army				
Front forces	137 RD, 2 DD (3, 4 DB)	563, 567 TDR, 5 GMD (22, 23 GMB, 323, 324 GMR), 286 GMBn, 16 AAAD (728, 1283, 1285, 1286 AAAR), 461 AAAR, 386, 617 AAABn	11 TC (53, 59, 160 TB, 12 MRB, 8 AcBn), 19 TC (101, 202 TB, 19 MRB, AcBn), 11G TB, 29G TR, 55 MtcBn, 45 AtrBn, 133, 134 AAAtr	3 BAC (241, 301 BAD), 225, 299 AAD, 284 NBAD, 286 BAD, 32 RAR, 778 LBAR	6 EMB, 8 SDEB, 12 GBnM, 49, 50, 131 PBBn, 231 EBn, 740 MSBn
Total (3 armies, 1 tank army, 1 air army)	21 RDs, 1 RB, 1 DD	2 ADs, 2 ARs, 7 TDRs, 7 MtrRs, 1 GMD, 3 GMRs, 1 GMBn, 1 AAAD, 3 AAARs, 2 AAABns	4 TCs, 3 TBs, 4 TRs, 2 MtcBns, 2 AeroSBns, 6 AtrBns	1 BAC, 2 BADs, 2 AADs, 1 FAD, 1 NBAD, 1 RAR, 1 LBAR	2 EBs, 10 EBns, 4 PBBns
Voronezh				
38th Army	167, 206, 232, 237, 240 RD, 7 DB	125 GunAR (41 GunAB), 1112 GunAR, 611, 1244 TDR, 491, 492 MtrR, 21 GMB (4 GMD), 66 GMR	180 TB		268 EBn, 1505 MSBn

—continued

1 FEBRUARY 1943 Continued

Fronts and Armies	Rifle, Airborne, and Cavalry	Artillery	Tank and Mechanized	Air	Engineers
40th Army	25G, 100, 107, 183, 303, 305, 309, 340 RD, 129, 253 RB, 16 DB	512 HowAR (29 HowAB), 76G GunAR, 4G, 595 TDR, 593, 594 MtrR, 36 GMR, 332 AAABn	116 TB, 26 AtrBn		14 EBn
60th Army	121, 141, 322 RD, 104, 248 RB, 8, 14 DB	1156 AAR, 522, 1148 HowARhp, 694, 1178 TDR, 128, 138 AMtrR, 495, 497 MtrR, 98 GMR, 326 GMBn, 217, 235 AAAR	150 TB, 44 AtrBn		317 EBn
3rd Tank Army	48, 62G, 111, 160, 184 RD, 37 RB	8 AD (2 LAB, 12 GunAB, 28 HowAB), 1172, 1245 TDR, 15 GMB, 62, 97, 315 GMR, 71, 470, 391 AAAR	12 TC (30, 97, 106 TB, 13 MRB, 6 AcBn), 15 TC (88, 113, 195 TB, 52 MRB, 5 AcBn), 179 TB, 39 AcBn		182 EBn
2nd Air Army				205, 269 FAD, 208 NBAD, 227, 291 AAD, 50 RAR, 375, 376, 878 MAR, 2 TAR, 13 CAS	
Front forces	18 RC (161, 180, 219, 270 RD), 4, 6, 8 SkiB, 37 RB, 6G CC (8, 13G CD, 161 MtrR, 20 CABn, 7 TDBn), 1 DD (2, 6, 10 DB)	10 AD (22 LAB, 27 GunAB, 29 HowAB), 1109 AAR, 875 HowAR, 1240 TDR, 4 GMD (16, 20 GMB, 16, 314 GMR), 496 AMtrR, 5 AAAD (670, 743, 1119, 1181 AAAR), 1288, 1289 AAAR, 626 AAABn	4 TC (45, 69, 102 TB, 4 MRB), 14, 86, 96, 173, 192, 201 TB, 262 TR, 43, 50 AeroSBn, 34 AtrBn		4 EMB, 60 ESB, 13 GBnM, 15, 23 PBBn, 235 EBn

Total (3 armies, 1 tank army, 1 air army)	1 RC, 25 RDs, 6 RBs, 3 SkiBs, 1 DD, 4 DBs, 1 CC, 2 CDs	2 ADs, 7 ARs, 9 TDRs, 9 MtrRs, 1 GMD, 1 GMB, 6 GMRs, 1 GMBn, 1 AAAD, 7 AAARs, 2 AAABns	3 TCs, 10 TBs, 1 TR, 2 AeroSBns, 1 AcBn, 3 AtrBns	2 AADs, 2 FADs, 1 NBAD, 3 MARs, 1 RAR	2 EBs, 7 EBns, 2 PBBns

Southwestern					
1st Guards Army	4G RC (35, 41G, 195 RD), 6G RC (38, 44, 58G RD), 57G, 58, 78, 244 RD	9 AD (407, 442, 456 LAR, 47, 127 GunAR, 212, 221, 230 HowAR), 40, 42G CAR, 302, 303 GMR, 115 GMBn, 4 AAAD (606, 633, 640, 658 AAAR), 139 AAABn	127 TR, 67 MtcBn		62 ESB, 26, 28, 100 PBBn, 350, 358 EBn, 538 MSBn
3rd Guards Army	14G RC (14, 50, 61G RD), 59, 60G, 203, 243, 266, 279 RD	7 AD (210, 525 LAR, 213, 1092 GunAR, 124, 320, 877 HowAR, 101, 103 MtrR) 1110 GunAR, 426, 532, 1243, 1249 TDR, 58, 100, 301 GMR, 579, 580, 626, 1257 AAAR, 60 AAABn	1G MC (1, 2, 3G MB, 16, 17G TR, 116G AR, 52G TDR, 407 GMBn), 2G TC (4, 25, 26G TB, 4G MRB, 9 AcBn), 2 TC (26, 99, 169 TB, 58 MRB, 12 AcBn), 23 TC (3, 39, 135 TB, 56 MRB, 11 AcBn, 442 GMBn), 5G MRB, 243 TR, 50, 54 MtcBn		37, 102 PBBn, 322 EBn
6th Army	15 RC (172, 350 RD), 6, 267 RD, 106 RB	870 LAR (7 AD), 150, 462 TDR, 45, 87 GMR, 1290, 1474 AAAR, 126 AAABn	115 TB, 212 TR		123 PBBn, 370 EBn
5th Tank Army	47, 54G, 321, 333, 346 RD, 8 CC (21, 35, 112 CD, 148 MtrR, 263 CABn, 8 TDBn)	396 AAR, 312, 518 GunAR, 152 HowAR, 33, 174, 179, 481 TDR, 107 MtrR (7 AD), 35, 75 GMR, 307 GMBn, 3 AAAD (1084, 1089,1114 1118 AAAR), 586 AAAR, 227 AAABn	5 MC (45, 49, 50 MB, 168, 188 TR, 64 MtcBn, 45 AcBn, 484 TDR, 406 GMBn), 3 GMtcR, 56 MtcBn		44 SDEB, 101, 130 PBBn, 181, 269 EBn

—continued

1 FEBRUARY 1943 Continued

Fronts and Armies	Rifle, Airborne, and Cavalry	Artillery	Tank and Mechanized	Air	Engineers
Mobile Op Gp			4G TC (12, 13, 14G TB, 3G MRB), 10 TC (178, 183, 186 TB, 11 MRB), 18 TC (110, 170, 181 TB, 32 MRB, 52 MtcBn, 1 AcBn)		15 EMB
17th Air Army				1 MAC (267 AAD, 288 FAD, 3 MAC (202 BAD, 207 FAD, 290 AAD), 221 BAD, 262 NBAD, 282 FAD, 208, 637 AAR, 282 MAR, 371 TAR, 34, 35 CAS	
Front forces	229 RB	534, 1176 TDR, 188 MtrR, 241, 247, 303, 878 AAAR	1G TC (15, 16, 17G TB, 1G MRB, 1G AcBn, 80G AAAR), 3 TC (50, 51, 103 TB, 57 MRB), 25 TC (111, 162, 175 TB, 16 MRB, 53 MtcBn, 3 AcBn, 219 AAAR), 126, 141 TR, 47, 64 AeroSBn		8 HPBR, 351 EBn
Total (3 armies, 1 tank army, 1 op gp, 1 air army)	4 RCs, 28 RDs, 2 RBs, 1 CC, 3 CDs	2 ADs, 7 ARs, 12 TDRs, 1 MtrR, 9 GMRs, 2 GMBns, 2 AAADs, 12 AAARs, 4 AAABns	2 MCs, 9 TCs, 1 TB, 1 MRB, 5 TRs, 1 MtcR, c4 MtcBns, 2 AeroSBns	2 MACs, 2 BADs, 2 AADs, 3 FADs, 1 NBAD, 2 AARs, 1 MAR	3 EBs, 1 PBR, 8 EBns, 8 PBBns

Don

Army	Units		
21st Army	51, 52, 66G, 96, 120, 173, 252, 298 RD, 1, 21, 99 SkiBns	1 AD (8 LAB, 19 GunAB, 13 HowAB, 4 MtrB), 4 AD (6 LAB, 3 GunAB, 14 HowAB, 8 MtrB), 99, 156 AAR, 1184, 1241, 1248 TDR, 19 GMB (3 GMD), 85 GMR, 309 GMBn, 1 AAAD (1068, 1085, 1090, 1116 AAAR), 1042, 1263 AAAR, 31, 307 AAABn	121 TB, 1, 5, 9, 10, 14, 15, 48G TR	205, 540 EBn
62nd Army	13, 39G, 45, 95, 138, 284 RD, 92 RB, 156 FR	266 AAR, 1103 GunAR, 397, 499 TDR, 141 AMtrR, 92 GMR, 242 AAAR		326, 327 EBn
64th Army	7 RC (93, 96, 97 RB), 15, 36G, 29, 38, 204, 422 RD, 143 RB, 20 DB, 45, 77, 115, 118 FR, 166, 172, 175, 177, 303 MGABn	19 HAD (70G, 123 AAR, 457, 1108, 1159 GunAR, 5 HowARhp, 400 GunABnhp), 1104, 1111, 1168 GunAR, 58, 184, 186, 493, 496, 500, 502, 536, 565, 762, 1188 TDR, 140 AMtrR, 18 GMB (3 GMD), 1261 AAAR	90, 254 TB, 38 MRB	175, 328, 329, 330 EBn
65th Army	27, 67G, 23, 24, 214, 233, 260 RD	11 AD (31 LAB, 45 GunAB, 40 HowAB), 101 HowAR, 110 HowARhp (19 HAD), 318 HowARhp, 93 GMR (3 GMD), 94 GMR, 18 AAAD (278, 297, 722, 1262 AAAR)	91 TB, 47G TR	321 EBn
66th Army	84, 99, 116, 226, 273, 299, 243 RD, 149 RB, 54, 159 FR	1102, 1158 GunAR, 406 GunABnhp, 1180 TDR, 136, 143 MtrR (4 MtrB), 56 GMR	7, 8G TR	431, 432 EBn
16th Air Army				2 BAC (223, 285 BAD), 220, 283 FAD, 228 AAD, 271 NBAD, 16 RAR, 45 CAS

—continued

1 FEBRUARY 1943 Continued

Fronts and Armies	Rifle, Airborne, and Cavalry	Artillery	Tank and Mechanized	Air	Engineers
Front forces	66, 154 NRB	119, 126 MtrR (4 MtrB), 137 MtrR, 2 GMD (3, 17 GMB, 5, 84, 310, 317 GMR), 3 GMD (4 GMB, 312, 313 GMR), 18, 57, 72, 89, 91 GMR, 325, 581, 1259 AAAR, 27, 67, 141, 436 AAABn	35, 234 TR, 48, 49, 52 AeroSBn, 39, 40, 59 AtrBn, 377 AAAtrBn		5, 8 EMB, 16 SDEB, 57 ESB, 14 GBnM, 6, 7, 9, 19, 20, 104 PBBn, 120, 257 EBn, 741 MSBn
Total (5 armies, 1 air army)	1 RC, 34 RDs, 8 RBs, 6 FRs, 1 DB	4 ADs, 11 ARs, 17 TDRs, 1 ABn, 3 MtrRs, 2 GMDs, 9 GMRs, 1 GMBn, 2 AAADs, 7 AAARs, 6 AAABns	4 TBs, 1 MRB, 12 TRs, 3 AeroSBns, 4 AtrBns	1 BAC, 2 BADs, 1 AAD, 2 FADs, 1 NBAD, 1 RAR	4 EBs, 15 EBns, 6 PBBns
Southern					
2nd Guards Army	1G RC (24, 33G, 98 RD), 13G RC (3, 49G, 387 RD), 300 RD	648 AAR, 506, 1095, 1100, 1101 GunAR, 435, 535, 1250 TDRs, 488 MtrR, 4, 23, 48, 88 GMRs, 15 AAAD (281, 342, 722, 1264 AAAR)	2G MC (4, 5, 6G MB, 21, 22G TR, 117G AR, 54G TDBn, 408 GMBn), 5G MC (10, 11, 12G MB, 53G TR, 2G MtcBn, 4G AcBn, 104G TDR, 409 GMBn), 3G TC (3, 18, 19G TB, 2G MRB, 3G AcBn, 324 GMBn), 52, 128, 136, 223 TR		1 PBB, 355 EBn, 742 MSBn
5th Shock Army	4, 40G, 258, 315 RD, 5 DB, 3G CC (5, 6G, 32 CD, 152 MtrR, 8 CABn, 3G TDBn)	1162 GunAR, 274, 331 HowAR, 507, 364 TDR, 21 GMR, 1086 AAAR (2 AAAD)	8G TB		61 ESB, 258, 827 EBn

28th Army	34G, 248 RD, 52, 79, 98, 99, 152, 156, 159 RB, 78, 116 FR	483, 484, 485 MtrR	6G TB, 51 TR, 35 AcBn, 30, 33, 46 AtrBn	57, 130 EBn, 121 PBBn
51st Army	87, 91, 126, 302 RD, 76 FR	1105 GunAR, 85G HowAR, 491, 492, 665, 1246 TDR, 486 AMtrR, 125 MtrR, 2, 19, 51, 80, 90 GMR, 2 AAAD (1069, 1113, 1117 AAAR), 77G AAAR 459 AAAR	3G MC (7, 8, 9G MB, 41G TR, 1G MtcBn, 175G AcBn, 334 GMBn), 4G MC (13, 14, 15G MB, 41 TR, 591 AAAR)	205, 275 EBn
8th Air Army			2 MAC (201, 235 FAD, 214 AAD), 206, 226 AAD, 268, 287 FAD, 270 BAD, 272 NBAD, 289 MAD, 8 RAR, 932 MAR, 678 TAR, 31, 32 CAS	
Front forces	4 CC (61, 81 CD, 149 TDR)	101G, 13, 14, 383, 521, 530 TDR, 487 AMtrR, 489 MtrR, 293, 416, 585, 607, 622, 1485 AAAR	13, 56 TB, 198 TR, 9, 10, 23, 27 AeroSBn, 28 AtrBn	2 PBB, 7, 9 EMB, 43 SDEB, 63 ESB, 1 HPBR, 17 GBnM, 119, 240 EBn, 1504 MSBn
Total (4 armies, 1 air army)	2 RCs, 17 RDs, 7 RBs, 1 DB, 2 CCs, 5 CDs, 3 FRs	10 ARs, 15 TDRs, 8 MtrRs, 10 GMRs, 2 AAADs, 8 AAARs	4 MCs, 1 TC, 4 TBs, 6 TRs, 4 AeroSBns, 1 AcBn, 4 AtrBns	1 MAC, 1 BAD, 3 AADs, 1 MAD, 4 FADs, 1 NBAD, 1 MAR, 1 RAR	5 EBs, 2 PBBs, 1 PBR, 12 EBns, 1 PBBn
North Caucasus				
9th Army	9 RC (43, 157, 256 RB), 11G RC (7, 8G, 34, 57 RB), 11 RC (19, 84, 131 RB)	98G, 807, 960 CAR, 117 TDR, 10 MtrR, 52 GMtrBn, 12, 13 MtrBn, 50 GMR, 1260 AAAR	207 TB, 562 TBn	61, 121 EBn, 85 PBBn

—continued

1 FEBRUARY 1943 Continued

Fronts and Armies	Rifle, Airborne, and Cavalry	Artillery	Tank and Mechanized	Air	Engineers
37th Army	2G, 223, 295, 389, 409, 414 RD	68G AAR, 1174 TDR, 132 AMtrR, 20 MtrBn, 25 GMR, 772 AAABn			112, 116, 336 EBn, 1574, 1605 SBn
44th Army	151, 271, 320, 347, 416 RD	1232 AAR, 747 TDR, 14 MtrBn			19 EBn, 1543, 1670 SBn
58th Army	77, 276, 317, 351, 417 RD	22 TDR, 133 AMtrR, 9 MtrR, 49 GMR, 594 AAAR			170, 334 EBn
4th Air Army				216 MAD, 217, 229 FAD, 218 NBAD, 219 BAD, 230 AAD, 446, 750 MAR	
Front forces	10 RC (89 RD, 59, 62, 164 RB), 4G CC (9, 10G, 30 CD, 149 MtrR, 2G CABn, 4 TDBn),5G CC (11, 12G, 63 CD, MtrBn, 13G CABn, 5 TDBn)	4G, 268, 337, 1169 AAR, 136, 1147 HowARhp, 92, 98, 103, 1255 TDR, 1 MtrB, 44 GMR, 59 GMBn (8 GMR) , 259 GMBn, 19 AAAD (1332, 1338, 1344, 1350 AAAR), 255, 740 AAAR, 179, 504, 540 AAABn	2, 15, 52, 63, 140 TB, 134, 221, 225 TR, 75, 132, 249, 266, 488 TBn, 62, 65, 66 MtcBn, 16, 36, 37, 42, 43, 46 AcBn, 8, 19, 36, 66 AtrBn		1, 2, 5 MtnEMB, 65 ESB, 9, 51, 123 EBn, 35, 37 PBBn, 97 MSBn, 1344, 1561 SBn
Total (4 armies, 1 air army)	4 RCs, 17 RDs, 13 RBs, 2 CCs, 6 CDs	1 AR, 8 TDRs, 1 MtrB, 4 MtrRs, 5 MtrBns, 4 GMRs, 1 GMBn, 1 AAAD, 5 AAARs, 3 AAABns	6 TBs, 3 TRs, 6 TBns, 3 MtcBns, 6 AcBns, 4 AtrBns	1 BAD, 1 AAD, 1 MAD, 2 FADs, 1 NBAD, 2 MARs	4 EBs, 18 EBns, 3 PBBns
Trans-Caucasus (Black Sea Gp of Forces)					
18th Army	236, 353, 395 RD, 10, 68, 119 RD	647 AAR, 418 TDR, MtrR, 67 GMR, 2G PackMtrBn, 2G PackMtrBtry, 236 AAAR			50, 332 EBn

46th Army	9 MtnRD, 31 RD, 40 RB, 2, 23, 33 MtnRR, 1, 2, 3, 4, 5, 6, 7, 8, 9, 10, 11, 12, 13, 14, 15 MtnRDet, 69 FR	195 PackMtrR, 1G PackMtrBn	11 AtrBn	68, 273 EBn
47th Army	3 RC (9, 60, 155 RB), 176, 216, 318, 337, 339, 383 RD, 242 MtnRD, 8G, 103 RB, 81, 255 NRB, 323, 324, 327 NIBn	1014 CAR, 69G, 25, 547, 1167, 1230, 1231 AAR, 81 HowAR, 350 HowARhp, 18, 490, 1115 TDR, 16 MtrBn, 8 (-59 GMBn), 305 GMR, 48 GMBn, 1, 3, 4, 5, 6G PackMtrBtry, 253 AAAR, 92G CAR, 377, 880 AR, 1195 HowAR, 489, 1187 TDR, 196, 197 PackMtrBn, 54 GMtrBn, 249, 257, 879, 1258 AAAR, 30, 57, 508 AAABn	151 TB, 62, 126, 563 TBn	91, 256 EBn
56th Army	10G RC (4, 5, 6G RB), 32, 55G, 61, 394 RD, 20, 83 MtnRD, 9G, 7, 16, 76, 111 RB, 1135 RR (339 RD)		564 TBn	16, 174, 333 EBn
5th Air Army				
Group forces	328 RD	20 AAAD (1333, 1339, 1345, 1351 AAAR), 574, 763 AAAR, 14, 17, 21, 364 AAABn	12 AtrBn, 3 Atr	132 BAD, 286, 295 FAD, 718 MAR, 742 RAR, 763 LBAR
Front forces	13 RC (hq), 16 RC (51, 107, 165 RB), 402 RD, 83 RB, 151 FR, MtnRBn, ParaR, ParaBn	39G GunAR, 526, 1023, 1150 HowARhp, 233 TDR, 2 MtrB, 1G TrollyMtrBn	5G TB, 258 TBn, 41, 42, 65 AtrBn	974 BAR	3 EMB, 13, 27 SDEB, 15 GBnM, 11 SBn, 8, 132 EBn, 19, 54, 97 PBBn
Total (4 armies, 1 air army)	4 RCs, 20 RDs, 23 RBs, 3 RRs, 1 AbnR, 2 FRs	18 ARs, 7 TDRs, 1 MtrB, 4 MtrRs, 3 MtrBns, 3 GMRs, 4 GMBns, 1 AAAD, 8 AAARs, 7 AAABns	2 TBs, 5 TBns, 5 AtrBns	1 BAD, 2 FADs, 1 MAR, 1 RAR, 1 BAR, 1 LBAR	3, 4 MtnEMB, 64 ESB, 16 GBnM, 21, 96, 98 PBBn, 75, 337, 338 EBn, 9 EBs, 17 EBns, 6 PBBns

—*continued*

1 FEBRUARY 1943 Continued

Fronts and Armies	Rifle, Airborne, and Cavalry	Artillery	Tank and Mechanized	Air	Engineers
Separate Armies					
7th Army	4 RC (272, 368 RD, 69 NRB), 21, 67, 114 RD, 70 NRB, 3 NIB, 162 FR	109 HowAR, 354 HGunABn, 460, 514 TDR, 530 AMtrR, 46, 64 GMR, 54, 268, 616 AAABn	363, 431 TBn, 14, 15, 16 AeroSBn	4G BAR, 415, 524 FAR, 716 LBAR, 119 RAS	1G SBn, 18 GBnM, 18, 36, 260 EBn, 40 PBBn
Total (1 army)	1 RC, 5 RDs, 3 RBs, 1 FR	1 AR, 2 TDRs, 1 ABn, 1 MtrR, 2 GMRs, 3 AAABns	2 TBs, 3 AeroSBn	1 BAR, 2 FARs, 1 LBAR	5 EBns, 1 PBBn
Moscow Defense Zone	119, 152, 153, 154, 155, 157, 160, 161 FR	1146 CAR, 402, 527, 1149, 1152 HowARhp, 402 GunABnhp, 12, 222, 520, 562, 1070, 1071, 1072, 1073, 1074, 1075, 1076, 1144 TDR, 408, 1160, 1161 HTDR, 253 AAABn	81 MtcBn		161, 162, 340, 341, 342, 693 EBn
Total	8 FRs	5 ARs, 15 TDRs, 1 ABn, 1 AAABn	1 MtcBn		6 EBns
Long-Range and Reconnaissance Aviation					
Total				1, 3, 17, 24, 36, 45, 50, 53, 62, 113, 222 LRAD, 747 LRAR, 2, 4, 40 LRRAR 11 LRADs, 1 LRAR, 3 LRRARs	
Grand Total (13 *fronts*, 64 armies, 3 tank armies, 13 air armies, 2 op gps, 1 def zone)	26 RCs, 364 RDs, 1 MRD, 139 RBs, 22 SkiBs, 2 DDs, 9 DBs, 6 CCs, 16 CDs, 27 FRs, 4 RRs, 1 AbnR	16 ADs, 177 ARs, 148 TDRs, 5 ABns, 2 MtrBs, 108 MtrRs, 8 MtrBns, 5 GMDs, 10 GMBs, 78 GMRs, 34 GMBns, 19 AAADs, 80 AAARs, 72 AAABns	9 MCs, 20 TCs, 68 TBs, 3 MBs, 2 MRBs, 47 TRs, 2 MtcRs, 38 TBns, 10 MtcBns, 11 AcBns, 48 AeroSBns, 46 AtrBns	3 BACs, 2 AACs, 3 MACs, 2 FACs, 11 LRADs, 15 BADs, 22 AADs, 2 MADs, 30 FADs, 9 NBADs, 1 LRAR, 4 BARs, 4 AARs, 3 FARs, 39 MARs, 11 RARs, 3 LBARs	43 EBs, 206 EBns, 3 PBBs, 2 PBRs, 64 PBBns

Stavka VGK Reserve

24th Army	Hq		
57th Army	156 MRBn		
2nd Res. Army	131, 259 RD, 32 RB		
Airborne forces	1, 2, 3, 4, 5, 6, 7, 8, 9, 10G AbnD		
Separate	49, 64, 152, 157, 169, 196, 229, 263, 277 RD, 124, 151 RB, 1, 2, 5, 7, 9, 10, 14, 15, 16, 17, 18, 19, 20, 21, 22, 23, 24, 25, 26, 27, 28, 29, 30 SkiB, 1G CC (1, 2, 7G CD, 150 MtrR, 4 CABn, 193 GMtrBn, 1G TDBn), 2G CC (3, 4G, 20 CD, 151 MtrR, 5 CABn, 194 GMtrBn, 2G TDBn), 7, 8, 24, 97 CD	29, 34, 140, 378, 419, 863 TDR, 11 MtrB (12 AD), 27 MtrB, 76 GMR, 9 AAAD (800, 974, 981, 993 AAAR), 1472, 1473, 1487, 1488 AAAR	9G, 92, 112, 135 TB, 2, 4, 6, 11, 12, 28, 30G, 58, 59, 60, 61, 114, 119, 166, 167, 189, 251, 257 TR, 1433, 1434 SPR, 1G MtcR, 410, 512 TBn, 13, 46, 51 AeroSBn, 17, 18, 20, 21 AcBn	2 AAC (hq), 3 FAC (265, 278 FAD), 1 FAC (294, 302 FAD), 244 BAD, 264 AAD, 303 FAD, 12, 48, 132, 140 BAR, 735 AAR, 133, 267, 298, 518, 519 FAR, 598 LBAR	122, 175 EBn 356 EBn
Total (2 armies, 1 res Army)	11 RDs, 10 AbnDs, 3 RBs, 23 SkiBs, 2 CC, 10 CDs	6 TDRs, 1 MtrB, 1 GMR, 1 AAAD, 5 AAARs	4 TBs, 18 TRs, 2 SPRs, 1 MtcR, 2 TBns, 3 AeroSBns, 4 AcBns	1 AAC, 2 FACs, 1 BAD, 1 AAD, 5 FADs, 4 BARs, 1 AAR, 5 FARs, 1 LBAR	2 EBs, 4 EBns

Military Districts and Nonoperating Fronts

Moscow MD	33, 137 RB, 1 Women's RB, 3 SkiB	13 AD (42 LAB, 33 GunAB, 47 HowAB, 17 MtrB), 14 AD (33 LAB, 48 GunAB, 43 HowAB, 16 MtrB), 15 AD (69 LAB, 44 GunAB, 35 HowAB, 18 MtrB), 16 AD (49 LAB, 36 GunAB, 32 HowAB, 14 MtrB), 17 AD (37 LAB, 53 GunAB, 50 HowAB, 13 MtrB), 20 AD	7 MC (93 TB, 76 MtcBn), 20, 25, 31, 32, 80, 144, 149, 154, 238 TB, 1 MtcB, 53 MRB, 26, 27, 34, 35, 49, 50G, 7, 27, 28, 29, 32, 36, 37, 38, 40, 62, 63, 64, 65, 184, 233, 240, 249, 255 TR, 1435, 1436, 1437,	2 SDAD, 173 BAR, 783 AAR;30G, 17, 21, 31, 92, 160, 191, 192, 238, 254, 297, 482, 486, 813, 927, 937 FAR, 18, 138, 201, 511, 626, 723 BAR, 372, 690, 714, 765, 989, 992, 994 LBAR (forming)	1 GBM, 14 EMB, 58, 59 ESB, 124 PBBn

—continued

1 FEBRUARY 1943 *Continued*

Fronts and Armies	Rifle, Airborne, and Cavalry	Artillery	Tank and Mechanized	Air	Engineers
		(54 LAB, 60 HowAB, 20 MtrB), 21 AD (66 LAB, 55 HowAB, 25 MtrB), 22 AD (62 LAB, 67 HowAB), 23 AD (63 HowAB), 24 AD (22 MtrB), 25 AD (hq), 65 LAB (18 AD), 1324, 1325, 1326 HowAR, 4, 137, 330, 324, 1016, 1017, 1018, 1020, 1021, 1022, 1145, 1153, 1154, 1191, 1196, 1197 HowARhp, 32, 40, 226, 245, 329, 331 ABnsp, 108, 120, 439, 449, 538, 552, 578, 614, 689, 727, 756, 881, 1000, 1001, 1312, 1313, 1317, 1318, 1322, 1323 TDR, 9 MtrB (11 AD), 28 MtrB, 6 GMD (24, 25 GMB), 47, 79, 83, 86, 316, 317, 325, 326 GMR, 247, 248 GMBn, 6 AAAD (146, 366, 516, 999 AAAR), 8 AAAD (797, 848, 978, 991 AAAR), 10 AAAD (802, 975, 984, 994 AAAR), 11 AAAD (804, 976, 987, 996 AAAR), 12 AAAD (836, 977, 990, 997 AAAR), 13 AAAD (1173, 1175, 1218, 1219 AAAR), 21 AAAD	1438, 1439, 1440, 1441, 1442, 1443 SPR, 51, 510, 511, 516, 517 TBn, 73, 74, 75, 77, 78, 79 MtcBn, 33 AeroSBn, 14, 40 AcBn, 7, 38, 56, 58, 60, 61, 79 AtrBn		

	(1334, 1340, 1346, 1352 AAAR), 22 AAAD (1335, 1341, 1347, 1353 AAAR), 23 AAAD (1336, 1342, 1348, 1354 AAAR), 24 AAAD (1337, 1343, 1349, 1355 AAAR), 120G, 121, 1044, 1045, 1062, 1063, 1065, 1067 AAAR		4 EBs, 1 PBBn
Total	3 RBs, 1 SkiB	11 ADs, 19 ARs, 20 TDRs, 6 ABns, 1 MtrB, 1 GMD, 8 GMRs, 2 GMBns, 10 AAADs, 9 AAARs	1 MC, 9 TBs, 1 MRB, 1 MtcB, 24 TRs, 9 SPRs, 5 TBns, 6 MtcBns, 1 AeroSBn, 2 AcBns, 7 AtrBns	1 SDAD, 7 BARs, 1 AAR, 16 FARs, 7 LBARs
Arkhangel'sk MD				
Total		1234 AAR, 310 GunAR, 1, 6 ABtrvhp, 31 MtrB 2 ARs, 1 MtrB	57, 58, 59, 60, 61 AeroSBn 5 AeroSBns	
Volga MD	37G, 112, 193, 308 RD, 25, 42, 115, 120, 160, 163 RB	1024, 1025, 1144, 1151 HowARhp, 317 ABnsp, 39 MtrB, 327 GMR	9 MC (69, 70, 71 MB, 148, 259 TR), 1 TC (89, 117, 159 TB, 44 MRB, 10 AcBn), 10, 232 TB, 2, 9 MB, 20 MRB, 82, 84, 85, 231, 258 TR, 565, 608 TBn, 25 AtrBn	27, 50, 149, 165, 233, 247, 270, 291, 431, 812 FAR, 135, 175, 211, 217, 237, 245, 431, 567, 569, 593, 594, 611, 617, 621, 624, 639, 655, 658, 672, 683, 694, 724, 811, 893, 944, 945, 947, 948, 949, 951, 952, 953, 954, 955, 956, 957, 958 AAR, 3 TAR, 13, 50, 320 RAS, 12, 47 CAS
Total	4 RDs, 6 RBs	4 ARs, 1 ABn, 1 MtrB, 1 GMR	1 MC, 1 TC, 2 TBs, 2 MBs, 1 MRB, 5 TRs, 2 TBns, 1 AtrBn	37 AARs, 10 FARs

—*continued*

1 FEBRUARY 1943 *Continued*

Fronts and Armies	Rifle, Airborne, and Cavalry	Artillery	Tank and Mechanized	Air	Engineers
Trans-Caucasus Front *(nonoperating)*	3 RBn			25, 36, 45, 88, 246, 265, 483, 743, 773, 805, 821, 862, 863, 926 FAR, 136, 214, 570, 590, 657 AAR, 8G, 242, 244, 454, 647, 762 MAR	321 SBn
45th Army	12 RC (261, 349, 392, 406 RD), 54, 55 FR	18 MtrBn			10 EBn, 22 PBBn
Forces in Iran	75 RD, 15 CC (1, 23 CD, 166 MtrR, 26 CABn, 15 TDBn)				
Total	1 RC, 5 RDs, 2 FRs, 1 CC, 2 CDs	1 MtrBn		4 BARs, 5 AARs, 14 FARs, 2 MARs	2 EBns, 1 PBBn
Ural MD	82 NRB	18 AD (51 GunAB, 38 HowAB, 15 MtrB), 39 GunAB (20 AD), 56 GunAB (22 AD), 61 GunAB (21 AD), 38 MtrB	66, 67, 68, 69, 70 AeroSBns		
Total	1 RB	1 AD, 1 MtrB	5 AeroSBns		
South Ural MD	122, 132, 134 RB	34, 315, 316, 322, 328, 330 ABnsp			
Total	3 RBs	6 ABns			
Siberian MD		36, 37 MtrB, 283, 288, 293 MtrR		13G, 260, 453 BAR, 15, 32, 43, 91, 163, 274, 347 FAR	
Total		2 MtrBs, 3 MtrRs		3 BARs, 7 FARs	

Central Asian MD				
Forces in Iran	213 RD, 64, 109, 118 RB, 72 RR, 245 CR	450 HowAR, 33, 34 MtrB, 179 MtrR, 28 AAABtry		136 MAD, 238 FAD, 300 AAD, 15 RAS	125, 136 EBn
Total	58 RC (68 MtnRD, 89 RB, 39 MtnCD) 1 RC, 2 RDs, 4 RBs, 1 CD, 1 RR, 1 CR	1 AR, 2 MtrBs, 1 MtrR		1 AAD, 1 MAD, 1 FAD	2 EBns
Trans-Baikal Front					
17th Army	36, 57 MRD, 227 RB, 1, 3 MRR	185, 624, 629, 1141 GunAR, 413 HowAR, 178 MtrR, 63, 66, 376, 382 AAABn	61 TD, 43 TB, 9 MArB, 30 MtcR, 68, 70, 82 TBn, 67 Atr		84 PBBn, 102 EBn
36th Army	94, 209, 210 RD, 226 RB, 31 FR	267, 390, 1233 GunAR, 259 HowAR, 177 MtrR, 120, 401, 405, 414 AAABn	33, 35 TBn, 68, 69 Atr		39 EBn
12th Air Army				30, 247 BAD, 245, 246 FAD, 248 AAD, 12 RAR, 846 LBAR, 847, 848 MAR, 849 TAR, 40, 41 CAS	
Front forces	2 RC (103 RD, 39 RB), 51 CD, 32 FR	1142, 1143 GunAR, 216 HowARhp, 106, 1146 HowARhp, 35 MtrB, 176 MtrR, 190 PackMtrR, 32 GMR, 410 AAABn	111 TD, 44, 205, 206 TB, 70, 79 Atr		1, 2, 17 PBBn, 51, 281, 282, 283 EBn
Total (2 armies, 1 air army)	1 RC, 4 RDs, 2 MRDs, 3 RBs, 1 CD, 2 FRs, 2 RRs	14 ARs, 1 MtrB, 4 MtrRs, 1 GMR, 9 AAABns	2 TDs, 4 TBs, 1 MB, 1 MtcR, 5 TBns	2 BADs, 1 AAD, 2 FAD, 2 MARs, 1 RAR, 1 LBAR	6 EBns, 4 PBBns
Far Eastern Front					
1st Army	5 RC (95, 246 RB), 26 RC (22, 59 RD), 59 RC (39 RD, 12, 29 RB), 187 RD, 105, 112 FR, 18 CC (246 CR, 185 MtrR, 18 TDBn)	50, 273, 1124, 1125, 1138, 1139 GunAR, 45, 87, 165, 182, 372, 1132, 1133 HowAR, 199, 1192 HowARhp, 168 MtrR, 33 GMR, 43, 44, 45, 103, 115, 129 AAABn	75, 77, 204, 208, 209, 210 TB, 42 MRB, 442, 670, 671, 675 TBn, 3, 78 AtrBn, 69 AAAtr	776 MAR, 26, 27 CAS	45 ESB, 132 PBBn

—continued

227

1 FEBRUARY 1943 Continued

Fronts and Armies	Rifle, Airborne, and Cavalry	Artillery	Tank and Mechanized	Air	Engineers
2nd Army	3, 12 RD, 17, 41, 258, 259 RB, 101 FR, 135 MGABn	42, 1120, 1140 GunAR, 114, 147, 238, 411, 1129 HowAR, 550 HowABn, 192 HGunABn, 181 MtrR, 9, 42 AAABn	73, 74 TB, 672, 673, 674, 676 TBn, 2 AtrBn, 5 Atr	777 MAR, 28 CAS	2 HPBR, 10 PBBn
15th Army	34 RD, 38, 260 RB, 102 FR	52, 424, 1121 GunAR, 145, 1128, 1130 HowAR, 1194 HowARhp, 183 MtrR, 46 AAABn	165, 171 TB, 677 TBn, 77 AtrBn, 59 AAAtr	781 MAR, 30, 39 CAS	3 HPBR, 11, 24, 29 PBBn, 129 EBn
25th Army	17 RC (190 RD, 261, 262 RB), 39 RC (40, 105 RD, 6, 8, 21, 158, 247 RB), 175 DR, 247 CR, 106, 107, 108, 110, 111, 113 FR, 84, 86 MGBn	282, 548, 1126 GunAR, 107, 148, 215, 386, 1134, 1135, 1136 HowAR, 549 HowARhp, 555 TDR, 180, 182 MtrR, 22, 24, 28 AAABn	72, 76, 218 TB, 302, 382 TBn, 9 AtrBn, 23, 62 AAAtr	912 MAR, 29 CAS	46 ESB
35th Army	35, 66 RD, 30 RB, 109 FR	76, 187, 1122, 1123 GunAR, 177, 181, 263, 1131 HowAR, 1193 HowARhp, 110 AAABn	125, 172 TB, 29 MtcR, 13 AtrBn, 53, 61 AAAtr	913 MAR, 130 CAS	3, 16, 58 PBBn, 280 EBn
9th Air Army				32, 249, 250 FAD, 33, 34 BAD, 251, 252 AAD, 6 RAR, 528 FAR	

10th Air Army			29 FAD, 53, 83 BAD, 253 AAD, 254 MAD, 7 RAR
11th Air Army			82 BAD, 96 FAD, 296 MAD, 140 RAS
Front forces	428, 433, 487, 1137 HowAR, 117, 362, 367, 428 HGunABn, 168, 181 MtrBn, 102 AAABn	203, 214 TB, 76 AtrBn	128, 255 MAR, 251 BAR, 799 RAR
Total (5 armies, 3 air armies)	Special RC (79, 101 RD, 2, 5 RB, 302, 540 RR, 5, 6, 206 RBn), 18, 88, 113 RB, 202 AbnB, 103, 104 FR 6 RCs, 14 RDs, 23 RBs, 1 AbnB, 3 RRs, 1 CC, 2 CRs, 13 FRs	17 TBs, 1 MRB, 1 MtcR, 11 TBns, 8 AtrBns	5 BADs, 3 AADs, 4 MADs, 5 FADs, 1 BAR, 1 FAR, 5 MARs, 3 RARs	3 EBs, 2 EBns, 2 PBRs, 8 PBBns
Grand Total (8 armies, 4 air armies)	9 RCs, 29 RDs, 2 MRDs, 43 RBs, 1 SkiB, 1 AbnB, 6 RRs, 2 CCs, 4 CDs, 17 FRs, 3 CRs	56 ARs, 1 TDR, 5 ABns, 5 MtrRs, 2 MtrBns, 1 GMR, 14 AAABns 12 ADs, 96 ARs, 21 TDRs, 18 ABns, 9 MtrBs, 13 MtrRs, 3 MtrBns, 1 GMD, 11 GMRs, 2 GMBns, 10 AAADs, 9 AAARs, 23 AAABns	2 MCs, 1 TC, 2 TDs, 32 TBs, 3 MBs, 3 MRBs, 1 MtcB, 29 TRs, 9 SPRs, 2 MtcRs, 23 TBns, 6 MtcBns, 11 AeroSBns, 16 AtrBns	7 BADs, 5 AADs, 5 MADs, 8 FADs, 1 SDAD, 12 BARs, 46 AARs, 48 FARs, 9 MARs, 4 RARs, 8 LBARs	7 EBs, 12 EBns, 2 PBRs, 14 PBBns

47 ESB

—continued

1 FEBRUARY 1943 Continued

PVO Fronts and Armies	PVO Formations	PVO Regions	PVO Separate Units	PVO Aviation
PVO Strany Forces: PVO Fronts and Armies				
Moscow PVO Front			72G, 82, 176, 250, 251, 329, 340, 347, 745, 751, 862, 864, 1201, 1202, 1203, 1204, 1205 AAAR, 1, 20, 22 AAMGR, 198, 205, 207, 232, 237, 240, 244, 247, 257, 270 AAABn, 1, 14, 30, 31 ProjR, 1, 12 VNOSR, 1, 9, 13 AeroObsR	6 FAC (12G, 16, 28, 34, 67, 126, 177, 178, 309, 429, 445, 488, 562, 564, 565, 736 FAR)
Leningrad PVO Army			115, 169, 189, 192, 194, 243, 351 AAAR, 2 AAMGR, 2 ProjR, 2 VNOSR, 3, 4, 11 AeroObsR, 192 AAATr	7 FAC (11, 26, 27G, 124, 158 FAR)
Baku PVO Army			180, 190, 195, 252, 335, 339, 513, 636, 654 AAAR, 3 AAMGR, 3 ProjR, 28 VNOSR, 67 VNOSBn, 5 AeroObsR, 179 AAAtr	8 FAC (82, 266, 480, 481, 961, 962 FAR)
PVO Strany Forces: Protecting Operating Armies				
Karelian Front		Murmansk DR (885 AAAR, 33, 135, 199, 426, 531 AAABn, 9 AABNBn, 6 AeroObstBn, 190 AAAtr)		122 FAD (767, 768, 769, 966 FAR)
Leningrad Front		Ladoga DR (Volkov and Osipovets AAAR, 65, 69, 225, 251, 253, 391, 434, 447 AAABn, 42, 47 VNOSBn)		

230

Northwestern and Kalinin Fronts	Bologoe DR (87, 215, 231, 248, 256, 271, 308, 380, 458 AAAR, 21, 32 VNOSBn, 57, 74, 75, 128, 182, 183 AAATr	106 FAD (33, 253, 441, 630, 926 FAR)
Briansk Front	Riazhsk-Tambov DR (733 AAAR, 16, 122, 290, 353 AAABn, 1, 2 AAMGBn, 7, 56, 65 VNOSBn, 73, 121, 131 AAATr)	36 FAD (591, 785, 827 FAR)
Voronezh Front	Voronezh-Borisoglebsk DR (183, 254, 317, 736, 746 AAAR, 86, 96 AAABn, 4, 7 AAMGR, 4 VNOSR, 5 ProjBn, 55, 56, 58, 127, 129, 130, 178, 184, 186, 187, 189 AAAtr)	101 FAD (487, 573, 826, 894 FAR)
Southern Front	Stalingrad CR (73G, 748, 1077, 1079, 1080, 1082, 1083 AAAR, 82, 106, 188, 267 AAABn), 72, 122, 126, 132, 135, 137, 141, 142, 181 AAAtr	102 FAD (572, 629, 788 FAR)
North Caucasus Front	Grozny DR (16, 454, 485, 744 AAAR, 11, 18, 23, 36, 151, 189, 265, 266, 375, 383, 411, 425 AAABn, 23, 74, 76 VNOSBn, 185 AAAtr; Krasnodar DR (734 AAAR, 53, 143, 201, 249, 286, 571 AAABn, 83 AABn, 33, 68 VNOSBn, 33 AAATr)	105 FAD (182, 234, 738, 822 FAR), 126 FAD (652, 833, 965 FAR)

PVO Strany Forces: Protecting Rear-Area Objectives

Moscow MD	Gor'kii CR (196, 583, 742, 784, 1291 AAAR, 13, 39, 58, 91, 202, 236, 238, 279, 281, 289, 310,	142 FAD (423, 632, 722, 786 FAR);

—*continued*

1 FEBRUARY 1943 *Continued*

PVO *Fronts* and Armies	PVO Formations	PVO Regions	PVO Separate Units	PVO Aviation
		379 AAABn, 45 ProjR); Rybinsk-Iaroslavl' DR (201 AAAR, 38, 40, 59, 61, 62, 148, 192, 197, 200, 212, 273, 287, 312, 362 AAABn); Tula DR (732 AAAR, 153, 252, 269, 283, 291, 511 AAABn, 1, 2 AAMGBn)		147 FAD (439, 731, 959 FAR); 125 FAD (495, 787, 960 FAR)
Arkhangel'sk MD		Arkhangel'sk DR (84, 160, 171, 213, 372, 480 AAAR); Cherepovets-Vologda DR (55, 74, 99, 272, 385, 413 AAABn)		104 FAD (348, 729, 730 FAR); 148 FAD (740, 964 FAR)
Volga and South Ural MDs		Kuibyshev DR (767, 861, 1088 AAAR, 90, 174, 199, 201, 285 AAABn, 15 AAMGBn, 40 ProjBn); Saratov-Balashov DR (720, 1078 AAAR, 56, 85, 89, 93, 243, 284, 296, 343, 374, 501 AAABn, 43 ProjR, 58, 139 AAAtr); Astrakhan DR (374, 679 AAAR, 194, 416, 471 AAABn, 1/317 AAAR, 140, 143, 144 AAAtr); Penza BR (79, 277, 510 AAABn)		141 FAD (631, 802 FAR); 144 FAD (405, 586, 963 FAR);

Trans-Caucasus Front	2 PVOB (345, 415, 443, 638 AAAR, 3, 381, 419, 422, 571 AAABn, 5 VNOSR, 162 AAMGBn, 21 ProjBn; 8 PVOB (352, 466 AAAR, 76, 365, 433 AAABn, 49 AAMGBn, 33 ProjBn, 7 AeroObsBn, 15, 24 VNOSBn)		298 FAD (35, 628, 982, 983 FAR)
Ural MD		Ural'sk DR (361 AAAR, 173, 178, 180, 182 AAABn)	
Central Asian MD Trans-Baikal PVO Zone		1 BR (10, 107, 132, 390 AAABn); 2 BR (150, 387, 408 AAABn); 3 BR (750 AAAR, 162, 166, 187, 262, 264 AAABn)	731 AAAR, 430 AAABn
Far Eastern PVO Zone		1 BR (757 AAAR, 138, 167, 175 AAABn, 2 AAMGBn); 2 BR (77, 137, 195 AAABn); 3 BR (749 AAAR, 147, 163, 190, 217 AAABn, 68 AAATr); 4 BR (4, 155, 398 AAABn); 5 BR (755 AAAR, 78, 152, 186 AAABn, 3 AAMGBn); 6 BR (752 AAAR, 463, 465 AAABn) 2 CRs, 15 DRs, 10 BRs	149 FAD (3, 18, 60 FAR)
Total (1 PVO front, 2 PVO armies)	2 PVOBs		34 AAAR, 5 AAMGRs, 10 AAABns, 6 ProjRs, 4 VNOSRs, 7 AeroObsRs	3 FACs, 17 FADs

1 JULY 1943

Fronts and Armies	Rifle, Airborne, and Cavalry	Artillery	Tank and Mechanized	Air	Engineers
Field Forces					
Karelian					
14th Army	10G, 14 RD, 72 NRB, 31 SkiB	1236 GunAR, 275, 297 MtrR, 41 GMR, 156 AAAR, 325, 487 AAABn			31 EBn
19th Army	104, 122 RD, 77 NRB	438 TDR, 566 MtrR, 53 GMR, 186 AAAR, 261, 298 AAABn	377, 429 TBn		279 EBn
26th Army	31 RC (45, 205 RD, 61, 85 NRB), 27, 54 RD, 32 SkiB	471 GunAR, 441, 444 TDR, 172, 278, 565 MtrR, 52 GMR, 297 GMBn (63 GMR) 272 AAAR, 48, 369 AAABn	374, 375 TBn, 2, 3, 24, 24 AeroSBn, 73 Atr		170 EBn
32nd Army	289, 313, 367 RD, 65, 80 NRB, 33 SkiB	1237 GunAR, 654 TDR, 173, 280, 298 MtrR, 63 GMR, 275 AAAR, 208, 446 AAABn 1598, 1599 AAAR	376 TBn (-KV TCo), 21, 22, 26 AeroSBn, 47 AtrBn		261 EBn
7th Air Army				258, 260, 261 MAD, 152, 195 FAR, 679 TAR, 108, 118 RAS, 42 CAS	
Front forces		32 AAABn	KV TCo (376 TBn), 28 AeroSBn, 27 AtrBn		1 SDEB, 6 GBnM, 733 MSBn
Total (4 armies, 1 air army)	1 RC, 11 RDs, 6 RBs, 3 SkiBs	3 ARs, 4 TDRs, 9 MtrRs, 4 GMRs, 6 AAARs, 9 AAABns	5 TBns, 8 AeroSBns, 2 AtrBns	3 MADs, 2 FARs	1 EB, 6EBns
Leningrad					
2nd Shock Army	43 RC (11, 128, 314 RD), 86, 376 RD, 55, 123 RB, 73 NRB, 16 FR	21G HowARhp, 311 GunAR (81 GunAB), 21, 28, 561, 1106 GunAR, 754 HowAR, 882, 884 TDR, 400 ABnhp,	98 TR, 86, 116 TBn		770 EBn, 734 MSBn

23rd Army	10, 92, 142, 201 RD, 17, 22 FR	230G, 104, 122, 144, 193, 281, 504 MtrR, 20, 23 GMR, 43 AAAD (464, 635, 1463, 1464 AAAR), 108 AAABn	14 AtrBn	234, 363 EBn
42nd Army	56, 85, 109, 125, 189 RD, 79 FR	260, 336 GunAR, 599 HowAR, 94, 883 TDR, 174, 276 MtrR, 618 AAABn	1 TB, 49G TR, 1439 SPR, 2 AcBn, 72 AtrBn	54, 585 EBn
		18 AD (65 LAB, 51 GunAB, 38 HowAB, 15 MtrB), 12, 14G, 73, 1486 GunAR, 324 HowARhp, 304, 384, 509, 705, 760 TDR, 533, 534 MtrR, 320 GMR, 7 AAAD (465, 474, 602, 632 AAAR), 631 AAAR, 72 AAABn		
55th Army	13, 46, 72, 131, 196, 224, 291 RD, 14 FR	28 AD (79 LAB, 81 GunAB, 80 HowAB, 42 MtrB), 126 GunAR, 289, 690 TDR, 301 HGunABn, 127, 134, 175 MtrR, 321, 322 GMR, 970 AAAR, 71, 613, 758 AAABn	152 TB, 1 AcBn, 71 AtrBn	325, 367 EBn
67th Army	30G RC (45, 63, 64G RD), 43, 90, 120, 123, 124, 268 RD	409 GunABnhp, 988 AAAR, 73 AAABn, 602 HGunBtry, 410 TDBtry	30G, 220 TB, 31G TR	53 EBn, 447 SBBn
Coastal Op Gp	48, 98, 168 RD, 50 RB, 48, 71 NRB, 73, 338 MGABn	519 HowAR, 184 MtrR, 190, 196, 197 ABnhp, 669, 1127 TDBtry, 92, 116 AAABn	287 TBn, 4 AcBn	295 EBn
13th Air Army				276 BAD, 277 AAD, 240, 275 FAD, 13 RAR, 12, 49 CAS

—continued

1 JULY 1943 Continued

Fronts and Armies	Rifle, Airborne, and Cavalry	Artillery	Tank and Mechanized	Air	Engineers
Front forces	6 NIR, 123, 124, 129, 130, 131, 132, 136 MGABn (Internal Defense of Leningrad)	5, 6 GMB, 38, 318 GMR, 167, 493, 519, 520 TDBtry 785, 803 AAAR, 15 AAABn	222 TB, 46G, 260, 261 TR, 5, 17, 39, 42 AeroSBn, 3 AcBn		2 SDEB, 52 ESB, 3 PBB, 5 PBR, 7 GMnM, 1G, 21, 43 PBBn, 106, 267 EBn
Total (5 armies, 1 op gp, 1 air army)	2 RCs, 33 RDs, 6 RBs, 5 FRs, 1 RR	2 AD, 1 AB, 16 ARs, 11 TDRs, 6 ABns, 15 MtrRs, 2 GMBs, 7 GMRs, 2 AAADs, 5 AAARs, 10 AAABns	5 TBs, 6 TRs, 1 SPR, 3 TBns, 4 AeroSBns, 3 AtrBns	1 BAD, 1 AAD, 2 FADs, 1 RAR	2 EBs, 1 PBB, 1 PBR, 14 EBns, 3 PBBns
Volkhov					
4th Army	44, 288 RD, 24, 53 RB, 206 MGABn	1096, 1097 GunAR, 192 MtrR, 214 GMBn (20 GMR), 1469 AAAR	32 AtrBn		365 EBn, 55 PBBn
8th Army	6 RC (hq), 18, 265, 286, 364, 372, 374, 379, 382 RD, 1, 22, 58 RB	2 AD (20 LAB, 7 GunAB, 10G HowAB, 5 MtrB), 71, 223G, 70 GunAR, 430, 1197 HowARhp, 500 MtrR, 29, 319 GMR, 41 AAAD (244, 245, 463 AAAR), 45 AAAD (737, 1465, 1466 AAAR), 177, 213 AAABn	185 TB, 32, 35, 50G, 25 TR, 107, 502 TBn, 47, 49 AcBn, 50 AtrBn, 32, 44 AeroSBn, 4 Atr		112 EBn
54th Army	80, 115, 177, 198, 281, 285, 311 RD, 14 RB	13G GunAR, 499 MtrR, 463 AAAR (41 AAAD)	124 TB, 48 AcBn		364 EBn
59th Army	7 RC (225, 229 RD), 2, 65, 191, 310, 377 RD, 2, 150 FR	367, 448 GunAR, 505, 506 MtrR, 1468, 1469 AAABn	29 TB, 48 AtrBn		109, 771 EBn, 32 PBBn

14th Air Army		1606, 1607 AAABn		
Front forces	165, 239, 256, 378 RD	8G GunAR, 315, 317 ABnhp, 30 MtrB, 7, 10, 12 GMB, 194 MtrR, 707 AAAR (45 AAAD), 1467 AAAR, 11G, 168, 461 AAABn	7G, 16, 122 TB, 33G TR, 1433, 1434 SPR, 500, 501, 503, 507 TBn, 34, 53 AeroSBn	280 BAD, 281 AAD, 845 FAR, 844 TAR, 8 RAS, 44 CAS	1 EMB, 2G SDEB, 8 GBnM, 2G, 40, 135 EBn, 539 MSBn, 34, 36, 38, 159 PBBn
Total (4 armies, 1 air army)	2 RCs, 28 RDs, 6 RBs, 2 FRs	1 AD, 11 ARs, 2 ABns, 1 MtrB, 6 MtrRs, 3 GMBs, 3 GMRs, 2 AAADs, 6 AAARs, 5 AAABns	6 TBs, 5 TRs, 2 SPRs, 6 TBns, 4 AeroSBns, 3 AtrBns	1 BAD, 1 AAD, 1 FAR	2 EBs, 10 EBns, 6 PBBns
Northwestern 1st Shock Army	23G, 188, 282, 391 RD, 33 RB	589 LAR (78 LAB), 701 GunAR, 1186 TDR, 282 MtrR (32 MtrB), 110, 274, 490 MtrR, 42 GMR, 1472 AAAR, 29 AAABn	27, 37, 226 TR		2, 28, 134 EBn, 67, 92 PBBn
22nd Army	44 RC (11, 15G NRB, 32, 46 RB), 8G, 33, 117 RD, 54 RB	164, 166G, 440 GunAR, 385 HowAR, 1198 HowARhp, 18 TDB, 1040 TDR, 268, 561, 562, 563 MtrR, 24 GMR, 43, 106 GMBn, 582, 1472 AAAR, 397 AAABn	81 TB, 170, 515 TBn		352, 903 EBn
34th Army	12G RC (1, 10G AbnD, 200 RD), 37, 171, 182, 245, 370 RD, 127, 144, 151 RB	26 AD (75 LAB, 72 GunAB, 77 HowAB, 24 MtrB), 27 AD (78 LAB, 76 GunAB, 74 HowAB), 11G, 151, 1235 GunAR, 395, 989 HowAR, 1199 HowARhp, 578, 641	60 TB, 3G, 32, 38, 65, 227, 239, 249 TR, 150, 514 TBn, 29, 35 AtrBn		13 EMB, 50, 238, 1391 EBn, 50, 54, 58, 86 PBBn

—continued

1 JULY 1943 Continued

Fronts and Armies	Rifle, Airborne, and Cavalry	Artillery	Tank and Mechanized	Air	Engineers
6th Air Army		TDR, 32 MtrB, 482 MtrR, 22, 26, 27, 70 GMR, 44 AAAD (508, 708, 710, 1274 AAAR), 729 AAAR (42 AAAD), 239, 242, 467 AAABn 1596, 1597, 1608 AAAR		3G AAD, 5G FAD, 242 NBAD, 58 BAR, 72 RAR, 699 TAR, 1, 25 CAS	
Front forces	14G RC (7, 53G RD, 137 RB), 43G, 26 RD, 365 MGABn	37G CAR, 283 MtrR, 42 AAAD (620, 709, 714 AAAR) 47 AAAD (1585, 1586, 1591, 1592 AAAR), 246, 250 AAABn	11, 18, 19, 35, 36, 57, 66 AeroSBn		41 SDEB, 9 GBnM, 222, 223 EBn
Total (3 armies, 1 air army)	3 RCs, 17 RDs, 2 AbnDs, 10 RBs	2 ADs, 13 ARs, 1 TDB, 4 TDRs, 1 MtrB, 9 MtrRs, 6 GMRs, 2 GMBns, 3 AAADs, 6 AAARs, 7 AAABns	2 TBs, 10 TRs, 4 TBns, 7 AeroSBns, 2 AtrBns	1 AAD, 1 FAD, 1 NBAD, 1 BAR, 1 RAR	2 EBs, 11 EBns, 6 PBBns
Kalinin					
3rd Shock Army	5G RC (19, 46G, 32 RD, 145 RB), 21G, 28, 357, 381 RD, 23, 31, 100 RB	41G CAR, 455, 1094, 1190 GunAR, 827 HowAR, 163G TDR, 203G, 550 MtrR, 205, 240 GMBn, 243, 1622 AAAR	46 MB, 78 TB, 57, 62 AtrBn		225, 289 EBn
4th Shock Army	47, 332, 334, 358, 360 RD, 101 RB, 26 DB	10G, 488 GunAR, 64, 1224 HowAR, 569, 759 TDR, 408 MtrR, 99 GMR, 1623, 1624 AAAR	143, 236 TB, 171 TBn		290 EBn, 736 MSBn

39th Army	134, 158, 178, 185, 234 RD, 124 RB	28G TB		17, 228, 251, 293 EBn, 122, 125 PBBn
43rd Army	145, 179, 262, 306 RD, 114 RB	106G, 545 GunAR, 472, 480 HowAR, 610 TDR, 554, 555 MtrR, 34 GMR, 621 AAAR, 490 AAABn	105 TR		273, 312 EBn, 106 PBBn
3rd Air Army		43, 1098 GunAR, 283, 376 HowAR, 759 TDR, 118 MtrR, 47 GMBn, 225, 1626 AAAR		211 AAD, 6G AAR, 11 RAR, 21 FAR, 279, 373 LBAR, 13, 36 CAS	
		1556, 1557, 1558 AAAR			
Front forces	2G RC (9, 17, 91G RD), 8 RC (7, 249 RD), 155 FR	38G, 85 CAR, 4, 17 TDB, 587 TDR, 31 MtrB, 551, 552, 556, 557, 559 MtrR, 46 AAAD (609, 617, 618, 717 AAAR), 246, 601, 1625 AAAR, 12, 183, 221, 622 AAABn	47 MB, 221 TR		2 EMB, 5 SDEB, 16, 56 ESB, 10 GBnM, 4G, 114, 210, 249, 348 EBn, 57, 60, 63, 93, 94 PBBn
Total (4 armies, 1 air army)	3 RCs, 26 RDs, 7 RBs, 1 DB, 1 FR	19 ARs, 2 TDBs, 6 TDRs, 1 MtrB, 11 MtrRs, 2 GMRs, 3 GMBns, 1 AAAD, 13 AAARs, 5 AAABns	4 TBs, 2 MBs, 2 TRs, 1 TBn, 2 AtrBns	1 AAD, 1 AAR, 1FAR, 2 LBAR, 1 RAR	4 EBs, 16 EBns, 8 PBBns
Western					
10th Guards Army	7G RC (29G RD), 15G RC (30, 85G RD), 19G RC (22, 56, 65G RD)	83G CAR	119 TR		263, 369 EBn

—*continued*

1 JULY 1943 Continued

Fronts and Armies	Rifle, Airborne, and Cavalry	Artillery	Tank and Mechanized	Air	Engineers
11th GuardsArmy	8G RC (11, 26, 83G RD), 16G RC (1, 16, 31G, 169 RD), 36G RC (5, 18, 84G RD), 108, 217 RD	8 APC: 3 APD (15 LAB, 5 GunAB, 1 HowAB, 117 HowARhp, 7 MtrB), 6 APD (21 LAB, 10 GunAB, 18 HowAB, 119 HowABhp, 2 MtrB);14 AD (54 LAB, 48 GunAB, 43 HowAB, 9 MtrB), 56G CAR, 1, 2, 17, 74, 75G, 39, 403, 537, 761, 995, 1093, 1165 GunAR, 15, 16G, 128, 360, 364 HowAR, 5G TDR, 545, 546 MtrR, 24, 25 GMB, 40, 59, 60, 74, 325 GMR, 14 AAAD (525, 715, 718, 721 AAAR), 17 AAAD (500, 1267, 1276, 1279 AAAR), 48 AAAD (231G, 50, 1277, 1278 AAAR), 716, 739, 1280, 1484 AAAR, 4, 614 AAABn	10, 29, 43G, 213 TB, 2, 4G TR, 1453 SPR		6G, 84, 226, 243, 367 EBn, 61 PBBn
5th Army	207, 208, 312, 352 RD	66G GunAR, 696 TDR, 537 MtrR, 41 GMBn, 1479 AAAR	153 TB		296, 297 EBn
10th Army	139, 247, 290, 330, 385 RD, 9 DB	188 GunAR (48 GunAB), 564, 572 GunAR, 520, 992 TDR, 544 AMtrR, 2 GMBn, 1268 AAAR	1 AtrBn		303, 345, 368 EBn

Army				
20th Army	152, 154 FR	1G TDB, 535 MtrR, 1265 AAAR (49 AAAD), 1270 AAAR, 64 AAABn		291, 301, 302 EBn
31st Army	36 RC (215, 274, 359 RD), 45 RC (88, 220, 331 RD), 82, 133, 251 RD	392, 542, 644, 646 GunAR, 529, 873 TDR, 536, 549 MtrR, 28, 201 GMBn, 49 AAAD (245, 1271 AAAR), 240, 341, 1269, 1478 AAAR	42G TB, 2G MtcR, 6, 20 AeroSBn	72 EBn
33rd Army	42, 144, 160, 164, 222 RD	1309 LAR (54 LAB), 55G CAR, 517, 557 GunAR, 2G TDR, 538 MtrR, 35 GMBn (60 GMR), 40 GMBn, 1266, 1480 AAAR	256 TB, 520 TBn	298, 321 EBn
49th Army	58, 146, 277, 338, 344 RD	570, 1099 GunAR, 49 HowAR, 3 TDB, 593 TDR, 540 MtrR, 317 GMBn, 1273, 1481 AAAR	23G TB, 1537 SPR, 138 TBn, 6, 52 AtrBn	305, 306 EBn
50th Army	38 RC (17, 326, 413 RD), 49, 212, 324 RD	447, 523, 1091 GunAR, 600 TDR, 541, 542 MtrR, 54 GMR, 1275, 1482, 1483 AAAR	196 TB, 1536 SPR, 21, 43 AtrBn	307, 309 EBn
1st Air Army		1550, 1551, 1552, 1553, 1604 AAAR	2 AAC (231, 232 AAD), 2 FAC (7G FAD), 8 FAC (215, 323 FAD), 204 BAD, 224, 233, 311 AAD, 303, 309 FAD, 213 NBAD, 10 RAR, 1 MedAR, 713 TAR, 65 CAS	

—continued

1 JULY 1943 Continued

Fronts and Armies	Rifle, Airborne, and Cavalry	Artillery	Tank and Mechanized	Air	Engineers
Front forces	371 RD, 36 RB	758 TDR, 307 GMR, 11 GMBn (59 GMR), 1272 AAAR (49 AAAD), 1281 AAAR, 324 AAABn	1 TC (89, 117, 159 TB, 44 MRB, 1437 SPR), 5 TC (24, 41, 70 TB, 5 MRB, 1435 SPR, 731 TDBn, 277 MtrR), 2G, 94, 120, 187 TB, 56G, 161, 233 248 TR, 7, 37, 38, 40 AeroSBn		11, 12 EMB, 33 SDEB, 11 GBnM, 6, 113, 122, 129, 133, 229, 230 EBn, 9, 51, 62, 87, 88, 89, 90, 91, 99 PBBn, 537, 738 MSBn
Total (9 armies 1 air army)	9 RCs, 54 RDs, 1 RB, 1 DB, 2 FRs	1 APC, 2 APDs, 1 AD, 35 ARs, 2 TDBs, 10 TDRs, 11 MtrRs, 2 GMBs, 8 GMRs, 5 GMBns, 4 AAADs, 24 AAARs, 4 AAABns	2 TCs, 13 TBs, 7 TRs, 3 SPRs, 1 MtcR, 2 TBns, 6 AeroSBns, 5 AtrBns	1 AAC, 2 FACs, 1 BAD, 5 AADs, 5 FADs, 1 NBAD, 1 RAR	3 EBs, 32 EBns, 10 PBBns

Briansk
3rd Army	235, 269, 283, 308, 342, 380 RD	20 APD (34 LAB, 53 GunAB, 60 HowAB, 93 HHowAB, 102 HowARhp, 20 MtrB), 420 GunAR, 584 TDR, 475 MtrR, 24 AAAD (1045, 1337, 1343, 1349 AAAR), 1284 AAAR	82, 114 TR, 1538 SPR, 10, 55 AtrBn		348 EBn
61st Army	9G RC (12, 76, 77G RD), 97, 110, 336, 356, 415 RD, 12 DB	60, 67G, 554 GunAR, 533 TDR, 547 MtrR, 13 AAAD (1065, 1173, 1175, 1218 AAAR), 1282 AAAR	68 TB, 36 TR, 1539 SPR, 31, 45 AtrBn		310, 344 EBn
63rd Army	5, 41, 129, 250, 287, 348, 397 RD	1071, 1311 TDR, 286 MtrR, 28 AAAD (1355, 1359, 1365, 1371 AAAR)	231 TR, 1452 SPR		356 EBn

15th Air Army			1G FAC (3, 4G FAD), 3 AAC (307, 308 AAD), 113 BAD, 225 AAD, 284 NBAD, 234, 315 FAD, 99G RAR	
Front forces	25 RC (186, 238, 362 RD)	2 APC: 13 APD (42 LAB, 47 HowAB, 88, 91 HHowAB, 101 HowABhp, 17 MtrB), 15 APD (69 LAB, 35 HowAB, 85, 87 HHowAB, 106 HowABhp, 18 MtrB), 3 GMD (15, 18, 19 GMB); 7 APC: 16 APD (49 LAB, 61 GunAB, 52 HowAB, 90 HHowAB, 109 HowABhp, 14 MtrB), 17 APD (37 LAB, 39 GunAB, 50 HowAB, 92 HHowAB, 108 HowABhp, 22 MtrB), 2 GMD (3, 17, 26 GMB); 44 GunAB, 12 TDB, 13 MtrB, 8 GMB, 85, 93, 310, 311, 312, 313 GMR, 10 GMBn, 1477 AAAR, 386 AAABn	1G TC (15, 16, 17G TB, 1G MRB, 34G TR, 65 MtcBn, 1001 TDR, 732 TDBn, 455 MtrR, 80G AAAR), 11, 12, 13, 26G, 253 TR, 1444, 1445, 1535 SPR, 55 MtcBn, 54 AtrBn	8 SDEB, 57 ESB, 3 GBnM, 131 SBn, 231, 740 EBn, 48, 53, 131, 136 PBBn
Total (3 armies, 1 air army)	2 RCs, 24 RDs, 1 DB	2 APCs, 5 APDs, 1 AB, 4 ARs, 1 TDB, 4 TDRs, 1 MtrB, 3 MtrRs, 2 GMDs, 1 GMB, 6 GMRs, 1 GMBn, 3 AAADs, 3 AAARs, 1 AAABns	1 TC, 1 TB, 9 TRs, 6 SPRs, 1 MtcBn, 5 AtrBns	1 AAC, 1 FAC, 3 AADs, 1 BAD, 4 FADs, 1 NBAD, 1 RAR	2 EBs, 8 EBns, 4 PBBns

—*continued*

1 JULY 1943 *Continued*

Fronts and Armies	Rifle, Airborne, and Cavalry	Artillery	Tank and Mechanized	Air	Engineers
Central Front					
13th Army	17G RC (6, 70, 75G RD) 18G RC (2, 3, 4G AbnD), 15 RC (8, 74, 148 RD), 29 RC (15, 81, 307 RD)	4 APC: 5 APD (16 LAB, 24 GunAB, 9 HowAB, 86 HHowAB, 100 HowABhp, 1 MtrB), 12 APD (46 LAB, 41 GunAB, 32 HowAB, 89 HHowAB, 104 HowABhp, 11 MtrB), 5 GMD (16, 22, 23 GMB); 19 GGunAR, 874 TDR, 476, 477 MtrR, 6, 37, 65, 86, 324 GMR, 1 AAAD (1042, 1068, 1085, 1090 AAAR), 25 AAAD (1067, 1356, 1362, 1368 AAAR), 1287 AAAR	129 TB, 27, 30G, 43, 58, 237 TR, 1442 SPR, 49 AtrBn		275 EBn
48th Army	42 RC (16, 202, 399 RD), 73, 137, 143, 170 RD	1168 GunAR, 2 TDB, 220G TDR, 479 MtrR, 16 AAAD (728, 1283, 1285, 1286 AAAR), 461 AAAR, 615 AAABn	45, 193, 229 TR, 1454, 1455 (9 TC), 1540 SPR, 37 AtrBn		313 EBn
60th Army	24 RC (112 RD, 42, 129 RB), 30 RC (121, 141, 322 RD), 55 RD, 248 RB	1156 GunAR, 1178 TDR, 128, 138, 497 MtrR, 98 GMR, 286 GMBn, 221G, 217 AAAR	150 TB, 58 AtrBn		59 ESB, 317 EBn
65th Army	18 RC (69, 149, 246 RD), 27 RC (60, 193 RD, 115 RB), 37G, 181, 194, 354 RD	120, 543 TDR, 143G, 218, 478 MtrR, 94 GMR, 235 AAAR	29G, 40, 84, 255 TR		14 EMB, 321 EBn

70th Army	28 RC (132, 211, 280 RD), 102, 106, 140, 162, 175 RD, 3 DB (2 DD)	1G AD (3G LAB, 1G GunAB, 2G HowAB), 378 TDR, 136 MtrR, 12 AAAD (836, 977, 990 AAAR), 581 AAAR		240, 251, 259 TR	169, 371, 386 EBn
2nd Tank Army			3 TC (50, 51, 103 TB, 57 MRB, 74 MtcBn, 881 TDR, 728 TDBn, 234 MtrR, 121 AAAR), 16 TC (107, 109, 164 TB, 15 MRB, 51 MtcBn, 1441 SPR, 614 TDR, 729 TDBn, 226 MtrR), 11G TB, 87 MtcBn		357 EBn
16th Air Army		1610, 1611, 1612 AAAR		3 BAC (241, 301 BAD), 6 MAC (221 BAD, 282 FAD), 6 FAC (273, 279 FAD), 2G, 299 AAD, 1G, 283, 286 FAD, 271 NBAD, 16 RAR, 6 MedAR, 14 CAS	
Front forces	2 DD (4 DB), 115, 119, 161 FR, 14 DB	68 GunAB, 1, 13 TDB, 130, 563 TDR, 21 MtrB, 84, 92, 323 GMR, 10 AAAD (802, 975, 984, 994 AAAR) 997 AAR (12 AAAD), 325, 1259, 1263 AAAR, 13G, 27, 31 AAABn	9 TC (23, 95, 108 TB, 8 MRB, 730 TDR), 19 TC (79, 101, 102 TB, 26 MRB), 1541 SPR, 40 AtrBn		1G SDEB, 6 EMB, 12 GBnM, 120, 257 EBn, 9, 49, 50, 104 PBBn

—*continued*

1 JULY 1943 Continued

Fronts and Armies	Rifle, Airborne, and Cavalry	Artillery	Tank and Mechanized	Air	Engineers
Total (5 armies, 1 tank army, 1 air army)	10 RCs, 38 RDs, 3 AbnDs, 1 RB, 1 DD, 1 DB, 3 FRs	1 AC, 2 APDs, 1 AD, 1 AB, 3 ARs, 3 TDBs, 8 TDRs, 1 MtrB, 10 MtrRs, 1 GMD, 10 GMRs, 1 GMBn, 5 AAADs, 12 AAARs, 4 AAABns	4 TCs, 3 TBs, 15 TRs, 3 SPRs, 1 MtcBn, 4 AtrBns	1 BAC, 1 MAC, 1 FAC, 3 BADs, 2 AADs, 6 FADs, 1 NBAD, 1 RAR	4 EBs, 11 EBns, 4 PBBns
Voronezh					
6th Guards Army	22G RC (67, 71, 90G RD), 23G RC (51, 52G, 375 RD), 80G RD	27, 33 GunAB, 628 GunAR, 27, 28 TDB, 493, 496, 611, 694, 868, 1008, 1240, 1666, 1667 TDR, 263, 295 MtrR, 5, 16, 79, 314 GMR, 26 AAAD (1352, 1357, 1363, 1369 AAAR), 1487 AAAR	96 TB, 230, 245 TR, 1440 SPR, 60 AtrBn		205, 540 EBn
7th Guards Army	24G RC (15, 36, 72G RD), 25G RC (73, 78, 81G RD), 213 RD	109, 161, 265G GunAR, 30 TDB, 114, 115G, 1669, 1670 TDR, 290 MtrR, 5 AAAD (670, 743, 1119, 1181 AAAR), 162, 258G AAAR	27G, 210 TB, 148, 167, 262 TR, 1438, 1529 SPR, 34, 38 AtrBn		60 ESB, 175, 329 EBn
38th Army	167, 180, 204, 232, 240, 340 RD	112G GunAR, 111G HowAR, 29 TDB, 222, 483, 1658, 1660 TDR, 491, 492 MtrR, 66 GMR, 441 GMBn (314 GMR), 981 AAAR (9 AAAD), 1288 AAAR	180, 192 TB		235, 268 EBn, 108 PBBn, 1505 MSBn
40th Army	100, 161, 184, 206, 219, 237, 309 RD	36 GunAB, 29 HowAB, 76G GunAR, 32 TDB, 4G, 12, 869, 1244, 1663, 1664 TDR, 493, 494 MtrR, 9, 10 PackMtrR, 9 AAAD (800, 974, 993 AAAR), 1488 AAAR	86 TB, 59, 60 TR		14 EBn

69th Army	107, 111, 183, 270, 305 RD	1661 TDR, 496 MtrR, 225G AAAR, 322 AAABn		328 EBn
1st Tank Army			316 GMR, 8 AAAD (797, 848, 978, 1063 AAAR)	3 MC (1, 3, 10 MB, 1G, 49 TB, 58 MtcBn, 35 TDR, 265 MtrR, 405 GMBn), 6 TC (22, 112, 200 TB, 6 MRB, 85 MtcBn, 1461 SPR, 538 TDR, 270 MtrR), 31 TC (100, 237, 242 TB)	71, 267 EBn
2nd Air Army		1554, 1555, 1605 AAAR		1 BAC (1G, 293 BAD), 1 AAC (266, 292 AAD), 4 FAC (294, 302 FAD), 5 FAC (8G, 205 FAD), 291 AAD, 203 FAD, 208 NBAD, 385, 454 LBAR, 50 RAR, 331 CAS	
Front forces	35G RC (92, 93, 94G RD)	1528 HowAR (29 HowAB), 522, 1148 HowARhp, 14, 31 TDB, 1076, 1689 TDR, 12 MtrB, 469 MtrR, 36, 80, 97, 309, 315 GMR, 22G AAABn		2G TC (4, 25, 26G TB, 4G MRB, 47G TR, 1500 TDR, 755 TDBn, 273 MtrR, 1695 AAAR), 5G TC (20, 21, 22G TB, 6G MRB, 48G TR, 1499 TDR, 454 MtrR, 1696 AAAR), TR	4, 5 EMB, 42 SDEB, 6 PBB, 13 GBnM, 6, 20 PBBn
Total (5 armies, 1 tank army, 1 air army)	5 RCs, 35 RDs	4 ABs, 9 ARs, 7 TDBs, 26 TDRs, 1 MtrB, 11 MtrRs, 11 GMRs, 4 AAADs, 9 AAARs, 2 AAABns		4 TCs, 1 MC, 6 TBs, 8 TRs, 3 SPRs, 3 AtrBns	1 BAC, 1 AAC, 2 FACs, 2 BADs, 3 AADs, 5 FADs, 1 NBAD, 1 RAR, 2 LBARs	4 EBs, 1 PBB, 12 EBns, 3 PBBns

—continued

1 JULY 1943 *Continued*

Fronts and Armies	Rifle, Airborne, and Cavalry	Artillery	Tank and Mechanized	Air	Engineers
Southwestern					
1st Guards Army	6G RC (57G, 53, 195 RD), 33 RC (50, 230, 243 RD, 253 RB), 44, 60G RD	7 AD (525 LAR/11 LAB, 17 GunAB, 25 HowAB, 3 MtrB), 42G CAR, 518 GunAR, 174, 536 TDR, 525 MtrR, 35, 301 GMR, 579, 580 AAAR, 139 AAABn	16, 17G TR (1G MC), 16 MtcBn		62 ESB, 351, 358 EBn
3rd Guards Army	34G RC (47, 59, 61G RD), 32 RC (259, 266, 279 RD), 78 RD	30 GunAB (9 AD), 222G, 312, 1232 GunAR, 152 HowAR, 179, 534, 1312 TDR, 23 MtrB, 526 MtrR, 58, 100 GMR, 586, 626, 1257 AAAR, 60 AAABn	5G MRB, 11 TB, 52, 243 TR, 50, 54 MtcBn		322 EBn
8th Guards Army	28G RC (39, 79, 88G RD), 29G RC (27, 74, 82G RD)	99 GunAR, 184 TDR, 141 MtrR, 302 GMR, 878 AAAR	5, 9G, 224 TR, 1443 SPR		326, 327 EBn
6th Army	4G RC (20, 35G, 228, 263 RD), 26G RC (41, 62G, 6 RD), 34 RC (152, 267 RD), 25, 38G RD	11 AD (31 LAB, 45 GunAB, 40 HowAB), 40G CAR, 170G GunAR, 33, 1176, 1249 TDR, 524 MtrR, 75, 87 GMR, 115 GMBn, 241, 1290 AAAR, 126 AAABn	115 TB, 212 TR		350, 370 EBn
12th Army	172, 203, 244, 333, 350 RD	103G GunAR, 1248 TDR, 531 MtrR, 1248 TDR, 531 MtrR, 1587 AAAR	141 TR, 56 MtcBn		181, 269 EBn
46th Army	31, 223, 236, 353, 394, 409 RD	437 TDR, 462 MtrR, 1651 AAAR			68, 273 EBn

248

57th Army	27G RC (14, 48, 58G RD), 19, 24, 52, 113, 303 RD, 1 DB	26 LAB (9 AD), 9G GunAB, 1110 GunAR, 374, 595 TDR, 523 MtrR, 45, 303 GMR, 71 AAAR, 227 AAABn	173, 179 TB
17th Air Army			1613, 1614, 1615 AAAR	1 MAC (5G AAD, 288 FAD), 3 MAC (290 AAD, 207 FAD), 9 MAC (305 AAD, 295 FAD), 244 BAD, 306 AAD, 262 NBAD, 39 RAR, 3 MedAR
Front forces	104 RB, 10 AWBn, 1G CC (1, 2, 7G CD, 143G TDR, 1 GMR, 1G TDBn, 49G MtrBn, 319 AAAR)	9 AD (456 LAR/26 LAB, 23 HowAB, 10 MtrB), 11 LAB (7 AD), 9, 10, 11 TDB, 61, 62 GMR, 405 GMBn, 3 AAAD (1084, 1089, 1114, 1118 AAAR), 4 AAAD (253, 254G, 606, 658 AAAR), 22 AAAD (1335, 1341, 1347, 1353 AAAR), 247, 303, 470, 1474 AAAR	1G MC (1, 2, 3G MB, 84 MtcBn, 116G AR, 1504 TDR, 267 MtrR, 1699 AAAR, 407 GMBn), 2 TC (26, 99, 169 TB, 58 MRB, 83 MtcBn, 1502 TDR, 269 MtrR, 1698 AAAR, 307 GMBn), 23 TC (3, 39, 135 TB, 56 MRB, 82 MtcBn, 1501 TDR, 457 MtrR, 1697 AAAR, 442 GMBn), 9G TB, 10G TR, 3G MtcR	15 EMB, 44 SDEB, 51 ESB, 4, 5 PBB, 8 PBR, 19 GBnM
Total (7 armies, 1 air army)	10 RCs, 51 RDs, 2 RBs, 1 CC, 3 CDs, 1 DB	3 ADs, 1 AB, 11 ARs, 3 TDBs, 13 TDRs, 1 MtrB, 7 MtrRs, 11 GMRs, 2 GMBns, 3 AAADs, 18 AAARs, 4 AAABns	1 MC, 2 TCs, 5 TBs, 1 MRB, 8 TRs, 1 SPR, 1 MtcR, 4 MtcBn	3 MACs, 1 BAD, 4 AADs, 3 FADs, 1 NBAD, 1 RAR	4 EBs, 2 PBBs, 1 PBR, 12 EBns

—continued

1 JULY 1943 Continued

Fronts and Armies	Rifle, Airborne, and Cavalry	Artillery	Tank and Mechanized	Air	Engineers
Southern					
2nd Guards Army	1G RC (24, 33, 86G RD), 13G RC (3, 49, 87G RD)	1095 GunAR, 483 MtrR, 18 AAAD (160, 166G, 297, 1262 AAAR), 1530 AAAR	2G MC (4, 5, 6G MB, 37G TB, 99 MtcBn, 408 GMBn)		63 ESB, 355 EBn
5th Shock Army	31G RC (4, 34, 40G RD), 96G, 126, 127, 221, 315 RD, 1G DB	506, 1162 GunAR, 85G, 331 HowAR, 507, 1255 TDR, 489 MtrR, 1617 AAAR	22G TR, 28 AtrBn		827 EBn
28th Army	55 RC (118, 271 RD), 1G, 78, 116 FR	110G GunAR, 521 TDR, 488 MtrR, 1485 AAAR	140 TB		57, 130 EBn
44th Army	37 RC (130, 248, 387 RD), 151, 320, 347, 416 RD	1101 GunAR, 274 HowAR, 491, 530, 747, 1250 TDR, 19 MtrB, 133G MtrR, 2 AAAD (1086, 1113, 1117 AAAR), 607 AAAR	32, 33G TB, 30 AtrBn		5G EBn
51st Army	3G RC (50, 54G, 91 RD), 54 RC (87, 99, 302 RD), 346 RD	2G AD (4G LAB, 6G, 114 GunAB, 5G HowAB), 1105 GunAR, 113G, 13, 14, 764, 1246 TDR, 486 MtrR (19 MtrB), 125 MtrR, 15 AAAD (281, 342, 723, 1264 AAAR), 77G AAAR	6G TB, 33 AtrBn		258, 275 Ebn, 121 PBBn
8th Air Army		1600, 1601, 1602, 1603 AAAR		10 MAC (289 AAD), 270 BAD, 1G AAD, 6G FAD, 2G NBAD, 8 RAR, 406 NBAR, 678 TAR, 5 MedAR, 87G ARCAF	
Front forces	8, 15 TDR, 2, 4, 19, 21, 23, 48, 51 GMR, 1069 AAAR		4G MC (13, 14, 15G MB, 36G TB, 62		7, 9 EMB, 43 SDEB, 1, 2

Army					
Total (5 armies, 1 air army)	7 RCs, 30 RDs, 1 DB, 3 FRs	(2 AAAD), 223, 416, 459, 622 AAAR	MtcBn, 348 GMBn, 591 AAAR), 5G AcBn, 46 AtrBn		PBB, 1 HPBR, 17 GBnM, 3G, 240 EBn, 1504 MSBn 4 EBs, 2 PBBs, 1 PBR, 11 EBns, 1 PBBn
North Caucasus					
9th Army		1 AD, 9 ARs, 2 TDBs, 12 TDRs, 1 MtrB, 5 MtrRs, 7 GMRs, 3 AAADs, 13 AAARs	2 MCs, 4 TBs, 1 TR, 4 AtrBns	1 MAC, 1 BAD, 2 AADs, 1 FAD, 1 NBAD, 1 RAR, 1 NBAR	121, 336EBn, 97 PBBn
18th Army	9 RC (34, 43, 157, 256 RB), 11 RC (19, 57, 84, 131 RB), 276, 351 RD	807, 960 CAR, 268, 547 GunAR, 489 TDR (16 TDB), 1187 TDR, 132 MtrR (29 MtrB), 159 PackMtrR, 253 MtrR, 12 MtrBn, 740, 1260 AAAR, 504 AAABn			50, 174, 332, 338 EBn
37th Army	20 RC (8G, 83, 255 RB), 176, 318 RD, 81 NRB, 107 RB	69G, 1167, 1169 GunAR, 81 HowAR, 350 HowARhp, 108G, 490 TDR, 574, 1258 AAAR, 21, 30 AAABn	132 TBn		112, 116 EBn
56th Army	11G RC (2, 32, 55G RD), 389, 395, 417 RD, 20 MtnRD	62 GunAB, 98G CAR, 647 GunAR, 1231 HowAR, 136 HowARhp, 29 MtrB, 19 AAAD (1332, 1338, 1344, 1350 AAAR), 772 AAAR, 52 GMBn			
	10G RC (5, 6, 7, 9, 10G RB), 3 RC (9, 83, 242 MtnRD), 10 RC (216, 328 RD, 62 NRB), 4G, 60 NRB	92G, 1014 CAR, 4G, 880 GunAR, 1195 HowAR, 1147 HowARhp, 29 TDR (16 TDB), 34 TDR, 260 MtrR (29 MtrB), 197 PackMtrR, 569 MtrR, 20 AAAD (879, 1339, 1345 AAAR), 257, 1351 AAAR, 51 GMBn	1448 SPR		8, 16 EBn

—continued

1 JULY 1943 Continued

Fronts and Armies	Rifle, Airborne, and Cavalry	Artillery	Tank and Mechanized	Air	Engineers
58th Army	77, 89, 295, 414 RD	68G GunAR, 22, 1174 TDR, 256 MtrR, 594 AAAR 1559, 1560, 1561, 1562, 1609 AAAR	8, 12, 66 AtrBn		170 EBn
4th Air Army				2 BAC (223, 285 BAD), 2 MAC (206, 214 AAD, 201 FAD), 219 BAD, 230 AAD, 9G, 229, 235, 236 FAD, 132, 218 NBAD, 7, 43G, 765 AAR, 269 FAR, 366 RAR, 5 MedAR, 23 CAS	
Front forces	16 RC (61, 317, 383 RD), 22 RC (339 RD), 4G CC (9, 10G, 30 CD, 152G TDR, 255 AAAR, 4G TDBn, 68 GMBn)	337, 377 GunAR, 6, 7, 16 TDB, 1 GMB, 8, 25, 43, 44, 49, 50, 67, 305 GMR, 196 PackMtrR, 1, 2, 3, 4 PackMtrBn, 1333 AAAR (20 AAAD), 210G, 249, 253, 763 AAAR, 14, 17, 57, 179, 364, 508, 540 AAABn	5G, 63 TB, 6G, 85, 244, 257, 258 TR, 1449 SPR, 75 TBn		13 SDEB, 15 GBnM, 9, 97, 123, 333 EBn, 19, 35, 37, 54 PBBn
Total (5 armies, 1 air army)	9 RCs, 24 RDs, 21 RBs, 1 CCs, 3 CDs	1 AB, 22 ARs, 3 TDBs, 6 TDRs, 1 MtrB, 6 MtrRs, 1 GMB, 3 MtrBns, 8 GMRs, 4 GMBns,2 AAAD, 17 AAARs, 10 AAABns	2 TBs, 5 TRs, 2 SPRs, 2 TBns, 3 AtrBns	1 BAC, 1 MAC, 3 BADs, 3 AADs, 5 FADs, 2 NBAD, 3 AARs, 1 FAR, 1 RAR	1 EB,16 EBns.5 PBBns
Separate Armies					
7th Army	4 RC (272, 368 RD, 69 NRB), 21, 67, 114 RD, 70 NRB, 3 NIB, 162 FR	460, 514 TDR, 354 HGunABn, 530 MtrR, 46, 64 GMR, 1650 AAAR, 54, 268, 616 AAABn	363, 431 TBn, 14, 16 AeroSBn	257 MAD, 119 RAS	1G SBn, 18 GBnM, 18 EBn

Total (1 army)	1 RC, 5 RDs, 3 RBs, 1 FR	2 TDRs, 1 ABn, 1 MtrR, 2 GMRs, 1 AAAR, 3 AAABns	2 TBns, 2 AeroSBns	1 MAD	3 EBns
Long-Range and Reconnaissance Aviation				1G AC (1, 6G LRAD), 2G AC (2, 8G LRAD), 3G AC (3, 7G LRAD), 6 AC (50, 62 LRAD), 7 AC (1, 12 LRAD) 4G, 36, 45 LRAD 47, 48, 98G RAR 6 LRACs, 15 LRADs, 3 RARs	
Total					
Grand total (12 *fronts*, 60 armies, 2 tank armies, 12 air armies)	64 RCs, 376 RDs, 5 AbnDs, 66 RBs, 3 SkBs, 2 CCs, 6 CDs, 6 DBs, 17 FRs, 1 RR	4 ACs, 20 ADs, 9 ABs, 154 ARs, 9 ABns, 24 TDBs, 106 TDRs, 9 MtrRs, 104 MtrRs, 3 MtrBns, 3 GMDs, 9 GMBs, 85 GMRs,18 GMBns, 32 AAADs, 133 AAARs, 64 AAABns	4 MCs, 13 TCs, 51 TBs, 2 MBs, 1 MRB, 76 TRs, 21 SPRs, 2 MtcRs, 25 TBns, 31 AeroSBns, 6 MtcBns, 36 AtrBns	3 BACs, 6 LRACs, 3 AACs, 6 MACs, 6 FACs, 14 BADs, 15 LRADs, 26 AADs, 4 MADs, 32 FADs, 9 NBADs, 1 BARs, 4 AARs, 5 FARs, 13 RARs, 5 LBARs	33 EBs, 6 PBBs, 3 PBRs, 162 EBns, 50 PBBns
***Stavka* VGK Reserve Steppe MD**					
4th Guards Army	20G RC (5,7, 8G AbnD), 21G RC (68, 69, 80G RD)	452, 1317 TDR, 466 MtrR, 96 GMR, 27 AAAD (1354, 1358, 1364, 1370 AAAR)	3G TC (3, 18, 19G TB, 2G MRB, 1436 SPR, 73 MtcBn, 1496 TDR, 266 MtrR, 1701 AAAR, 749 TDBn, 324 GMBn)		48 EBn
5th Guards Army	32G RC (13, 66G RD, 6G AbnD), 33G RC (95, 97G RD, 9G AbnD), 42G RD	301, 1322 TDR, 308 GMR, 29 AAAD (1360, 1366, 1372, 1374 AAAR)	10 TC (178, 183, 186 TB, 11 MRB, 1450 SPR, 77 MtcBn, 727 TDR, 287 MtrR, 1693 AAAR)		256, 431 EBn

—continued

1 JULY 1943 Continued

Fronts and Armies	Rifle, Airborne, and Cavalry	Artillery	Tank and Mechanized	Air	Engineers
27th Army	71, 147, 155, 163, 166, 241 RD	680, 1070 TDR, 480 MtrR, 47 GMR, 23 AAAD (1064, 1336, 1342, 1348 AAAR)	93 TB, 39 TR		25, 38 EBn
47th Army	21 RC (23, 218, 337 RD), 23 RC (29, 30, 38 RD)	269, 1593 TDR, 466 MtrR, 83 GMR, 21 AAAD (1044, 1334, 1340, 1346 AAAR)			91 EBn
53rd Army	28G, 84, 116, 214, 233, 252, 299 RD	232, 1316 TDR, 461 MtrR, 89 GMR, 30 AAAD (1361, 1367, 1373, 1375 AAAR)	34, 35 TR		11, 17 EBn
5th Guards Tank Army		678 GunAR, 689 TDR, 76 GMR, 6 AAAD (146, 366, 516, 1062 AAAR)	5G MC (10, 11, 12G MB, 24G TB, 4G AcBn, 2G MtcBn, 1447 SPR, 104G TDR, 285 MtrR, 737 TDBn, 409 GMBn), 29 TC (25, 31, 32 TB, 53 MRB, 1446 SPR, 38 AcBn, 75 MtcBn, 108 TDR, 271 MtrR, 747 TDBn), 53G TR, 1549 SPR, 1G MtcR	994 LBAR	377 EBn
5th Air Army				7 MAC (202 BAD, 287 FAD), 8 MAC (4G, 264 AAD, 256 FAD), 3 FAC (265, 278 FAD), 7 FAC (259, 304 FAD), 69G FAR, 511 RAR	

254

MD forces	35 RC (hq), 3G CC (5, 6G, 32 CD, 144G TDR, 3G TDBn, 64 GMtrBn, 1731 AAAR), 5G CC (11, 12G CD, 63 CD, SPBn, 150G TDR, 5G TDBn, 72 GMtrBn, 585 AAAR), 7G CC (14, 15, 16G CD, 145G TDR, 7G TDBn, 57 GMtrBn, 1733 AAR)	11 AAAD (804, 976, 987, 996 AAAR)	4G TC (12, 13, 14G TB, 3G MRB, 1451 SPR, 76 MtcBn, 756 TDR, 264 MtrR, 752 TDBn, 120G AAAR), 3G MC (7, 8, 9G MB, 35G TB, 1G MtcBn, 1510 TDR, 129 MtR, 743 TDR, 334 GMBn, 1705 AAAR), 1 MC (19, 35, 37 MB, 219 TB, 57 MtcBn, 75 TDR, 294 MtrR), 2 MC (18, 34, 43 MB, 33 TB, 68 MtcBn, 79 TDR, 468 MtrR, 734 TDBn, 410 GMBn, 1706 AAAR), 78 MtcBn	8 ESB, 27 SDEB, 7, 19, 40 PBBn, 246, 247, 248, 250, 284 EBn
MD Total (5 armies, 1 tank army, 1 air army)	7 RC, 27 RDs, 5 AbnDs, 3 CCs, 9 CDs	1 AR, 11 TDRs, 4 MtrRs, 6 GMRs, 7 AAADs	4 MCs, 4 TCs, 1 TB, 4 TRs, 1 SPR, 1 MtcR, 1 MtcBn	2 MACs, 2 FACs, 1 BAD, 2 AADs, 6 FADs, 1 FAR, 1 RAR, 1 LBAR	2 EBs, 14 EBns, 3 PBBns

Separate Armies
Stavka VGK Reserve

11th Army	53 RC (135, 197, 369 RD), 4, 96, 260, 273, 323 RD	1179, 1321 TDR, 481 MtrR, 30 GMR, 31 AAAD (1376, 1380, 1386, 1392 AAAR)	225 TR	202, 277 EBn
52nd Army	93, 136, 138, 253, 254, 294, 373 RD	17 GMR		366 EBn
68th Army	153, 154, 156, 157, 159, 173, 192, 199 RD	211G GunAR, 1427 TDR, 77 GMR, 726 AAR		122, 175 EBn

—*continued*

1 JULY 1943 *Continued*

Fronts and Armies	Rifle, Airborne, and Cavalry	Artillery	Tank and Mechanized	Air	Engineers
3rd Reserve Army	51, 62, 63, 70, 76, 95, 119, 174 RD	649, 1072 TDR, 456 MtrR, 95 GMR			260 EBn
3rd Guards Tank Army			12 TC (30, 97, 106 TB, 13 MRB, 1417 SPR, 66 MtcBn, 1498 TDR, 757 TDBn, 272 MtrR, 1703 AAAR), 15 TC (88, 113, 195 TB, 52 MRB, 1418 SPR, 39 AcBn, 1503 TDR, 733 TDBn, 467 MtrR, 1704 AAAR), 91 TB, 50 MtcR		182 EBn
Stavka forces	1, 2, 3, 4, 5, 6, 7, 8, 9, 10, 11, 12, 13, 14, 15, 16, 17, 18, 19, 20G AbnB, 2G CC (3, 4G, 20 CD, 149G TDR, 2G TDBn, 60G MtrBn, 1730 AAAR), 6G CC (8, 13G, 8 CD, 142G TDR, 6G TDBn, 47 GMtrBn, 1732 AAAR)	23 APD (58 HowAB, 96 HHowAB, 28 MtrB), 137, 1150 HowARhp, 753, 754, 756 TDBn, 1 GMD (2 GMB)	5 MC (2, 9, 45 MB, 233 TB, 64 MtcB, 1228 TDR, 745 TDBn, 458 MtrR, 1700 AAAR), 18 TC (110, 170, 181 TB, 32 MRB, 36 GTR, 1000 TDR, 736 TDBn, 292 MtrR, 1694 AAAR), 25 TC (111, 162, 175 TB, 20 MRB, 53 MtcBn, 1497 TDR, 746 TDBn, 459 MtrR, 1702 AAAR), 126, 127 TR, 1547, 1548 SPR, 86, 98 MtcBn, 22, 59 AtrBn	227 AAD, 269, 322 FAD, 4G LRAC (5G LRAD), 8 LRAC (48 LRAD), 73 LRAD, 42, 761, 976 FAR, 22G LBAR, 173 BAR, 742 RAR	56, 85 PBBn, 14 GBnM

Total (8 armies, 2 tank armies, 1 air army, 1 res Army)	8 RCs, 58 RDs, 5 AbnDs, 20 AbnBs, 5 CCs, 15 CDs	1 AD, 4 ARs, 16 TDRs, 6 MtrRs, 3 TDBns, 1 GMD, 10 GMRs, 8 AAADs, 1 AAAR	5 MCs, 8 TCs, 2 TBs, 7 TRs, 3 SPRs, 2 MtcRs, 3 MtcBns, 2 AtrBns	2 LRACs, 2 MACs, 2 FACs, 1 BAD, 3 LRADs, 3 AADs, 8 FADs, 4 FARs, 2 RARs, 1 BAR, 2 LBARs	2 EBs, 22 EBns 5 PBBns

Military Districts and Nonoperating Fronts

Moscow Defense Zone: 54, 77, 91, 118, 153, 156, 157, 159, 160 FRs; 105, 112, 113, HowABhp, 1638 GunAR, 1074 HowAR, 508, 562, 1073, 1075, 1160, 1161, 1642, 1643, 1644, 1645, 1646 TDR, 402, 406 ABnhp, 1639 AAAR, 577, 578 AAABn; 81 MtcBn; 162, 340, 341, 693 EBn

Total: 9 FRs; 3 ABs, 2 ARs, 2 ABns, 11 TDRs, 1 AAAR, 2 AAABns; 1 MtcBn; 4 EBns

Moscow MD: 1 Women's RB; 5 APC: 3G APD (7G LAB, 22G GunAB, 8G HowAB, 99 HHowAB, 107 HowARBhp, 43 MtrB), 5G APD (71 LAB, 17G GunAB, 67 HowAB, 95 HHowAB, 18G HowABhp, 27 MtrB); 7 GMD (4, 9, 11 GMB); 21 APD (66 LAB, 64 GunAB, 55 HowAB, 94 HHowAB, 103 HowABhp, 25 MtrB), 22 AD (59 GunAB), 56 GunAB, 97, 98 HHowAB, 20G HowABhp, 8, 116, 129, 154, 1157, 1517, 1518, 1519, 1520, 1521, 1522 CAR, 19, ...; 6G MC (16, 17G, 49 MB, 29, 56 TR, 1G SPR, 51G TDR, 31G AAABn), 7 MC (16, 63, 64 MB), 8 MC (66, 67, 68 MB), 11 TC (20, 36, 65 TB, 12 MRB, 1493 SPR, 1507 TDR, 243 MtrR, 728 TDBn), 20 TC (8G, 80, 155 TB, 7G MRB, 1419 SPR, 1505 TDR, 291 MtrR, 1711 AAAR, 735 TDBn), 30 TC (197, 243, 244 TB, 30 ...; 2, 4 SDAD, 312, 314 NBAD, 35, 132 BAR, 136, 208, 214, 570, 637, 657, 723, 724 AAR, 21G, 9, 17, 149, 161 FAR, 386, 887 LBAR, 918 TAR; 1 GBM, 1, 2, 3, 4, 5, 6, 7, 8, 9, 10, 11, 12, 13, 14, 15 AESB, 61, 88, 132, 233, 245 EBn, 737, 742 MSBn, 124 PBBn

—continued

1 JULY 1943 *Continued*

Fronts and Armies	Rifle, Airborne, and Cavalry	Artillery	Tank and Mechanized	Air	Engineers
		20 TDB, 1506, 1508, 1509, 1511, 1512, 1514, 1515, 1723, 1724, 1725, 1726, 1727, 1728, 1729 TDR, 32, 40, 226, 245, 329, 331 ABnsp, 739, 741, 744, 748, 750, 751 TDBn, 33 MtrB, 108 MtrR, 4 GMD (20, 21 GMB), 6 GMD (13, 14 GMB), 27 GMB, 3, 7, 9, 10, 11, 12, 18, 39, 56, 57, 72, 88, 91, 326, 328 GMR, 32 AAAD (1377, 1381, 1387, 1393 AAAR), 33 AAAD (1378, 1382, 1388, 1394 AAAR), 34 AAAD (1379, 1383, 1389, 1395 AAAR), 35 AAAD (1384, 1390, 1396, 1398 AAAR), 36 AAAD (1385, 1391, 1397, 1399 AAAR), 1707, 1708, 1709, 1710, 1712, 1713, 1714, 1715, 1716, 1717, 1718, 1719, 1720, 1721 AAAR, 67, 141 AAABn	MRB, 1621 SPR, 88 MtcBn, 1513 TDR, 299 MtrR, 219 AAAR, 742 TDBn, 248 GMBn), 31, 34G, 88, 92, 118, 144, 149, 151, 154, 177, 184, 232, 238 TB, 1, 7, 8, 14, 28G, 28, 41, 42, 53, 54, 57, 128, 134, 136,139, 160, 166, 184, 189, 198, 223 TR, 51, 52 MtcR, 991, 999, 1219, 1416, 1456, 1457, 1458, 1459, 1460, 1462, 1494, 1495, 1542, 1543, 1544, 1545, 1546 SPR, 51, 62, 510, 511, 512, 513, 516, 517, 519, 565 TBn, 90, 91, 92, 93, 94, 95, 96, 97, 98 MtcBn, 12, 33, 41, 56 AeroSBn, 7, 16, 23, 24, 26, 39, 44, 51, 53, 56, 61, 79 AtrBn		

258

Total	1 RB		1 AC, 3 APDs, 1 AD, 4 ABs, 11 ARs, 6 ABns, 2 TDBs, 14 TDRs, 6 TDBns, 1 MtrB, 1 MtrR, 3 GMDs, 1 GMB, 15 GMRs, 5 AAADs, 14 5 AAARs, 2 AAABns	3 MCs, 3 TCs, 13 TBs, 21 TRs, 17 SPRs, 2 MtcRs, 10 TBns, 9 MtcBns, 4 AeroSBn, 12 AtrBns	2 SDADs, 2 NBADs, 2 BARs, 8 AAR, 5 FARs, 2 LBARs	16 EBs, 7 EBns, 1 PBBn
Arkhangel'sk MD	24 RD, 24, 25, 26 AWBn		310, 1234 GunAR, 1, 6 ABtryhp	9, 10, 13, 23, 27, 43, 45, 50, 51, 54, 55, 58, 59, 60, 61, 64, 67 AeroSBn	909 FAR	
Total	1 RD		2 ARs	17 AereoSBns	1 FAR	
Volga MD	41, 42, 43, 44, 45, 46, 47, 48, 49, 50, 51, 52 AWBn		484 TDR, 327 GMR, 38 AAAD (1401, 1405, 1409, 1413 AAAR), 39 AAAD (1406, 1410, 1414, 1526 AAAR), 40 AAAD (1407, 1411, 1415, 1527 AAAR)	9 MC (69, 70, 71 MB), 41G, 2, 10, 14, 15, 116, 207, 254 TB, 51, 61, 104, 154, 250 TR, 126, 249, 258, 563, 564, 608 TBn, 48, 49, 52 AeroSBn, 25 AtrBn	13G BAR, 245, 567, 569, 593, 594, 611, 658, 694, 811, 944, 945, 954, 958 AAR, 515 FAR, 3 TAR, 13 RAS, 60, 62, 63, 64, 67, 68, 69, 70, 71, 72, 73, 74, 75, 76, 77, 78, 79, 80, 82, 83, 84 CAS	376 EBn, 147, 216 SBn
Total			1 TDR, 1 GMR, 3 AAADs	1 MC, 8 TBs, 5 TRs, 6 TBns, 3 AeroSBns, 1 AtrBn	1 BAR 13 AARs, 1 FAR	3 EBns
Stalingrad MD Total	46, 47 AWBn		115 HowAB (hq), 5 TDB 1 AB, 1 TDB			
Trans-Caucasus Front 45th Army	261, 349 RD, 55, 69 FR		39G CAR, 140, 233 TDR, 20 MtrR, 18 MtrBn	226, 227 TB, 65 AtrBn		10 EBn
Forces in Iran	75 RD, 90 RB, 15 CC (1, 23 CD, 1595 TDR, 15 TDBn, 17 MtrBn)					

—continued

1 JULY 1943 Continued

Fronts and Armies	Rifle, Airborne, and Cavalry	Artillery	Tank and Mechanized	Air	Engineers
Front forces	12 RC (392, 406 RD) 13 RC (402 RD, 94, 133 RB), 54, 151 FR	1667 CAR, 526, 1023 HowARhp, 44 MtrB, 1561, 1562, 1652, 1653 AAAR, 481 AAABn	230 TB, 271 TR, 11, 15, 19, 36, 41, 42 AtrBn, 20 Atr	453 BAR, 25, 66, 246, 494, 773, 805, 821, 863, 978 FAR, 149, 335 RAS	4 MtnEMB, 16 GBnM, 321 SBn, 337 EBn, 21, 22, 98 PBBn
Total (1 army)	2 RC, 6 RDs, 3 RBs, 1 CC, 2 CDs, 4 FRs	4 ARs, 2 TDRs, 1 MtrB, 1 MtrR, 1 MtrBn, 4 AAARs, 1 AAABn	3 TBs, 1 TR, 7 AtrBns	1 BAR, 9 FARs	1 EB, 4 EBns. 3 PBBns
Ural MD Total					
South Ural MD Total	2, 3, 4, 5 AWBn	135 HowAR, 1292 TDR, 34, 316, 322, 328, 330 ABnsp 1 AR, 1 TDR, 5 ABns	46, 68 AeroSBn 2 AeroSBns		
Siberian MD Total	27, 32, 33, 34 AWBn			265, 283, 483 FAR 3 FARs	
Central Asian MD	93 RB, 3, 6, 7, 8, 9, 11, 12, 13, 15, 16, 17, 18, 19, 20, 21, 22, 23, 29 AWBn	24 GunAR, 450 HowAR, 179 MtrR		136 MAD, 238 FAD, 300 AAD, 15 RAS	125, 136, 384, 385 EBn
Forces in Iran	58 RC (68 MtnRD, 89 RB, 39 MtnCD)	28 AAABtry			
Total	1 RC, 1 RD, 2 RBs, 1 CD	2 AR, 1 MtrR		1 MAD, 1 AAD, 1 FAD	4 EBns
Trans-Baikal Front 17th Army	36, 57 MRD, 227 RB, 1, 3 MRR	185, 629, 1141 GunAR, 413, 624 HowAR, 178 MtrR, 63, 66, 376, 382 AAABn	61 TD, 25 MB, 43 TB, 30 MtcR, 70, 82 TBn, 67 Atr		102 EBn, 84 PBBn

Army	Units	Units	Units	Units
36th Army	94, 209, 210 RD, 226 RB, 59 CD, 31 FR	267, 390, 1233 GunAR, 259 HowAR, 176, 177 MtrR, 190 PackMtrR, 120, 401, 405, 414 AAABn	33, 35 TBn, 68, 69 Atr	39 EBn
12th Air Army				30, 247 BAD, 248, 316 AAD, 245, 246 FAD, 12 RAR, 846 LBAR, 23 BAS, 40, 41 CAS
Front forces	2 RC (103 RD, 39 RB), 32 FR	1142, 1143 GunAR, 106, 1146 HowARhp, 32 GMR, 410 AAABn	111 TD, 44, 205, 206 TB, 70, 79 Atr	281, 283, 382, 383 EBn, 1, 2, 17 PBBn
Total (2 armies, 1 air army)	1 RC, 4 RDs, 2 MRDs, 3 RBs, 1 CD, 2 FRs, 2 RRs	13 ARs, 4 MtrRs, 1 GMR, 9 AAABns	2 TDs, 4 TBs, 1 MB, 1 MtrR, 4 TBns	2 BADs, 2 AAD, 2 FAD, 1 RAR, 1 LBAR	6 EBns, 4 PBBns

Far Eastern Front

Army	Units	Units	Units	Units
1st Army	5 RC (187 RD, 95, 246 RB), 26 RC (22, 59 RD), 59 RC (39 RD, 12, 29 RB), 18 CC (67, 84 CD, 1594 TDR, 18 TDBn, MtrBn), 105, 112 FR	50, 273, 1124, 1125, 1138, 1139 GunAR, 45, 87, 1133 HowAR, 199, 1192 HowARhp, 1471, 1627, 1630, 1631 TDR, 168, 296, 451, 452 MtrR, 33 GMR, 1588, 1647 AAAR, 43, 44, 45, 103, 115, 129, 300 AAABn	Ussuriisk TB, 75, 77, 204, 208, 209, 210 TB, 42 MRB, 3, 78 AtrBn	26, 27 CAS	45 ESB, 132 PBBn
2nd Army	3, 12 RD, 17, 41, 258, 259 RB, 101 FR	42, 1120, 1140 GunAR, 147, 1129 HowAR, 550 HowARhp, 1628, 1632 TDR, 192 HGunABn, 181, 465 MtrR, 1589 AAAR, 9, 42 AAABn	2 Amur TB, 73, 74 TB, 2, 5 AtrBn	28 CAS	2 HPBR, 10 PBBn
15th Army	34 RD, 38, 260 RB, 102 FR	52, 145, 424, 1121 GunAR, 1194 HowARhp, 183, 470 MtrR, 1648 AAAR, 46, 302 AAABn	165, 171 TB, 77 AtrBn	29 CAS	129 EBn, 11, 24, 29 PBBn

—*continued*

1 JULY 1943 Continued

Fronts and Armies	Rifle, Airborne, and Cavalry	Artillery	Tank and Mechanized	Air	Engineers
25th Army	17 RC (190 RD, 261, 262 RB, 175 RR), 39 RC (40, 105 RD, 6, 8, 21, 158, 247 RB), 106, 107, 108, 110, 111, 113 FR, 84, 86 MGBn	282, 548, 1126, 1127, 1136 GunAR, 107, 148 HowAR, 549 HowARhp, 555, 1629, 1634, 1635 TDR, 180, 182, 453, 463, 464, 473 MtrR, 1590 AAAR, 22, 24, 28, 721 AAABn	Coastal TB, 72, 76, 218 TB, 9 AtrBn, 23, 62 Atr	38 CAS	46 ESB
35th Army	35, 66 RD, 30 RB, 109 FR	76, 187, 1122, 1123 GunAR, 177, 263 HowAR, 1193 HowARhp, 1636 TDR, 472 MtrR, 1649 AAAR, 110, 355 AAABn	125, 172 TB, 29 MtcR, 13 AtrBn	30, 39 CAS	280 EBn, 3, 16, 58 PBBn
9th Air Army				33, 34 BAD, 251, 252 AAD, 32, 249, 250 FAD, 6 RAR, 528 FAR	
10th Air Army				53 BAD, 83, 253, 254 MAD, 29 FAD, 7 RAR	
11th Air Army				82 BAD, 96, 296 MAD, 140 RAS	

Front forces	Special RC (79, 101 RD, 2, 5 RB, 302, 540 RR, 5, 6, 206 RBn), 18, 88, 113 RB, 202 AbnB, 103, 104 FR	433, 1637 GunAR, 428, 487 HowAR, 1633 TDR, 117, 362, 367, 428 HGunABn, 471 MtrR, 102, 505, 726 AAABn	203, 214 TB, 76 AtrB	128, 255 MAR, 251 BAR, 799 RAR	47 ESB, 3 HPBR
Total (5 armies, 3 air armies)	6 RCs, 14 RDs, 23 RBs, 1 AbnB, 1 CC, 2 CDs, 13 FRs, 3 RRs	41 ARs, 12 TDRs, 5 ABns, 16 MtrRs, 1 GMR, 6 AAADs, 20 AAABns	20 TBs, 1 MRB, 1 MtcR, 8 AtrBns	4 BADs, 2 AADs, 7 MADs, 4 FADs, 1 BAR, 1 FAR, 3 RARs	3 EBs, 2 PBRs, 2 Ebns 8 PBBns
Grand total (8 armies, 4 air armies)	10 RCs, 26 RDs, 2 MRDs, 32 RBs, 1 AbnB, 2 CCs, 6 CDs, 28 FRs, 5 RRs	1 AC, 3 APDs, 1 AD, 8 ABs, 76 ARs, 18 ABns, 3 TDBs, 41 TDRs, 6 TDBns, 2 MtrRs, 23 MtrRs, 3 GMDs, 1 GMB, 18 GMRs, 1 MtrBn, 8 AAADs, 25 AAARs, 34 AAABns	4 MCs, 3 TCs, 2 TDs, 48 TBs, 1 MBs, 1 MRB, 27 TRs, 17 SPRs, 4 MtcRs, 20 TBns, 26 AeroSBns, 10 MtcBns 28 AtrBns	6 BADs, 5 AADs, 8 MADs, 7 FADs, 2 NBADs 2 SDADs, 5 BARs, 21 AARs, 20 FARs, 4 RARs, 3 LBARs	20 EBs,2 PBRs, 30 EBns, 15 PBBns

—continued

1 JULY 1943 Continued

PVO Fronts and Armies	PVO Formations	PVO Regions	PVO Separate Units	PVO Aviation
PVO Strany Forces **Western PVO Front**		Murmansk DR (361, 746, 885 AAAR, 33, 135, 199, 311, 313, 403, 404, 407, 426, 531 AAABn, 9, 30, 31 AAMGBn, 6 AeroObsBn, 6, 73 VNOSBn, 190, 201 AAtr); Bologoe DR (87, 178, 215, 224, 248, 256, 271, 284, 308 AAAR, 10 AAMGR, 21, 32, 98, 107 VNOSBn, 57, 74, 75, 128, 182, 182, 193, 197 AAAtr); Tula DR (732, 1573, 1574 AAAR, 56, 80, 153, 252, 269, 283, 291, 511 AAABn, 15 AAMGBn, 29 ProjBn, 58, 124, 125, 138, 188 AAAtr); Riazhsk-Tambov DR (733, 1423 AAAR, 58, 85, 180, 201, 290, 353 AAABn, 11 AAMGR, 13, 30, 34 AAAMGBn, 26 ProjBn, 7, 11, 56, 65 VNOSBn, 73, 121, 131, 139, 198, 202, 205 AAAtr); Voronezh CR (183, 254, 317, 736, 1572 AAAR, 86, 96, 173, 374, 379, 416, 430 AAABn, 4, 7, 8 AAMGR, 23 AAMGBn, 4 VNOSR, 29 VNOSBn, 5, 15 ProjBn, 55, 122, 126, 127, 129, 135, 141, 142, 143, 199, 200,		122 FAD (767, 768, 769 966 FAR); 106 FAD (33, 253, 441, 630, 926 FAR); 125 FAD (495, 651, 787, 960 FAR); 36 FAD (383, 591, 785, 827 FAR); 9 FAC (487, 586, 826, 894, 907, 910 FAR);

	203, 206 AAAtr); Khar'kov DR (374, 1575 AAAR, 9 AAMGR, 182 AAABn, 22, 57 VNOSBn, 72, 130, 132, 137, 178, 181, 184, 186, 187, 189, 204 AAAtr); Rostov CR (485, 1079, 1080, 1563, 1564 AAAR, 18, 82, 188, 189, 266, 267, 297, 299, 303, 383, 419 AAABn, 5 AAMGR. 16, 162 AAMGBn, 33, 43, 46 VNOSBn, 54, 144, 194, 195, 196 AAAtr); North Caucasus CR (454, 734, 1425, 1576 AAAR, 3, 11, 23, 36, 53, 143, 211, 249, 265, 286, 381, 433 AAABn, 16 ProjBn, 33, 140 AAAtr); Arkhangel'sk DR (84, 160, 171, 213, 318, 372, 480 AAAR, 41 VNOSBn); Cherepovets-Vologda DR (55, 74, 99, 194, 272, 385, 413 AAABn, 13, 106 VNOSBn, 183, 191 AAAtr); Rybinsk-Iaroslavl' DR (201, 1424, 1566, 1567, 1875, 1876 AAAR, 38, 40, 62, 148, 192, 197, 212, 231, 273, 287, 362, 380, 458 AAABn, 14, 18 AAMGBn, 77, 105 VNOSBn)	310 FAD (573, 802 FAR); 105 FAD (182, 234, 266, 628, 738, 833, 961 FAR); 104 FAD (348, 729, 730 FAR); 148 FAD (740, 964 FAR); 147 FAD (439, 959 FAR);
Total	3 CRs, 8 DRs	1 FAC, 9 FADs
Moscow PVO Front	1G, 50, 51, 52, 53, 54, 55, 56, 57, 58, 59, 60, 61, 62, 63 AAAD, 1, 2, 3 AAAMGD, 1, 2, 3, 4 ProjD, 1, 2 VNOSD, 1, 2, 3, 4 AeroObsD	340, 347, 1866, 1867, 1868 AAAR, 198, 205, 207, 232, 237, 240, 244, 257, 260, 263, 270, 349, 350 AAABn, 26, 27 AAMGBn, 71 VNOSBn

—continued

1 JULY 1943 Continued

PVO *Fronts* and Armies	PVO Formations	PVO Regions	PVO Separate Units	PVO Aviation
1st Fighter Air Army				317 FAD (34, 67, 736 FAR), 318 FAD (28, 562, 564, 565 FAR), 319 FAD (11, 177, 178, 309, 445 FAR), 320 FAD (12G, 16, 126, 429, 488 FAR)
Total (1 air army)	15 AAADs, 3 AAAMGDs, 4 ProjDs, 2 VNOSDs, 4 AeroObsDs		5 AAARs, 13 AAABns, 2 AAMGBns	4 FADs
Leningrad PVO Army		Ladoga DR (Volkov and Osipovets AAAR, 65, 69, 225, 251, 253, 391, 434, 447 AAABn, 42, 47 VNOSBn)	115, 169, 189, 192, 194, 351, 1804 AAAR, 2 AAMGR, 2 ProjR, 3, 4, 11 AeroObsR, 2 VNOSR	7 FAC (11, 26, 27G, 124, 158 FAR)
Total		1 DR	7 AAARs, 1 AAMGR, 1 ProjR	1 FAC
Eastern PVO Front		Gor'kii CR: Izhevsk AAAB (1869 AAAR, 356, 358 AAABn, 25 AAMGBn, 5 VNOSBn), 196, 742, 784, 1291, 1571, 1578, 1579, 1580, 1872, 1873, 1874, 1877 AAAR, 13, 39, 91, 200, 202, 236, 238, 279, 281, 289, 310, 384, 389 AAABn, 33, 37 AAMGR, 19 AAMGBn, 38, 45 ProjR, 8, 28 AeroObsBn, 8, 39, 101, 104 VNOSBn; Saratov-Balashov DR (720, 1078, 1860, 1861, 1864, 1865 AAAR, 89, 93, 106, 243, 296, 343, 425, 501 AAABn, 36 AAMGR, 43 ProjR,		142 FAD (423, 632, 722, 743, 786 FAR); 144 FAD (405, 963 FAR);

266

4 AeroObsBn, 16, 17, 99, 100, 103 VNOSBn); Stalingrad CR: 16 AAAB (1805, 1806 AAAR, 30 AAMGR, 19, 20 ProjBn, 26 AeroObsBn), 17 AAAB (1807, 1808 AAAR, 31 AAMGR, 22, 24 ProjBn, 27 AeroObsBn), 73G, 679, 748, 1077, 1082, 1083, 1568, 1569, 1570 AAAR, 471 AAABn, 1/731 AAAR, 6 AAAMGR, 12, 13, 17 ProjBn, 10, 14, 19, 44, 70 VNOSBn, 136 AAAtr; Grozny DR (16, 744, 1879 AAAR, 38 AAMGR, 151, 375, 411, 571 AAABn, 67, 76 VNOSBn, 179, 185 AAAtr); Ural'sk DR: 6 AAAB (1870 AAAR, 359 AAABn, 4 AAMGBn, 2 VNOSBn), 9 AAAB (1871 AAAR, 361 AAABn, 5 AAMGBn, 4 VNOSBn); Astrakhan BR (1809 AAAR, 32 AAMGR, 28 ProjBn); Kuibyshev DR (767, 861, 1088, 1855, 1856, 1857, 1858, 1859, 1862, 1863 AAAR, 90, 174, 285, 366, 368, 370, 378 AAABn, 34, 35 AAMGR, 40 ProjR, 10, 11, 21, 22 AAMGBn, 50, 97 VNOSBn, 2 AeroObsBn); Penza BR (79, 277, 510 AAABn, 24 AAMGBn)	2G FAD (38, 83, 84G FAR); 126 FAD (652, 822, 965 FAR); 141 FAD (631, 908 FAR);
Total 2 CRs, 4 DRs, 2 BRs	5 FADs

—*continued*

1 JULY 1943 *Continued*

PVO *Fronts* and Armies	PVO Formations	PVO Regions	PVO Separate Units	PVO Aviation
Trans-Caucasus PVO Zone Baku PVO Army			180, 190, 195, 252, 335, 339, 513, 636, 654, 1880, 1881 AAAR, 3, 39 AAMGR, 3 ProjR, 28 VNOSR, 5 AeroObsR, 128, 137 AAMGBn, 23 VNOSBn	8 FAC (82, 480, 481, 922, 962 FAR)
Zone Forces	2 AAAB (345, 415, 443, 638, 1882, 1883, 1884 AAAR, 40 AAMGR, 5 VNOSR, 21 ProjBn, 180 AAAtr), 8 AAAB (352, 466 AAAR, 76, 365, 392, 393, 422 AAABn, 20, 49 AAMGBn, 33 ProjBn, 24 VNOSBn, 7 AeroObsBn)			298 FAD (982, 983 FAR), 35 FAR
Total (1 PVO army)	2 AAABs		11 AAARs, 2 AAMGRs, 1 ProjR, 1 VNOSR, 1 AeroObsR	1 FAC, 1 FAD, 1 FAR
Central Asian PVO Zone Total			731 AAR 1 AAAR	

Trans-Baikal PVO Zone		1 BR (10, 132, 162, 390 AAABn, 25 VNOSBn);2 BR (150, 187, 262, 264, 387, 408 AAABn, 80 VNOSBn); 3 BR (750 AAAR, 107, 166 AAABn, 55 VNOSBn)	297 FAD (938, 939 FAR)
Total		3 BRs	1 FAD
Far Eastern PVO Zone	5 AAAB (749 AAAR, 8 AAMGBn, 25 ProjBn, 12 AeroObsBn, 559 VNOSBn)	Kuibyshev BR (757 AAAR, 138, 167, 175, 195 AAABn, 38 VNOSBn; Khabarovsk BR (1877 AAAR, 163, 217 AAABn, 20, 53 VNOSBn); Birobidzhan BR (147, 155, 190, 398 AAABn, 12 VNOSBn); Spaask BR (4, 152 AAABn, 54 VNOSBn); Voroshilov BR (755 AAAR, 78, 186 AAABn, 37, 565 VNOSBn); Komsomol BR (752 AAAR, 305, 463, 465 AAABn)	149 FAD (3, 18, 60 FAR)
Total	1 AAAB	6 BRs	1 FAD
Grand total (3 PVO *fronts*, 2 PVO armies, 4 PVO zones, 1 air army)	15 AAADs, 3 AAABs, 3 AAMGDs, 4 ProjDs, 2 VNOSDs, 3 AeroObsDs	5 CRs, 13 DRs, 11 BRs 24 AAAR, 13 AAABns, 2 AAMGRs	3 FACs, 21 FADs, 1 FAR

31 DECEMBER 1943

Fronts and Armies	Rifle, Airborne, and Cavalry	Artillery	Tank and Mechanized	Air	Engineers
Field Forces					
Karelian					
14th Army	10G, 14 RD, 72 NRB, 31 SkiB, MGBn	1236 GunAR, 275, 297 MtrR, 41 GMR, 156 AAAR, 325, 487 AAABn			31 EBn
19th Army	104, 122 RD, 7 NRB, MGBn	1293 GunAR, 566 MtrR, 53 GMR, 186 AAAR, 261 AAABn	377, 429 TBn, 24 AeroSBn		279 EBn, 193 FlameCo
26th Army	31 RC (45, 205 RD, 61, 85 NRB), 27, 54 RD, 32 SkiB, MGBn	471 GunAR, 441 TDR, 172, 278, 565 MtrR, 52 GMR, 272 AAAR, 48, 369 AAABn	374, 375 TBn, 73 Atr		170 EBn, 194 195 FlameCo
32nd Army	289, 313, 367 RD, 65, 80 NRB, 33 SkiB, MGBn	1237 GunAR, 173, 280, 298 MtrR, 63 GMR, 275 AAAR, 208, 446 AAABn	376 TBn, 1, 2, 3, 21, 22, 25, 26, 28 AeroSBn		261 EBn, 196 FlameCo
7th Air Army		1598, 1599 AAAR		1G, 260, 261 MAD, 324 FAR, 679 TAR, 108, 118 RAS, 42 LRRAS	
Front forces		32, 298 AAABn	27, 47 AtrBn		1 SDEB, 733 EBn, 6 GBnM, 6 FlameBn
Total (4 armies, 1 air army)	1 RC, 11 RDs, 6 RBs, 3 SkiBs	4 ARs, 1 TDR, 9 MtrRs, 4 GMRs, 6 AAARs, 9 AAABns	5 TBns, 9 AeroSBns, 2 AtrBns	3 MADs, 1 FAR	1 EB, 6EBns, 1 FlameBn, 4 FlameCos
Leningrad					
2nd Shock Army	43 RC (48, 90, 98 RD), 122 RC (11, 131, 168 RD), 43 RD, 50 RB, 48, 71 NRB, 16 FR	116, 154 CAR, 754 HowAR, 533, 535 HGumABn, 760 TDR, 230G, 144, 184, 281 MtrR, 30, 318, 322 GMR, 803 AAAR, 92, 116 AAABn	152 TB, 98, 204, 222 TR, 17, 42 AeroSBn, 4 AcBn		295, 447, 734 EBn

23rd Army	10, 92, 142 RD, 17, 22 FR		5 AeroSBn, 1 AcBn	
42nd Army	30G RC (45, 63, 64G RD), 109 RC (72, 109, 125 RD), 110 RC (56, 85, 86 RD), 189 RD, 79 FR	8 CAR, 336 GunAR, 94, 883 TDR, 276 MtrR, 618 AAABn 18 APD (65 LAB, 58 HowAB, 3, 80 HHowAB, 120 HowABhp, 42 MtrB), 23 APD (79 LAB, 38 HowAB, 2, 96 HHowAB, 21 GHowABhp, 28 MtrB), 1157 CAR, 1106, 1486 GunAR, 52G HGunABn, 304, 384, 509, 705, 1973 TDR, 104, 174, 533, 534 MtrR, 20 (-211 GMBn), 38, 320, 321 GMR, 7 AAAD (465, 474, 602, 632 AAAR), 32 AAAD (1377, 1387, 1393, 1413 AAAR), 631 AAAR, 72 AAABn	1, 220 TB, 31, 46, 49G, 205, 260 TR, 1439, 1902 SPR, 2 AcBn, 71, 72 AtrBn	54, 585 EBn
67th Army	116 RC (13, 46, 376 RD), 118 RC (124, 128, 268 RD), 291 RD, 14 FR	81 GunAB, 267G, 21, 260, 561 GunAR, 599 HowAR, 532 HGunABn, 289, 690, 882, 884 TDR, 122, 127, 134, 175, 193, 504, 567 MtrR, 970, 988 AAAR, 71, 73, 108, 613 AAABn	14 AtrBn	53, 234, 325, 367 EBn, 8 FlameBn
13th Air Army			276 BAD, 277 AAD, 275 FAD, 283 FAD, 13 RAR, 12, 49, 52 CRAS	
Front forces	108 RC (196, 224, 314 RD), 117 RD (120, 123, 201 RD), 123 RC (hq)	3 APC (hq), 51 GunAB, 12, 14G, 73, 126, 129 GunAR, 409 HGunABn, 1 GMD (2, 5, 6 GMB), 536 TDR, 1, 8 AeroAObsBn, 43 AAAD (464, 635, 1463, 1464 AAAR), 785 AAAR, 758 AAABn	30G TB, 17G, 261 TR, 1811 SPR, 3 AcBn	2 SDEB, 52 ESB, 5 HPBR, 7 GMnM, 34, 106 EBn, 1G, 21, 42 PBBn, 175 FlameCo

—*continued*

31 DECEMBER 1943 Continued

Fronts and Armies	Rifle, Airborne, and Cavalry	Artillery	Tank and Mechanized	Air	Engineers
Total (4 armies, 1 air army)	10 RCs, 33 RDs, 3 RBs, 5 FRs	1 AC, 2 APDs, 2 ABs, 18 ARs, 5 ABns, 12 TDRs, 1 TDBn, 16 MtrRs, 1 GMD, 7 GMRs, 3 AAADs, 5 AAARs, 9 AAABns	4 TBs, 10 TRs, 3 SPRs, 3 AeroSBns, 4 AcBns, 3 AtrBns	1 BAD, 1 AAD, 1 FAD, 1 FAR, 1 RAR	2 EBs, 1 PBR, 12 EBns, 3 PBBns, 1 FlameBn, 1 FlameCo
Volkhov					
8th Army	119 RC (286, 374 RD), 18, 364 RD, 1, 22 RB	258 LAR (20 LAB), 8, 71, 223G GunAR, 500 MtrR, 18 GMR, 41 AAAD (245, 634 AAAR), 1468 AAAR, 177 AAABn	33G, 185 TR, 32 AeroSBn, 49 AcBn, 50 AtrBn, 4 Atr		112 EBn
54th Army	111 RC (44, 288 RD), 115 RC (281, 285 RD, 14, 53 RB), 80, 177, 198 RD, 2 FR	1097 GunAR, 194, 499 MtrR, 29 GMR, 224 and 463 AAAR (41 AAAD), 1467, 1469 AAAR, 15 AAABn	124 TR, 107, 510 TBn, 48 AcBn, 32, 48 AtrBn, 22 AAAtr		2 GSDEB, 9 AESB, 8 GBnM, 364, 539 EBn
59th Army	6 RC (65, 239, 310 RD), 14 RC (191, 225, 378 RD), 112 RC (2, 372, 377 RD, 24 RB), 150 FR	2 AD (20 LAB, 7 GunAB, 10G HowAB), 121 HowABhp, 13G, 70, 367, 448, 1096 GunAR, 5, 30 MtrR, 192, 505, 506 MtrR, 10, 12 GMB, 28, 319 MGR, 211 GMBn (20 GMR), 3 AeroAObsBn, 45 AAAD (707, 737, 1465, 1466 AAAR), 1470 AAAR, 213, 461 AAABn, 1606, 1607 AAABn	16, 29, 122 TB, 32, 35, 50C, 25 TR, 1433, 1434 SPR, 500, 502, 503 TBn, 34, 44 AeroSBn, 47 AcBn		1 ESB, 2G, 35, 40, 109, 135, 365 EBn, 34, 36, 55 PBBn, 9 FlameBn
14th Air Army				280 BAD, 281 AAD, 269 FAR, 386 NBAR, 742 RAR, 844 TAR, 4 ARCAF, 44, 59 CRAS	

Front forces	7 RC (256, 382 RD), 58 RB	11G, 168 AAABn	7G TB, 123 Atr		12 ESB, 38 PBBn
Total (3 armies, 1 air army)	7 RCs, 22 RDs, 6 RBs, 2 FRs	1 AD, 1 AB, 9 ARs, 2 MtrBs, 6 MtrRs, 2 GMBs, 4 GMRs, 2 AAADs, 6 AAARs, 6 AAABns	4 TBs, 7 TRs, 2 SPRs, 5 TBns, 3 AeroSBns, 3 AcBns, 3 AtrBns	1 BAD, 1 AAD, 1 FAD, 1 RAR, 1 NBAR	4 EBs, 10 EBns, 4 PBBns, 1 FlameBn
2nd Baltic					
1st Shock Army	12G RC (7G, 26 RD), 14G RC (23, 53G RD), 182 RD, 137 RB	37G CAR, 11G, 701 GunAR, 385 HowAR, 1186 TDR, 110, 274 MtrR, 42 AAAD (620, 709, 714, 729 AAAR), 1473 AAAR, 63G, 29 AAABn	37, 227, 239 TR, 514 TBn, 11, 35, 36, 66 AeroSBn, 29, 35 AtrBn		13 ESB, 2, 28 EBn, 54, 58 PBBn, 13 FlameBn, FlameCo
3rd Shock Army	79 RC (171, 219 RD), 90 RC (115, 200, 245 RD), 93 RC (326, 370 RD), 100 RC (21, 46, 119G RD), 28, 146 RD	455, 1190 GunAR, 827 HowAR, 163G TDR, 203G, 550 MtrR, 90 GMR, 243, 1622 AAAR, 12 AAABn	29G, 78, 92, 118 TB, 1453 SPR		19 AESB, 225, 289 EBn
6th Guards Army	23G RC (51, 52G, 37 RD), 96 RC (282, 379 RD), 97 RC (67, 71G, 165, 391 RD), 98 RC (1, 185 RD), 150 RD	20 APD (53 GunAB, 93 HHowAB, 102 HowABhp, 20 MtrB), 27 AD (78 LAB, 76 GunAB, 74 HowAB), 19G GunAB, 25, 1235 GunAR, 6G TDB, 496, 1240 TDR, 295 MtrR, 21 GMB, 26, 27, 42, 70 GMR, 14 AAAD (715, 718, 721, 2013 AAAR), 47 AAAD (1585, 1586, 1591, 1592 AAAR), 1487 AAAR, 64G, 386, 467 AAABn	38G TB, 3, 27, 30G, 32, 38, 65, 221, 249 TR, 1539 SPR		8 SDEB, 205, 540 EBn, 18 FlameBn
10th Guards Army	7G RC (207, 208, 312 RD), 15G RC (29, 30, 85G RD), 19G RC (22, 56, 65G RD), 31 ATRBn	564 GunAR, 758 TDR, 536 MtrR, 240 AAAR	119 TR		263, 369 EBn, 206 FlameCo

—*continued*

31 DECEMBER 1943 *Continued*

Fronts and Armies	Rifle, Airborne, and Cavalry	Artillery	Tank and Mechanized	Air	Engineers
22nd Army	44 RC (33, 319 RD, 54 RB), 8, 43G, 178 RD, 23 RB, 118 FR	395 GunAR, 1040 TDR, 561 MtrR, 1472 AAAR, 239, 397 AAABn	81, 82 TR, 515 TBn, 56, 57, 62 AtrBn		352 EBn
15th Air Army		1596, 1597, 1608, 1639 AAAR		11 MAC (4, 148, 293 FAR, 658, 724 AAD), 3G, 225 AAD, 5G, 315 FAD, 284, 313 NBAD, 1 NBAR, 55 BAR, 99G RAR, 699 TAR, 1003 MedAR, 15 SAR, 1G, 50, 54, 57, 64 CRAS	
Front forces	8 RC (7, 249 RD)	2 APC (hq), 34 LAB and 60 HowAB (20 APD), 85 CAR, 18 TDB, 13 MtrB, 40 GMR, 36 AAAD (1385, 1391, 1397, 1399 AAAR), 44 AAAD (508, 708, 710, 1274 AAAR), 1477 AAAR, 242 AAABn	55 MtcBn, 133, 134 AAAtr		5 AESB, 3, 16 GBnM, 36, 134, 222, 223, 231, 738 EBn, 56, 67, 86, 88 PBBn
Total (5 armies, 1 air army)	15 RCs, 45 RDs, 3 RBs, 1 FR	1 AC, 1 APD, 1 AD, 1 AB, 12 ARs, 2 TDB, 6 TDRs, 1 MtrB, 7 MtrRs, 1 GMB, 6 GMRs, 5 AAADs, 11 AAARs, 9 AAABns	5 TBs, 14 TRs, 2 TBns, 2 SPRs, 4 AeroSBns, 5 AtrBns, 1 MtcBn	1 MAC, 2 AADs, 2 FADs, 2 NBADs, 1 BAR, 2 AARs, 3 FARs, 1 RAR, 1 NBAR	4 EBs, 17 EBns, 6 PBBns, 2 FlameBns, 2 FlameCos
1st Baltic					
4th Shock Army	2G RC (29, 166, 381 RD), 22G RC (51, 154, 156 RD), 60 RC (119, 357 RD, 101 RB), 83 RC (117, 234, 360	66 LAB (21 APD), 27G GunAB (8 GunAD), 38G CAR, 166G, 488 GunAR, 17 TDB, 556 MtrR, 99, 310	5 TC (24, 41, 70 TB, 5 MRB, 161, 1515, 1546 SPR, 92 MtcBn, 277 MtrR, 731 TDBn,		1 GAESB, 290, 736 EBn, 94 PBBn, 12 FlameBn

11th GuardsArmy	RD), 155 FR, 3G CC (5, 6G, 32 CD, 1814 SPR, 144G TDR, 3 GMR, 64G MtrBn, 3G TDBn, 1731 AAAR) 8G RC (5, 26, 83G RD), 16G RC (1, 11, 31G RD), 36G RC (16, 84G, 235 RD), 18, 90G RD		47 GMBn, 1708 AAAR), 34G, 236 TB, 171 TBn
	GMR, 1624 AAAR		
	15 APD (69 LAB, 35 GunAB, 58, 87 HHowAB, 106 HowABhp, 18 MtrB), 21 APD (64 GunAB, 94 HHowAB, 25 MtrB), 523, 1093, 1165 CAR, 403, 537 GunAR, 480 HowAR, 551 TDR, 545 MtrR, 2 GMD (3, 17, 26 GMB), 22, 24, 34, 93 GMR, 17 AAAD (1267, 1276, 1279, 1483 AAAR), 46 AAAD (609, 617, 618, 717 AAAR), 1280 AAAR	1 TC (89, 117, 159 TB, 44 MRB, 1437 SPR, 86 MtcBn, 1514 TDR, 388 TDBn, 108 MtrR, 10 GMBn, 1720 AAAR), 10G TB, 2G TR	10 AESB, 6G, 226, 243 EBn, 174, 178 FlameCo
39th Army	5G RC (9, 17, 19, 91G RD), 84 RC (134, 158, 262 RD), 124 RB	8 GunAD (26, 28G GunAB), 55 HowAB and 103 HowABhp (21 APD), 41G CAR, 545 GunAR, 472 HowAR, 4 TDB, 610 TDR, 558 MtrR (31 MtrB), 408, 552, 554, 555 MtrR, 20 GMB, 326 GMR, 39 AAAD (1406, 1410, 1414, 1526 AAAR), 225, 621 AAAR, 490 AAABn	28, 39G TB, 47 MB, 11G TR	17, 228 EBn, 122 PBBn
43rd Army	1 RC (145, 204 RD), 91 RC (179, 270, 306 RD), 92 RC (332, 334, 358 RD, 145 RB), 114 RB	43 GunAR, 64, 283, 376, 1224 HowAR, 587, 759 TDR, 31 MtrB (-558 MtrR), 118 MtrR, 39 GMR, 246, 1626 AAAR, 221 AAABn	60, 143 TB, 46 MB, 105 TR	273, 312 EBn, 106 PBBn

—continued

31 DECEMBER 1943 Continued

Fronts and Armies	Rifle, Airborne, and Cavalry	Artillery	Tank and Mechanized	Air	Engineers
3rd Air Army		1556, 1557, 1558 AAAR		3 AAC (307, 308 AAD), 1G FAC (3, 4G FAD), 2 FAC (7G, 322 FAD), 211, 335 AAD, 240, 259 FAD, 314 NBAD, 11 RAR, 6G AAR, 373 NBAR, 763 TAR, 105G ARCAF	
Front forces	103 RC (16 RD), 47 RD	85 GMR, 601, 1623, 1625, 1714 AAAR, 183, 622 AAABn		13, 36 CRAS	2 ESB, 4 AESB, 5 SDEB, 10 GBnM, 4G, 37, 114, 210, 249, 293 EBn, 57, 60, 93 PBBn
Total (4 armies, 1 air army)	13 RCs, 39 RDs, 4 RBs, 1 CC, 3 CDs, 1 FR	2 APDs, 1 AD, 17 ARs, 2 TDBs, 4 TDRs, 1 MtrB, 7 MtrRs, 1 GMD, 1 GMB, 9 GMRs, 3 AAADs, 13 AAARs, 4 AAABns	2 TCs, 7 TBs, 2 MBs, 3 TRs, 1 TB	1 AAC, 2 FACs, 6 FADs, 4 AADs, 1 NBAD, 1 AAR, 1 RAR, 1 LBAR	5 EBs, 16 EBns, 6 PBBns, 1 FlameBn, 2 FlameCos
Western					
5th Army	72 RC (153, 159, 277 RD)	646 GunAR, 696 TDR, 283 MtrR, 95 GMBn, 726 AAAR	1537 SPR		296, 297 EBn, 16 FlameBn
10th Army	38 RC (64, 212, 385 RD), 70 RC (49, 139, 330 RD), 76, 160, 290 RD	1091 CAR, 572 GunAR, 43 TDB, 992 TDR, 544 MtrR, 1268 AAAR	1 AtrBn		6, 229, 303, 345 EBn, 177 FlameCo

Army				
31st Army	71 RC (220, 331 RD), 114 RC (88, 251 RD), 152 FR	31G HHowAB, 117 HowABhp, 392 CAR, 542, 557, 644, 1099 GunAR, 83G, 49, 56 HowAR, 529 TDR, 537, 549 MtrR, 77 GMR, 2 AeroAObsBn, 33 AAAD (1378, 1710, 1715, 1718 AAAR), 341, 1275, 1478, 1479 AAAR, 4, 614 AAABn	42G TB, 1435 SPR, 2G MtcR, 52 AtrBn	72, 113, 233, 537 EBn, 51, 90 PBBn, 14, 15 FlameBn, 186 FlameCo
33rd Army	36 RC (199, 215, 274 RD, 36 RB), 45 RC (32, 97, 184 RD), 65 RC (42, 173, 222 RD), 69 RC (144, 164 RD), 81 RC (95, 157 RD)	3G APD (7G LAB, 22G GunAB, 8G HowAB, 99 HHowAB, 107 HowABhp, 43 MtrB), 6G HGunAD (15, 29, 30G, 4 GunAB), 119 HowABhp, 517 CAR, 761 GunAR, 16G TDB, 873 TDR, 538 MtrR, 24 GMB, 54, 74, 307, 325 GMR, 34 AAAD (1379, 1383, 1389, 1395 AAAR), 49 AAAD (1265, 1271, 1272, 2012 AAAR), 739, 1266, 1480 AAAR	2, 23G, 213, 256 TB, 1445, 1494, 1830 SPR	1 AESB, 129, 133, 230, 298 EBn, 185 FlameCo
49th Army	61 RC (62, 174, 192 RD), 62 RC (63, 247, 352 RD), 113 RC (70, 344 RD), 154 FR	468, 995 GunAR, 1G TDB, 593 TDR, 540, 542 MtrR, 1273, 1709 AAAR	196 TB, 6 AtrBn	305 EBn, 17 FlameBn
1st Air Army		1550, 1551, 1552, 1553, 1604 AAAR		2 AAC (7G, 231 AAD), 3G, 113 BAD, 233, 311 AAD, 303, 309 FAD, 213, 325 NBAD, 10 RAR, 713 TAR, 1 MedAR, 21, 32, 62, 65 CRAS

—continued

31 DECEMBER 1943 Continued

Fronts and Armies	Rifle, Airborne, and Cavalry	Artillery	Tank and Mechanized	Air	Engineers
Front forces	338, 371 RD	5 APC: 5G APD (71 LAB, 17G GunAB, 67 HowAB, 95 HHowARB, 18G HowABhp, 27 MtrB), 7 GMD (4, 9, 11 GMB); 4G HGunAD (11, 12, 13, 14G GunAB), 570 CAR, 16, 55G HowAR, 13 TDB, 535 MtrR, 317 GMR, 48 AAAD (231G, 1277, 1278, 2011 AAAR), 1270, 1281, 1481, 1482 AAAR, 64, 324, 500, 525 AAABn	2G TC (4, 25, 26G TB, 4G MRB, 1819, 1833 SPR, 79 MtcBn, 19 AcBn, 1500 TDR, 755 TDBn, 273 MtrR, 28 GMBn, 1695 AAR), 43G, 120, 153 TB, 56, 63, 64G, 248 TR, 1495 SPR, 12, 41 AeroSBn, 145 AAAtr		3 AESB, 11 EMB, 33 SDEB, 11 GBnM, 122, 132 EBn, 9, 62, 87, 89, 91, 99, 137, 159 PBBn
Total (5 armies, 1 air army)	13 RCs, 39 RDs, 1 RB, 2 FRs	1 AC, 2 APDs, 2 ADs, 3 ABs, 18 ARs, 4 TDBs, 5 TDRs, 8 MtrRs, 1 GMD, 1 GMB, 7 GMRs, 4 AAADs, 20 AAARs, 6 AAABns	1 TC, 9 TBs, 4 TRs, 6 SPRs, 1 MtcR, 2 AeroSBns, 3 AtrBns	1 AAC, 2 BADs, 4 AADs, 2 FADs, 2 NBAD, 1 RAR	4 EBs, 18 EBns, 10 PBBns, 4 FlameBns, 3 FlameCo
Belorussian Front					
3rd Army	41 RC (120G, 186 RD), 80 RC (5, 283, 362 RD), 17, 269 RD	295G GunAR, 584 TDR, 475 MtrR, 1284 AAAR	36 TR, 31, 55 AtrBn		57 ESB, 9G EBn
48th Army	25 RC (4, 197, 273 RD), 29 RC (102, 137, 307 RD), 42 RC (170, 194, 399 RD), 73, 175, 217 RD	1168 GunAR, 3G TDB, 220G, 1179 TDR, 479 MtrR, 84 GMR, 31 AAAD (1376, 1380, 1386, 1392 AAAR), 461 AAAR	42, 231 TR, 1897 SPR		277, 313 EBn, 142 FlameCo

Army				
50th Army	46 RC (238, 369, 380 RD), 108, 110, 324, 413 RD		44 TDB, 1321 TDR, 481 MtrR, 13 AAAD (1065, 1173, 1175, 1218 AAAR), 1484 AAAR	233 TR, 21, 43 AtrBn	2 AESB, 307, 309 EBn, 173 FlameCo
61st Army	9G RC (12, 76, 77G RD), 89 RC (15, 55, 81 RD), 356 RD, 2G CC (3, 4, 17G CD, 149G TDR, 2G TDBn, 10 GMR, 60G MtrBn, 1730 AAAR), 7G CC (14, 15, 16G CD, 145G TDR, 7G TDBn, 7 GMR, 57G MtrBn, 1733 AAAR)		6 APD (21 LAB, 10 GunAB, 18 HowAB, 118 HHowAB, 2 MtrB), 60G CAR, 67G GunAR, 1 TDB, 533 TDR, 547 MtrR, 6, 56 GMR, 1282 AAAR	68 TB, 1459 SPR	310, 344 EBn, 20 FlameBn
63rd Army	35 RC (129, 250, 348 RD), 40 RC (41, 169 RD), 53 RC (96, 260, 323 RD)		554 GunAR, 40 TDB, 1311 TDR, 286 MtrR, 28 AAAD (1355, 1359, 1365, 1371 AAAR)	26G TR, 1901 SPR	
65th Army	18 RC (69, 162, 193 RD), 19 RC (38G, 82 RD), 27 RC (60, 106, 354 RD), 95G RD (37, 44G, 172 RD), 105 RC (75G, 132, 253 RD)		4 APC: 5 APD (23G LAB, 24 GunAB, 9 HowAB, 86 HHowAB, 100 HowABhp, 1 MtrB), 12 APD (46 LAB, 41 GunAB, 32 HowAB, 89 HHowAB, 104 HowABhp, 11 MtrB), 5 GMD (16, 22, 23 GMB); 22 AD (13 LAB, 59 GunAB, 63 HowAB), 20, 41 TDB, 543 TDR, 143G, 478 MtrR, 37, 92, 311, 313 GMR, 2G AAAD (302, 303, 304, 306G AAAR), 3G AAAD (297, 307, 308, 309G AAAR), 235 AAAR	1G TC (15, 16, 17G TB, 1G MRB, 237, 1001, 1541 SPR, 1G, 65 MtcBn, 732 TDR, 455 MtrR, 43 GMBn, 80G AAAR), 255 TR, 1816, 1888 SPR	8 AESB, 84, 356 EBn, 53 PBBn, 141, 207 FlameCo 14 ESB, 202, 321 EBn, 19 FlameBn

—continued

31 DECEMBER 1943 *Continued*

Fronts and Armies	Rifle, Airborne, and Cavalry	Artillery	Tank and Mechanized	Air	Engineers
16th Air Army		325, 1610, 1611, 1612, 1974 AAAR		3 BAC (241, 301 BAD), 6 MAC (221 BAD, 282 FAD), 6 FAC (234, 273 FAD), 2G, 299 AAD, 1G, 283, 286 FAD, 271 NBAD, 16 RAR, 62G ARCAF	
Front forces	121 RC (23, 218 RD), 115, 119, 161 FR, 6G CC (8, 13G, 8 CD, 1813 SPR, 142G TDR, 6G TDBn, 11 GMR, 47G MtrBn, 1732 AAAR)	44, 68 GumAB, 4G TDB, 120, 1071 TDR, 35G MtrB, 218 MtrR, 94 GMR, 12 AAAD (836, 977, 990, 997 AAAR), 24 AAAD (1045, 1337, 1343, 1349 AAAR), 221G, 1259, 1263 AAAR, 13G, 27, 31, 615 AAABn	193, 251, 253 TR, 1444, 1538 SPR, 39, 40, 59 AtrBn	6 MedAR, 11G, 47, 53, 69 CRAS	1G SDEB, 6 ESB, 18 AESB, 7 PBB, 12 GBnM, 63 120, 257, 341, 386, 693, 740, 741 EBn, 48, 85, 92, 104, 131 PBBn,
Total (6 armies, 1 air army)	17 RCs, 57 RDs, 1 RB, 3 CCs, 9 CDs, 3 FRs	1 AC, 3 APDs, 1 AD, 2 ABs, 5 ARs, 7 TDBs, 9 TDRs, 1 MtrB, 8 MtrRs, 1 GMD, 8 GMRs, 7 AAADs, 13 AAARs, 4 AAABns	1 TC, 1 TB, 9 TRs, 7 SPRs, 7 AtrBns	1 BAC, 1 MAC, 1 FAC, 3 BADs, 2 AADs, 6 FADs, 1 NBAD, 1 RAR	7 EBs, 1 PBB, 20 EBns, 6 PBBns, 2 FlameBns, 4 FlameCos
1st Ukrainian 1st Guards Army	11 RC (271, 276, 316 RD), 94 RC (30, 99, 350 RD), 107 RC (127, 304, 328 RD)	3 APD (15 LAB, 5 GumAB, 1HowAB, 116 HHowAB, 7 MtrB), 518 GunAR, 22 TDB, 163, 1642, 1644 TDR, 12 MtrB, 496, 525 MtrR, 65	93 TB, 1831, 1832 SPR		9 ESB, 235, 351, 1505 EBn

13th Army	24 RC (140, 149, 287 RD), 28 RC (4G AbnD, 70C, 246, 415 RD), 76 RC (6, 121G, 112 RD), 77 RC (143, 181, 397 RD)	GMR, 25 AAAD (1067, 1356, 1362, 1368 AAAR), 580 AAAR 19G GunAR, 23 TDB, 130, 645, 868, 1643, 1645, 1660 TDR, 128, 476, 477, 497 MtrR, 5, 47, 323 GMR, 10 AAAD (802, 975, 984, 994 AAAR), 1287 AAAR	25 TC (111, 162, 175 TB, 20 MRB, 41, 1829 SPR, 53 MtcBn, 1497 TDR, 746 TDBn, 459 MtrR, 2 GMBn, 1702 AAAR), 129, 150 TB, 999, 1889, 1890 SPR	7 AESB, 275 EBn
18th Army	22 RC (129G, 71, 317 RD), 52 RC (117G, 24, 395 RD), 101 RC (161 RD)	17 APD (37 LAB, 39 GunAB, 50 HowAB, 92 HHowAB, 108 HowABhp, 22 MtrB), 69, 112G GunAR, 1528 HowAR, 108, 312G, 408, 493 TDR, 569 MtrR, 37 AAAD (1400, 1404, 1408, 1412 AAAR), 269G AAAR	12G TR	50 EBn
27th Army	47 RC (38, 136, 180 RD), 206, 309, 337 RD	680, 1672 TDR, 480, 492 MtrR, 33 GMB, 83 GMR, 249 AAAR		25, 38 EBn
38th Army	17G RC (68G, 211, 241 RD), 21 RC (100, 135, 155 RD), 74 RC (107, 183, 305 RD), 125 ATRBn	13 APD (42 LAB, 47 HowAB, 88, 91 HHowAB, 101 HowABhp, 17 MtrR), 24G GunAB, 76C, 628 GunAR, 805 HowAR, 315, 316G, 222, 1076, 1593, 1663, 1689 TDR, 3 AeroAObsBn, 491 MtrR, 314 GMR, 21 AAAD (1044, 1334, 1340, 1346 AAAR), 1288 AAAR	7, 9G, 39 TR	15 AESB, 7, 268 EBn

—continued

31 DECEMBER 1943 Continued

Fronts and Armies	Rifle, Airborne, and Cavalry	Artillery	Tank and Mechanized	Air	Engineers
40th Army	50 RC (74, 163, 240 RD), 51 RC (167, 232, 340 RD), 1 InfB (Czech)	33 GunAB, 25G HowABhp, 8G TDB, 4, 317G, 1666, 1667 TDR, 9, 10, 493 MtrR, 16, 328 GMR, 9 AAAD (800, 974, 981, 993 AAAR)	1812 SPR		14 EBn, 4, 21, 22 FlameBn
60th Army	15 RC (322, 336 RD), 18G RC (148, 280, 351 RD), 23 RC (8, 147, 226 RD), 30 RC (121, 141 RD), 108 ATRBn	1156 GunAR, 839 HowAR, 7G, 28 TDB, 350, 563, 640, 1075, 1178, 1506, 1646 TDR, 138 MtrR, 88, 98 GMR, 23 AAAD (1064, 1336, 1342, 1348 AAAR), 217 AAAR	59 TR, 1219 SPR, 37, 49, 58 AtrBn		59 ESB, 317 EBn, 1, 2 FlameBn
1st Tank Army	138 ATRBn	79 GMR, 8 AAAD (797, 848, 978, 1063 AAAR)	8G MC (19, 20, 21G MB, 1G TB, 354G, 1451 SPR, 8G MtcBn, 353G TDR, 756 TDBn, 265G MtrR, 405 GMBn, 358G AAAR), 11G TC (40, 44, 45G TB, 27G MRB, 293G, 1535 SPR, 9G MtcBn, 362G TDR, 391 TDBn, 270G MtrR, 53 GMBn), 64G TB, 81 MtcBn		71, 267 EBn
3rd Guards Tank Army		36, 91 GMR, 1381, 1394 AAAR	6G TC (51, 52, 53G TB, 22G MRB, 1442, 1893 SPR, 3G MtcBn, 55G TDBn, 272G		182 EBn

2nd Air Army		1554, 1555, 1605 AAAR	MtrR, 286G AAAR), 7G TC (54, 55, 56G TB, 23G MRB, 1419, 1894 SPR, 4G MtcBN, 56G TDR, 467G MtrR, 287G AAAR), 9 MC (69, 70, 71 MB, 47, 59G TR, 1454, 1823 SPR, 100 MtcBn, 396 TDR, 616 MtrR, 1719 AAAR), 91 TB, 166 TR, 1835, 1836 SPR, 50 MtcR, 39 AcBn	5 AAC (4G, 264 AAD), 5 FAC (8G, 256 FAD), 10 FAC (10G, 235 FAD), 202 BAD, 227, 291 AAD, 208 NBAD, 50 RAR, 4 MedAR, 8 ARCAF, 51, 60, 66 CRAS	
Front forces	42G, 237, 389 RD, 1G CC (1, 2, 7G CD, 1461 SPR, 143G TDR, 1G TDBn, 1 GMR, 49 MtrBn, 319 AAAR), 54, 159 FR	7 APC: Hq and 3 GMD (15, 18, 19 GMB); 1 GAD (3 GLAB, 1 GGunAB, 2 GHowAB), 1950 GunAR, 111 GHowAR, 9G, 24, 32 TDB, 269, 330, 372, 874, 1292, 1664 TDR, 494 MtrR, 32 GMB, 1954 AAAR, 22 GAAABn		4G TC (12, 13, 14G TB, 3G MRB, 76 MtcBn, 756 TDR, 752 TDBn, 264 MtrR, 240 GMBn, 120G AAAR), 5G TC (20, 21, 22G TB, 6G MRB, 1416, 1458, 1462 TDR, 80 MtcBn, 754 TDBn, 454 MtrR, 1696 AAAR), 45 AtrBn	4 ESB, 6 AESB, 42 SDEB, 3, 6 PBB, 13 GBnM, 27 EBn, 9, 20, 49, 50, 108 PBBn

—continued

31 DECEMBER 1943 Continued

Fronts and Armies	Rifle, Airborne, and Cavalry	Artillery	Tank and Mechanized	Air	Engineers
Total (7 armies, 2 tank armies, 1 air army)	20 RCs, 62 RDs, 1 AbnD, 1 CC, 3 CDs, 2 FRs	1 AC, 3 APDs, 1 AD, 3 ABs, 12 ARs, 8 TDBs, 39 TDRs, 1 MtrB, 15 MtrRs, 1 GMD, 2 GMBs, 13 GMRs, 7 AAADs, 12 AAARs, 2 AAABns	6 TCs, 2 MC, 5 TBs, 6 TRs, 9 SPRs, 1 MtcR, 1 AcBn, 1 MtcBn, 4 AtrBns	1 AAC, 2 FACs, 1 BAC, 4 AADs, 4 FADs, 1 NBAD, 1 RAR	7 EBs, 2 PBBs, 16 EBns, 6 PBBns, 5 FlameBns
2nd Ukrainian					
4th Guards Army	20G RC (5G AbnD, 66G, 375 RD), 21G RC (69G, 138 RD)	33 TDB, 452 TDR, 466 MtrR, 27 AAAD (1354, 1358, 1364, 1370 AAAR)			48 EBn
5th Guards Army	32G RC (6G AbnD, 95, 97, 110G, 214 RD), 33G RC (9G AbnD, 13G, 111 RD) 35G RC (93, 94G, 78, 84 RD), 123 ATRBn	49 LAB (16 APD), 91 HHowAB (13 APD), 265G, 1110, 1327 GunAR, 11, 34 TDB, 301, 444 TDR, 469 MtrR, 8, 27 GMB, 308 GMR, 29 AAAD (1360, 1366, 1372, 1374 AAAR), 225G AAAR	57 GTR		256, 328, 431 EBn, 3 FlameBn
7th Guards Army	24G RC (8G AbnD, 36, 41G RD), 25G RC (72, 81G, 409 RD), 303 RD, 3 ATRBn	11 AD (45 GunAB, 40 HowAB), 161G GunAR, 30 TDB, 114, 115G, 1661, 1669 TDR, 263, 290 MtrR, 97, 302, 309 GMR, 5 AAAD (670, 743, 1119, 1181 AAAR), 162G AAAR	27G TB, 34, 38 AtrBn		175, 329 EBn, 27 FlameBn
37th Army	27G RC (48, 58G RD), 57 RC (15, 92G, 228 RD), 82 RC (10G AbnD, 28G, 188 RD), 1G AbnD	42 LAB (13 APD), 381 GunAR, 10 TDB, 324, 1008 TDR, 562 MtrR, 315 GMR, 35 AAAD (772, 1390, 1396, 1398 AAAR)	61 AtrBn		8 ESB, 112, 116 EBn

Army				
52nd Army	73 RC (7G AbnD, 62G RD), 78 RC (254, 373 RD), 294 RD	568 GunAR, 438, 1322 TDR, 490 MtrR, 17 GMR, 38 AAAD (1401, 1405, 1409, 1712 AAAR)	173 TB, 378, 379 TBn	133 SBn, 366 EBn, 32, 40 PBBn
53rd Army	48 RC (14G, 252, 299 RD), 75 RC (116, 213, 233 RD), 63, 122 ATRBn	16 APD (61 GunAB, 52 HowAB, 90 HHowAB, 14 MtrB), 31 LAB (11 AD), 1328 GunAR, 6 TDB, 232, 1316 TDR, 461 MtrR, 89, 96 GMR, 30 AAAD (1361, 1367, 1373, 1375 AAAR)	34 TR	11, 17 EBn
57th Army	49 RC (19, 223 RD), 64 RC (73, 78G, 52 RD), 68 RC (80G, 93, 113 RD), 53 RD, 93 ATRBn	374, 595 TDR, 523 MtrR, 80 GMR, 258G, 71 AAAR, 227 AAABn	96 TB	251, 252 EBn, 176 FlameCo
5th Guards Tank Army	678 GunAR, 689 TDR, 76 GMR, 6 AAAD (146, 366, 516, 1062 AAAR)	5G MC (10, 11, 12G MB, 24G TB, 104G, 1447, 1529 SPR, 2G MtcBn, 737 TDBn, 285 MtrR, 409 GMBn), 18 TC (110, 170, 181 TB, 32 MRB, 1438, 1543 SPR, 78 MtcBn, 1000 TDR, 736 TDBn, 292 MtrR, 106 GMBn, 1694 AAAR), 29 TC (25, 31, 32 TB, 53 MRB, 1446, 1549 SPR, 75 MtcBn, 108 TDR, 271 MtrR, 11 GMBn), 53G TR, 1G MtcR	994 NBAR	377 EBn

—continued

31 DECEMBER 1943 *Continued*

Fronts and Armies	Rifle, Airborne, and Cavalry	Artillery	Tank and Mechanized	Air	Engineers
5th Air Army		1561, 1562 AAAR		1 BAC (1G, 293 BAD), 1 AAC (266, 292 AAD, 203 FAD), 4 FAC (294, 302 FAD), 7 FAC (205, 304 FAD), 312 NBAD, 511 RAR, 1001 MedAR, 18 ARCAF, 85 CRAS	
Front forces	26G RC (25G, 6, 31 RD), 33 RC (50, 297 RD), 89 GRD, 5G CC (11, 12G, 63 CD, 1896 SPR, 150G TDR, 5G TDBn, 9 GMR, 72G MtrBn, 585 AAAR), 130 ATRBn	109 HowABhp (16 APD), 27 GunAB, 1073 TDR, 303 GMR, 11 AAAD (804, 976, 987, 996 AAAR), 26 AAAD (1352, 1357, 1363, 1369 AAAR)	1 MC (19, 35, 37 MB, 219 TB, 57 MtcBn, 75 TDR, 751 TDBn, 294 MtrR, 41 GMBn, 1382 AAAR), 7 MC (16, 63, 64 MB, 41G TB, 1440, 1821 SPR, 109 TDR, 94 MtcBn, 614 MtrR, 40 GMBn, 1712 AAAR), 8 MC (66, 67, 68 MB, 116 TB, 69 TR, 1822 SPR, 97 MtcBn, 114 TDR, 395 TDBn, 615 MtrR, 205 GMBn, 1716 AAAR), 20 TC (8G, 80, 155 TB, 7G MRB, 1834, 1895 SPR, 96 MtcBn, 1505 TDR, 735 TDBn, 291 MtrR, 406 GMBn, 1711 AAAR), 167 TR, 10 AtrBn		5, 60 ESB, 14 AESB, 27 SDEB, 1 PBB, 1, 8 PBB, 61, 69, 246, 247, 248, 250 EBn 6, 7, 19, 125 PBBn

Total (7 armies, 1 tank army, 1 air army)	19 RC, 52 RDs, 7 AbnDs, 1 CC, 3 CDs	1 APD, 1 AD, 1 AB, 8 ARs, 6 TDBs, 17 TDRs, 8 MtrRs, 2 GMBs, 11 GMRs, 9 AAADs, 6 AAARs, 1 AAABn	3 TCs, 4 MCs, 3 TBs, 4 TRs, 1 MtcR, 2 TBns, 4 AtrBns	1 BAC, 1 AAC, 2 FACs, 2 BADs, 2 AADs, 5 FADs, 1 NBAD, 1 RAR, 1 NBAR	5 EBs, 1 PBB, 2 PBRs, 21 EBns, 6 PBBns, 2 FlameBns, 1 FlameCo

3rd Ukrainian

6th Army	66 RC (60G, 203, 244, 333 RD)				4 PBB, 181, 370 EBn
8th Guards Army	4G RC (35, 47, 57G RD), 28G RC (39, 79, 88G RD), 29G RC (27, 74, 82G RD)	103G GunAR, 152 HowAR, 1248 TDR, 531 MtrR, 35 GMR, 1353 AAAR (22 AAAD), 1587 AAAR	9 APD (26 LAB, 30 GunARB, 23 HowAB, 113 HowABhp, 10 MtrB), 40G CAR, 170G, 99, 547 GunAR, 19 TDB, 266G, 184 TDR, 251 TDBn, 141, 524 MtrR, 45, 58, 87 GMR, 3 AAAD (1084, 1089, 1114, 1118 AAAR), 22 AAAD (1335, 1341, 1347 AAAR), 271G, 878 AAAR	11 TB, 10G TR, 991 SPR, 53 MtcR		11 AESB, 62 ESB, 326, 327, 350, 358 EBn, 23, 24 FlameBns
46th Army	6G RC (20G, 152, 353 RD), 34 RC (195, 236, 394 RD)	115 GunAB (9 APD), 42G CAR, 109G GunAR, 437, 1312 TDR, 462, 563 MtrR, 61, 301 GMR, 579, 1384, 1651 AAAR, 60, 139 AAABn 1613, 1614, 1615 AAAR	4G, 52, 187 TR		51 ESB, 68, 269 EBn
17th Air Army				1 MAC (5G AAD, 288 FAD), 9 MAC (305, 306 AAD, 295 FAD), 244 BAD, 11G FAD, 262 NBAD, 39 RAR, 371 NBAR, 282 SAR, 3 MedAR, 14 ARCAF, 50 RAS, 34, 58, 63, 67 CRAS	

—continued

31 DECEMBER 1943 Continued

Fronts and Armies	Rifle, Airborne, and Cavalry	Artillery	Tank and Mechanized	Air	Engineers
Front forces	10 AWBn	870 LAR (11 LAB), 5, 9 TDB, 1249 TDR, 23 MtrB, 28, 29 GMB, 62 GMR, 4 AAAD (253, 254, 268G, 606 AAAR), 241, 247, 303, 470, 586, 626, 1474 AAAR	23 TC (3, 39, 135 TB, 56 MRB, 1443 SPR, 82 MtcBn, 1501 TDR, 739 TDBn, 457 MtrR, 442 GMBn, 1697 AAAR), 5, 60G, 141 TR, 1818, 1891 SPR, 3G MtcR, 67 MtcBn		44 SDEB, 5 PBB, 2 HPBR, 19 GBnM, 64 EBn
Total (3 armies, 1 air army)	6 RCs, 19 RDs	1 APD, 8 ARs, 3 TDBs, 6 TDRs, 1 TDBn, 1 MtrB, 5 MtrRs, 2 GMBs, 7 GMRs, 3 AAADs,16 AAARs, 2 AAABns	1 TC, 1 TB, 7 TRs, 3 SPRs, 2 MtcRs, 1 MtcBn	2 MACs, 1 BAD, 3 AADs, 3 FADs, 1 NBAD, 1 RAR, 1 NBAR	4 EBs, 2 PBBs, 1 PBR, 10 EBns, 2 FlameBns
4th Ukrainian					
2nd Guards Army	1G RC (33, 86G RD), 13G RC (3, 49, 87G RD), 295 RD), 1G, 116 FR	377, 1095 GunAR, 113G TDR, 483 MtrR, 19 GMR, 1530 AAAR			3G, 355 EBn
3rd Guards Army	32 RC (259, 266, 279 RD), 34G RC (59, 61G, 243 RD), 37 RC (248, 416, 417 RD), 130 RD, 5, 62, 94, 95 ATRBn	7 APD (11 LAB, 9G, 17 GunAB, 25 HowAB, 105 HowABhp, 3 MtrB), 26 AD (75 LAB, 56 GunAB, 77 HowAB), 506 CAR, 312 GunAR, 1231 HowAR, 5G TDB, 179 TDR, 488, 526 MtrR, 4, 21, 23, 51, 100 GMR, 2 AAAD (1069, 1086, 1113, 1117 AAAR), 160G AAAR (18 AAAD), 1257 AAAR	4G MC (13, 14, 15G MB, 36G TB, 292G, 1828 SPR, 5G AcBn, 62 MtcBn, 1512 TDR, 748 TDBn, 348 GMBn), 19 TC (79, 101, 202 TB, 26 MRB, 1824 SPR, 91 MtcBn, 1511 TDR, 179 MtrR, 1717 AAAR), 32G TB, 5G MRB, 243 TR, 52 MtcBn		130, 322 EBn, 25 FlameBn

5th Shock Army	3G RC (50, 54, 96G RD), 63 RC (118, 267 RD)	1162 GunAR, 7 TDB, 507, 521 TDR, 484 and 485 MtrR (19 MtrB), 489 MtrR, 48 GMR, 270G AAAR (18 AAAD), 1617 AAAR	238 TB, 14G TR, 28 AtrBn		827 EBn, 5 FlameBn
28th Army	9 RC (230, 301 RD), 10G RC (24, 109G, 61, 77 RD), 320 RD	4G LAB and 6G GunAB (2G APD), 92G CAR, 110G, 880, 1101 GunAR, 274 HowAR, 530 TDR, 133G MtrR, 25 GMR, 607 AAAR	34, 40G TR		5G, 57 EBn
51st Army	10 RC (216, 257, 263, 346 RD), 54 RC (91, 126, 315 RD), 55 RC (87, 347, 387 RD), 78 FR	2G APD (114 GunAB, 5G HowAB, 20G HowABhp, 33 MtrB), 647, 1105 GunAR, 85G, 331 HowAR, 14, 764, 1246, 1250 TDR, 125 MtrR, 2, 67 GMR, 15 AAAD (281, 342, 723, 1264 AAAR), 18 AAAD (166G, 297 AAAR) 77G AAAR, 126 AAABn 459, 591, 622, 1600, 1601, 1602, 1603 AAAR	6G TB, 512 TBn, 25, 30, 33 AtrBn		7 ESB, 275 EBn
8th Air Army				7 AAC (206, 289 AAD), 3 FAC (265, 278 FAD), 6G BAD, 1G AAD, 6, 9G, 236 FAD, 2G NBAD, 8 RAR, 406 NBAR, 10, 678 TAR, 5 MedAR, 87G ARCAF, 23, 61, 68 CRAS	
Front forces	4G CC (9, 10G, 30 CD, 1815 SPR, 152G TDR, 4G TDBn, 12 GMR, 68G MtrBn, 255 AAAR)	15, 21 TDB, 13, 491 TDR, 19 MtrB, 4 GMD (14, 30, 31 GMB), 13 GMB, 223, 416, 1485 AAAR	2G MC (4, 5, 6G MB, 37G TB, 1452 APR, 99 MtcBn, 1509 TDR, 744 TDBn, 408 GMBn), 22, 61G TR, 46, 54 AtrBn		12 AESB, 63 ESB, 43 SDEB, 2 PBB, 17 GBnM, 65, 240, 258,

—*continued*

31 DECEMBER 1943 *Continued*

Fronts and Armies	Rifle, Airborne, and Cavalry	Artillery	Tank and Mechanized	Air	Engineers
Total (5 armies, 1 air army)	12 RCs, 38 RDs, 3 FRs, 1 CC, 3 CDs	2 APDs, 1 AD, 15 ARs, 4 TDBs, 11 TDRs, 1 MtrB, 6 MtrRs, 1 GMD, 1 GMB, 10 GMRs, 3 AAADs, 15 AAARs, 1 AAABn	1 TC, 2 MCs, 3 TBs, 1 MRB, 6 TRs, 1 MtcR, 1 TBn, 6 AtrBns	1 AAC, 1 FAC, 1 BAD, 3 AADs, 5 FADs, 1 NBAD, 1 RAR, 1 NBAR	1504 EBn, 35, 121 PBBn, 102 PBBn (5 PBB), 4 EBs, 1 PBB, 13 EBns, 2 PBBns, 2 FlameBns
Separate Armies					
7th Army	4 RC (272, 368 RD, 69 NRB), 21, 67, 114 RD, 70 NRB, 3 NIB, 162 FR, 31 NIBn	354 HGumABn, 460, 514 TDR, 530 MtrR, 46, 64 GMR, 1650 AAAR, 54, 268, 616 AAABn	363, 431 TBn, 14, 16, 30, 31 AeroSBn	257 MAD	1G SBn, 18 GBnM, 18 EBn, 7 FlameBn
Coastal Army	3 MtnRC (128G, 242 MtnRD, 414 RD), 11G RC (2, 32, 55G RD, 83 NRB), 16 RC (89, 227, 339, 383 RD), 20 RC (20 MtnRD, 318 RD), 9 RD, 255 NIB	62 GumAB, 98G CAR, 4G, 268, 1167, 1169 GunAR, 81 HowAR, 1/125 HowABhp, 16 TDB, 34, 1174 TDR, 29 MtrB, 195, 197 PackMtrR, 1 GMB, 8, 44, 49, 50 GMR, 1, 2, 3G PackMtrBn, 19 AAAD (1332, 1338, 1344, 1350 AAAR), 210, 272G, 257, 763, 1260 AAAR, 14, 17, 21, 30, 179, 504, 508, 540 AAABn	63 TB, 85, 244, 257 TR, 1449 SPR		13 SDEB, 15 GBnM, 97 EBn, 19, 37 PBBn, 26 FlameBn, 179, 180 FlameCo
4th Air Army		1559, 1560, 1609 AAAR		132 BAD, 214, 230 AAD, 229, 329 FAD, 366 RAR, 55 CRAS	

Total (2 armies, 1 air army)	5 RCs, 18 RDs, 5 RBs, 1 FR	1 AB, 6 ARs, 1 ABn, 1 TDB, 4 TDRs, 1 MtrB, 3 MtrRs, 1 GMB, 6 GMRs, 3 GMBns, 1 AAAD, 9 AAARs, 11 AAABns	1 TB, 3 TRs, 2 TBns, 1 SPR, 5 AeroSBns	1 BAD, 2 AADs 1 MAD, 2 FADs, 1 RAR	1 EB, 5 EBns, 2 PBBns, 2 FlameBns, 2 FlameCos

Long-Range and Reconnaissance Aviation

Total				1G LRAC (1, 6G LRAD), 2G LRAC (2, 8G LRAD), 3G LRAC (3, 7G LRAD), 4G LRAC (4, 5G LRAD), 5 LRAC (53, 54 LRAD), 6 LRAC (9G, 50 LRAD), 7 LRAC (1, 12 LRAD), 8 LRAC (36, 48 LRAD), 45 LRAD, 47, 48, 98G RAR	
Grand total (11 fronts, 55 armies, 3 tank armies, 12 air armies)	138 RCs, 435 RDs, 8 AbnDs, 29 RBs, 3 SkiBs, 7 CCs, 21 CDs, 20 FRs	5 ACs, 17 APDs, 9 ADs, 14 ABs, 132 ARs, 6 Abns, 37 TDBs, 114 TDRs, 2 TDBns, 9 MtrBs, 98 MtrRs, 6 GMDs, 13 GMBs, 92 GMRs, 3 GMBns, 47 AAADs, 132 AAARs, 64 AAABns	15 TCs, 8 MCs, 53 TBs, 2 MBs, 1 MRB, 73 TRs, 33 SPRs, 6 MtcRs, 18 TBns, 8 AcBns, 26 AeroSBns, 3 MtcBns, 37 AtrBns	8 LRACs, 17 LRADs, 3 RARs	2 BACs, 8 LRACs, 4 MACs, 5 AACs, 8 FACs, 13 BADs, 17 LRADs, 4 MADs, 28 AADs, 38 FADs, 10 NBADs, 1 BARs, 3 AARs, 4 FARs, 14 RARs, 6 LBARs	48 EBs, 7 PBBs, 4 PBRs, 164 EBns, 51 PBBns, 25 FlameBns, 19 FlameCos

Stavka VGK Reserve
Northwestern Front (hq)

20th Army	120 RC (hq)	5 GunAR, 165, 648 TDR, 618 MtrR				302 EBn
21st Army	99 RC (229, 265, 311 RD)	1072 TDR, 456 MtrR, 716 AAAR				260 EBn

—continued

31 DECEMBER 1943 Continued

Fronts and Armies	Rifle, Airborne, and Cavalry	Artillery	Tank and Mechanized	Air	Engineers
34th Army	(hq)				
47th Army	106 RC (58, 133, 359 RD), 102 RC (hq)	123 GunAR, 460 MtrR, 1488 AAAR			91 EBn
69th Army	31G RC (4, 34, 40, 108G RD), 67 RC (151, 221, 302 RD)	68G GunAR, 22 TDR, 256 MtrR, 594 AAAR			170 EBn
70th Army		378 TDR, 136G MtrR, 581 AAAR		395 MAR	371 EBn
2nd Tank Army		86 GMR	3 TC (50, 51, 103 TB, 57 MRB, 1540 SPR, 74 MtcBn, 881 TDR, 728 TDBn, 234 MtrR, 126 GMBn, 121 AAAR);16 TC (107, 109, 164 TB, 15 MRB, 1441, 1542 SPR, 51 MtcBn, 298G TDR, 729 TDBn, 226 MtrR, 89 GMBn, 1721 AAAR, 11G TB, 87 MtrCBn		357 EBn
4th Tank Army		312 GMR	6G MC (16, 17G, 49 MB, 29, 56 TR, 1G SPR, 95 MtcBn, 51G TDR, 740 TDBn, 240 MtrR, 52, 31G AAABn), 10G TC (61, 62, 63G TB, 29G MRB, 356G, 1545 SPR, 7G MtcBn,		88 EBn

6th Air Army	104 RC (hq), 202 RD, 2, 3, 11, 12, 13, 14, 15, 16G AbnD, 3, 8G AbnB	8 AC (hq), 124 HowABhp, 989 HowAR, 8, 12, 14, 25, 31, 42 TDB, 32 MtrB, 268 MtrR, 316 GMR	357G TDR, 62G TDBn, 299G MtrR, 248 GMBn, 359G AAAR), 51 MtcR	1G MC (1, 2, 3G MB, 9G TB, 1504, 1544 AR, 741 TDBn, 267 MtrR, 407 GMBn, 1699 AAAR), 3G MC (7, 8, 9G MB, 35G TB, 1510 SPR, 1G MtcBn, 743 TDR, 129 MtrR, 334 GMBn, 1705 AAAR), 7G MC (24, 25, 26G MB, 57G TB, 291G SPR, 5G MtcBn, 57G TDBn, 468G MtrR, 410 GMBn, 288G AAAR), 3G TC (3, 18, 18G TB, 2G MRB, 1436, 1496 SPR, 10G MtcBn, 749 TDR, 266 MtrR, 324 GMBn, 1701 AAAR), 8G TC (58, 59, 60G TB, 28G MRB, 15G TR, 301G SPR, 6G MtcBn, 58G TDBn, 269G MtrR, 307 GMBn, 300G AAAR), 9 TC (23, 95, 108 TB, 8	242 NBAD 1G BAC (4, 5G BAD), 1G MAC (6G AAD), 8 FAC (215, 323 FAD), 56 LRAD, 326 NBAD, 2, 4 SDAD, 73 LRTAD, 765 AAR, 821 FAR, 48, 70 CRAS 17 AESB, 1391 EBn, 10, 11, 519 FlameBn
Stavka forces					

—continued

31 DECEMBER 1943 Continued

Fronts and Armies	Rifle, Airborne, and Cavalry	Artillery	Tank and Mechanized	Air	Engineers
			MRB, 1455 SPR, 90 MtcBn, 1508 TDR, 730 TDBn, 286 GMBn), 10 TC (178, 183, 186 TB, 11 MRB, 1450 SPR, 30 AcBn, 77 MtcBn, 727 TDR, 390 TDBn, 287 MtrR, 1693 AAAR), 11 TC (20, 36, 65 TB, 12 MRB, 1493, 1507 SPR, 93 MtcBn, 738 TDBn, 243 MtrR, 115 GMBn, 1388 AAAR), 31 TC (100, 237, 242 TB, 65 MRB, 1244, 1548 SPR, 98 MtcBn, 753 TDR, 617 MtrR, 201 GMBn, 396 AAAR), 144, 201 TB, 35, 128, 134, 223, 224, 225, 230, 259, 262, 513, 517 TR, 1536 SPR, 510 TBn, 38 AeroSBn, 7, 22, 26 AtrBn		
Total (1 *front* hq, 6 armies, 2 tank armies, 1 air army)	7 RCs, 14 RDs, 8 AbnDs, 2 AbnBs	1 AC, 1 AB, 4 ARs, 6 ATBs, 5 TDRs, 1 MtrB, 6 MtrRs, 3 GMRs, 4 AAARs	4 MCs, 9 TCs, 3 TBs, 11 TRs, 1 SPR, 1 MtcR, 1 TBn, 1	1 BAC, 1 MAC, 1 FAC, 2 LRADs, 1 AAD, 2 BADs, 2	1 EB, 8 EBns, 3 FlameBns

294

Military Districts and Nonoperating Fronts

Moscow MD	124 and 131 RC (hq), 77, 91, 153, 156, 157, 160 FR: 1 Polish AC (1, 2, 3 InfD, 1 TB, 1 AB, 3 MtrR)	97, 98 HHowAB, 112, 122 HowABhp, 4, 28, 110, 136, 137, 138, 633, 1517, 1518, 1519, 1520, 1521, 1522 CAR, 51, 93, 95, 1074, 1638 GunAr, 315, 317, 329, 331 ABnsp, 402, 406 ABnhp, 2, 3, 26, 27, 45, 46, 47 TDB, 1070, 1160, 1161 TDR, 385, 386, 387, 750 TDBn, 619, 620, 621 MtrR, 6 GMD (7, 25 GMB), 43, 57, 59, 60, 66, 72, 75, 305, 324, 329 GMR, 127, 128, 129 GMBn, 64 AAAD (1979, 1983, 1987, 1991 AAAR), 65 AAAD (1980, 1984, 1988, 1992 AAAR), 66 AAAD (1981, 1985, 1989, 1993 AAAR), 67 AAAD (1982, 1986, 1990, 1994 AAAR), 72 AAAD (79, 82, 250, 309 AAAR), 73 AAAD (205, 402, 430, 442 AAAR), 74 AAAD (445, 457, 498, 499 AAAR), 159, 216 AAR, 67, 141, 449, 577, 578 AAABn	5 MC (2, 9, 45 MB, 233 TB, 156 TR, 1228, 1820, 1827 SPR, 64 MtcBn, 745 TDBn, 458 MtrR, 35 GMBn, 1700 AAR), 86, 94, 149, 232 TB, 8, 13, 16, 28, 29, 36, 48, 58G, 27, 40, 45, 57, 58, 60, 114, 148, 184, 189, 203, 226, 245, 258 TR, 1456, 1457, 1460, 1898, 1899, 1900 SPR, 33 AeroSBn, 44, 60, 79 AtrBn	218, 219, 327, 334 BAD, 224, 300, 332 AAD, 330 FAD, 9 BAR, 136 AAR, 72, 859 RAR, 74, 75, 76, 77, 78, 79 CRAS	13, 16 AESB, 41 SDEB, 4 PBR, 5 RearAreaB, 9, 14 GBnM
			AeroSBn, 1 MtcBn, 3 AtrBns	FADs, 2 NBADs, 2 SDADs, 1 AAR, 1 FAR, 1 MAR	
Total	2 RCs, 6 FRs	4 ABs, 19 ARs, 6 ABns, 7 TDBs, 3 TDRs, 4 TDBns, 3 MtrRs, 1 GMD, 10 GMRs, 3 GMBns, 7 AAADs, 2 AAARs, 5 AAABns	1 MC, 4 TBs, 22 TRs, 6 SPRs, 1 AeroSBn, 3 AtrBns	4 BADs, 3 AADs, 1 FAD, 1 BAR, 1 AAR, 2 RARs	3 EBs, 1 PBB, 2 EBs

—continued

31 DECEMBER 1943 Continued

Fronts and Armies	Rifle, Airborne, and Cavalry	Artillery	Tank and Mechanized	Air	Engineers
Arkhangel'sk MD	24 RD, 143, 488 MGABn	310 GunAR, 1, 6 ABtryhp	6, 7, 9, 10, 13, 20, 23, 27, 37, 38, 40, 43, 45, 47, 50, 51, 54, 55, 58, 59, 60, 61, 64, 67 AeroSBn	909 FAR	
Total			24 AereoSBns		
Baltic MD	1 RD	1 AR		1 FAR	
Total		151 GunAR, 641 TDR, 482 MtrR, 582 AAAR 1 AR, 1 TDR, 1 MtrR, 1 AAAR			
Belorussian MD					38, 162, 340 EBn
Total					3 EBns
Orel MD		127 GunAB, 1066, 1216, 1942, 1943, 1944 CAR, 172, 181, 182 GunAR	15, 254 TB, 51 TR, 511, 516 TBn, 48, 49 AeroSBn, 724, 819 Atr	321 BAD, 279, 331 FAD, 336 RAS	926, 927 SBn
Total		1 AB, 8 ARs	2 TBs, 1 TR, 2 TBns, 2 AeroSBns	1 BAD, 2 FADs	2 EBns
Khar'kov MD			31, 33G, 140 TB, 1, 62G, 43, 212 TR, 1892 SPR	336 FAD	2, 3 RearAreaB, 238, 376 EBn
Total			3 TBs, 4 TRs, 1 SPR	1 FAD	2 EBns
Volga MD		327 GMR, 40 AAAD (1407, 1411, 1415, 1527 AAAR), 68 AAAD (1995, 1999, 2003, 2007 AAAR), 69 AAAD (1996, 2000, 2004, 2008	23 AtrBn	41, 567, 594, 618, 694 AAR, 518 FAR, 54, 73, 80 CRAS	

Total		AAAR), 70 AAAD (1997, 2001, 2005, 2009 AAAR), 71 AAAD (1998, 2003, 2006, 2010 AAAR), 57, 364 AAABn	5 AARs, 1 FAR	
North Caucasus MD		1 GMR, 5 AAADs, 2 AAABns	1 AtrBn	4 MtnESB, 1 RearAreaB, 336 EBn, 97 PBBn
		125 HowABhp (-1 Bn), 1945, 1946, 1947, 1948, 1949 CAR, 337 GunAR, 1195 HowAR, 196 PackMtrR, 253 MtrR, 20 AAAD (1333, 1339, 1345, 1351 AAAR), 253, 740, 879 AAAR	5G TB, 6G TR, 8, 12, 66 AtrBn	
Total		1 AB, 7 ARs, 2 MtrRs, 1 AAAD, 3 AAARs	1 TB, 1 TR, 3 AtrBns	1 EB, 1 EBn, 1 PBBn
Trans-Caucasus Front				
45th Army	261, 349 RD, 55, 69 FR	39G GunAR, 140, 233 TDR, 20 MtrR, 1653 AAAR	226, 227 TB, 20 Atr	25, 978 FAR, 149 RAS, 335 LRRAS	10 EBn
Forces in Iran	75 RD, 90 RB, 15 CC (1, 23 CD, 1595 TDR, 15 TDBn, 17 MtrBn)			
Front forces	12 RC (392, 406 RD) 13 RC (296, 402 RD), 94, 133 RB, 54, 151 FR	126 HowBhp, 1667 CAR, 44 MtrB, 862, 1562, 1652 AAAR	230 TB, 263, 270, 271 TR, 11, 19, 36, 41, 42, 65 AtrBn, 15 MtrAtr	246, 773 FAR	337 EBn
Total (1 army)	2 RC, 7 RDs, 3 RBs, 1 CC, 2 CDs, 4 FRs	1 AB, 2 ARs, 2 TDRs, 1 MtrB, 1 MtrR, 4 AAARs	3 TBs, 3 TRs, 6 AtrBns	4 FARs	2 EBns
Ural MD		32, 40, 226, 245 ABnsp	46, 65, 68 AeroSBns		4 RearAreaB, 67, 68, 69 EBn
Total		4 ABns	3 AeroSBns		3 EBns

—continued

31 DECEMBER 1943 Continued

Fronts and Armies	Rifle, Airborne, and Cavalry	Artillery	Tank and Mechanized	Air	Engineers
South Ural MD Total		34, 316, 322, 328, 330 ABnsp 5 ABns			
Central Asian MD	58 RC (68 MtnRD, 89, 93 RB) in Iran: 39 MtnCD, 20, 31 AWBns			136 MAD, 333 AAD, 238 FAD, 15 RAS	125, 136, 384, 385 EBn
Total	1 RC, 1 RD, 2 RBs, 1 CD			1 AAD, 1 MAD, 1 FAD	4 EBns
Trans-Baikal Front 17th Army	85 RC (36, 57 MRD, 284 RD, 1, 3 MRR)	185, 624, 629, 1141 GunAR, 413 HowAR, 1910 TDR, 178 MtrR, 1914 AAAR, 63, 66, 376, 382 AAABn	61 TD, 43 TB, 25 MB, 30 MtcR, 70, 82 TBn		102 EBn, 84 PBBn
36th Army	86 RC (hq), 94, 209, 210 RD, 278, 298 RD, 31 FR	267, 390, 1233 GunAR, 259 HowAR, 1912 TDR, 177 MtrR, 190 PackMtrR, 1915, 1916 AAAR, 120, 401, 405, 414 AAABn	33, 35 TBn		39 EBn
12th Air Air Army				30, 247 BAD, 248, 316 AAD, 245, 246 FAD, 846 AAR, 12 RAR, 23 HBAS, 40, 41 CRAS	
Front forces	2 RC (103, 275, 292, 293 RD, 368 MtnRR), 59 CD, 32 FR, 1, 2 ParaBn	1142, 1143 GunAR, 106, 1146 HowARhp, 1913 TDR, 176 MtrR, 32 GMR, 1917, 1918 AAAR, 410 AAABn	111 TD, 44, 205, 206 TB		281, 283, 382, 383 EBn, 1, 2, 17 PBBn
Total (2 armies, 1 air army)	3 RCs, 10 RDs, 2 MRDs, 1 CD, 2 FRs, 3 RRs	13 ARs, 3 TDRs, 4 MtrRs, 1 GMR, 5 AAADs, 9 AAABns	2 TDs, 4 TBs, 1 MB, 4 TBns, 1 MtcR	2 BADs, 2 AADs, 2 FADs, 1 AAR, 1 RAR	6 EBns, 4 PBBns

Far Eastern Front
Coastal Group of Forces

Army	Rifle/Infantry	Artillery	Armor	AA/Other	Engineer
1st Army	26 RC (22, 59 RD), 59 RC (39 RD, 29 RB), 187 RD, 84 CD, 6, 105, 112 FR	50, 273, 1124, 1125, 1139 GunAR, 45, 87 HowAR, 199 HowARhp, 1594, 1630, 1631 TDR, 24, 168, 451, 452 MtrR, 33 GMR, 1588, 1647 AAAR, 43, 115, 129, 300 AAABn	75, 77, 210, 257 TB, 3, 78 AtrBn		45 ESBn
25th Army	17 RC (190 RD, 21, 247 RB), 39 RC (40 RD, 8, 158, 262 RB), 12, 261 RB, 175, 1407 RR, 7, 106, 107, 108, 110, 111, 113 FR, 84 MGBn	282, 548 CAR, 1127, 1136 GunAR, 107, 148 HowAR, 1192 HowARhp, 100 ABn, 555, 1627, 1629 TDR, 180, 453, 464, 473 MtrR, 1590 AAAR, 22, 24, 28, 721 AAABn	76, 218, 259 TB, 42 MRB, 9 AtrBn		46 ESB, 334 EBn
9th Air Army				34 BAD, 251, 252 AAD, 33 MAD, 32, 249, 250 FAD, 6 RAR, 528 FAR	
Group forces	87 RC (223, 300 RD, 113 RB), 88 RC (105, 256 RD, 6 RB)	1126 GunAR, 1138 HowAR, 1471, 1634 TDR, 182 MtrR	72, 204 TB		
2nd Army	3, 12 RD, 17, 41, 258, 259 RB, 101 FR, 8 RBn, 135 MGBn	42, 1120, 1140 GunAR, 147, 1129 HowAR, 550 HowARhp, 192 HGunABn, 1628, 1632 TDR, 181, 465 MtrR, 1589 AAAR, 9, 42 AAABn	73, 74, 258 TB, 2, 5 AtrBn, 5 RRTrolleyBn		277 EBn, 10 PBBn
15th Army	34, 255 RD, 18, 38, 260 RB, 4, 102 FR, 20 RBn	52, 424, 1121 GunAR, 145, 1637 HowAR, 1194 HowARhp, 117 HGunABn, 183, 470 MtrR, 1648 AAAR, 46, 302 AAABn	165, 171, 203 TB, 77 AtrBn		129 EBn, 11, 24, 29 PBBn

—continued

31 DECEMBER 1943 Continued

Fronts and Armies	Rifle, Airborne, and Cavalry	Artillery	Tank and Mechanized	Air	Engineers
16th Army	56 RC (79, 101 RD, 2, 5 RB, 302, 432, 540 RR, 5, 6, 7, 206 RBn), 103, 104 FR, Sakhalin RR	433 GunAR, 428, 487 HowAR, 82, 362, 367, 428 HGunABn, 726 AAABn	214 TB		
35th Army	5 RC (35, 66, 264 RD, 30, 95, 246 RB, 1408 RR), 109 FR	76, 187, 1122, 1123 GunAR, 177, 263, 1133 HowAR, 549, 1193 HowARhp, 1635, 1636 TDR, 472 MtrR, 1649 AAAR, 110, 355 AAABn	125, 172, 208, 209 TB, 72 MB, 13 AtrBn		280 EBn, 3, 16, 58, 132 PBBn
10th Air Army				53, 83 BAD, 253 AAD, 254 MAD, 29 FAD, 7 RAR, 19 FAS, 29 CRAS	
11th Air Army				82 BAD, 96, 296 MAD, 3 FAR, 140 LRRAS	
Front forces	88 RB, 202 AbnB	505 AAABn	678 TBn, 76 AtrBn	128, 255 MAR, 251 HBAR, 799 RAR, 26, 27, 29, 30, 38, 39 CRAS, 111 RAS	47 ESB, 3 HPBR, 26 EBn
Total (6 armies, 3 air armies)	8 RCs, 19 RDs, 23 RBs, 1 AbnB, 1 CD, 16 FRs, 7 RRs	41 ARs, 7 ABns, 13 TDRs, 14 MtrRs, 1 GMR, 6 AADs, 16 AAABns	20 TBs, 1 MB, 1 MRB, 1 TBn, 8 AtrBns	4 BADs, 6 MADs, 3 AADs, 4 FADs, 1 BAR, 2 FARs, 3 RARs	3 EBs, 1 PBR, 5 Ebns, 8 PBBns
Grand total (3 fronts, 9 armies, 4 air armies)	16 RCs, 38 RDs, 2 MRDs, 28 RBs, 1 AbnB, 1 CC, 5 CDs, 28 FRs, 10 RRs	7 ABs, 92 ARs, 22 ABns, 7 TDBs, 22 TDRs, 4 TDBns, 1 MtrR, 25 MtrRs, 1 GMD, 13 GMRs, 3 GMBns, 13 AADs, 21 AAARs, 32 AAABns	1 MC, 2 TDs, 37 TBs, 2 MBs, 1 MRB, 31 TRs, 7 SPRs, 1 MtcR, 7 TBns, 30 AeroSBns, 21 AtrBns	11 BADs, 7 MADs, 9 AADs, 11 FADs, 2 BARs, 7 AARs, 8 FARs, 6 RARs	7 EBs, 2 PBRs, 30 EBns, 13 PBBns

PVO *Fronts* and Armies	PVO Regions	Separate PVO Units	PVO Aviation
PVO Strany Forces			
Western PVO Front	Murmansk CR (361, 746, 885, 1082, 1855, 1863 AAAR, 33, 135, 199, 311, 313, 403, 404, 407, 426, 531 AAABn, 30 AAMGR, 9, 30, 31 AAMGBn, 17 ProjBn, 6 AeroObsBn, 6, 73 VNOSBn, 190, 201 AAAtr); Bologoe DR (242 AAAR, 87, 178, 188, 215, 224, 248, 256, 271, 284, 308, 378 AAABns, 10, 42, 44 AAMGR, 24 AAMGBn, 23 AABtry, 670, 808 AAAMGCo, 32, 64, 98, 107 VNOSBn, 56, 57, 74, 75, 128, 182, 193, 197, 207, 215, 216 AAAtr); Smolensk DR (1088, 1883 AAAR, 56, 148, 243, 274 AAABn, 37 AAMGR, 25 AAMGBn, 1127, 1128 AAMGCo, 34 ProjBn, 7, 90, 104 VNOSBn, 217, 220, 222 AAAtr); Tula DR (732, 1573, 1574 AAAR, 80, 153, 269, 511 AAABn, 1, 2, 15 AAMGBn, 3, 4 AABtry, 2, 120, 636 AAMGCo, 29 ProjBn, 58, 82 VNOSBn, 58, 124, 125, 138, 188, 208 AAAtr); Orel DR (733, 1569, 1876 AAAR, 173, 212, 238, 252, 265, 283, 290, 306, 343, 356, 358 AAABn, 35, 45 AAMGR, 13, 22, 34, 35, AAMGBn, 664 AAMGCo, 24, 26 ProjBn, 11, 69, 103 VNOSBn, 73, 127, 131, 198, 202, 205 AAAtr); Kursk DR (254, 736, 1808, 1874 AAAR, 180, 374, 416 AAABn, 41 AAMGR, 23 AAMGBn, 29, 85 VNOSBn, 55, 124,		122 FAD (767, 768, 769 FAR); 106 FAD (145, 147G, 33, 441, 926 FAR); 328 FAD (495, 960 FAR); 125 FAD (651, 787, 1006 FAR); 36 FAD (383, 591, 785, 827 FAR);

—continued

31 DECEMBER 1943 Continued

PVO Fronts and Armies	PVO Regions	Separate PVO Units	PVO Aviation
	214, 221 AAAtr); Voronezh DR (183 AAAR, 58, 85, 96, 201, 353, 361 AAABn, 8 AAMGR, 5 AAMGBn, 802 AAMGCo, 15 ProjBn, 2, 56, 62, 65 VNOSBn); Kiev CR (251, 317, 1423, 1572, 1869, 1871 AAAR, 18, 86, 93, 254, 259, 291, 379, 395, 415, 430, 471, 510 AAABn, 4, 7, 11, 31 AAMGR, 42 ProjR, 4 VNOSR, 28 ProjBn, 72, 121, 122, 126, 129, 135, 137, 141, 143, 184, 199, 203, 206, 209, 211, 212 AAAtr); Khar'kov DR (374, 383, 583, 1575, 1806, 1870 AAAR, 37, 79, 191, 255, 266, 294, 381, 501 AAABn, 9 AAMGR, 671 AAMGCo, 35 ProjBn, 5, 22, 23, 44 VNOSBn, 130, 178, 181, 187, 200, 204, 213, 218 AAAtr); Donbas CR (11, 82, 182, 319, 334, 370, 383 AAAR, 32 AAMGR, 729 AAMGCo, 36 ProjBn, 74 VNOSBn, 54, 132, 140, 144, 179, 186, 194, 195, 196, 219 AAAtr); Rostov CR (485, 1079, 1080, 1563, 1564 AAAR, 211, 299 AAABn, 5 AAMGR, 16, 162 AAMGBn, 730, 732 AAMGCo, 41 ProjBn, 9 AeroObsBn, 33, 46, 57 VNOSBn); North Caucasus CR (454, 734, 1425, 1576 AAAR, 36, 53, 143, 286, 433 AAABn, 60, 61, 790 AAMGCo, 15, 68 VNOSBn, 140, 179 AAAtr); Arkhangel'sk DR (1568, 1805 AAAR, 84, 160, 171, 213, 318, 372, 480 AAABn, 34 AAMGR, 24 AABtry, 736 AAMGCo, 13,	9 AAAB (hq) 16 AAAB (91, 267, 279, 310 AAABn, 46 AAMGR, 189 AAAtr) 3 AAAB (1862 AAAR, 189, 282, 292, 419 AAABn, 4 AAMGBn, 16 ProjBn, 19, 63, 99 VNOSBn, 17 AAAB (329, 415, 1858, 1884 AAAR, 3, 23, 151, 249, 280, 297, 303, 359, 366, 375 AAABn, 40, 43 aamgr, 89 aabTRY, 1129 AAMGCo, 43 VNOSBn, 139 AAAtr);	9 FAC (39, 146, 148G, 234, 586, 894, 907 FAR), 148 FAD (hq) 310 FAD (348, 573, 802 FAR); 10 FAC (182, 266, 628, 738, 833, 961, 1008 FAR); 104 FAD (729, 730 FAR);

Special Moscow PVO Army	19 ProjBn, 26 AeroObsBn, 41 VNOSBn; Cherepovets-Vologda DR (55, 74, 99, 194, 272, 385, 413 AAABn, 20, 21 AABtry, 29 AAMGBn, 13, 106 VNOSBn, 183, 191 AAAtr); Rybinsk-Iaroslavl' DR (201, 1424, 1566, 1567, 1875 AAAR, 38, 40, 62, 192, 197, 231, 273, 287, 362, 380, 458 AAABn, 14, 18 AAMGBn, 659, 660 AAMGCo, 1 AeroObsBn, 77, 105 VNOSBn)	147 FAD (439, 740, 959, 964, 966, 1005 FAR);
1st PVO Fighter Air Army	1G, 50, 51, 52, 53, 54, 55, 56, 57, 58, 59, 60, 61, 62, 63 AAAD, 1, 2, 3 AAMGD, 340, 347, 1866, 1867, 1868 AAAR, 198, 205, 206, 207, 232, 237, 240, 244, 257, 258, 260, 263, 270, 349, 350 AAABn, 1, 2, 3, 4 ProjD, 1, 2, 3 AeroObsD, 1, 2 VNOSD, 26, 27 AAMGBn, 53 AABtry, 635 AAMGCo, 18 VNOSRadioR, 210 AAAtr	317 FAD (34, 67, 736 FAR), 318 FAD (11, 28, 562, 564, 565 FAR), 319 FAD (177, 178, 309, 445 FAR), 320 FAD (12G, 16, 126, 429, 488 FAR)
Total (1 PVO Army, 1 air army)	5 CRs, 10 DRs	2 FACs, 13 FADs
Leningrad PVO Army	Ladoga DR (Volkov and Osipovets AAAR, 36G, 25, 37, 65, 69, 225, 253, 391, 432, 434, 447 AAABn, 124 AAMGCo, 42, 47 VNOSBn)	2G FAC (11, 26, 27, 102, 103G FAR)
	115, 169, 189, 192, 194, 351, 1804 AAAR, 20 AAABn, 2 AAMGR, 1, 2, 3, 5, 6 AABtry, 2, 3, 4, 11 AeroObsR, 2 ProjR, 2 VNOSR, 72 VNOSBn	
Total	1 DR 7 AAARs, 1 AAABn, 1 AAMGR	1 FAC

—continued

31 DECEMBER 1943 Continued

PVO Fronts and Armies	PVO Regions	Separate PVO Units	PVO Aviation
Eastern PVO Front	Gor'kii CR (196, 742, 784, 1291, 1571, 1579, 1580, 1877, 1878 AAAR, 13, 39, 200, 236, 289, 384, 389 AAABn, 33 AAMGR, 38, 45 ProjR, 19 AAMGBn, 8, 28 AeroObsBn, 4, 8, 39 VNOSBn); Kuibyshev DR (767, 861, 1856, 1857, 1859 AAAR, 90, 174, 277, 285, 368 AAABn, 40 ProjR, 10 AAMGBn, 2 AeroObsBn, 50, 52, 97 VNOSBn; Saratov-Balashov DR (720, 1078, 1860, 1861, 1864, 1865 AAAR, 89, 106, 296, 425 AAABn, 36 AAMGR, 43 ProjR, 20 ProjBn, 4 AeroObsBn, 16, 17, 100 VNOSBn); Stalingrad CR (73G, 748, 1077, 1083, 1570, 1807 AAAR, 6 AAMGR, 546, 547, 548, 549, 550, 551, 552, 553, 554 AABtry, 123, 791 AAMGCo, 22 ProjBn, 10, 70 VNOSBn, 136 AAAtr; Astrakhan BR (679, 1809 AAAR, 545 AABtry, 1131, 1132 AAMGCo, 12 ProjBn, 14 VNOSBn);	10 AAAB (1872, 1873 AAAR, 202, 281 AAABn)	142 FAD (423, 632, 722, 743, 786 FAR); 141 FAD (268, 862, 908 FAR); 144 FAD (405, 631, 743, 963 FAR); 2G FAD (38, 83, 84G, 933, 934 FAR); 936 FAD (2G FAD)
Trans-Caucasus PVO Zone			
Baku PVO Army		180, 190, 195, 252, 335, 339, 513, 636, 654, 1880, 1881 AAAR, 3, 39 AAMGR, 128, 137 AABtry, 3 ProjR, 5 AeroObsR, 28 VNOSR	8 FAC PVO (82, 480, 481, 922, 962 FAR)
Zone forces	Groznyi DR (16, 744, 1879 AAAR, 411, 422 AAABn, 38 AAMGR, 64 AAMGCo, 67, 76 VNOSBn, 185 AAAtr)	2 AAAB (345, 443, 638, 1882 AAAR, 5 VNOSR, 62 AAMCo, 21 ProjBn), 8 AAAB (352, 466 AAAR, 76, 365, 392,	126 FAD (652, 822, 965 FAR), 298 FAD (35, 982, 983 FAR)

	393, 571 AAABn, 124, 127 AABtry, 20, 49 AAMGBn, 97 AAMGCo, 33 ProjBn, 7 AeroObsBn, 24 VNOSBn, 180 AAAtr	
Total (1 PVO army, 1 PVO zone)	2 AAABs, 11 AAARs, 2 AAMGRs	1 FAC, 6 FADs
Trans-Baikal PVO Zone		
1 BR (10, 132, 162, 390 AAABn, 25 VNOSBn); 2 BR (150, 187, 262, 264, 408 AAABn, 80 VNOSBn);3 BR (750 AAAR, 107, 166 AAABn, 55 VNOSBn)	387 AAABn, 79 VNOSBn	297 FAD (938, 939 FAR)
Total 2 CRs, 3 DRs, 1 BR		
3 BRS	1 AAABn	1 FAD
Far Eastern PVO Zone		
Khabarovsk BR (1887 AAAR, 163, 217 AAABn, 20, 53 VNOSBn); Kuibyshev BR (757 AAAR, 138, 167, 175, 195 AAABn, 38 VNOSBn; Bikin BR (147, 155, 190, 398 AAABn, 12 VNOSBn); Spaask BR (639 AAAR, 4, 152, 543 AAABn, 54 VNOSBn); Voroshilov BR (755 AAAR, 78, 186 AAABn, 37 VNOSBn); Komsomol BR (752 AAAR, 305, 465 AAABn, 75 VNOSBn); Nikolaev BR (1919 AAAR, 102, 456, 457 AAABn, 61 VNOSBn)	5 AAAB (749 AAAR, 8 AAMGBn, 25 ProjBn, 12 AeroObsBn)	149 FAD (18, 60 FAR)
Total 7 BRs	1 AAAB	1 FAD
Reserve Central PVO Headquarters		
Total	1 AAAR 731 AAAR	
Grand total (2 PVO fronts, 3 PVO armies, 3 PVO zones, 1 air army) 7 CRs, 14 DRs, 11 BRs	1 AAAR 15 AAADs, 3 AAMGDs, 4 ProjDs, 3 AeroObsDs, 2 VNOSDs, 8 AAABs, 24 AAARs, 3 AAMGRs, 16 AAABns	4 FACs, 21 FADs

Abbreviations

Infantry, Airborne, and Cavalry
RC – rifle corps
CC – cavalry corps
AbnC – airborne corps
RD – rifle division
MtnRD – mountain rifle division
AbnD – airborne division
CD – cavalry division
MtnCD – mountain cavalry division
DD – destroyer division
DNO – people's militia division
RB – rifle brigade
MtnRB – mountain rifle brigade
GrenRB – grenadier rifle brigade
NRB – naval rifle brigade
NIB – naval infantry brigade
AbnB – airborne brigade
MvrAbnB – maneuver airborne brigade
SkiB – ski brigade
RR – rifle regiment
MRR – motorized rifle regiment
MtnRR – mountain rifle regiment
SkiR – ski regiment
CR – cavalry regiment
MtnCR – mountain cavalry regiment
ParaR – parachute regiment
DR – destroyer regiment
FR – fortified region
NIBn – naval infantry battalion
SkiBn – ski battalion
ParaBn – parachute battalion
MGABn – machine gun-artillery battalion
MGBn – machine-gun battalion
AWBn – automatic weapons battalion
Spetsnaz Det– special-designation detachment
MtnR Det – mountain rifle detachment

Artillery
AC – artillery (penetration) corps
APD – artillery penetration division
AD – artillery division
HAD – heavy artillery division
GunAD – gun artillery division
TDD – tank destroyer division
GMD – guards-mortar division
AAAD – antiaircraft artillery division
AB – artillery brigade
LAB – light artillery brigade
GunAB – gun artillery brigade
HowAB – howitzer artillery brigade
HHowAB – heavy howitzer artillery brigade
HowABhp – high-power heavy howitzer artillery brigade
GHowAB – gun-howitzer artillery brigade
GHowABhp – high-power gun-howitzer artillery brigade
MtrB – mortar brigade
ATB – antitank brigade
GMB – guards-mortar brigade
TDB – tank destroyer brigade
AR – artillery regiment
AAR – army artillery regiment
LAR – light artillery regiment
CAR – corps artillery regiment
GunAR – gun artillery regiment
HowAR – howitzer artillery regiment
HowARhp – high-power howitzer artillery regiment
MtrR – mortar regiment
AmtrR – army mortar regiment
PackMtrR – pack mortar regiment
ATR – antitank regiment
TDR – tank destroyer regiment
HTDR – heavy tank destroyer regiment
GMR – guards-mortar regiments
AAAR – antiaircraft artillery regiment
ABn – artillery battalion
HGunABn – heavy gun artillery battalion
ABnhp – high-power artillery battalion
GunABnhp – high-power gun artillery battalion
CaBn – cavalry artillery battalion
MtrBn – mortar battalion
PackMtrBn – pack mortar battalion
TDBn – tank destroyer battalion
GMBn – guards-mortar battalion
AAABn – antiaircraft artillery battalion
AeroObsBn – aerial obstacle battalion
TrollyMtrBn – trolley mortar battalion

ABtrysp – special-power artillery battery
HGunABtry – heavy gun artillery battery
PackMtrBtry – pack mortar battery
TDBtry – tank destroyer battery

Tank and Mechanized Forces
MC – mechanized corps
TC – tank corps
MD – motorized division
MRD – motorized rifle division
TD – tank division
MB – mechanized brigade
MRB – motorized rifle brigade
TB – tank brigade
MtcB – motorcycle brigade
MotArB – motorized armored brigade
TR – tank regiment
SPR – self-propelled gun regiment
MtcR – motorcycle regiment
TBn – tank battalion
AcBn – armored car battalion
AeroSBn – aerosleigh battalion
MtcBn – motorcycle battalion
AtrBn – armored train battalion
Atr – armored train
AAATr – antiaircraft artillery train
TCo – tank company

Engineer Forces
EB – engineer brigade
SB – sapper brigade
SDEB – special-designation engineer brigade
ESB – engineer-sapper brigade
EMB – engineer-miner brigade
MtnEMB – mountain engineer-miner brigade
AESB – assault engineer-sapper brigade
GBM – guard brigade of miners
ER – engineer regiment
PBR – pontoon-bridge regiment
HPBR – heavy pontoon-bridge regiment
EBn – engineer battalion
MotEBn – motorized engineer battalion
SBn – sapper battalion
MSBn – mine-sapper battalion
PBBn – pontoon-bridge battalion
MotPBBn – motorized pontoon-bridge battalion
GBnM – guards battalion of miners
FlameBn – flamethrower battalion
FlameCo – flamethrower company

PVO Strany Forces
PVOF – PVO *front*
PVOA – PVO army

PVOC – PVO corps
PVOZ – PVO zone
PVOCR – PVO corps region
PVOD – PVO division
PVODR – PVO division region
AAAD – antiaircraft artillery division
AAMGD – antiaircraft machine-gun division
VNOSD – early detection and warning division
AeroObsD – aerostatic obstacle division
PVOB – PVO brigade
PVOBR – PVO brigade region
AAAB – antiaircraft artillery brigade
PVOFAD – PVO fighter aviation division
PVOFAR – PVO fighter aviation regiment
AAAR – antiaircraft artillery regiment
AAAMGR – antiaircraft machine-gun regiment
ProjR – projector (searchlight) regiment
VNOSR – early detection and warning regiment
VNOSRadioR – early detection and warning radio regiment
AeroObsR – aerostatic obstacle regiment
AAABn – antiaircraft artillery battalion
AAMGBn – antiaircraft machine-gun battalion
ProjBn – projector battalion
VNOSBn – early detection and warning battalion
AAMGCo – antiaircraft machine-gun company
AABtry – antiaircraft battery
AeroObsD – aerial obstacle detachment

Air (Aviation) Forces
BAC – bomber aviation corps
FAC – fighter aviation corps
AAC – assault aviation corps
MAC – mixed aviation corps
Res AvGp – reserve aviation group
AD – aviation division
LRAD – long-range aviation division
BAD – bomber aviation division
HBAD – heavy bomber aviation division
LRBAD – long-range bomber aviation division
LBAD – light bomber aviation division
NBAD – night bomber aviation division
SDAD – special-designation aviation division
FAD – fighter aviation division
AAD – assault aviation division
MAD – mixed aviation division
AB – aviation brigade

BAR – bomber aviation regiment
LRBAR – long-range bomber aviation regiment
LBAR – light bomber aviation regiment
FAR – fighter aviation regiment
AAR – assault aviation regiment
MAR – mixed aviation regiment
RAR – reconnaissance aviation regiment
HRAR – heavy reconnaissance aviation regiment
TAR – transport aviation regiment
MedAR – medical aviation regiment

Organized by size, largest to smallest.

LBAS – light bomber aviation squadron
RAS – reconnaissance aviation squadron
CAS – corrective-aviation squadron
CRAS – corrective reconnaissance aviation squadron
CAF – civil aviation fleet
ARCAF – aviation regiment civil air fleet

Other

G (prefix) – guards (with all other abbreviations)
Op Gp – operational group